Library of
Davidson College

MIGRATIONS AND INVASIONS IN GREECE AND ADJACENT AREAS

MIGRATIONS AND INVASIONS IN GREECE

AND ADJACENT AREAS

by

N.G.L. HAMMOND, C.B.E., D.S.O., F.B.A.

NOYES PRESS
PARK RIDGE, NEW JERSEY

Copyright © 1976 by Nicholas Hammond
Library of Congress Catalog Card Number: 76-17379
ISBN: 0-8155-5047-2

Published in the United States by
NOYES PRESS
Noyes Building
Park Ridge, New Jersey 07656

Library of Congress Cataloging in Publication Data

Hammond, Nicholas Geoffrey Lemprière.
   Migrations and invasions in Greece and adjacent areas.

   Includes index.
   1. Ethnology—Greece. 2. Ethnology—Balkan Peninsula. 3. Migrations of nations. 4. Man—Migrations.
I. Title.
DF135.H35   301.32'938   76-17379
ISBN 0-8155-5047-2

*TO FRIENDS IN THE BALKANS FOR SHARED EXPERIENCES AND INTERESTS
WITH GRATITUDE AND AFFECTION*

PREFACE

When Robert Noyes invited me to write a book on the subject of migrations and invasions in Greece, I hesitated to accept a task of such wide scope in space and time; but I have taken up the challenge in the belief that my past experiences have given me perhaps some of the qualifications which seem desirable.

The first is a working knowledge of the physical geography and the human conditions (especially those prior to post-war developments) of Albania, south Yugoslavia, southwest Bulgaria and Greece north of the Gulf of Corinth. I laid the basis of such a knowledge by living with peasants and travelling mainly on foot for three years—partly before the war and partly during it—in Albania, Epirus, Macedonia and the whole Pindus range down to Galaxidhi and Itea. It did not take long for me to question the correctness of the views then current in learned circles that "the spine of Pindus" and "the trough of the Achelous" were natural routes of migration. Since the war it has been possible for me to travel extensively in Yugoslavia south of the Priština with the help of a grant from the British Academy, revisit Albania in 1972 through the kindness of the Albanian Government, and traverse the Strymon valley and see many museums and sites in Bulgaria as the guest of the Bulgarian Academy of Sciences in 1970. And I have also been able to revisit Greece, where I have taken every opportunity to extend my knowledge of the geography and the people.

The second qualification is a working knowledge of the archaeological discoveries which have been made in four separate countries. For it is not sufficient for a study of this subject to stay within the frontiers of one country. To take an example, the complex of migrations which shaped the "Dark Age" of Greece c. 1100–800 B.C. can only be understood within a wider geographical and sociological framework than that of the Mycenaean world, south of Mt Olympus and the Gulf of Arta. This became clear to me in the writing of my books *Epirus* and *A History of Macedonia I–II*, and I have become accustomed to grappling with reports of Albanian, Yugoslav and sometimes Bulgarian scholars as well as with those concerning sites in Greece. It is to be hoped that others will be attracted into this field, which is little worked by Aegean archaeologists of the Mycenaean and subsequent periods.

The third qualification is a readiness to look for historical analogies. The study of almost all migrations and a good many invasions from palaeolithic to modern times has brought me into contact with much unfamiliar archaeological evidence and not a few literary texts and ideas which were new to me. This has been refreshing in itself and has fulfilled a long-felt desire to become acquainted with the movements of the Vlachs and the Albanians into Greece. It seems to me that the analogies between some events of the prehistoric period and some of the historic period are both close and illuminating. They are perhaps particularly valuable when they are focused upon the complex of migrations which forms the subject of the last chapter. And they may help to answer the sort of question which is put at International Conferences of Prehistorians: "are the Greeks 'autochthonous', and are 'migrations' myths rather than facts?"

My debts to colleagues are innumerable, and I hope I may be pardoned if I mention only a few of them, some unfortunately no longer with us. In England A. J. B. Wace, W. A. Heurtley, Sylvia Benton, and V. R. d'A. Desborough. In U. S. A. Homer Thompson, Dorothy Thompson and Charles Edson. In Greece S. I. Dakaris, Julia Vokotopoulou, Ph. M. Petsas, M. Andronikos, B. Laourdas and Sp. Marinatos. In Albania Frano Prendi, Zhaneta Andrea, Muzafer Korkuti, Dhimosten Budina, G. Karaiskaj, L. Papajani, and Neritan Ceka. In Yugoslavia Milutin Garašanin and Fanoula Papazoglu. And in Bulgaria Goranka Toncheva, Christo Danov, Georgi Mihailov and Vladimir Georgiev. They and others have helped me in many ways in the past, though they may be unaware that I am writing this book and quite certainly may not share my views. Lastly my special thanks to David Cox, the cartographer of Cox Cartographic, Ltd., Pippin Cottage, Waterstock, Oxford, who has turned my draft maps into such a high degree of respectability; to Martha Gillies who has seen my typescript through the press with the greatest care and consideration; to Laurie Levich who drew the vases for Plate 5b; and to Robert Noyes who has helped me in obtaining satellite photographs of the area.

Cambridge *N. G. L. Hammond*
June 1, 1976

CONTENTS

List of Maps xi
List of Plates xiii
Abbreviations xiv
Part One – The Historic Period 1
I. The Geographical Setting 19
    The Southwestern Balkans as a Geographical Entity 19
    The Longitudinal Routes, from North to South 21
    The Latitudinal Routes, from West to East 29
    Invasions and Migrations 33
II. The Nomadic Peoples: Vlachs and Sarakatsani 37
    The Vlachs 37
    The Sarakatsani 46
III. The Settled Peoples: Albanians, Slavs, Bulgars, Turks and Greeks 52
    The Albanians 52
    The Slavs and the Bulgars 63
    The Turks and the Greeks 68
    The Pattern of Historical Invasions and Migrations 69
Part Two – The Prehistoric Period 79
Comparative Chronologies c. 4000–1500 B.C. 80
IV. The First Impressions Made by Man on the Southwest Balkans 81
    Movements in Pursuit of Animals 81
    Movements in Pursuit of Lands 84
    Migrations and Invasions Leading to the First Population Overlappings 89
    Summary of Developments 95
V. Trade, Power and Conquests 100
    The Late Neolithic Period 100
    Early Helladic I–II and Corresponding Phases in the Southwest Balkans 107
    Early Helladic III and Middle Helladic 113
VI. Destruction and Migration in the So-Called Dark Age of the Southwest Balkans 129
    The Decline of the Mycenaean World 129
    The Decisive Invasions 135
    The Subsequent Migrations 149
Retrospect 161
Plates 165
Index 177

LIST OF MAPS

A. Satellite photographs and corresponding maps, 1:1,000,000
   1. and 1a. Peć to Elbasan...2, 3
   2. and 2a. Kačanik to Verria..4, 5
   3. and 3a. Radomir to Serres...6, 7
   4. and 4a. Pogradec to Margariti..8, 9
   5. and 5a. Verria to Viniani...10, 11
   6. and 6a. Larissa to Corinth...12, 13
   7. and 7a. Magnesia to Athens..14, 15
   8. and 8a. Athens to Kalamata..16, 17

B. Maps conveying specific information
   9. Areas occupied by the Vlachs c. 1912..44
 10. Vlachs, Kupatshari and Sarakatsani in the highlands of Grammus and Pindus...........................47
 11. Migrations in Epirus Nova c. 1300–1500 A.D..55
 12. Migrations of Goths and Albanians, the latter sometimes with Vlachs......................................58
 13. Migrations of the fourteenth century A.D..60
 14. Dialects of Albanian and summer pastures of the Vlachs in the 1930s.......................................64
 15. Invasions from the North-East and the East: Persians, Sitalces and Turks.................................72
 16. The Mirditë-Mati culture (zenith c. 600–800 A.D.)...75
 17. Palaeolithic settlements in the S. W. Balkans..82
 18. Early Neolithic Sites..87
 19. Cultures of the Middle Neolithic Period..90
 20. Late Neolithic Settlements..101
 21. Distribution of Tumuli of E. H. and M. H. date...117
 22. Situation in Early Helladic III..132
 23. Migrations and Invasions c. 1230–1050 B.C..142
 24a. Probable distribution of Greek dialects c. 1200 B.C..145
 24b. Probable distribution of Greek dialects c. 900 B.C..147
 25. Migrations of the Early Iron Age...150

PLATES

		PAGE
1a	Korakou bridge on the Achelous	165
1b	The Acheron cutting its way through limestone ranges in a series of gorges	165
2a	Alpine pastures near the sources of the Achelous	166
2b	Alpine pastures on greenstone formation	166
3a	Shepherd and sheep in the plain of Ioannina	167
3b	Vlach shepherds near the summer pastures of Khaliki	167
4a	Threshing in Albania in 1932	168
4b	Albanian-speaking family in Tsamouria	168
5a	Animal figurines from Porodin in Pelagonia	169
5b	Four-legged fertility vase	169
6a	Anchor-amulets of clay	170
6b	Double tumulus at Pazhok in central Albania	170
7a	Double tumulus at Vodhinë in southern Albania	171
7b	A tumulus with two circles at Marathon in Attica	171
8	Bronze and stone objects from Macedonia	172
9	Pottery of "northwest geometric style" and fluted ware	173
10	Designs on "northwest geometric style" pottery from Malik and Tren	174
11	Illyrian pendants of bronze, and other objects	175
12	Early Iron Age bronzes, and hair-grips of gold and iron	176

Abbreviations

AAA	*Athens Annals of Archaeology*
AD	*Archaiologikon Deltion*
AI	*Archaeologia Iugoslavica*
AM	*Athenische Mitteilungen*
AR	*Archaeological Reports*
Arch. Anz.	*Archäologischer Anzeiger in Jahrbuch des deutschen archäologischen Instituts*
BSA	*The Annual of the British School at Athens*
BUSS	*Buletin për shkencat shoqërore* (Tirana)
CAH	The Cambridge Ancient History, 1923–39
CAH³	The Cambridge Ancient History, edited by I. E. S. Edwards, C. J. Gadd, N. G. L. Hammond and E. Sollberger, 1970–
CP	*Classical Philology*
CSHB	*Corpus Scriptorum Historiae Byzantinae* (Bonn, 1828–97)
DgL	A. Philippson, *Die griechischen Landschaften*
Epirus	N. G. L. Hammond, *Epirus* (Oxford, 1967)
FGrH	F. Jacoby, *Fragmente der griechischen Historiker* (Berlin, 1923)
Gimbutas, *Indo-Europeans*	M. Gimbutas in *Indo-European and Indo-Europeans: Papers Presented at Third Indo-European Conference at the Univ. of Pennsylvania.* Ed. by George Cardona, et. al. (Philadelphia, 1971)
Hesp.	*Hesperia*
HG²	N. G. L. Hammond, *A History of Greece to 322 B.C.* (2nd ed. Oxford, 1967)
ITEE	*Istoria tou Ellenikou ethnous* (Athens, 1970)
JHS	*The Journal of Hellenic Studies*
JRS	*The Journal of Roman Studies*
MGH	*Monumenta Germaniae Historica* (Hanover, 1826–)
Macedonia	N. G. L. Hammond, *A History of Macedonia*, vol. 1 (Oxford, 1972)
Mus. Helv.	*Museum Helveticum*
Op. Ath.	*Opuscula Atheniensia*
PAE	*Praktika tes en Athenais Arkhaiologikes Etaireias*
PM	W. A. Heurtley, *Prehistoric Macedonia* (Cambridge, 1939)
PPS	*Proceedings of the Prehistoric Society*
PTh	A. J. B. Wace and M. S. Thompson, *Prehistoric Thessaly* (Cambridge, 1912)
SA	*Studia Albanica* (Tirana)
StGH	N. G. L. Hammond, *Studies in Greek History* (Oxford, 1973)
StH	*Studime Historike* (Tirana)
Wace and Thompson	A. J. B. Wace and M. S. Thompson, *The Nomads of the Balkans* (London, 1914)
Weigand *(A)*	G. Weigand, *Die Aromunen* (Leipzig, 1895)
Weigand *(EvM)*	G. Weigand, *Ethnographie von Makedonien* (Leipzig, 1924)
WMBH	*Wissenschaftliche Mitteilungen aus Bosnien und Hercegovina*

Part One

The Historic Period

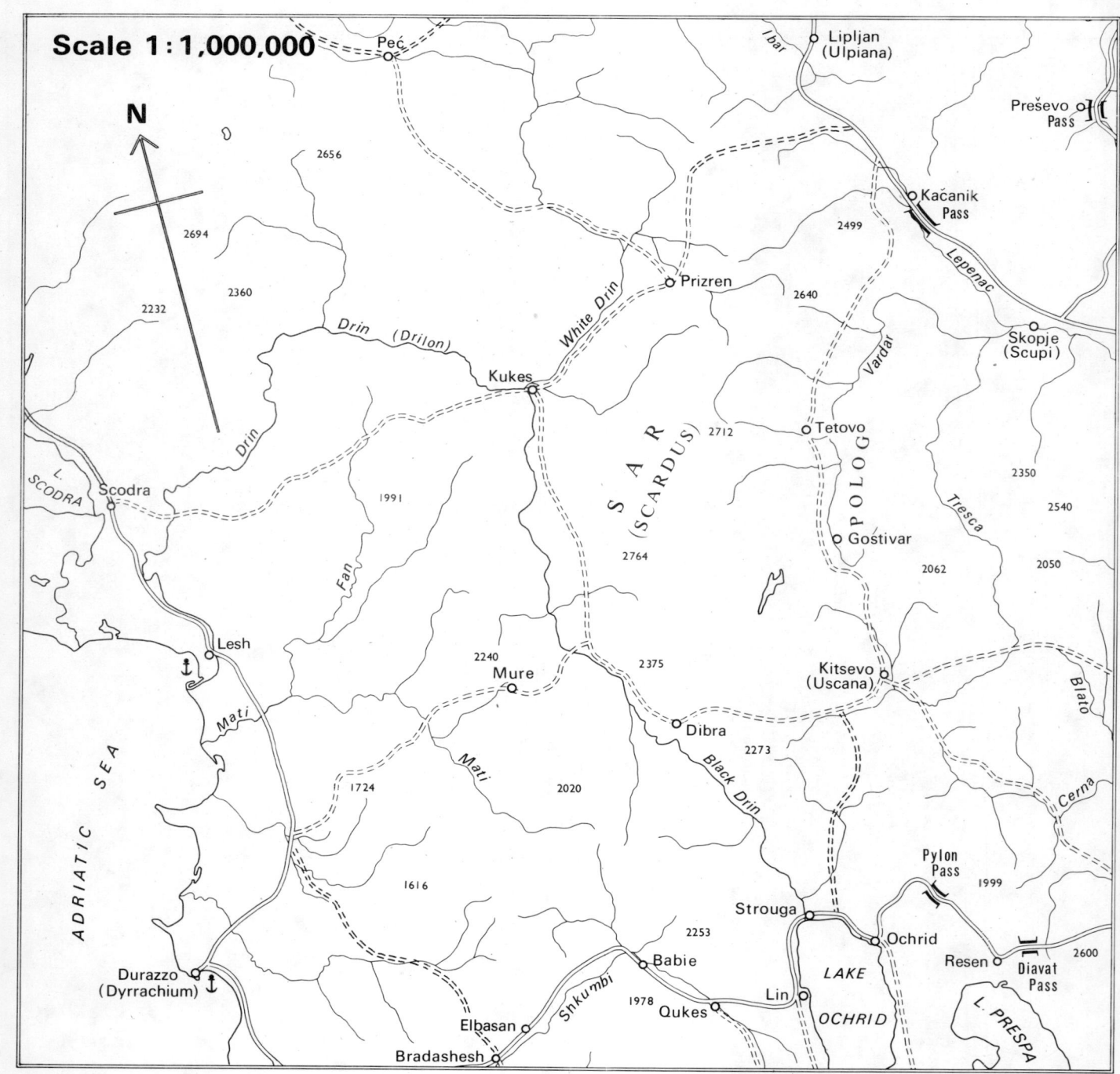

1. Peć to Elbasan

1a. Peć to Elbasan

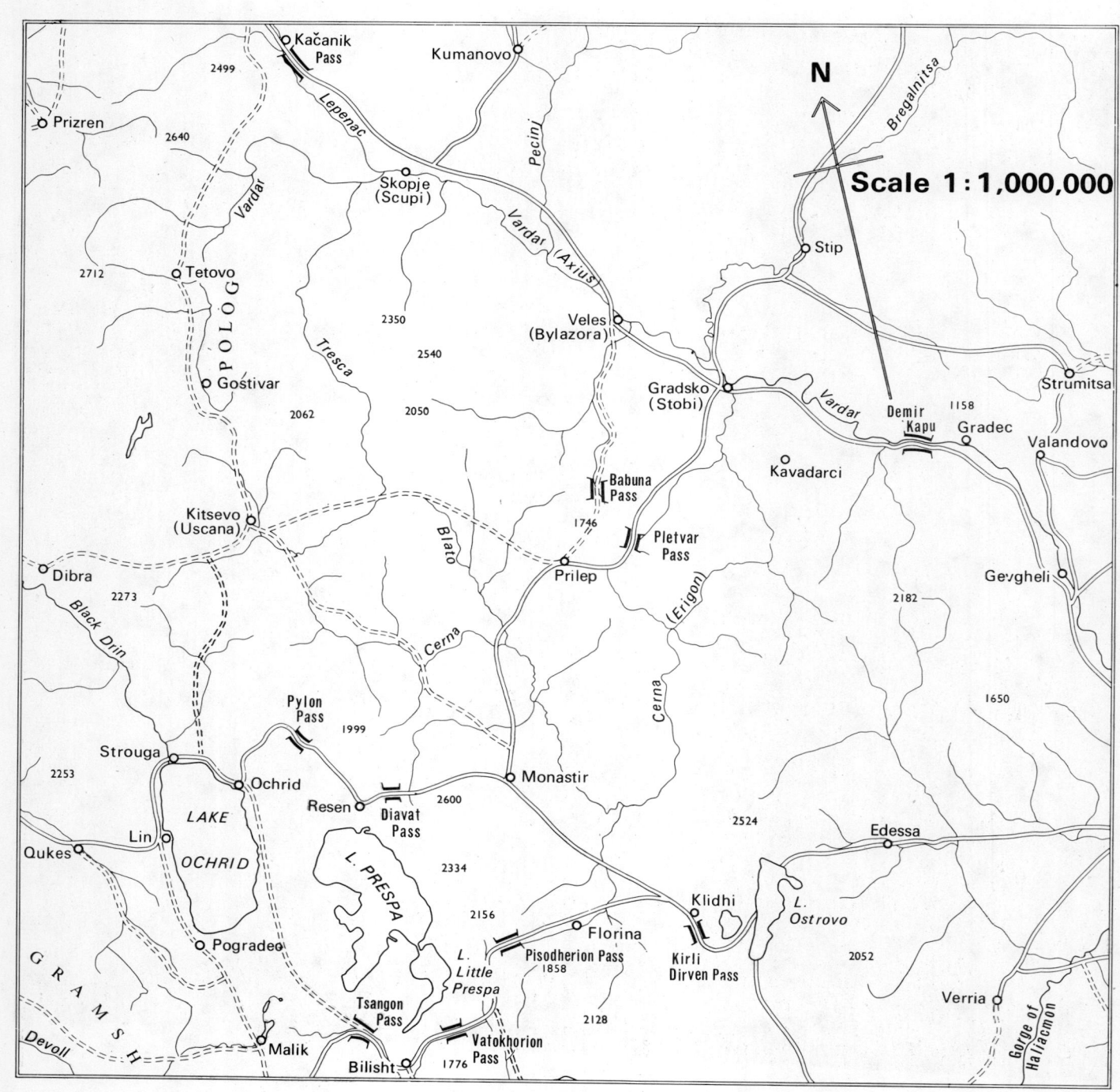

2. Kačanik to Verria

2a. Kačanik to Verria

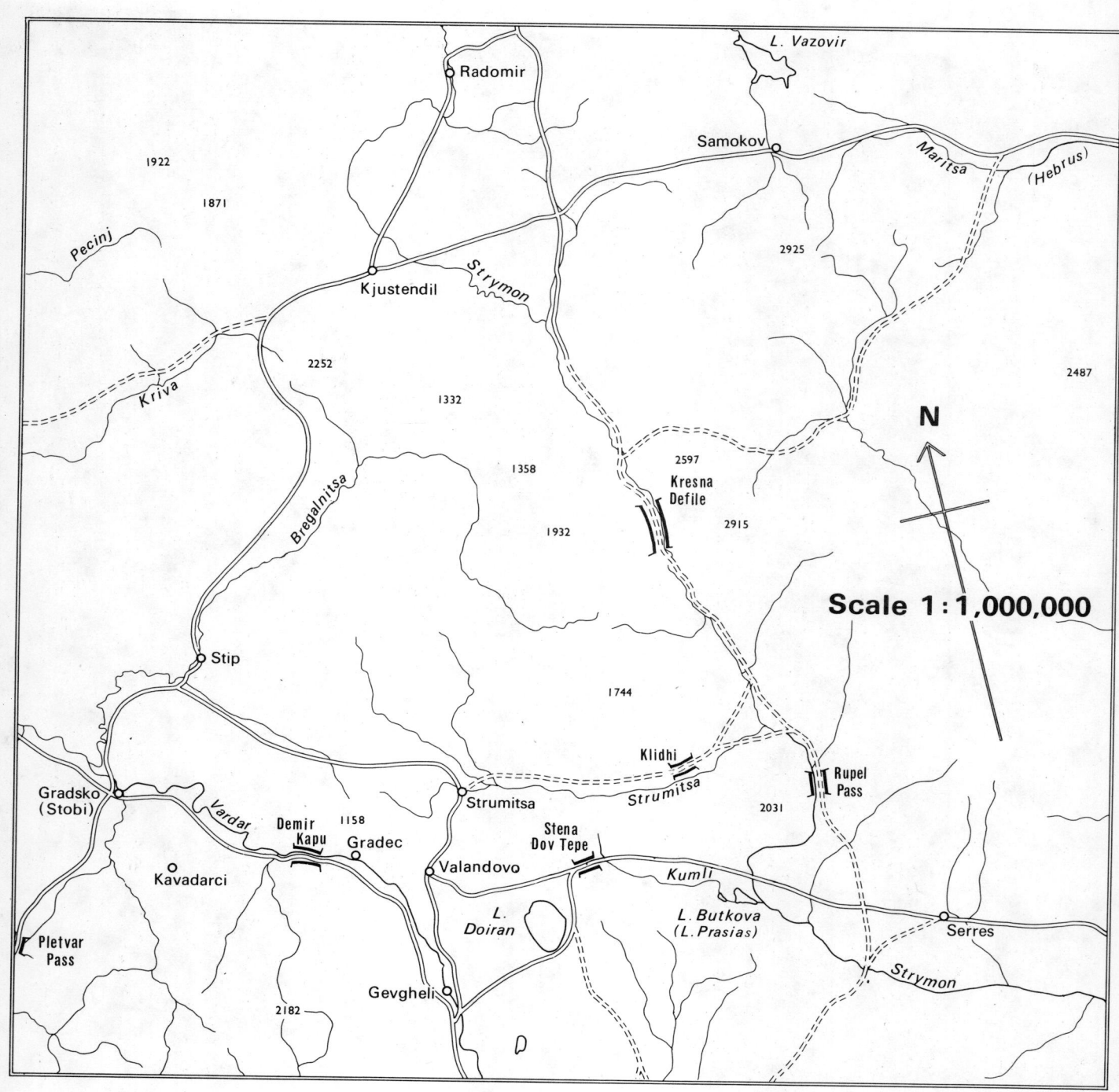

3. Radomir to Serres

3a. Radomir to Serres

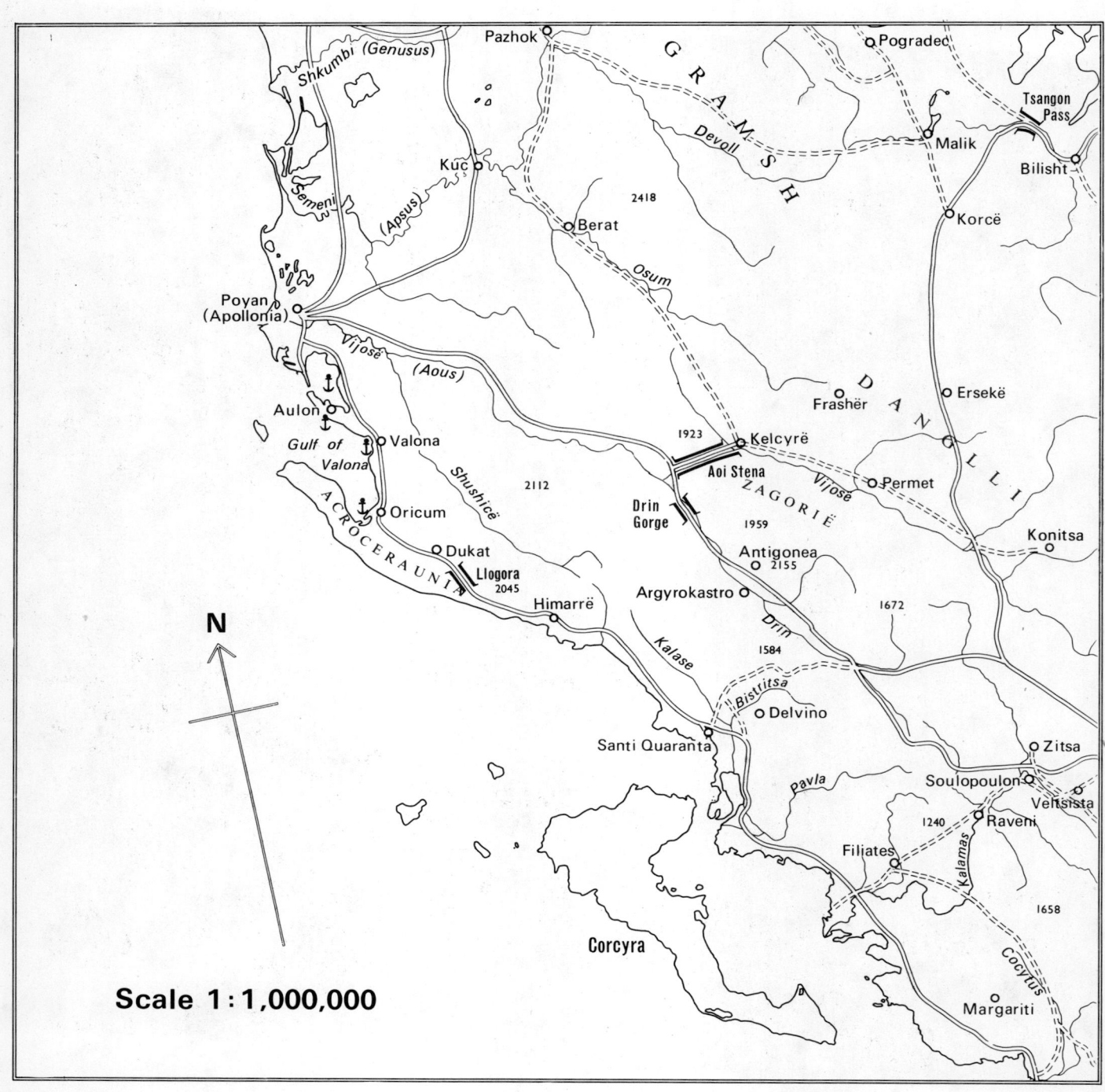

4. Pogradec to Margariti

4a. Pogradec to Margariti

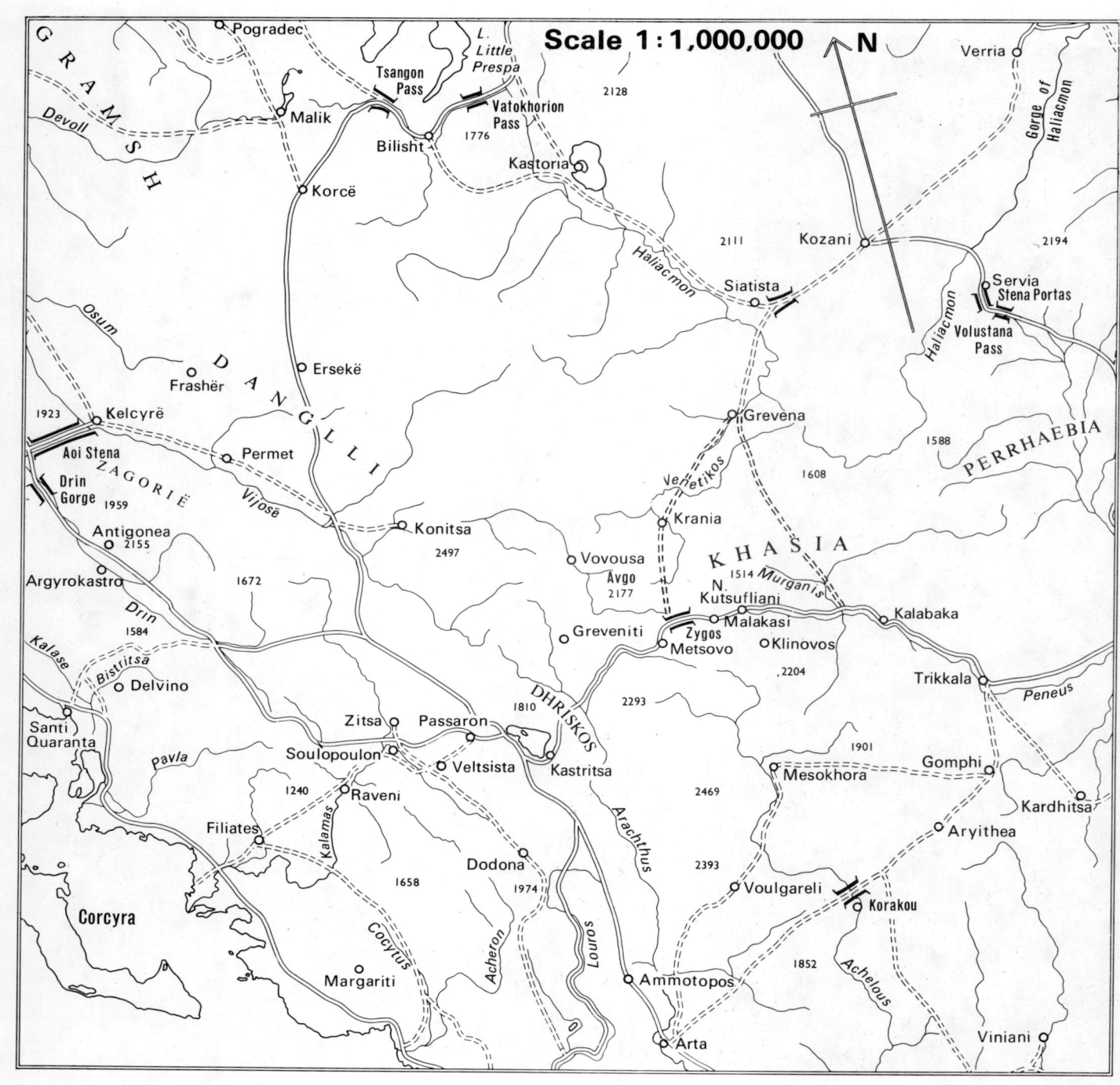

5. Verria to Viniani

5a. Verria to Viniani

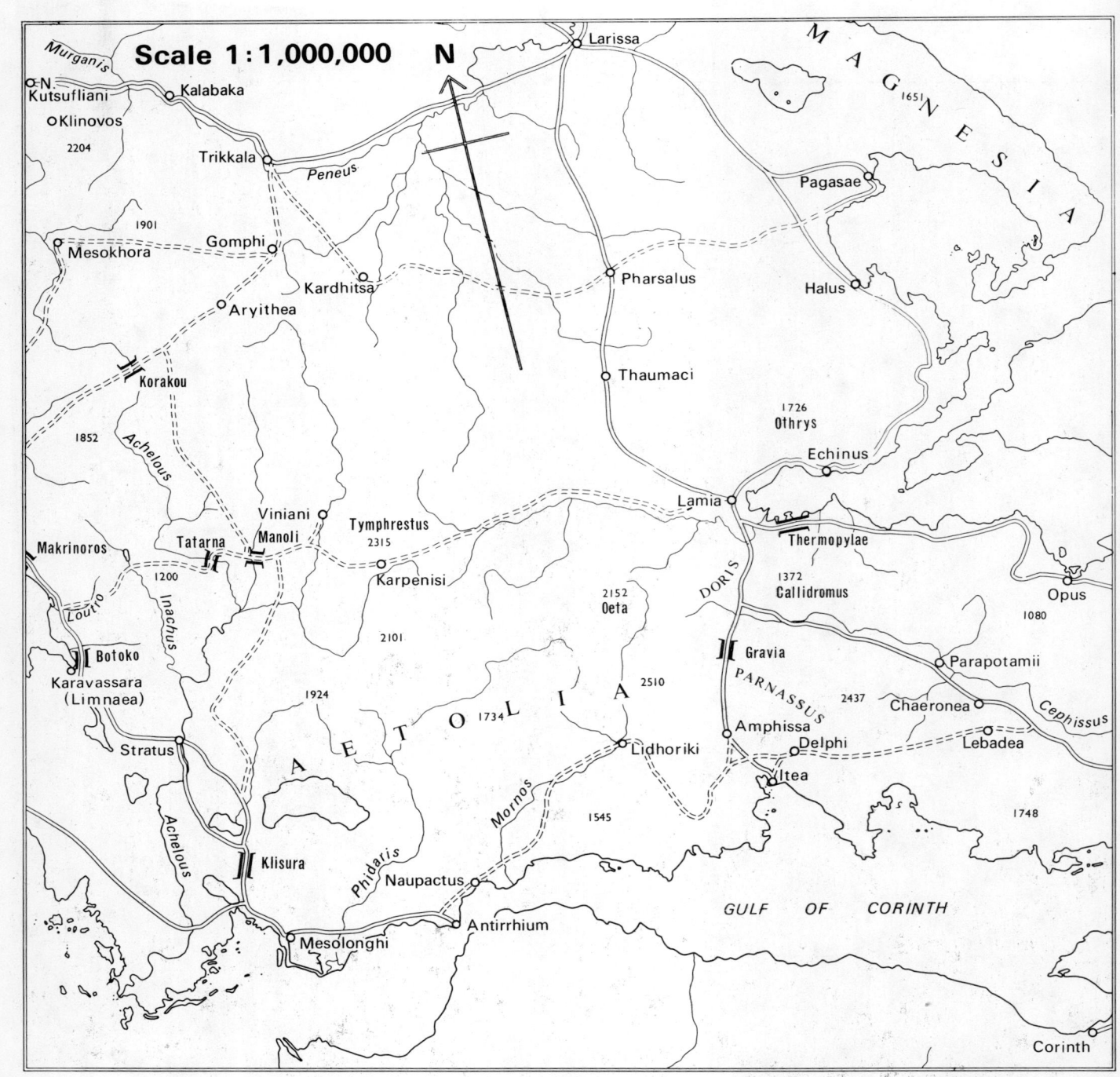

6. Larissa to Corinth

6a. Larissa to Corinth

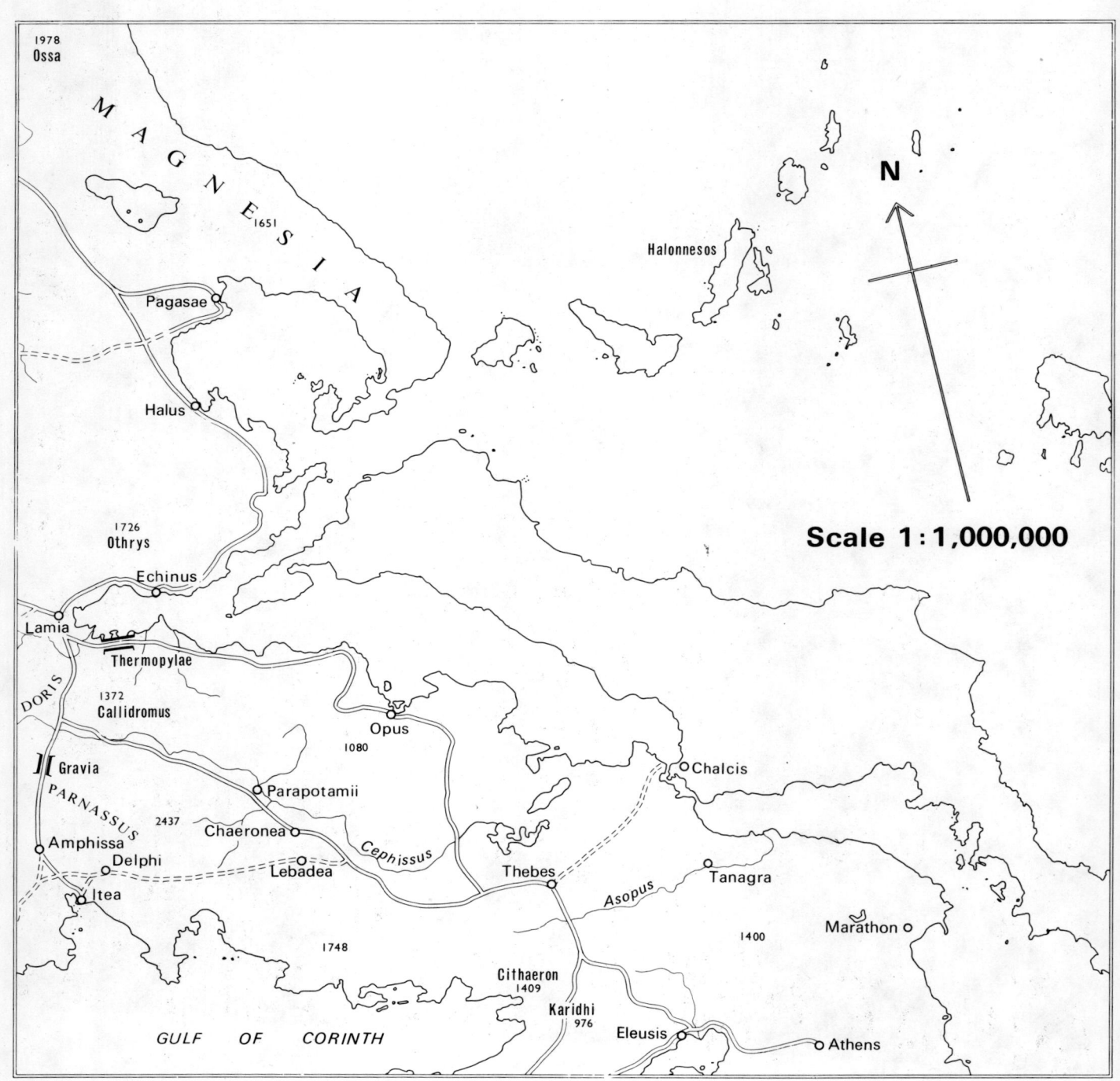

7. Magnesia to Athens

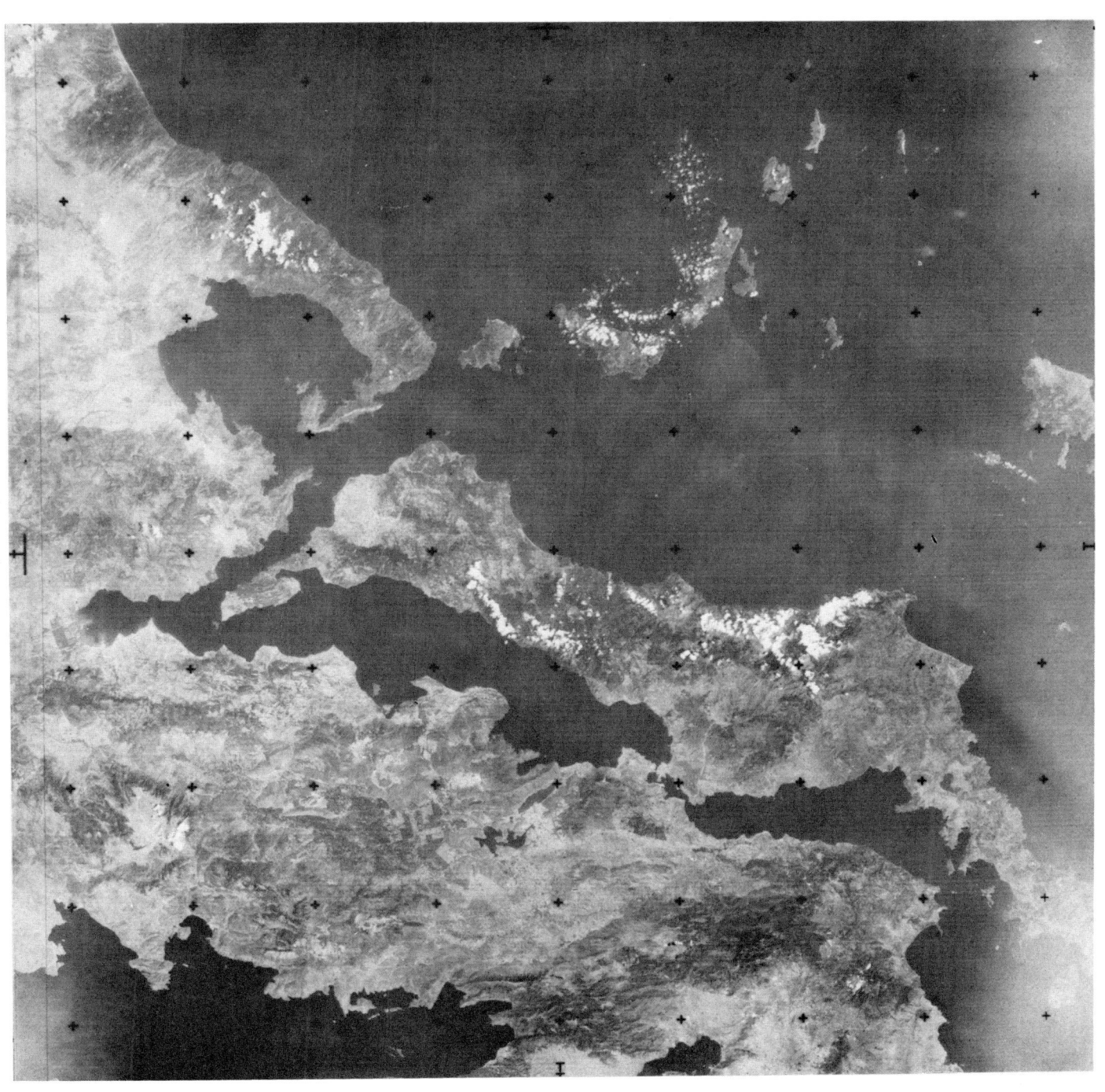

7a. Magnesia to Athens

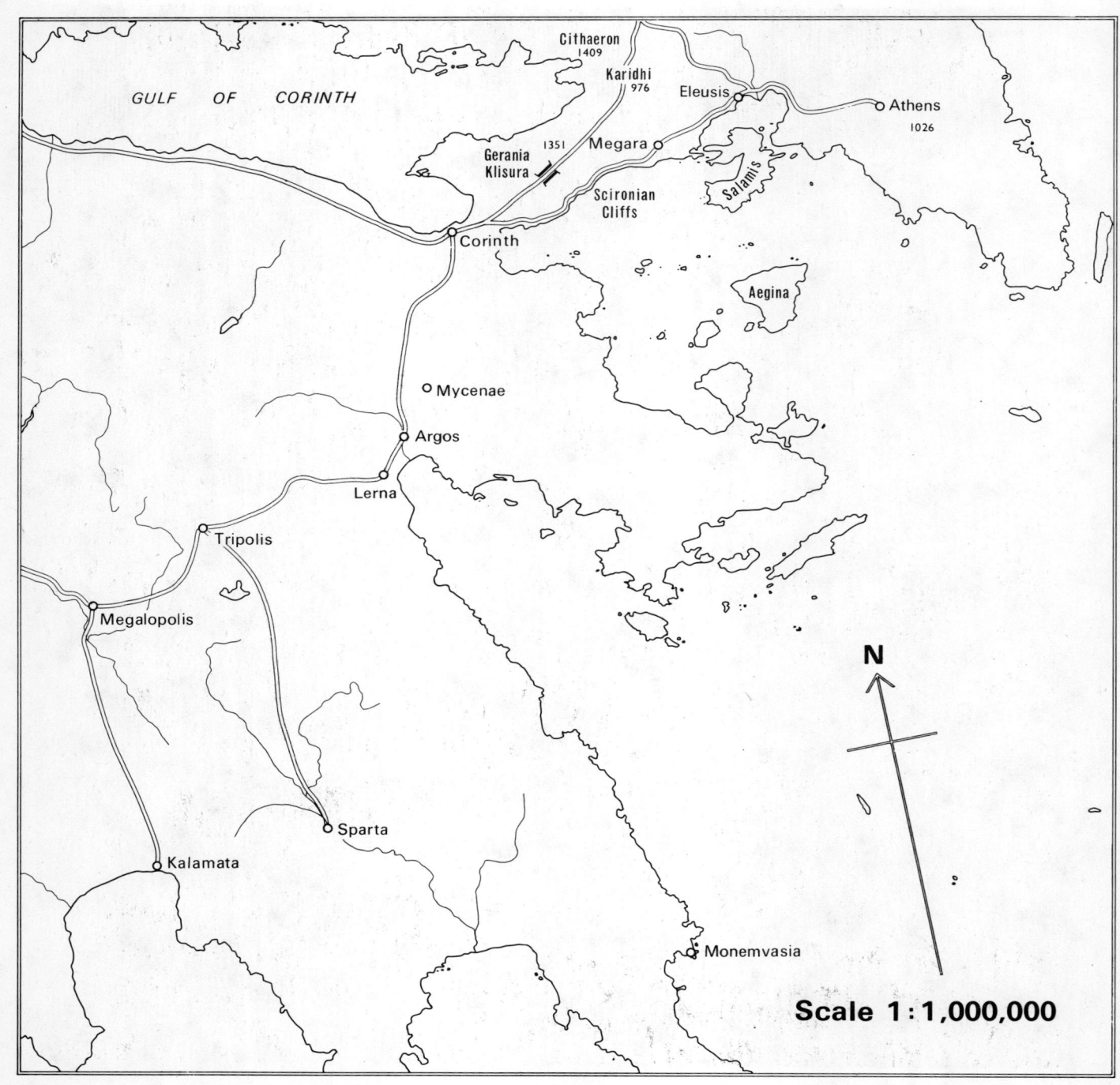

8. Athens to Kalamata

8a. Athens to Kalamata

I

The Geographical Setting

The Southwestern Balkans as a Geographical Entity

(See Maps 1 to 8a)

For the purpose of this study I am using the term "the southwest Balkans" in the following sense. The dividing line between the northern Balkans and the southern Balkans is set by great mountain ranges which form the watershed between the Danube and the rivers entering the southern Adriatic Sea and the Aegean Sea. If we start from the west, these ranges make up the mountainous masses of Montenegro and northern Albania which turn the course of the Drin (anc. Drilon) westwards into the Adriatic Sea below Scodra. The ranges of the next group, consisting of the Šar Planina (anc. Scardus, 2702 m), Crna Gora (1651 m), Duka Planina (1922 m), and Osogovska Planina (anc. Messapium, 2252 m), contain the headwaters of the Vardar (anc. Axius), which makes its entry into the sea to the west of Salonica (anc. Thessalonica). These ranges are in the shape of a horseshoe facing north, and the central part of the convex edge happens to be much lower than the sides. Last are the ranges which enclose the uppermost valley of the Struma (anc. Strymon). The most easterly of these is Mt Vitosha (anc. Scombrus, 2286 m), a very beautiful and thickly wooded mountain. The dividing line between the western Balkans and the eastern Balkans runs southwards from Mt Vitosha through the ranges of Rila (2925 m) and Pirin (2914 m) and then, east of Serres, to Mt Pangaeum (1956 m) and the sea.

Because the mountain ranges are very high, forested and generally steep, there are very few entries into the southwest Balkans from the north which an invading army or an organised group of migrants could use.

The easiest entry into the northwestern part of this area is certainly by sea, sailing down the Adriatic. Anyone who has visited the deep inlet of Kotor is aware of the forbidding mountains of the coastal range which make land travel so difficult. Yet just behind this coastal range there is a long, fertile depression which extends in the south to the Lake of Scodra (now Shkodër). This area, known as Zeta,[1] was the centre of the Serb kingdom which broke away from Byzantium in 1042. There are routes into it from Kotor and from Dubrovnik, but the main route in Roman times came from the plain of Nikšić over the pass of Ostrog. The best route of egress from Zeta leads to the coast of northern Albania, where a coastal plain extends from Scodra southwards to the Gulf of Valona. On the other hand, the mountains of Montenegro north and east of Zeta and the mountains of northern Albania present an almost impassable barrier, which not only has great width, but also great depth. The nature of this wild country has been vividly described by Margaret Hasluck from her personal knowledge of northern Albania.[2]

> In the Accursed Alps (Bjeshkët ë Nemuna) . . . the close-set summits of Radohinë (8690 feet), Jezercë (8790 feet [2694 m]), Rosh (8720 feet), and Kolatë (8370 feet) wall off Yugoslavia from Upper Shalë in spectacular fashion. East of Shalë, the monster Peak of the Irons (Majë e Hekuravë, 8530 feet) divides the

tribe of Mertur from the open plateau of Krasniqë. The passes across the mountains are often lofty and arduous. To take an extreme example, the only way from Shalë to Bogë, its western neighbour, is by the Sheep Track Pass, to the northern frontier by the Pejë Pass, and to Nikaj on the east by the Ndermajnë Pass, which are respectively 5900, 5600 [1708 m] and again 5600 feet above sea level and take a day to traverse. It is self-evident that the tribesmen of Shalë have never seen much of their neighbours. Elsewhere geographical conditions are less formidable, yet generally severe enough to limit intercourse between communities.

Nor is entry from the east into northern Albania any less difficult. The Šar Planina (2712 m), Mt Gjalicë (2480 m) and Mt Korab (2765 m) present a continuous and massive wall which faces the onlooker from Ochrid or from Skopje citadel. The only breakthrough is made by the White Drin which cuts its way between the mountains of northern Albania and the Šar Planina to join the Black Drin at Kukës. This breakthrough does not present an easy route. Yet it is an important one, since it alone connects the Black Drin valley with Prizren and Peć in the Metohija plateau and further to the northeast with the Kossovo plateau, both of which are fertile and rich.[3]

By contrast there are two easy routes leading from the north into the western part of the upper Vardar valley. One route passes through a gently rising, vast and fertile tableland of deep and stoneless soil, peaty or pinkish, which extends to the foot of the mountains on either side and runs unbroken from Priština on the upper Ibar, a tributary of the Danube, to Kačanik on the upper Lepenac, a tributary of the Vardar. The traveller hardly notices that he is crossing a watershed because the rise is so gradual and the ridge is not high in relation to neighbouring peaks. This is the low part of the horseshoe of ranges. From the tableland by Kačanik there is a very easy route into the flat and fertile basin, called Polog, between Tetovo and Gostivar, where the headwaters of the Vardar are collected; but the route from that basin southward is not so easy, as we shall see later. Alternatively, from Kačanik itself there is a route down the Lepenac valley. This begins with a defile which has almost sheer sides—the so-called Kačanik Pass, 475 m above sea level. The valley is thereafter narrow and steep-sided as far as Krekapak, where it opens out and soon joins the wide valley of the Vardar.

The other easy route from the north starts from Niš (anc. Naissus). It comes up the valley of the Morava, a tributary of the Danube, by-passes the gorge at Grdelica, and crosses an open and surprisingly flat watershed at the so-called Preševo Pass, only 426 m above sea level, to enter the basin of the Pecinj, a tributary of the Vardar. Nowadays the main road uses the Kačanik Pass, and the main railway, preferring lesser gradients and lower height, uses the Preševo Pass. The two routes meet at Skopje (anc. Scupi), today the most important city on the Vardar.

Farther to the east, the best entry from the north into the head of the Strymon valley is from Sofia (anc. Serdica). On leaving Sofia one crosses the outlying, thickly-wooded spurs of Mt Vitosha by a narrow man-made route from which there is a fine view of the pyramidal peak of Osovo, often snowclad. From the last spur one descends through a gentle plateau to Pernik on the Strymon and soon enters the wide and fertile plain by Radomir alongside the river.

Entries from the east into the southwest Balkans are even fewer. The ranges of Rila and Pirin are exceptionally steep and fantastically forested, as one would expect of the home of Dionysus, god of exuberant life and growth. The main route of entry, which I followed, is the one running from Razlog on the Mesta (anc. Nestus) to Gradevo and Blagoevgrad on the Strymon. The top of the pass over Mt Pirin was not far from the snowline in May, and then came a terrifying descent through a steep-sided, thickly-forested gorge with a rushing river. The descent to the low-lying plain on either side of Mt Pangaeum is quite different. There the going is easy, although there is a narrow bottleneck at the so-called Acontisma Pass. The historian Ammianus Marcellinus, writing late in the fourth century A.D., described it as "narrow and precipitous" (27.4.8). It was the gateway between Thrace and Macedonia.

Thus the southwest Balkans is a natural citadel into which the routes of entry are remarkably few. The inhabitants of the mountainous areas which lie on the side of these routes have always been hardy, warlike and eager for independence. In ancient times the Illyrians held Montenegro and North Albania;[4] the Dardanians the approaches to Kačanik and Preševo; the Paeonians the range of Osogovska; the Agrianes the mountain of Vitosha; and the Thracians the ranges of Rila, Pirin and Pangaeum.[5] In medieval times the Albanians, the Serbs, the Vlachs, and the

Bulgars were no less formidable to the settled Byzantine peoples of the lowlands; under the Turkish empire they maintained some freedom in their mountain fastnesses. The main roads in Macedonian, Roman, Byzantine, Turkish and modern times have always used these same points of entry: Scodra, Prizren-Kukës, Kačanik, Preševo, Sofia-Radomir, and Acontisma on the coast.

The Longitudinal Routes, from North to South

Those who enter the southwest Balkans from the north have a restricted choice of routes towards the south. From Scodra and Kukës the best route is to Lesh (anc. Lissus) on the coast and then along the inland side of the coastal plain, passing close to Durazzo (anc. Dyrrachium) where the hills come near to the coast, and going through Poyan (anc. Apollonia) to the north coast of the Gulf of Valona, where the coastal plain ends. The peculiar feature of this plain is that, having been formed over the millennia by the silt-deposits of the great Albanian rivers, it is extremely low-lying and swampy (unless scientifically drained), and that it is therefore subject to immense floods (unless the rivers are scientifically controlled).[6] It is for that reason that the coastal road has, in fact, followed the inland side of the plain, hugging the edge of the foothills. A grave defect of the route is the need to cross seven rivers, of which the Drin (anc. Drilon), Mati, Shkumbi (anc. Genusus), Semeni (anc. Apsus) and Vijosë (anc. Aous) are considerable in summer and enormous in flood-times. It is difficult to build bridges in the alluvium of the coastal plain, and ferries have often been the only way of crossing the rivers.

If one wishes to avoid the need to cross so many rivers as they enter the coastal plain, it is possible to turn inland at the latitude of Durazzo and follow a flat valley-floor to Tirana, from which there is a formidable climb through a forested mountainside up to a high ridge which provides an even highway. From this ridge one descends very steeply indeed to Bradashesh in the valley of the Shkumbi, just west of Elbasan. Here there is a chance of fording the river, which has a wide bed of limestone rubble. Indeed, there is also a place between limestone bluffs where the river was bridged in antiquity.[7] One then proceeds southwards through a remarkably low trough past Pazhok to the river Devoll, which can be crossed more easily as it has not yet joined the Osum, and then goes on to Berat.

From Berat one can either enter the coastal plain and proceed along its inland side to Poyan (anc. Apollonia), or take advantage of the SSE direction of the valleys and continue on an inland route, going up the valley of the Osum and crossing a watershed ridge to enter the valley of the Deshnicë, a tributary of the Vijosë (anc. Aous), which one joins at Kelcyrë. The side of the river can then be followed up to Konitsa. Again it has not been necessary to cross any large rivers on this route, although much of the going is arduous between Berat and Kelcyrë.

The other route from Kukës follows the valleyside of the Black Drin and leads to the shore of Lake Ochrid at Strouga. It is more arduous for man and beast than the coastal route, but it does not involve the crossing of such dangerous and even impassable rivers. The route southward from Gostivar also reaches the north shore of Lake Ochrid, not at Strouga but at St. Erasmus. It passes through virgin forests of oak and beech, and there are high ridges to cross and deep descents and climbs, but it links three fertile and flat but elevated areas by Gostivar, Kitsevo (anc. Uscana) and Trebenište-Ochrid. From the northern end of Lake Ochrid there is an exceptionally easy route through the Balkan lakeland, leaving Lake Ochrid and then Lake Malik to the west and Lake Prespa and Lake Ventrok (or Little Prespa, as it is also called) to the east. One can follow either side of Lake Ochrid without serious difficulty. Then there is a climb over some steep hills of flysch formation with a yellowish soil and a descent into an undulating plain which merges later into the flat plain of Malik. The river Devoll (in medieval writers 'Diabolis') is crossed by Malik town after which one proceeds into the even larger plain of Korcë (in Greek 'Koritsa').[8] These great plains of fenlike, black soil stand 800 m and more above sea level; they are extremely healthy, and produce excellent crops and also provide abundant pastures. The ratio between agriculture and pastoralism depends partly on the number of drainage operations. Thus today Lake Malik has disappeared through an efficient drainage scheme carried out by the present Albanian government, although it was a considerable lake with a swampy surround at the end of the last war. Even so this lakeland string of plains, which extends from Trebenište in the north to Bozhigrad in the south, has long been renowned as the best cultivated part of Albania. Indeed, the ancient name of some of its inhabitants, 'the Caloecini', may refer to their good husbandry. There are in addition excellent fisheries in the lakes and fine pastures on the surrounding mountains. In consequence this highway route has great attractions for conquerors from the north who have been accustomed to this sort of terrain, for instance in Metohija and Kossovo. One must also bear in mind that the inhabitants of these plains, if efficiently organised, can put up a strong resistance at the narrow passages which exist at St. Erasmus and Old Ochrid (anc. Lychnidus), where the cliffs come close to the lakeside, and further south at Lin on the west side of Lake Ochrid or at Sveti Naum on the east side.

Let us now consider the route southwards from Skopje. The valley of the middle part of the Vardar is generally open and fertile, and it is at a much lower level than the highland route through the lakeland. There is a short defile north of Titov Veles (anc. Bylazora) and a long, precipitous defile below it. The valley is again open and fertile, especially in the Kavadarci (Tikvetch) area, where the soil is a sandy yellow and one has a sniff of the Mediterranean air for the first time. Then comes the tremendous defile known as the Demir Kapu, where the river is squeezed between limestone cliffs. There was no passage at all for a traveller on foot until c. 400 B.C. when a roadway was cut on the right bank and a Macedonian colony was founded at the northern entry of the defile.[9] The defile itself is a kilometre or so in length, and after that the valley is narrow as far as Gradec. There are no convenient routes over the mountains on either side of the Demir Kapu. Since the defile was completely blocked until 400 B.C. and afterwards was easily held because it offered such a narrow passage, it was never used by invading armies or migrating hordes. They had to make a wide detour either to the west or to the east if they wished to gain entry to the coastal plain of Macedonia.

Moving now to the entry from Sofia into the upper valley of the Strymon, we traverse the rich plain of Radomir and then the even more extensive plain below Kjustendil (anc. Pataulia). As we proceed south towards the snowy mass of the Rila range, the Strymon cuts its way through hilly country in an impassable bed, but a detour is easy. Thereafter the valley is open again until we reach Tserovo, where there is an impassable defile between steep and sometimes precipitous mountainsides with rocky outcrops and thick forest. This defile, known as the Kresna Defile or the Klisura Pass,[10] reaches as far as Pirin; it corresponds to the Demir Kapu in the Vardar valley. Detours over the mountains on either side are very difficult. The modern road alongside the defile has been skillfully engineered. There is no doubt that in ancient times the Klisura Pass was a block to movement by armies or groups of migrants down the Strymon valley. Thus in 429 B.C. the large army of Sitalces, king of the Odrysians in Central Thrace, whose capital was at or near Plovdiv (anc. Philippoupolis), marched through his realm as far as the upper Strymon and the land of the Laeaei (around Kjustendil) and then passed "through an uninhabited part of Mt Cercine along a road which had been cut through the forest on a previous campaign against the Paeonians."[11] He chose this high route not through any personal caprice but because he was unable to follow the valley of the Strymon beyond Tserovo.

When we come to the end of the coastal plain at Poyan (anc. Apollonia) or to the north coast of the Gulf of Valona and its ancient harbour called Aulon, we have a choice of routes. The reason for this is that we are entering an entirely different kind of terrain. It is known as Epirus, "mainland," as seen for instance from the off-lying island of Corfu (anc. Corcyra). It is characterised by five parallel ranges, all running NNW by SSE. The most westerly forms the coast, which is generally steep-to and inhospitable, with the famous storm-breeding range of the Acroceraunia or 'Highlightningers' in the north (with high peaks of 2018 and 2045 m) and with Mt Zalongo's coastal spurs 548 and 563 m high in the south. The most easterly forms the central spine of the peninsula, and is known from north to south as Grammus (2036 m) and Pindus (with peaks of 2238, 2249, and 2177 m) as far as the Zygos or 'cross-bar'—the one and only pass through the central spine—and thereafter it becomes a double range, containing the river Aspropotamos (anc. Achelous), and is named by its peaks (e.g., Peristeri, 2295 m; Kakarditsa, 2429 m; Tsoumerka, 2392 m; Tringia, 2204; and Karava, 2184 m). The further south one goes in Epirus, the more tightly packed the parallel ranges become, until they are squeezed tight together as we draw near the Gulf of Arta. With this geological formation[12] it is inevitable that the routes run down the valleys, NNW to SSE, and they become squeezed almost out of existence in the extreme south.

The pattern of parallel ranges is repeated in the river-system. This is seen most clearly in the northern part of the terrain. The Vijosë (Aous), drawing its headwaters from Pindus, breaks through the next parallel range in a vast gorge between Smolika (2639 m) and Gamila (2480 m), and picks up the Voïdhomati river in the parallel valley. Then at Kelcyrë the river turns westwards, breaking through a double range (Trebeshin, 1923 m and Dhëmbel, 1280 m), and picks up the river Drin in the parallel valley. It passes through the next parallel range at Klos and picks up the river Shushicë in the next parallel valley before it passes by Apollonia and enters the Adriatic Sea. Similarly in the south the Arachthus or 'Tearer', rising close to the source of the Vijosë and taking its headwaters from the Zygos area, breaks its way past Peristeri and picks up the Zagoritikos in the parallel valley. It passes through many impenetrable gorges, pinched between the ranges of Xerovouni (1600 m) and Tsoumerka (2392 m), until it breaks through the Xerovouni range at Arta and enters the Gulf of Arta. Here the sea has captured the river's lower basin. Before that happened, it was joined by the Louros river and its tributaries, themselves draining the tight-packed parallel valleys of southwest Epirus.

The best route southwards from Poyan (Apollonia) goes up the valley of the Vijosë, which has a narrow but flat bed and affords easy going as far as its junction with the Drin. At this point, if not earlier, one has to cross the river, which is not easy to ford even in midsummer. One then follows the valley of the Drin. First there is a narrow defile, but thereafter the valley is flat-bottomed and wide, narrowing down by Ktismata. The ancient Roman road went by Vodhinë in the valley of a small tributary, the Kseria, or 'dry streambed', and by similar valleys via Soulopoulon to Dodona and thence to the north shore of the Gulf of Arta. The pack-horse track in Turkish times crossed the Kalamas higher up near Zitsa, using a natural rock-bridge called Theogephyra ('God's Bridge'). The modern road continues up the narrowing Drin valley, passes east of Mt Soutista (1316 m) and follows a dry limestone coombe to enter the high plateau of Ioannina. The modern road descends from this plateau by a skillfully engineered system of bridges through the tight valley of the river Louros, whereas the main Turkish road ran high up along the western flank of the Xerovouni range. One ancient route did likewise, as we may judge from the position of some fortifications. Another ancient route took the valley west of the Louros river.[13]

There are two subsidiary routes leading southwards from the Gulf of Valona. One starts with a long, steep climb from sea level to the ridge of the Acroceraunia, where the so-called Llogora Pass is 1055 m high, and then there is an even steeper scramble down to a lower level. On the occasion in January 48 B.C. when Julius Caesar and some 20,000 men made a crossing of the Llogora Pass, Appian wrote of this "rugged and narrow track" (Appian, *Bella Civilia* 2.54). Nor does the route southwards along the lowest spurs of the mountains improve until one reaches the Bay of Palermo, from which the going is good to Santi Quaranta (anc. Onchesmus).

An alternative route from the Gulf of Valona begins more easily by ascending the lower valley of the Shushicë, but is then much worse in the western part of the Kurvelesh—a very rugged, wooded and remote area. This route descends the Kalasë valley and enters the plain of Delvino, inland of Santi Quaranta. Proceeding southwards in the proximity of the coast one has to cross three considerable rivers which rise not from the central range, as the Vijosë and the Arachthus do, but from one or another of the intermediary ranges. Each of the rivers—the Bistritsa, the Kalamas (anc. Thyamis) and the Acheron—has created a swampy plain near the coast, and the first and last have made lakes too (that of the Acheron having been drained in the 1930s).[14] These plains and rivers are not easy for armies to cross. Any traveller taking the coastal route has to surmount the watersheds between the rivers and go against the grain of the country. There is a good deal of climbing and descending over very rough and rugged ground, especially over the last stretch from the mouth of the Acheron to the vicinity of the northern shore of the Gulf of Arta.

Let us consider now the highland route which we had followed as far as Korcë. We have a choice of two routes southwards, one on the west of Grammus and the other on the east of it. Taking the former we climb over a low ridge and cross the fertile plateau of Ersekë (1036 m high), and then make a long, rough descent via Leskoviq to the bed of the Sarandaporos ('the forty-forder'), which is crossed just before it flows into the Vijosë (anc. Aous). Close by is the picturesque town of Konitsa, situated below the immense cliffs of Mt Smolika (2639 m) and beside the entry into an impassable gorge of the Vijosë. Here a fine Turkish bridge enables one to cross the river. Continuing southwards one crosses the Voïdhomati and climbs over a low pass to enter the plateau of Pogoniani, which is a smaller version of that of Ioannina. Descending from this plateau one joins the main north-south route before it enters the dry coombe on the way to Ioannina.

The route from Korcë to the east side of Grammus goes through the pass of Tsangon, where the hills close in on the river Devoll, and crosses the small plain of Poloskë (c. 850 m high); one then climbs over the watershed ridge, some 1000 m high, and descends into the upper basin of the Haliacmon, where one can pass over the river to Kastoria (anc. Celetrum). An easy route takes one down the Haliacmon valley to Grevena near the great bend in the river's course. Here one can cross the Cambunian range at a relatively low altitude (between summits of 812 m and 697 m) and traverse a heavily wooded region of oak-scrub, known as the Khasia, and then follow the lower valley of the Murganis (or Mikanis) until it joins the river Peneus above Kalabaka. It is then easy going to Trikkala (anc. Tricca) in the western Thessalian plain, and from there to Thaumaci on the southern edge of the plain. An alternative route from Grevena ascends the valley of the Venetikos to Monakhiti and Krania and then crosses the watershed between the Haliacmon and the Peneus by an easy pass, called the Pass of Velemishti. One comes down to the Peneus valley at Nea Kutsufliani (anc. Aeginium). From there one can climb up to Ambelokhori and work round to Kastania, from which there is a route via Klinovos and Pertouli into the valley of the upper Achelous. This journey from Grevena via Nea Kutsufliani to Pertouli is one made only by shepherds and muleteers in normal circumstances.[15] It is not practicable during much of the winter.

Let us now consider the Vardar valley below Skopje, where the Demir Kapu blocks the way, and a detour must be made either to the west or to the east. If we go to the west, we leave the valley bed either at Titov for the Babuna Pass or at Gradsko (anc. Stobi) for the Pletvar Pass; in either case one has to go through a long, narrow defile during the ascent. From either pass one descends to Prilep, which is a town on a hill overlooking the Pelagonian plain, a great expanse of flat, peaty soil, drained by the Blato and the Cerna (anc. Erigon). On the Pelagonian side, once one has crossed the Cerna, it is quite fast going. Next comes the so-called Monastir Gap (which is simply a narrowing of the plain) and then the plain of Lyncus up to the first narrow place at Klidhi ('Key'), the so-called Kirli Dirven Pass, which is a narrow, winding, dry coombe of limestone formation.[16] This pass gives access to a lower plain, that of Eordaea, which has some lakes. Again the going is easy as one descends to the valley of the Haliacmon by Servia.

As one proceeds southwards, the climb by foot from Servia is steep but not very long, and the watershed ridge is crossed between the Haliacmon and the Sarandaporos (anc. Titaresius), a tributary of the Peneus, at a point flanked by high summits of 1379 and 1324 m. There is an easily defended defile on the Macedonian side at Stena Portas and another on the Thessalian side at the narrow place known as the Volustana Pass. At first the descent is gradual and open, but then there are many steep climbs and long descents as one moves across a number of ridges, until the entry into the flat, high plain of Elassona, which is the centre of this canton, called Perrhaebia. One descends along the valley of the Titaresius, which becomes narrow and defensible at and below Dhamasi, and finally emerges into the plain of Thessaly, where once one is across the Peneus the going is easy as far as Thaumaci, at the same latitude as the north coast of the Gulf of Arta.

The detour from the middle valley of the Vardar towards the east takes one to a gap between the range of Barnous-Gradeska (through which the Vardar cuts its way at Demir Kapu) and that of Belasitsa (anc. Orbelus). This gap in the mountain ring enclosing Lower Macedonia gives access also from the Strumitsa valley to the lower Vardar valley. The easiest route is via Valandovo. There is a further defile through which the river flows between Gevgheli and Axioupolis, but the country to the east is not difficult and one can circumvent the defile. Thereafter all is straightforward to Thessalonica on the Thermaic Gulf.

If one wants to go south, one crosses the river well inland and proceeds via Pella on the inland side of the swampy plain, which until quite recently had a large lake, named after Yiannitsa.[17] For the coastal plain has been formed by the deposits of the great rivers—the Gallikos (anc. Echedorus), the Vardar (anc. Axius) and the Vistritsa (anc. Haliacmon)—and of two lesser but considerable rivers, the Ludias (an ancient name) and the Vodhas (anc. Astraeus). The plain has grown in extent with the centuries and has always been swampy towards the coast, like the similarly-formed plains of Albania and Epirus.

After circling the inland side of the great plain and passing below Verria (anc. Beroea), one crosses a very low ridge and enters the coastal plain of Pieria, which narrows down to a thin strip of flat land south of Dium. Then at Platamona (anc. Heracleum) where a spur of the mountain is washed by the sea, there is a natural site for a strong fort, which can control the entire route. Soon afterwards one comes to the river Peneus and the defile, five miles long, known as the 'Vale of Tempe', where the Peneus cuts its way through the limestone sides of Lower Olympus and Mt Kissavos (anc. Ossa). As we learn from Livy, there was hardly room for a loaded pack-horse to get through the defile in the second century B.C., and even ten well-armed men were able to hold the pass with ease (44.6.8 and 11). It was probably the Romans who first cut the rocks and made a road on the south side of the defile. Once in Thessaly the going is easy via Pharsalus to Thaumaci.

On the western side of the peninsula, we can either cross by sea from Preveza to the spit of Acarnania, which was called Actium in antiquity, or we can march round the east side of the Gulf. On the latter course we cross the Arachthus where it enters the plain at Arta (anc. Ambracia). Here a small force can hold the crossing, which is between low limestone bluffs, and the town itself, being on a hill washed by the river on three sides,[18] is a further obstacle to any invader. Proceeding southward along a narrow plain, one comes to the eastern coast of the Gulf, which is rock-bound, steep and wooded. The coast itself was impassable until a motor road was constructed. Men and horses climbed to the top of the coastal range (402 m), which is called Makrinoros ('Long Mountain'), and followed the ridge until it was possible to drop down to the river Loutro to cross the coastal plain towards Karavassara (anc. Limnaea). The entry to Karavassara is pinched between the sea and a limestone spur and can be held by a small force. This pass can be turned by taking a route further inland which follows the ridge of the parallel range (Mt Thyamus in antiquity) and then the upper valley of the Botoko.

A long rift affords easy going from Karavassara to Stratus; then one has to cross the Achelous and the plain of western Aetolia. Next comes a remarkable pass, the Klisura, a limestone gorge with high walls which extends for some three and a half kilometres.[19] It was probably created by a remote predecessor of the Achelous, but the bed of the gorge is now dry, being higher than the level of the plain. From the exit of this impressive gorge—easily held against invaders—the waters of the Gulf of Corinth and the Peloponnese are visible. One descends past the lagoons of Mesolonghi (rich in fish, like the lagoons on the north shore of the Gulf of Arta), crosses the Phidaris (anc. Euenus), and reaches Antirrhium where there is the shortest sea route between central Greece and the Peloponnese.

Advancing southwards from Thaumaci one crosses the Othrys range, where there is a choice of passes between 750 and 620 m high, and descends rather steeply to the plain of Lamia. A much longer route from Thessaly to Lamia follows the coast from Halus on the Gulf of Pagasae to Echinus on the Maliac Gulf. From Lamia one also has the choice of a route inland or along the coast. The latter is the less arduous. In the fifth century B.C., it involved going through the 'pass of Thermopylae' between the cliffs and the sea, the passage varying between 15 and 2 metres, but the coastal strip is now quite wide because of the erosion of the coastal range and the deposit of silt by the Spercheus river in the Maliac Gulf. The route turns south beyond Opus and enters the central plain of Boeotia.

The inland route from Lamia begins with a long climb up to a high pass on the ridge between Mt Oeta and Mt Callidromus and drops only a little into the small upland plain of Doris, at the head of the long valley of the Cephissus. From there there are two routes. The first heads south, leaving the Cephissus valley at Gravia by a pass 850 m high, which is narrow, long and easily defensible. The country becomes more open as one reaches Amphissa and walks through the olive-groves to the shore of the Gulf of Corinth at Itea, below Delphi. The other route follows the Cephissus valley into the central plain of Boeotia. The going is easy, but there are defensible narrows at Parapotamii and at Chaeronea.

If one is going south from the central plain of Boeotia to the Peloponnese, one climbs first over Mt Cithaeron and then over Mt Karidhi ('Walnut'), and descends through a narrow cleft to enter the shelving plain of the Megarid. Then comes a long and steady climb up to the saddle in the range of Mt Gerania, from which one has a fine view of the mountains of the eastern Peloponnese. One descends through woods to Platanos, from which more than one easy route leads to the flat part of the Isthmus just before Corinth.[20]

This route from Boeotia is far shorter and less arduous than the long detour through Attica via Mandra (near Eleusis) and Megara. In ancient times the coastal route from Megara to the flat part of the Isthmus was difficult and dangerous, especially by the Scironian cliffs, later called the Kaki Skala ('Bad Ascent'), until the emperor Hadrian had the narrowest part of the passage widened. Even so the route through Gerania was preferred in the Turkish period.

In order to put the importance and the nature of these routes to the test of experience, I shall use as examples a number of campaigns. In January 48 B.C. Julius Caesar landed on the Acroceraunian coast and took his army over the Llogora Pass. See Maps 4 and 4a. He then captured Oricum at the head of the Gulf of Valona, won over Apollonia (now Poyan) and advanced on the inland side of the plain to the Semeni river by Kuç. There his enemy, Pompey, held the far bank, thus deterring Caesar from ferrying his army across the river. Reinforcements for Caesar, sailing from Italy, managed to slip through the Pompeian blockade of the lower Adriatic, but strong winds drove them to the north of Durazzo, where they landed safely. Their commander, Mark Antony, now had to join hands with Caesar. He evidently took the inland route via Tirana and reached a point above Bradashesh. Meanwhile, Pompey, having heard of Antony's landing, guessed what he would do and slipped away at night to intercept Antony in the Shkumbi valley. Pompey took the route through the low sink past Pazhok. But Antony stayed out of reach, and Caesar crossed the Semeni unopposed and followed Pompey through the low sink. As Pompey was now between two armies, he withdrew down the valley of the Shkumbi and encamped on its north bank at a place called Asparagium.

Some weeks later, when Caesar found himself at a disadvantage at Petra near Durazzo, he disengaged and retreated southwards with Pompey in pursuit. It was now early spring and the rivers must have been in flood. Reaching the Genusus (Shkumbi), Caesar's cavalry fought off the enemy cavalry, which had caught him up because "the banks of the river were troublesome," i.e., for troops scrambling down to embark on ferries (*Bellum Civile* 3.75.5, "ad flumen Genusum quod ripis erat impeditis"). When the army had been transported across the river ("traductoque exercitu flumen Genusum"), Caesar occupied the camp he had used earlier and Pompey stayed in his old camp on the north side of the river at Asparagium. Supposing that the day's march was done, and knowing that Caesar would not recross the river, Pompey let his troops disperse to forage and to collect baggage from Petra which they had left in a hurry. Caesar then resumed the march and gained an eight-mile lead by nightfall (reaching the vicinity of Lushnje). He kept ahead for three days, although "the rivers were very high and the journey troublesome" (*Bellum Civile* 3.77.2, "altissimis fluminibus atque impeditissimis itineribus"). He had to cross the Semeni (anc. Apsus) and some smaller rivers which entered the plain. Pompey abandoned the pursuit on the fourth day. Caesar then turned aside from the direct route ("directo itinere") in order to leave his wounded and make dispositions at Apollonia. We infer from this that "the direct route" ran not via Apollonia but through the hills inland of Apollonia, so as to enter the Aous valley and proceed from there up the Drin valley. When Caesar left Apollonia, he took the Aous-Drin route into Epirus and so "through Epirus and Athamania" to Thessaly (*Bellum Civile* 3.79.4). Thus he went from the Drin valley to the plateau of Ioannina and so to Ambracia, which he intended to use as his base of supplies, and from there through Athamania to Thessaly.

In A.D. 1096 the army of the First Crusade defeated Alexius, the Byzantine Emperor, at Durazzo and then marched south "in vallem de Andronopoli," that was to Hadrianopolis near Argyrokastro in the Drin valley, no doubt following Caesar's route. See Maps 1 and 4. They were probably anxious to obtain supplies in Epirus. The Emperor based himself upon Ochrid in the lakeland area and drew troops from 'Diabolis', the region of the Devoll, whose name does not come from the river but from the plain. After suffering a further defeat near Ioannina, the Emperor withdrew to Ochrid, and the Crusaders advanced "from town to town" until they reached "Castoria." The route they must have used was that from Konitsa via Leskoviq and Ersekë to Korçë, and then from Korcë via Bilisht over the watershed to Kastoria.[21] Later the Crusaders returned from Kastoria to the lakeland area by the same route and massacred a settlement of Christian heretics on an island in one of the lakes (probably the island of St. Achilleiou in Lake Little Prespa). These operations show how these routes in the lakeland area occupied a central position in the strategy of the southwest Balkans.

In October 1940 the Italians on the southern frontier of Albania invaded Epirus. See Maps 4 and 5. They delivered a three-pronged attack.[22] The first army drove down the coastal sector and reached the plain of Margariti. The second army attacked from the head of the Drin valley and aimed for Ioannina. The third army seized Konitsa, but being thwarted by the impenetrable gorges of the Aous and the Voïdhomati, made a detour east of Mt Smolika to Samarina, rejoined the Aous higher up, and so reached Vovousa. The Greeks concentrated their defence on the main route, that is in the central sector east of Mt Soutista. First they held up the second Italian army while the other two were advancing; then they counterattacked and drove this army back into the upper Drin valley. The Greeks now swung right to cut off the Italian army which was hurrying back from Vovousa, causing it to retreat along the Aous to Kelcyrë.

By December 1940 the Greek line ran from Himarrë (on the coastal road) through the Kurvelesh to Lekel at the defile of the Drin just before it joins the Aous, along the south side of the Aoi Stena to Brezhdan, and then across the districts of Danglli and Gramsh via Fratar to Pogradec at the southwestern angle of Lake Ochrid. The chief lines of supply ran along the coastal road; the central road via Ioannina and the Drin valley; the roads from Konitsa to Permet along the Aous; and from Konitsa via Korcë to Lake Ochrid. Supplies came also from Macedonia into the lakeland area.

The importance of the Makrinoros ridge and the Pass by Karavassara (anc. Limnaea) is apparent from several campaigns. See Maps 6 and 6a. In 430 B.C. a large army drawn mainly from Epirus, under Spartan command, was mustered in the territory of Ambracia (now Arta) for the purpose of conquering Acarnania and capturing Naupactus on the Gulf of Corinth. Being unopposed at first, they marched "through Argive territory" (which began south of the Makrinoros ridge), captured Limnaea, and went on by the long rift to Stratus, where they were defeated. Had they been successful, they could have continued on the direct route across the western Aetolian plain and through the Klisura to the coast of the Gulf of Corinth.[23] In 426 B.C., when his enemies were lying in wait just north of the Pass by Karavassara, another Spartan general marching from the south crossed the Achelous, marched past Stratus and up the long rift into the territory of Limnaea; but he then turned inland and entered the territory of the Agraei, where he followed the ridge of Mt Thyamus and came down to the north of his enemies.[24]

In A.D. 1829 an English general, in command of Greek troops at Vonitsa on the south shore of the Gulf of Arta, positioned on the flank of the Turkish line of communications which ran from Arta via Karavassara to Mesolonghi and Naupactus, planned a surprise attack on the northern end of the Makrinoros ridge by land and from the sea. His land forces marched to the south and then to the east of Karavassara; they then ascended the south end of Mt Makrinoros. Meanwhile, the English fleet landed troops at night on the shore below the northern end of the ridge. The two forces then captured all the Turkish posts on the ridge. They consolidated their position by occupying the northern ends of both the Makrinoros ridge and the neighbouring ridge inland. As all communication with Arta was now severed, the Turkish garrisons at Karavassara, Mesolonghi and Naupactus capitulated.[25]

In 1912, when the Turkish frontier ran just north of Arta, the Greeks delivered a two-pronged attack from Arta against the Turkish bases at Preveza and at Ioannina. The first force was held up at Strongili on the north shore of the Gulf, but the second force captured first the defile at the southern end of Mt Xerovouni and then the bridge over the Louros, thus cutting the two lines of communication from Ioannina to the Gulf of Arta; as a French historian noted at the time: "tenant ainsi les débouchés dans la plaine d'Arta des deux routes venant de Janina."[26] Preveza fell a week later, and the combined Greek forces then drove the Turks back along the flank of Mt Xerovouni towards Ioannina, winning a victory at Pende Pigadhia ('Five Wells').

In April 1941 the German forces, operating from Bulgaria, failed to break through the Greek resistance at Rupel in the gorge of the river Strymon. See Maps 2, 3, 5 and 6. The breakthrough came further west. There the Germans had gained control of the Strumitsa valley and Strumitsa town in Yugoslavia. One force entered the head of the Kumli valley and occupied the Stena Dov Tepe Pass. The other force moved from Strumitsa to Valandovo and from there into the Axius valley at Polykastro. The force holding Stena Dov Tepe opened the way for a further advance from Strumitsa to Kilindir and Kilkis. On April 9th the Germans entered Salonica. Their main force, however, crossed the Vardar and advanced from Axioupolis via Skydhra to Verria and then to Katerini. Attacks on the British positions on the Petra Pass (leading inland to Elassona) and on the narrowing coast by Platamona were repulsed.

Meanwhile another German force entered the upper Vardar valley, advanced to Prilep and came through the Monastir Gap on April 9th. Greek forces were then protecting the Pisodherion Pass (west of Florina) and the left of the British line was at the Kirli Dirven Pass by Klidhi. On the 12th, the British withdrew southwards and proceeded to adopt a line along the Cambunian range from the low part between Grevena and the Khasia region to the passes above Servia, and so joined hands with the British coastal group which held the Petra Pass and the narrows at Platamona.

The weak point was at the hinge between the Greek forces to the west and the southwest of the Kirli Dirven Pass and the British force retreating southeastwards by Ptolemaïs and Kozani to take up the new line of defence.[27] In this area the Germans pushed through the Siatista Pass into the Haliacmon valley, from which one group swung north to capture Kastoria on April 15th and another group of armoured cars and tanks went southwest through Grevena and broke through to the Peneus valley west of Kalabaka, making use of the Venetikos valley and the route to Nea Kutsufliani and perhaps also of the lower Murganis valley. Thus the whole British position was turned, and the British forces withdrew to hold a new line at Thermopylae.

The route of this German breakthrough had been used by one of Julius Caesar's commanders, Domitius, in 48 B.C. His army then lay at Monastir, and it was in danger of being overwhelmed by the stronger army of Pompey who was about to arrive there from Durazzo via Ochrid (anc. Lychnidus). At the time Julius Caesar was in southern Epirus and was about to march from Ambracia "through Athamania" to Gomphi (now Mouzaki) in Thessaly. Caesar and Domitius were completely out of touch with one another, but some Gauls in Pompey's army passed the news of Caesar's southward movement and of Pompey's imminent arrival to Domitius, who fled south and met Caesar at Nea Kutsufliani[28] (anc. Aeginium: Caesar, *Bellum Civile* 3.79.7 "ad Aeginium, quod est obiectum oppositumque Thessaliae, Caesari venienti occurrit").

In 480 B.C., when the Persian king Xerxes brought his huge army from Therme (near Salonica) to the vicinity of Katerini, he made a reconnaissance by sea of the mouth of the Peneus. See Map 15. He was able to confirm what he had been told, that the Vale of Tempe, although undefended, was too narrow for the passage of his forces.[29] He therefore had a wide road constructed through the Petra Pass over "the Macedonic mountain" (the Pierian range) into Perrhaebia, and his army marched by this route past Elassona into the Thessalian plain. The Greeks had decided not to defend the Vale of Tempe, because they realised that the position could be turned by an army using the Petra Pass. Their position at Thermopylae proved very strong at first; but it was turned by a Persian force which moved at night along a high mountain track and surprised the Greeks guarding it at dawn.[30] When the Greeks withdrew up the mountainside, the Persians passed on and came down to the sea in the rear of the Greek force at Thermopylae. There the Spartans, led by their king Leonidas, fought to the death. The main body of the Persian army did not proceed through the very narrow pass of Thermopylae but climbed up to the pass between Mt Oeta and Mt Callidromus, entered Doris and followed the valley of the Cephissus through the narrows of Parapotamii into the plain of Boeotia.

In 339 B.C. Philip of Macedon entered Doris in the same way and intended to reach Boeotia. See Maps 6 and 7. Demosthenes persuaded the Boeotians to ally themselves with Athens, and their joint forces held the narrows at Parapotamii. In addition they placed troops in the Gravia Pass above Amphissa. In 338 Philip, operating from his base in Doris, broke through the Gravia Pass and thereby turned the Greek position at Parapotamii. When the Greeks adopted a new position at Chaeronea, Philip attacked in strength and gained a decisive victory.

The route from southern Boeotia over Mt Cithaeron and through the northern Megarid and then "through Gerania" has been of great importance. In 479 B.C. a Greek army of more than 100,000 men, holding the southern bank of the Asopus river below Plataea, had to be supplied from the Peloponnese. Wheeled vehicles were used at the time (Herodotus 9.39.2). In 457 B.C. a Peloponnesian army marched from Tanagra in southern Boeotia into the Megarid, and going on "through Gerania and the Isthmus" it regained the Peloponnese.[31] In A.D. 1258, in a war between the Prince of Achaea in the Peloponnese and the Duke of Athens, the Prince occupied "the Skala of Megara" (the Kaki Skala or passage by the Scironian cliffs) and "the Klisura" (the pass through Gerania), while the Duke took up defensive positions covering the entry to Attica and the pass of Mt Karidhi (leading to Boeotia). The Prince forced this last pass and drove the Duke back into Boeotia.[32] See Map 8.

The Latitudinal Routes, from West to East

The routes which cross our area from west to east, connecting the coast of the Adriatic Sea with those of the Black Sea and the Sea of Marmara, and connecting the coast of the Sicilian Sea with that of the Aegean Sea further south, have played almost as important a role in the history of the Balkans as those from north to south. All such passages on the western side of the spinal range or ranges (Šar Planina to Parnassus) are of an order of difficulty which western Europeans regard as daunting, but they have been accepted as tolerable by Balkan traders who used caravans of pack-horses.

The first route runs from the basin of Zeta over the mountains between the masses of Montenegro and Northern Albania and descends into the basin of Peć in the district Metohija, from which there is easy access to Priština and Lipljan (anc. Ulpiana), which lie on the great north-south route of the Ibar and Vardar valleys.

Next (Maps 1 and 2) is the 'Via Egnatia', the Roman name for an age-old passage which the Romans paved and improved and which was in constant use throughout medieval and Turkish times.[33] It started from two terminals on the Adriatic coast, Durazzo and Apollonia (as long as the navigable Aous river ran close to it) and later Aulon on the north coast of the Gulf of Valona, when the Aous changed its course away from Apollonia. The roads from these terminals met in the valley of the Shkumbi (anc. Genusus), which offers a direct and easy passage on its right bank for a long distance inland, up to the point east of Elbasan where the river changes its course to cut through the tangle of the Candavian Mountains. Here one crosses the river and makes an arduous climb high above the friable flysch formation of the valley to the limestone mountainside by Babië. A long traverse with many ups and downs and zigzags round the heads of ravines brings one to Qukës, from which there is a steep descent to the riverside, where a narrow limestone bed makes bridging possible. We now leave the Shkumbi and climb up, first through the tilted plateau of Domousova and then through a high marshy basin, to reach the top of the pass from which the waters of Lake Ochrid are visible. The descent is long and steep, but the route becomes flat round the north shore of the lake to Old Ochrid (anc. Lychnidus), where it joins the important north-south routes via the Black Drin and Kitsevo to the lakeland.

At this point we may break off and return to the Shkumbi bed below Qukës. An alternative route from there follows the upper valley of the Shkumbi which is now easy going, as the country is open and cultivated, for instance by Ano Selcë. From the head of the valley one way goes over the watershed and descends to Pogradec at the southwest corner of Lake Ochrid; the other proceeds through the mountains towards the plain of Korcë (Koritsa).[34]

From Old Ochrid the Via Egnatia climbed over two very high passes: one north of Mt Petrina (1734 m) from which one descends to Resen above Lake Prespa, and the other north of Mt Peristeri (2601 m)—the so-called Diavat Pass—from which one descends to Monastir. The climbs and the descents are arduous, but the ground is firm and often grassy, there are forests of beech and pine, and the air in the summer is of Alpine freshness. In winter it is a different matter, because the passes are well above the snow line. But the worst is over on reaching the Monastir Gap. From there the Via Egnatia followed the north-south route into Eordaea which we have already described. Within Eordaea the Via Egnatia turned northeast at Amyntaion (anc. Cellis) and ran through the basin which now holds Lake Ostrovo, much smaller in ancient times, and climbed over a pass by Karaburun (669 m) between Mt Barnous and Mt

Bermion. There is a gradual descent along the river Skirtos ('the leaper') to Edessa, a fine city on the escarpment, overlooking the coastal plain. The going is now excellent as far as Salonica.[35]

Beyond Salonica there is an easy ascent into the Langadha basin and the Via Egnatia runs along the southern side of its two lakes.[36] We leave the basin by a limestone coombe with steep sides; this is the Pass of Rendina, which can be easily defended. It gives access to the Strymonian plain. The river Strymon was crossed at Amphipolis, which lay between Lake Cercinitis and the sea. From Amphipolis the Via Egnatia followed the route north of Mt Pangaeum to Philippi, rather than the coastal route south of Mt Pangaeum. The two routes met at Kavalla (anc. Neapolis). From there the Via Egnatia proceeded through the narrow Pass of Acontisma into the valley of the Mesta (anc. Nestus) and eventually to Constantinople (now Istanbul) on the Sea of Marmara. This great road picks up all the north-south routes, namely at Salonica, Amphipolis, the mouth of the Nestus and so on.

Between the latitude of Peć-Lipljan and that of the Via Egnatia there are some west-east routes which cover all or a part only of the southwest Balkans. One route (Map 1) proceeds from the Adriatic coast up the valley of the Mati river to a pass of some 1400 m at Murë and descends to the valley of the Black Drin at Dibër (Dibra). Crossing the north-south route which runs along this valley, one passes through a low saddle of the Šar Planina-Korab range and descends to Kitsevo (anc. Uscana), which is on a tributary of the Vardar.[37] Here one crosses the north-south route from Gostivar to Ochrid, and proceeds by a rather easy route through the hills to Prilep. Continuing (Map 2) through the Pletvar Pass to Gradsko (anc. Stobi) on the Vardar, one meets the north-south route of the Vardar valley and proceeds up the valley of the Bregalnitsa past Štip (anc. Astibus) into the upper valley. Then (Map 3) one takes an easy pass by Kratovo (anc. Tranupara) into the head of the valley of the Kriva, and on from there over another easy pass to Kjustendil (anc. Pautalia) on the side of the Strymon valley, where one picks up the north-south route from Sofia (anc. Serdica), which runs down the Strymon.

In the region between the Vardar and the Strymon there are two short transverse routes of some importance. One of them proceeds from Stobi into the Strumitsa valley (anc. Doberus) and follows the valley through a narrow pass, called Klisura, to the junction with the Strymon just above the Rupel pass. This passage was much used in medieval and Turkish times because it avoided the defiles of the lower Vardar valley.[38] The other route starts from a little north of Gevgheli (anc. Eidomene) and follows a sink on the south side of the Belasitsa range, crossing the watershed at a pass called the Stena Dov Tepe and descending by the valley of the Kumli to the Strymon river.[39] On crossing the river one can proceed via Serres to Drama and Philippi, where one joins the Via Egnatia. This route enables one to by-pass Amphipolis, Rendina and the Langadha basin.

Another (Maps 2 and 4) starts from the coastal plain of Albania and proceeds from the spectacular defile of Berat (anc. Antipatrea) through very difficult wooded country (Gramsh) either to join the upper Devoll at Malik or direct to Korcë (Koritsa).[40] Proceeding through the Tsangon Pass and the plain of Poloskë, which we have mentioned before, one turns eastward at Bilisht and climbs over the Pass of Vatokhorion between summits of 1749 and 1538 m of the range which forms the watershed. Ascending the valley of the Haliacmon to its source one crosses the Pass of Pisodherion between peaks of 2110 and 1858 m. From this lofty pass one has a long descent to Florina and enters the plain of Lyncus to join the Via Egnatia north of Klidhi.

In ancient times it seems that there was a shorter and better route, one that cut out the Vatokhorion Pass. This route turned east by the foot of Lake Little Prespa and followed the south side of the lake to Drenovo, from which the ascent was made to the Pisodherion Pass. At that time the lake drained into the Devoll, and the river left a very narrow passage at the foot of the lake, a passage which might be called the Tren Pass after a nearby village.[41] It was possible then to proceed along the eastern side of both Prespa Lakes and to reach Resen on the Via Egnatia. The remarkable feature of the route by Korcë and the Passes of Tsangon and Tren is that once one has reached the western side of Korcë plain the going is flat to Drenovo, and there is only one range to cross before entering Lyncus.

On the other hand, if one takes the Via Egnatia route from Ochrid to Monastir, one has to climb over two high passes, that between Ochrid and Resen over Mt Petrina and that between Resen and

Monastir over Mt Peristeri. Thus the Malik-Tren-Resen-Monastir route is much easier.

From the coast of Epirus (Maps 4 and 5) two routes lead inland. One is short, from Santi Quaranta or Butrinto to join the main north-south route in the Drin valley; this involves a gradual climb and a steep descent.[42] The other starts from the delta of the Kalamas (anc. Thyamis) and keeps on the north side of the river to Filiates, from which one follows the long valley of the Dhafnis and climbs steeply over a ridge of shale to descend to the Kalamas at Raveni (anc. Phanote). The route follows one side and then the other side of the river, and then turns up the valley of a tributary, the Veltsiotikos. From the village of Veltsista (now Klimatia) it is a short climb over the ridge to enter the plateau of Ioannina. One descends past a fortified hill-site, called Gardhiki, which was probably the ancient Passaron, the administrative centre of the Molossian kingdom.[43] Here one joins the main north-south route through Epirus.

Leaving the plateau via Kastritsa (probably anc. Eurymenae), we embark on the best route over the central range between the area of Korcë and the Gulf of Corinth. It is not by any means easy even in summer and it can be impossible in winter. A long ascent brings one to a saddle of flysch formation, called Dhriskos, from which it is a steep descent to the valley of the Arachthus ('Tearer', so called because it makes impassable gorges in limestone rock). One crosses the Zagoritikos or Dhipotamos (a large tributary flowing from Zagori) and follows the right bank of the Arachthus, which is often steep and affords little passage, as far as Tria Khania ('Three Inns'), which lies below a Vlach village, Voutonosi. Then comes a long climb, crossing and recrossing the river, up to Metsovo, the leading village of the Pindus Vlachs. There is a steep descent and then a long steep climb past precipitous screes of green serpentine to the head of the Zygos ('Crossbar') Pass, just over 5,000 feet high.

The descent follows a long grassy ridge through forests first of beech and then of pine, until one reaches the Peneus river and crosses over to go up to Malakasi, the first village on the Thessalian side. It is a long and gradual descent down the valley of the Peneus, which becomes wider below Murgani. One route from Grevena is joined at Nea Kutsufliani and another at Murgani. After a two hour journey one enters Kalabaka which is overshadowed by the tall sentinels of rock on which are the Meteora monasteries, looking out over the Thessalian plain.[44] If one continues across the plain to the east, the main north-south route from Larissa is crossed and one reaches Volos, on the Gulf of Pagasae. A fast walker, under good conditions, can make the journey from Kastritsa to Kalabaka in twenty-four hours.

There are other routes through Pindus, but they are used now only by shepherds and by mountain villagers who transport hay or timber on pack-animals. Such routes run from Konitsa to Kastoria, and from Greveniti in Zagori to Grevena.[45] Routes south of the Zygos Pass had some importance during the wars waged by the Romans in Greece, and again in the period 1831–1912 when the Greco-Turkish frontier ran just north of the line from Arta to Volos. See Map 5. The villages south of Paliokhori in the upper valley of the Achelous and its tributaries, being at a lower altitude than those of northern Pindus, are inhabited during the winter and are much more numerous, although less prosperous; and this has encouraged more intercommunication with adjacent areas.[46] The best route, from Arta (anc. Ambracia) to Mouzaki (anc. Gomphi), takes thirty-one hours for a fast walker under good conditions.[47] One climbs over a range of flysch formation at Katavothra, crosses the Achelous at Korakou bridge built in the Turkish period (Pl. *1a*), ascends the long valley of an eastern tributary to Mezilo, climbs over a ridge and descends through the fertile plateau of Nevropolis to Mouzaki on the edge of the Thessalian plain. Alternatively, over the last stretch one can go via Aryithea to Porta Panayia.

A more direct but also more arduous route runs farther north: Arta–Voulgareli–Mesokhora bridge–ridge between Stournareika and Paliokaria–Porta Panayia. This takes some twenty hours. Another route further south (Map 6), from the east side of the Gulf of Arta to Karpenisi near the head of the Spercheus valley, is also a matter of some twenty hours for a fast walker, but it too is arduous, with many climbs and descents. One crosses the ridge of the third range parallel to the coast at Xerakia, then the ridge west of the Achelous near Khalkopouloi, and then the Tatarna bridge over the Achelous. Another climb and descent and one crosses the Agrafiotikos by the bridge of Manolis, built in 1659; the same again and one crosses the Megdovas below Viniani; and finally a very high and arduous pass over Mt Tymphrestus (2315 m) and down to Karpenisi.

To the south the tangle of high Aetolian mountains makes movement from west to east even more difficult. This is true also, if one keeps close to the coast of the Gulf of Corinth, because one has to cross river after river and climb the watersheds between them. It is only on the eastern side of this mountainous tract that we can speak of a west-east route, leading from Itea-Delphi past Arachova to Lebadea in the Boeotian plain and leaving Mt Parnassus (2457 m) on our left.[48] See Map 6.

When we consider the military use of these west-east routes, the most important was the Via Egnatia, improved by the Romans to serve as a 'via militaris'. See Map 1. When Pompey and Caesar disengaged near Dyrrachium, Pompey marched through the Candavian mountains to Heraclea (near Monastir) in Macedonia; so too the Emperor Alexius, having been defeated at Dyrrachium by the First Crusaders, fled by 'Babagora' (now Babië) to Ochrid and retired later to 'Butella' (Monastir). The strategic value of the Dibër gap and the Dibër-Kitsevo-Prilep route was shown most strikingly in the campaigns of the Turks against Skanderbeg in the fifteenth century. Battle after battle was fought in the vicinity of Dibër, "cette porte de l'Albanie centrale," as it has been called by A. Gegaj.[49] One of the defeats of the Turkish army occurred in the plain of Polog, which shows that the Turks were using the route from Kossovo via Gostivar to Kitsevo. The Dibër gap was important also in the wars between Rome and Macedon. For instance in 170–169 B.C., when the Romans held Dibër and Kitsevo (anc. Uscana), Perseus had to send envoys by the route north of Šar Planina (anc. Scardus) via Peć to negotiate with the king of the Ardiaei, Genthius, whose capital was in the district of Zeta.[50] Farther east, the route from Stobi via Štip and Kjustendil to Sofia was used by Alexander the Great, when he marched from Macedonia "towards the Agrianes and the Paeones" in 335 B.C., and by Philip V, when he marched from Stobi to attack the Maedi in the valley of the Strymon in 181 B.C.[51]

To the south of the Via Egnatia the passes of the lakeland area were used by Roman armies in the campaigns of the Second Macedonian War.[52] See Map 4. In 199 B.C. Sulpicius marched from his camp south of the Apsus (Semeni), probably at Kuç, through the district of Gramsh via Codrion (probably Kalaja Rrmait near Mirakë) to Malik, from which he turned north to camp somewhere near Pogradec by the river Bevus (now Molca). Later that year he marched from Celetrum (Kastoria) to Pelium (near Tren), using either the Vatokhorion Pass or the more direct one southeast of Bilisht. The route from Pelium to Lyncus through the Pass of Tren and over the Pisodherion Pass seems to have been used by Alexander the Great in 335 B.C.[53] In east Macedonia the route along the Strumitsa valley was the scene of the defeat of Samuel the Bulgar by the Byzantine Emperor at the Klidhi Pass in A.D. 1014. See Map 3. When Alexander set out to conquer Persia, he used the route by Stena Dov Tepe and the Kumli valley, just as Xerxes had done when he was marching against the Greeks. It was during his retreat that Xerxes took the southernmost route through the Langadha basin and tried to cross the Strymon by Amphipolis, where the ice broke under the weight of the army.[54]

The short route between the coast and the Drin valley played a role in 230 B.C. (Map 4). The Illyrians under Scerdilaïdas came through the "Pass of Antigonea" (just before the Drin joins the Aous) and went on from the Drin valley to Phoenice.[55] It is probable that the consul Hostilius followed the route from the delta of the Kalamas (anc. Thyamis) to enter the plateau of Ioannina at Gardhiki (anc. Passaron) and took the Zygos Pass over Pindus, in order to take up an appointment in Boeotia.[56] The shorter of the routes from Ambracia to Gomphi, that via Aryithea, was used by Roman forces, including cavalry, for instance in 198 B.C. and it was described by Livy (32.15.6) as very short but difficult and troublesome.[57] I do not know of any campaign in which the route from the east coast of the Gulf of Arta to Karpenisi was used. On the other hand the route from Delphi to the plain of Boeotia was the line of communications between the Greek forces by Amphissa and those by Parapotamii in the winter of 339–8 B.C.

Many of the passes which we have mentioned become snowed up in the winter months, and it was therefore exceptional to undertake campaigns in northern or central Greece in the winter. In 169 B.C., when Perseus was hemmed in by the Romans and their allies, he made a desperate attempt to break the circle by undertaking a winter campaign which involved crossing the Pindus range. His only allies in Epirus were the Molossians of the Ioannina plateau. See Maps 2, 5 and 6. The Chaonians were hostile in northern Epirus, a Roman garrison held Ambracia, and the Aetolians were on the Roman side. Perseus hoped to arrive unannounced at Stratus; the town was garrisoned by the Aetolians, but one of the commanders was disaffected and had offered to betray the place to Perseus. Starting somewhere from Elimea (probably from Kozani) with 10,000 infantry, 300 cavalry (so few "owing to the narrow places and roughness of the roads"), a baggage-train and supplies, he took the direct route across Pindus via Grevena and Monakhiti and on the third day reached Mt Citius (probably Avgo, 2177 m). There the snow lay so deep that he had great difficulty in crossing the high ground, and it was almost impossible to find a suitable camp for the night. Next day the weather and the going were very bad, and his pack-animals suffered especially severely ("ingenti vexatione iumentorum"). As the snow is usually deeper and the ground steeper on the west side of the range, he was probably descending at this stage. But he pressed on and reached the southern part of the plateau of Ioannina, where he could obtain fresh horses and some supplies from the Molossians.

Next day, the fifth, he made a huge march (Livy 43.21 "ingens iter") which brought him to the bank of the Arachthus somewhere north of Ambracia (Arta). As the Arachthus proceeds through impassable gorges in this part of its course, Perseus took the route via Pende Pigadhia as far as Ammotopos, from which there is a route by the Kiafa stream down to the river. (My walking time for this march would have been some fourteen hours). At the Arachthus Perseus was unlucky. The river was too high for him to cross, and it took his engineers some days to construct a bridge, no doubt with tall trees felled on the spot.

Once across the Arachthus, he gave Arta and Karavassara (Limnaea) a wide berth by taking a route through Skoulikaria into the valley of the Sindekiniotikos river (anc. Inachus) which is flat-bottomed and provides good going. Having covered some 40 kilometres, he reached the frontier of Agraïs (near Khalkopouloi) where he met the disaffected officer from Stratus and planned to enter Stratus during the following night. He arrived at Stratus on time after a march of equal length, only to find that the commander of the Roman garrison at Ambracia and a body of troops had entered the town after dark, just ahead of him.[58] The dice seemed to be loaded against Perseus.

It is essential to have personal knowledge of the ground or to use the work of someone who has that knowledge in order to relate this and other campaigns to the topography of the area. Otherwise absurdities arise. For example, writing of Perseus' campaign, W. M. Leake, who was the greatest topographer of the nineteenth century, thought that Perseus "pursued the course of the river (Arachthus) . . . seeking for a passage." Now Leake had ridden from Arta to Ioannina in fourteen hours (his baggage taking two hours more) via Pende Pigadhia, but he had not crossed the mountain, as I did, e.g. at Kalenji, to look at the valley of the middle Arachthus.[59] It is in fact a series of gorges, such as those shown on Plate 1a.

Again, A. W. Gomme, who was usually attentive to topographical matters, made the error of supposing that Xerxes and his huge army went "up the Haliacmon valley and then south by the pass now called Servia."[60] In fact the Haliacmon cuts its way between the Pierian mountains and Mt Bermion in a deep gorge, which I walked up with Heurtley in December 1929 and knew again in 1943. See Map 5. It is difficult on foot, impossible for wheeled vehicles and narrow in places; no army, let alone a very large one, would march that way. The main route from the coast to the middle valley of the Haliacmon now runs 1000 metres above the river past the Zoödokos Pege on the north side, and a longer, more arduous and equally high route has been made recently along the Pierian mountains on the south side. It is most unlikely that Xerxes used either of these routes through these mountains,[61] for he would have had to have made a road in addition to the one over the Petra Pass, which a third of his army was said to have constructed (Herodotus 7.131).

Invasions and Migrations

There is a difference between a march with armed forces only, such as that of Perseus to Stratus, and campaigns which are conducted in search of land when the men are accompanied by women and probably children. The latter partake of both invasion and migration. Thus the forces of Theodoric the Goth were accompanied by women and carried their chattels and booty on some thousands of waggons and on large numbers of baggage-animals, evidently pack-horses.[62] See Map 12. His forces, like those of other Gothic chieftains, were eager to obtain good land on which to settle; indeed those of Sidimund were already cultivating "a fertile allotment and a grant of territory" near Dyrrachium. In A.D. 479 Theodoric and his Goths sacked Stobi on the Vardar and then went on to Heraclea (near Monastir), probably by the Pletvar Pass and Prilep. He sent cavalry ahead to occupy the high points of the passes, then set in motion the main body with the waggons and the baggage animals, and let the rearguard follow under the command of Theodimund. The people of Lychnidus (Old Ochrid) beat Theodoric off, 'Scampia' was abandoned by its inhabitants, and Dyrrachium was taken. His method of supply was a simple one: to demand food from any inhabited centre, and, if it was not provided, to sack the place. Meanwhile two Roman commanders came up the Via Egnatia from Thessalonica via Edessa to Lychnidus, where they halted their troops and opened negotiations.

Preliminary arrangements for the Goths to receive a land settlement in Dardania (perhaps in the Kossovo area) were well advanced between Theodoric and one of the Roman commanders who had joined him near Durazzo, when the other commander saw an opportunity of destroying the unsuspecting Goths who were still on the way from Lychnidus to Dyrrachium. He sent some infantry ahead to seize the heights above the Goths at night, and he set out in the evening with a force of cavalry. At dawn, when the long column of waggons was already under way towards or on the terrible descent from Babië towards the river, the Roman cavalry attacked the Gothic rear guard and the Roman infantry appeared on the overhanging rocks. Theodimund and his mother, with their guards, fled down to the level ground, where they destroyed "the bridge over a deep gorge" and prevented pursuit. After a short battle the Romans took about 2,000 waggons and more than 5,000 prisoners, together with much booty. They returned in triumph to Lychnidus but had to burn some of the waggons on the way, because it was so difficult to draw them through such precipitous country.[63]

On another occasion, when Thiudimer was in possession of Naissus (Niš), he sent a force ahead to occupy Ulpiana (Lipljan) and this force opened up the entry to "some inaccessible places of Illyricum."[64] Then it occupied Heraclea (by Monastir) and "Larissa" (which is probably an error for Arnissa, perhaps Petres) on the Eordaean side of the Kirli Dirven Pass. Thus his plans were like those of Theodoric, when he was at Heraclea, but this time the intention was to advance along the Via Egnatia into Lower Macedonia. Thiudimer came up from Naissus and advanced to Thessalonica, where he found the defences strong and came to terms with the Roman governor. He gave the Goths a number of places to inhabit ("quae incolerent"): Pella, Cyrrus, Europus (NE of Pella), Beroea, Methone, Pydna and Dium, i.e. the chief cites of Lower Macedonia west and southwest of the Vardar.[65] This time too we may assume that the Goths had their waggons, their horses and their families with them, as well as cattle, sheep and other forms of loot.[66] They were evidently pastoralists rather than peasant farmers, and their large numbers of horses and their use of cavalry made them particularly dangerous to the settled Byzantine peoples.

We hear also of Scythian invaders in A.D. 268, who overran Lower Macedonia as Sitalces had done in 429 B.C. "They then withdrew into the interior and as they went they ravaged the areas of Doberus and Pelagonia, every single place" (Zosimus I. 43). It is interesting to note their route of withdrawal. They avoided the narrow defile of Demir Kapu, although the Romans at this time maintained a good road through it. Instead they went from the lower valley of the Vardar via Valandovo into Doberus (the Strumitsa valley) and from there back to the Vardar valley and on by the Pletvar Pass or the Babuna Pass into Pelagonia. Their strength being in cavalry, they kept to the more open country and avoided a defile when they could do so. See Maps 2 and 3.

We shall find other examples of this kind of invasion-migration in the next chapter. Then too the invaders were pastoralists with many horses and flocks, especially of sheep. As their descendants are still in this area, they figure in the next chapter.

Lastly, let us consider the sea routes. The marshy coastal plains of Albania and of Macedonia have no tradition of seafaring whatever, and their changing shoals and flat, featureless coasts have always been dangerous for mariners. But the Bay of Kotor and the Gulf of the Drin are different. They were the centres of the naval power of the Ardiaei in the third century B.C., and this part of the Adriatic coast together with the offshore islands farther north is a natural training-area for sailors. Indeed the Dalmatian coast, the peninsula of Istria and the head of the Adriatic Sea have rivalled the Aegean Sea in the art of seamanship, and there have been times when the ships of these regions, whether Illyrian or Venetian, have practised piracy and trade in the Aegean Sea with success. On the other hand, to the south the peoples of Epirus, Acarnania and Aetolia have usually left all seafaring to the inhabitants of the islands—Corcyra, Leucas, Ithaca, Cephallenia and Zacynthos—and it has often happened that such ports as exist on the mainland coast have been acquired by seafaring nations, such as Corinth in ancient times, and Venice or Britain thereafter. On the east side of the peninsula, the Gulf of Pagasae plays the same role as the Gulf of the Drin: it is a natural training-area for sailors, and the offshore islands lead the sailor on into the Aegean Archipelago. Yet most of the mainland population from Olympus to Cithaeron are landlubbers, and the leading seamen of this latitude have always come from the long offshore island of Euboea.

The safest crossing in the days of sail was from Bari in Apulia to the Gulf of the Drin or to Durazzo (Dyrrachium), because there was plenty of sea room and conspicuous landmarks could be sighted in clear weather. The crossing from Apulia to the Gulf of Valona was hazardous by comparison, because the seas are often steeper in these narrower waters and the dreaded Acroceraunian coast is close at hand. The crossing from the heel of Italy to the west coast of Corcyra was almost as hazardous, but it had the advantage of by-passing the Acroceraunian coast. Ships travelling down the Adriatic and into the Aegean sailed from island to island, except in the dangerous area of the Albanian coast, and then they had a difficult passage round the tips of the Peloponnese. From the eastern side of the peninsula passage across the Aegean is easy and there are several good routes; but entry into the Black Sea was rendered difficult for sailing ships by the strong current flowing into the Mediterranean and by the northerly winds which prevail at some seasons of the year.

Invasions of the southwestern Balkans by sea have come more often from the Adriatic than from the Aegean. Illyrians, Romans, Normans, Venetians, Genoese, and to a marginal extent the French and the British made use of the sea lanes from the west, but Persians, Huns, Goths, Slavs, Bulgars and Turks came preferably and sometimes exclusively by land. Migrating bands have crossed the Adriatic in both directions in historical times, but they have more often crossed the Aegean from west to east than vice versa. Thus, perhaps paradoxically, the Adriatic has played a much more important part in seaborne invasions and migrations of the southwest Balkans than the Aegean Sea in historical times.

NOTES

1. For this area (which I have not visited) see J. Cvijić, *La péninsule balkanique* (Paris, 1918), p. 24 and for the Roman road Arthur Evans in *Archaeologia* 49 (1885) 1, 80 f.

2. M. Hasluck, *The Unwritten Law in Albania* (Cambridge, 1954), p. 3.

3. C. J Jireček, *Die Heerestrasse von Belgrad nach Constantinopel und die Balkanpässe* (Prague, 1877), pp. 22 f., took the Roman road from Ulpiana (Lipljan, north of Kačanik) to Lissus (Lesh) by this route. Arthur Evans, loc. cit., argued from the report of an Albanian friend that it ran through Djakova, Brizza and Toplana to Lesh, that was north of the Drin bend. Probability lies with Jireček.

4. Arthur Evans, loc. cit., described this area as "among the wildest and most inaccessible of the Balkan peninsula and peopled for the most part by savage and fanatical mountaineers."

5. Herodotus 7.111.1 remarked that one of these tribes, "the Satrae, who lived in lofty mountains, clad in forests of all kinds and capped with snow," had never been conquered by anyone. This is still the boast of the Bulgarians of Rila.

6. In late March 1932 I crossed the Shkumbi by ferry, when the floods covered the greater part of the coastal plain.

7. The piles remain in the river bed; see *Epirus*, p. 235 with fig. 3.

8. I visited this area in 1972 and have described it more fully in *JHS* 94 (1974) 66 f.

9. See *Macedonia*, p. 174. The Yugoslav excavations there are reported in *Archaeologia Iugoslavica* 5 (1964) and *Starinar* 12 (1961) 222 f.

10. The Kresna defile is illustrated in S. Casson, *Macedonia, Thrace and Illyria*, p. 20, fig. 10.

11. Thucydides 2.97.2 and 98.1.

12. See map 1 in *Epirus*.

13. For the Roman roads see *Epirus*, p. 700, map 18.

14. The swamps of the Bistritsa valley were mentioned by Procopius, *De Aedificiis* 4.1.37, writing in A.D. 555 or so.

15. I used it in 1943.

16. See *Macedonia*, p. 105 for a detailed description of the pass and for the action of Brasidas there.

17. For changes in the plain see *Macedonia*, pp. 142 f. and maps 15 and 16.

18. See *Epirus*, p. 141 map 6.

19. A picture of the gorge may be found in W. J. Woodhouse, *Aetolia* (Oxford, 1897), p. 14.

20. This route is described in *StGH*, pp. 417 f.

21. For further details see *JHS* 94 (1974) 69.

22. See A. Papagos, *The Battle of Greece 1940–1941* (Athens, 1949), pp. 259 f.

23. Thucydides 2.80-81, discussed in *Epirus*, p. 500; see also pp. 246 f.

24. Thucydides 3.106, discussed in *StGH*, pp. 471 f. with fig. 21.

25. See *StGH*, pp. 474 f.

26. Lt.-Col. Boucabeille, *La Guerre turco-balcanique* (Paris, 1913), pp. 68 f.

27. As the Greek forces had almost no motor transport, they were unable to keep up with the withdrawal of the British forces from Klidhi and had to abandon their plans. For instance, one Greek unit which intended to withdraw from Korcë to Grevena by the route to the east of Grammus had no time to do so, see Papagos (op. cit., note 22), p. 367.

28. For this identification see *Epirus*, p. 681.

29. Herodotus 7.128.

30. See fig. 17 in HG^2, p. 233.

31. Thucydides 1.108.2

32. See the *Chronicle of the Morea* 3259-69, cited in *StGH*, p. 435.

33. For this part of the Via Egnatia see my article in *JRS* 64 (1974) 185-94.

34. I visited Ano Selcë in 1972 and was told there of these two routes.

35. For this part of the Via Egnatia see *Macedonia*, pp. 37-58 with maps 6-8.

36. See *Macedonia*, pp. 195 f. and map 17.

37. For Kitsevo see *Macedonia*, p. 43.

38. So D. Obolensky, *The Byzantine Commonwealth* (London, 1971), p. 22.

39. See *Macedonia*, pp. 200 and 169.

40. W. M. Leake, *Travels in Northern Greece* (London, 1835), 1, p. 335, went from Korcë to Berat.

41. See my article in *JHS* 94 (1974) 71 f.

42. See *Epirus*, pp. 119 f. and 206.

43. See *Epirus*, pp. 86 f., 186 f. and 576 f.

44. See *Epirus*, pp. 259 f. The motor-road, built in 1939, follows a different route on the Epirus side most of the time.

45. See *Epirus*, pp. 275 f. and 34.

46. See *Epirus*, pp. 257 f. with maps 11 and 12.

47. *Epirus*, p. 256; an ancient geographer, Dionysius son of Calliphon, reckoned it a journey of three days "from Ambracia to Thessaly."

48. *Epirus*, pp. 243 f. The dimensions of the bridges are given by Lt.-Col. Baker, "Memoir on the Northern Frontier of Greece," *Geographical Journal*, 7, 81 f.

49. A Gegaj, *L'Albanie et l'invasion turque* (Louvain, 1937), p. 72.

50. See *BSA* 61 (1966) 250 with fig. 2.

51. Arrian, *Anabasis* 1.5.1; Livy 40.20.1.

52. See *JRS* 56 (1966) 42 f. and *Macedonia*, pp. 61 and 100.

53. See *JHS* 94 (1974) 81 f.

54. Aeschylus, *Persae* 494-506.

55. *Epirus*, pp. 595 f. and *JRS* 61 (1971) 112.

56. *Epirus*, p. 676.

57. Also Cicero, *Epistulae ad Brutum* 1.6.1.

58. See *Epirus*, pp. 281 f. for more detail. Perseus had to move at speed and avoid main routes in areas under enemy control; that is why his marches seem excessive and his detours surprising. The logic of his movements was made clear to me by experience in taking guerila forces down to the German-occupied coastal area of Macedonia in 1943.

59. Leake (op. cit., note 40), 1, pp. 298 f.

60. A. W. Gomme, *Commentary on Thucydides* 3, p. 545; he was following F. Geyer, *Makedonien bis zur Thronbesteigung Philipps II* (Oldenburg, 1930) p. 46, "den Haliakmon aufwärts," and was followed by A. R. Burn, *Persia and the Greeks* (London, 1962), p. 342 "by way of the Haliacmon" and map on p. 340.

61. For a description of the route by Zoödokos Pege see *Macedonia*, pp. 158 f. The natural route for any army going from the coastal plain to Thessaly was via Edessa and Lake Ostrovo (anc. Begorritis) to Servia and Perrhaebia; this route was taken by Perseus, for instance, when he marched with 43,000 men from Citium in the coastal plain and entered the Perrhaebian Tripolis on the third day in 171 B.C. (Livy 42.51 f.; see *Macedonia*, p. 166).

62. We learn of them from a fragment of the History of Malchus (*CSHB*). On 266-67 the women are mentioned, and the men are said to have had two or three horses each, before they suffered losses.

63. See *Macedonia*, pp. 34 f. for more detail.

64. The account is in Jordanes *Getica* (*MGH*) 56. 286.

65. See *Macedonia*, pp. 108 f. for another case of Larissa as an error for Arnissa, and for the names of the cities which are corrupt in the manuscripts of Jordanes.

66. Malchus (loc. cit., note 62), p. 265 mentions that the Goths had "flocks [*poimnia*, used especially of sheep] and horses and other booty."

II

The Nomadic Peoples: Vlachs and Sarakatsani

The Vlachs

(See Maps 9, 10 and 14)

The Vlachs (an abbreviated form of 'Wallachs') speak a dialect of the Rumánian language.[1] Their dialect is closer than any other dialect to Latin, which means that the Vlach language broke away from the Rumanian language at an early stage and its development since then has been arrested by comparative isolation and by primitive conditions of life. In theory the distant ancestors of the Vlachs could have learnt Latin in any part of the Roman world which was in contact with Dacia, the Roman province in which the Rumanian language is believed to have grown. In practice there is one important restriction. The Greek language has been a dominant language throughout historical times; there is no instance of Greek speakers adopting another language in the place of their own, even, say, Persian or Turkish in areas where Greek speakers lived, even though they were a tiny minority. It follows that the Vlachs did not come originally from a Greek-speaking area and then change their language from Greek to Latin, as has sometimes been argued, chiefly for reasons of political propaganda. In the time of the Roman Empire the common people of the Balkan peninsula as far north as the northern limits of Pelagonia spoke Greek, for that was the language used in the inscriptions of the period.[2] It follows that the distant ancestors of the Vlachs came from north of the Kačanik pass, that is, from the basin of the lower Danube. Once that is established, we may well accept the tradition which was expressed by Cecaumenus in the eleventh century A.D. (but which was, no doubt, centuries older) that they had come from Dacia when the Romans abandoned the province in the third century A.D. This tradition has the added advantage that it explains the affinity of the Vlach language to the Rumanian language and may help to account for the distinctive way of life still practised by some Vlachs.[3]

Those Vlachs who are still nomadic practise the transhumance of sheep, that is to say they move large herds of sheep late in April from the lowland pastures towards the alpine pastures of the high mountains (see Map 14), returning to the lowlands late in October. Other peoples in the Balkans practise transhumance in the same way. But a particular feature of the Vlachs (shared by the Sarakatsani) is that, whereas only the shepherds among other peoples move with the sheep, the whole society of Vlachs—men, women, children, mules, horses and other animals—accompanies the journeys of the sheep. Until some two or three hundred years ago the nomadic Vlachs lived in temporary hut-encampments only. This is apparent from their language: Latin words are native to the language for the essentials of a hut (*kasă*), namely a door (*poartă*) and a hearth (*vatră*), but loan words from Turkish and Greek are used for divisions of a house. Conversely the loan words taken from Vlach into Greek have to do with flocks, herds and muleteering. The earliest indication that the Vlach language was being spoken in the Balkan peninsula comes from two Greek writers of the sixth century A.D., Procopius and Theophanes. The former gave in his list of fortified places some typically Vlach names, such as Sceptecasas ('conspicuous huts') and Gemellomuntes ('twin mountains'). Theophanes reported an incident in a campaign in the Balkans against the Avars, when the Byzantine army was pursuing the enemy. The pack on a mule slipped, and a man using the native dialect shouted out "*Torna, torna fratre.*" His words, intended for the muleteer, meant "Its slipping, slipping, brother." But they were interpreted by others as "Turn back, turn back, brother." So the army beat a hasty retreat.[4]

As we have seen, the primitive nature of the Vlach language in such matters as words in connection with housing shows that the Vlachs had been nomadic for very many centuries and at least from the time when they left Dacia. What form of life had they practised in Dacia? Some have argued that they were Roman settlers (or descendants of such) who came to Dacia as Latin-speakers and undoubtedly lived in towns, and that they took to a nomadic way of life only on being expelled from Dacia. This is possible in theory but improbable in practice, as history leads us to expect the change from nomadism to settled life rather than the opposite. Moreover, the Vlach way of life is feasible only if a community already possesses capital in the form of thousands of sheep and a considerable number of pack-animals. It seems unlikely that refugees from Dacia would have wished to convert any capital they had into livestock or would have chosen to adopt for the first time such a way of life.

The view expressed by A.J.B. Wace seems more probable.[5] A combination of nomadism and stock-raising has always been indigenous to northwestern Asia. The Scythians provided a good example in antiquity. In the words of Herodotus 4.2 they were "not agriculturalists but nomads." They dispossessed the Cimmerians of their lands, and the Cimmerians—also nomads—migrated southwards on both sides of the Black Sea; but then the Scythians themselves, being dispossessed of their lands by the Massagetae, migrated southwards on both sides of the Black Sea and more particularly into the great plains of south Russia which terminate eventually in the mountains of Dacia and the Balkans. So too the nomadic Magyars migrated from Asia into Rumania and thence into their present home, Hungary, and the nomadic Bulgars passed through Rumania and spread into many parts of the Balkans. It is then not unlikely that the original Vlachs came as nomads to Dacia. There they maintained their nomadic way of life but adopted Latin as their language. When the defences of Dacia fell, the Vlachs escaped with their flocks and found new pastures in the northern Balkans. During the course of the centuries they moved southwards under various pressures until the most southerly of them reached the confines of Greece. Thus the small numbers of nomadic Vlachs today may be seen as the last link in a long chain which reaches back through Dacia to the steppes of Asia.

Nomadism breeds independence of spirit, self-reliance and readiness for change, and inevitably brings the nomad into contact with other people. He is physically tough. He must be prepared to defend his flocks and his women and children against the attacks of wolves and bears and against the onslaughts or raids of other people. Travelling in 1889, the German scholar G. Weigand met the Vlachs of Avdhella on high Pindus just when they were beginning their migration to the lowlands of Thessaly.[6] First came a number of strong, well-armed men at the head of the column; next horses and mules heavily laden with rugs, utensils, children and women; and at the end more well-armed men. The sheep, divided into flocks by their age and sex, and whether or not they were due to lamb, moved separately, grazing as they went, and were protected not only by well-armed men but by large and ferocious dogs, a pack of which could kill a wolf or a man.

In the troubled times of the Byzantine empire, the Vlachs were a powerful people, possessing weapons, horses, and wealth on the hoof, and being tightly organised into patriarchal groups. Cecaumenus mentioned a principality of Vlachs in "Hellas" in 980.

They obtained special treatment from the Byzantine emperor, as we learn from documents of the period c. 1100–5, which belong to the Lavra monastery on Mt Athos.[7] An order and a letter from the Emperor Alexius were concerned with three kinds of transhumant shepherds who pastured their flocks on monastery land in Moglena in the summer and on some state land called Krabista in the winter. The three kinds were Vlachs, Bulgars and Koumani. Of these the Vlachs had a favoured position because they were exempt from some form of state taxation throughout the whole of the 'Thema' (an administrative district, like a county). In his letter Alexius further exempted the Vlachs who were attached to the monastery of Lavra from paying to the monastery a tax for the use of the monastery pastures. On the other hand it seems that the Bulgars and the Koumani were forced to pay these and other dues to the state authorities and to the monastery. Such concessions to the Vlachs were made not through kindness but under duress. Settled peoples and the government which depended on maintaining settled conditions for the survival of the state had good reason to be afraid of these well-armed nomads.

Cecaumenus described the Vlachs of Thessaly and of the Pindus range as treacherous and faithless in the eleventh century, and a travelling Jew, one Benjamin of Tudela, wrote of them c. 1160 when he came from the south to Lamia: "here are the confines of Wallachia, a country of which the inhabitants are called Vlachi. They are as nimble as deer, and they descend from their mountains into the plains of Greece committing robberies and taking booty. Nobody ventures to make war on them, nor can any king bring them to submission."

In 1186 the Bulgarians and the Vlachs rose against the Byzantine emperor under the leadership of two Vlachs,[8] Peter and Asan. They defeated one Byzantine army in a night-attack, and then another, commanded by the emperor himself, who relied upon his cavalry. The Vlachs used the traditional tactics of the nomads, peppering the cavalrymen with javelins and arrows and then retiring until they drew the enemy onto unfavourable ground, whereupon the Vlachs drew their swords and attacked at close quarters. Another victory in 1192 enabled the Vlachs and the Bulgarians to pass to the offensive, and they captured towns such as Varna on the coast of the Black Sea. Peter and Asan were murdered, but the succession remained in their family. At the height of their power the Vlachs and the Bulgarians controlled the central part of the southern Balkans, extending their authority westwards into Albania, southwards to the borders of Thessaly and eastwards to Serres in the valley of the Strymon river. But they made the great mistake of pillaging and destroying the towns and united the settled population in opposition.

When the Vlacho-Bulgarian kingdom collapsed in 1241, the Vlachs remained strong in Thessaly. Their leader, Taron, entered into alliance with John Ducas, a son of the Despot of Epirus, and Ducas and his descendants maintained a principality there until 1308. The capital was at Hypate on the southern side of the Spercheus valley. Thereafter Thessaly passed into the control of Byzantium, and in 1334 the Emperor Andronicus III accepted the submission of a group of people from the mountainous areas of Thessaly who "lived in no town but in inaccessible places." They submitted because they were afraid of being attacked during the time of heavy snows. According to John Cantacuzenus I. 474, they were "Albanians with no king, called after their tribal chiefs (*phylarchi*) Malakasii, Bouii and Mesaritae." They were in fact Vlachs; for the Vlach-speaking Malakasii and Bouii, who live today in central Pindus and in southern Thessaly, are undoubtedly descendants of these same people.[9] They were called "Albanians" by Cantacuzenus, because they had come in a geographical sense from the area which he called "Albania"; this included the lowland plain of Malakasa (Malakastër in Albanian today) and the highland pastures of the "Beuaei" (Stephanus Byzantinus s.v. *Beue*) to the south of Lake Ochrid.[10] The connection between the Vlachs and the Albanians dated in fact from very early times; for Weigand noted that the Albanians were particularly expert in sheep-raising and that many Albanian words for the sheep-milking industry appear as loan-words in Vlach speech.[11] It is probable that these words were acquired when the Vlachs first came into close contact with the Albanians in the region, for instance, of Peć in Metohija in the middle of the first millennium, as the Vlachs moved gradually southwards. Another indication of this connection may be seen in the so-called "Arvanitovlachi," who speak Vlach but have a good many Albanian loan-words and only a few Greek loan-words. These people are semi-nomadic and are found in Tsamouria in southwestern Epirus, near Larissa in Thessaly and in small numbers in western Macedonia.[12]

The economic system of the nomadic Vlachs is simple and has persisted probably unchanged from the earliest times. The sheep are kept for milk, wool and meat in that order of priority. Lambs are born in December or January in the lowlands and are strong enough for the spring migration to the mountains; but the young rams are killed for meat. Roasted whole on a spit over a barbecue, they are a feature of the celebration of Easter. The ewes are milked until the end of July; the milk being thick and rich makes excellent yoghurt and several kinds of cheese, and the shepherds on the mountainside have buttermilk and curds, which are kept in skin bags, suspended from the branch of a great tree which gives deep shade. Shearing is done just before or just after the spring migration, and the wool is cleaned and worked into rugs and clothing by the women throughout the summer. The name of a Vlach village, 'Fourka', is taken from the wooden distaff which is the Vlach woman's constant companion; and I have seen old looms in some hill-villages. The rugs are made with geometric designs and are brightly coloured, being dyed until recently with vegetable dyes; they are sold at fairs in the market towns and are sent to the cities for sale at home and abroad. The homespun cloth is thick, warm and hard-wearing; the shepherd's cape (Pl. 3a), often stiffened with goat-hair wool, sits on him like a small tent and withstands the torrential rain of summer and autumn and the winter snow. The same clothing is worn summer and winter, indeed several thicknesses of it, by men, women and children, which is understandable as they live and sleep so much in the open.

Horses and mules are used as pack-animals, a man on a horse leading a string of ten mules or so which are trained to follow. They are indispensable for the transportation of the families and their possessions in spring and autumn, and they carry bales of woollen goods, ricks of hay, and above all sawn planks to the market-towns throughout the summer. Sheep, horses and mules are sold at various fairs in the spring or autumn. Timber is abundant on the central range of the peninsula, which is clad with natural forests of oak, beech, fir, pine; and on the eastern side there is also sweet chestnut. Vlach communities controlled the cutting of trees and the replanting until recent times. The wood then was sawn in mills driven by water-power. In the 1930s I often passed caravans of fifty to a hundred mules bringing their awkward loads of long planks down to the market towns.

When conditions were peaceful, the nomadic Vlachs amassed considerable wealth. Their own needs in an open-air life were of the simplest, for they made their own huts and clothes, ate their own milk products and cooked their own meat. Most of their tools and utensils were of wood; thus carding-combs, looms, machinery for beetling mills and water mills were made of wood, and the famous wooden town-clock of Vovousa was keeping good time when I saw it in the 1930s. Bowls, cups, dishes and cutlery were wooden, the show pieces being painted; indeed even today, if one is given a souvenir plate or vase at Ioannina or at Tirana, it is usually of painted wood, skillfully carved to imitate pottery. Bags of skin or woollen cloth or gourds were much in use. Pottery, so breakable under the conditions of nomadic life, was hardly used except in the form of coarse cooking pots. Metal pots and pans of copper or pewter were much prized, and two Vlach communities at Sirrakou and Kalarritai were famous for their working of copper and pewter receptacles, and also of gold and silver jewelry. During the winter months many of the Vlach men plied a trade or practised a craft in the lowlands or worked with their string of mules. Their expenses were relatively small. They owned their animals, their summer pastures and the timber of their mountains, and they had to pay for pasture only in the winter and on the migrations. Their wealth was displayed in gold coins and in large gold and silver brooches and belt ornaments, worn by the women and young girls;[13] for it had to be in a portable form.

The prosperity of the nomadic Vlachs spread also to the settled Vlachs, who had taken up permanent residence in the market-towns and engaged in trade, at times on an international scale. The settled Vlachs tended to lose their racial identity; for they were quick to learn Greek or Albanian or Serbian or Bulgarian as the case might be, because they brought a quick intelligence and a spirit of enterprise and self-reliance into all they undertook. Within the period of Turkish rule, which lasted from 1430 to 1912, the Vlachs reached their highest level of prosperity between the late seventeenth century, when trading privileges were granted to the Vlach communities which lay near the route through the mountains from Ioannina to Trikkala, and the early nineteenth century when Turkish control began to collapse. During that time woollen goods, goathair capes, homespun clothing, cheese and pewter were sent far and wide into Europe, and the Vlachs kept the trade mainly in their own hands by establishing merchant houses in the cities of Europe, for instance at Marseilles, Vienna, Moscow, Odessa and Constantinople.

It was during this prosperous period that the nomadic Vlachs combined their hut-encampments on the alpine pastures and formed summer villages. A few of these grew into small towns; thus Muskopole ('the plain of Musk') and Shipiska, in what is now eastern central Albania, each had perhaps 8,000 houses and some 40,000 inhabitants by 1700, while

Samarina and Metsovo, in what is now northern Greece, had about 5,000 and 1,000 houses respectively. The people of Samarina in about 1850 owned 80,000 sheep. Although Perivoli owned more territory than any other Vlach village, its population of sheep outgrew its resources, and colonies were planted far to the north at Istok between Ochrid and Resen, and far to the east in the hills above Volos. The important thing to observe is that in times of prosperity Vlach centers such as Muskopole, Samarina and Metsovo developed only in the mountains and never in the lowlands, the reason being that the Vlachs became concentrated in the summer when their flocks were grazing on the wide pastures of the central range, but they were usually dispersed in the winter by the need to rent pastures piecemeal.

As the rule of Turkey relaxed, raiding and brigandage developed, especially in Albania, and in 1788 Ali Pasha, an Albanian chieftain from Tepelenë in northern Epirus, became the more or less independent ruler of Ioannina. Many of the Vlach towns and villages in the north were sacked and destroyed by the Albanians; thus Muskopole was looted twice, in 1769 and 1788, and the depredations of Ali Pasha reduced it to the small hamlet which it is today. During the Greek War of Independence and the many Balkan wars which followed up to 1912, the changing frontiers ran through the summer pastures of the Vlachs who were robbed repeatedly by raiders and brigands of both sides. At this time the decline of the Vlachs was completed; for example, in 1854 Metsovo was captured first by Greeks and then by Turks and plundered by both. In the first World War static fronts were formed in Central Albania and Macedonia, running through the chief winter pastures of the shepherds; and in the second World War the Andartai of the Resistance Movements and then the participants on both sides in the Civil War up to 1950 stole the sheep and robbed the houses of the summer villages. Today one thinks of the nomadic Vlachs as a small and impoverished element in the populations of four quite separate and not always mutually friendly nations—Greece, Albania, Yugoslavia and Bulgaria. Indeed their number is still declining because with the development of intensive agriculture and mechanised farming most of the lowland areas are no longer available for winter pasture. Vlachs today are a mere shadow of a once powerful people.

What made the Vlachs great and what still saves them from extinction is the mountainous area of the central Balkan range. In general Greeks do not like high mountains, and they are afraid of the dogs, which are trained to attack wolves and men. (They thought I was demented when I went alone and unarmed into the highlands of Pindus and Agrapha, and it must be admitted that I was once bitten in the leg by a sheepdog.) Consequently the Vlachs have had most of the high mountains to themselves, and in particular the richest pastures and the finest timber, which are both found on the volcanic formation running from Mt Shpat in the north to Pindus south of the Zygos. (Such pasturelands are shown in Plate 2b, the photograph having been taken from the top of the pass between Metsovo and Milea, looking towards Milea.) As long as external conditions allow, a family of Vlachs migrates to the same spot, like a family of swallows. Because conditions deteriorated, they lost most of their northern territory to the Albanians early in the nineteenth century, but they have clung to their territory on the Pindus in spite of every difficulty.

The strength of their tradition lies in the family and in the patriarchal and tribal system within which the family is set like a fly in amber. In their nomadic society man, woman and child undertake work of importance to the economy; they live together at close quarters, and they migrate together twice a year. But the man is the keeper of the sheep (Pl. 3b), hunter and warrior. He is the head of the family. He and other senior members of a family decide whom a girl is to marry, and in most cases the bridegroom comes from a related family within a small tribal group. There is no dowry system and there are no wedding presents, but precedence in marriage is observed, running from the eldest daughter to the youngest and then from the eldest son to the youngest (so too among Albanians in southern Albania in the 1930s). When marriages are made between two villages, as between Samarina and Fourka, it is due to affinity within a tribe, which is indicated by a common dialect or by similar features of costume.

The tribes are small; Weigand reckoned from twenty to two hundred families constituted a tribe.[14] In the past they were certainly very numerous, and they maintained their individuality by practising endogamy and by migrating to the same district each summer. The chief of each tribe acted as its ruler, and the chiefs of several tribes sometimes joined together in the face of danger from without. Already in 1334 Cantacuzenus referred to these chiefs as *phylarchi*, a Greek word meaning 'rulers of tribes'. It was through the initiative of the chiefs that the change from hut-encampments to summer villages came about, mostly in the years before and after 1700. The chiefs are called *tshelnikadzi* by the Vlachs. Each is head of a community, and the members of the community own sheep, pastures, timber and land in common. The chief is sometimes termed 'chief shepherd'. One *tshelniku* may rule over from fifty to two hundred families.

Each village has its own foundation-story. Thus Samarina was founded in the form of four small hamlets or hut-encampments by four *tshelnikadzi*, whose family names are still remembered. These small hamlets were later joined together into one village by an act of what is called in Greek *synoikismos*, probably in the sixteenth century. Vovousa (in Vlach Baieasa) grew out of the union of four summer hut-encampments, and one of them—Baietan—is said to have helped in the founding of Perivoli, which in turn grew from a union of three hamlets. As Vovousa and Perivoli belong to the same dialect group, the tradition may well be true. Avdhella is said to have grown from the union of five hut-encampments, which carried the names of their original founders; the union itself was made for greater security and may have been enacted about 1700, when the Albanians became a menace to the Vlachs generally.[15] Sometimes groups of tribes joined together, as we see from John Cantacuzenus; for the Malakasii and the Bouii of 1334 were the forerunners of the Malakasii whose villages extend now from Malakasi in the upper Peneus valley to Gardhiki in the upper Achelous valley and of the Bouii who live now in several villages of southern Thessaly. And it seems that earlier still, from 1186 to 1241, Peter and Asan and their successors were able to unite most of the Vlach tribes against the emperor of Byzantium.

That during the centuries the Vlachs have moved a long way from the north and mainly on the western flank of the Balkan peninsula is indicated by the survival of a Vlach dialect among people who call themselves Vlachs in Istria near the head of the Adriatic Sea, and by the presence of Morlachs or 'Black Vlachs' in Dalmatia. In the 1880s, when Arthur Evans was travelling in Dalmatia, he found a large Vlach element at Dubrovnik (Ragusa), and he collected a number of place-names in Dalmatia which were of Vlachic derivation. He concluded that the region of Peć (just to the north of Albania) had once been a stronghold of Vlach tribes, and he noted also two Vlach villages near the important pass of Preševo. During their gradual shift southwards some Vlachic tribes were firmly entrenched in central Albania by the fourteenth century at the latest; for John Cantacuzenus then described the Vlachic tribesmen as "Albanoi" in a geographical and not an ethnological sense. One of the tribal names used by Cantacuzenus, 'Malakasii', was derived most probably from the plain 'Malakasa' or 'Malakastra' between Valona and Berat, which provides superb winter pasture. The name is evidently of Vlach origin, and means 'bad encampments', so called probably because of the malaria which was the scourge of this area until the post-war period. Another tribe he mentioned, the Bouii, came probably from the ancient Beuia north of Muskopole. They belonged later to the so-called Frasherot Vlachs whose homeland was in central Albania, where the villages of Frashër and Fratar still preserve the name. So too Kolonjë, the district on the western side of Mt Grammus, has been given that name by the Albanians after the Vlach name 'Colonia', a group of summer encampments. The Vlachs who settled later by Stratus in Acarnania and by Almiros in Thessaly preserved the memory that they had come originally from central Albania, and some of the Vlachs at Almiros visited Pliasa, their original home near Koritsa,[16] every summer until 1881, when a new frontier impeded them.

Central Albania was evidently the centre of gravity in the Vlach world from 1300 (if not earlier) until 1700. By the latter date Shipiska and Muskopole and other large villages, now almost deserted, such as Lunka and Gopeš, were exceedingly prosperous, and it is clear that the Vlachs were then in control of the lakeland area of Ochrid, Prespa and Malik and its alpine pastures. Throughout this period the Vlachs held the pastures also of Grammus and Pindus, as we know from the earlier evidence of Benjamin of Tudela. During this long period the chief winter pastures of the Vlachs of the lakeland area were in the coastal plains of Albania, called Muzeqijë and Malakasa, but some lay eastwards in the lower Haliacmon valley and in the coastal plain of Macedonia. The Vlachs of Grammus had winter pastures by Valona and Butrinto on the Albanian coast, but some of them too went eastwards into the Haliacmon valley. The Vlachs of the Pindus range turned to southern Epirus, Acarnania and Aetolia—known as 'Little Vlachia'—and more particularly to Thessaly—known as 'Great Vlachia'—for their winter pastures. It is probable that some flocks went as far as the north coast of the Corinthian Gulf and the coastal plains of Boeotia and Attica.[17]

The chief factor in the decline of Vlach prosperity in the late eighteenth century was the expansion of the Albanians, marked by raiding and brigandage, which accompanied the weakening of Turkish authority in this part of the Turkish empire. The Albanians did most damage in what is now central Albania; for they destroyed Shipiska and Muskopole and caused the Vlachs of the lakeland area to move eastwards and southwards, some as far as the Strymon basin and the slopes of Mt Rhodope and others to Acarnania and Thermopylae. Others settled in abject poverty in the unhealthy Malakasa plain on the Albanian coast.[18] The centre of gravity shifted southwards to the Pindus range, but here too the depredations of Ali Pasha, the despot of Ioannina, led to migrations from Avdhella, Perivoli and Samarina to southwest Macedonia, where the refugees settled in the hills west of Verria. Frasherot Vlachs migrated from central Albania and joined the Verria group; others settled at Pisodherion above Florina in westernmost Macedonia, and still others moved from Pliasa near Koritsa to settle by Almiros (the ancient Pherae) in eastern Thessaly. Conditions deteriorated even further in the nineteenth century when the Turks struggled against the rising tide of nationalism in the Balkans. Then many Vlachs sought employment in the towns or emigrated, particularly to the United States.

The last description of the Vlachs before the final disruption of the Turkish empire into national units—Greece, Albania, Serbia and Bulgaria—in 1912-13 was written by Wace and Thompson. They listed the regions in which the Vlachs were then living, and divided them into groups according to differences of dialect and/or costume.[19] As they did not visit the Vlachs of the upper Aspropotamos (Achelous) valley and as I did do so in the 1930s, I have added some points to their account. The pattern of Vlach settlement as it was c. 1912 is shown on Map 9.

The chief concentration of Vlachs was on the Pindus range, which lay by then in Greece. The continuous area of pastures (Pl. 2a-b) and natural forest extended from Fourka in the north to Gardhiki in the south. The Vlachs of northern Pindus, from Fourka to Vovousa, formed a distinct group, which wintered mainly in Thessaly in the lower valleys of the Titaresius and Peneus. The Aspropotamos group in southern Pindus, from Metsovo and Krania to Gardhiki, wintered mainly in the coastal areas of southern Epirus (especially in the peninsula of Preveza) and of Acarnania, and also in the plains of southern Thessaly and farther south in low-lying areas of central Greece.

In 1912 the groups to the north of Pindus were mere shadows of their former selves: namely the Gramosteani in Kolonjë, the Frasherots still living north of the middle Aous valley, and the survivors of the once very large group in the lakeland area on both sides of Koritsa. Offshoots from this last area were living in the hills between Resen and Monastir; there they had joined a much earlier settlement of Vlachs at Gopeš and Molovište, who claimed to have been there since at least 1600 and spoke a distinctive dialect, shared only by the Vlachs of Istria and the Vlachs of Moglena.[20] The small group at Lunka was all that remained of a northern extension of the Koritsa communities.[21] The bulk of these peoples went for winter pastures to the coastal plains of Albania,[22] but some preferred to go eastwards into the low-lying parts of the Haliacmon valley, before the present national frontiers were created. Two Vlach villages near the Preševo Pass were noted by Arthur Evans c. 1880.

Within what is now Greek Macedonia the small group of Vlachs at Pisodherion and the large group by Verria were descendants of refugees from central Albania and from northern Pindus. On the other hand the group by Klisoura and Sisanion to the east of Kastoria had been settled there for some centuries before the refugees came; they had ceased to be nomadic and were engaged mainly in trade.

Another group of Vlach descent, which must have taken to a settled existence many centuries ago, occupies the hill country between the summer villages of northern Pindus and Grevena, itself a great centre for the nomadic Vlachs during their seasonal migrations. This group still wore Vlach dress in 1912 and they spoke Greek with a pronounced Vlach accent and with an admixture of Vlach words; but they had

Map 9

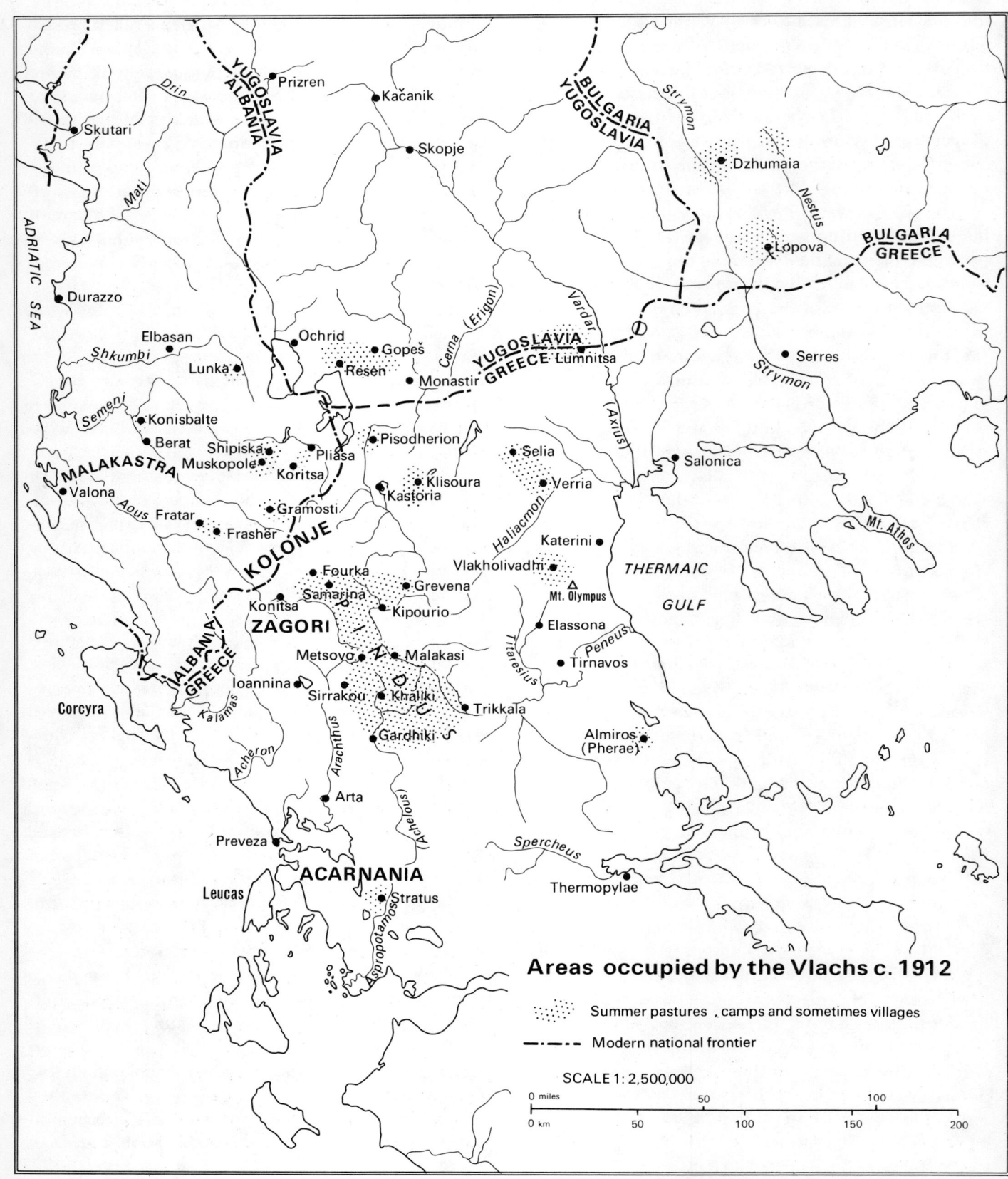

adopted Greek entirely, and only the older generation of men and many women of all ages were still bilingual in Greek and Vlach. They intermarried with the neighbouring Greek villages, partly because they were scorned and rejected by the nomadic Vlachs of northern Pindus. They are called Kupatshari, 'men of the oak tree' (*kupatshu* being Vlach for oak tree), because the district Grevena is covered in oak scrub and forest.[23] The people of the highest of their villages, such as Kipourio and Philippaei, engage in shepherding, timber-cutting and muleteering; in this they resemble the nomadic Vlachs, but the Kupatshari villages are partly inhabited throughout the winter. The community as a whole is primarily engaged in agriculture and trade (see Map 10).

The Vlachs of Olympus, or more precisely of Pieria, with their centre of Vlakholivadhi ('Vlach Meadow'), are again different. Their dialect in 1912 showed them to have been in touch with Greek-speaking people for longer than any other group of Vlach-speakers. On the other hand they have had little contact with the nomadic Vlachs of the Pindus range, because their summer pastures are on Mt Olympus and the Pierian range and their winter pastures are close at hand, on the coast by Katerini.

Another group of unique character lived round Lumnitsa in Moglena, a secluded upland basin on the range of Mt. Païko on the west side of the lower Vardar valley. When Wace and Thompson visited these Vlachs, they found their dialect to be almost unintelligible. It was a dialect shared only by the Vlachs of Istria and by those of the Resen-Monastir group, and therefore stemmed from a time when the ancestors of these now far-flung groups were in close contact. In any case we should put the diaspora of these Vlachs well within the first millennium on other grounds. We have already seen from the documents of the monastery of Lavra that Vlachs were pasturing their flocks on monastery lands in the Moglena c. 1100. We learn also of Vlachs in Macedonia from the *Regnum Slavorum* 4, written c. 1150 by the Presbyter of Doclea, who stated that Symeon the Bulgar in his conquest of Macedonia reduced groups "Latinorum qui illo tempore [c. 980–90] Romani vocabantur modo vero Morovlachi, hoc est nigri Latini, vocantur." The change of name from 'Romani (c. 980–90) to 'Morovlachi' (from the Greek form 'Mavrovlachi', meaning 'Black Vlachs') by 1150 is interesting because the name 'Morlachs' has survived for the Vlachs in Dalmatia. Wace and Thompson noted at the time of their visit that the Vlachs of Moglena called themselves not 'Arumani' ('Romans'), as the other Vlachs do, but 'Vlachs'. This distinctive group still maintained the traditional dress, but they were unusual in that they practised agriculture and many of them were Mohammedans. The survival of a very early group of Vlachs in the Moglena has an analogy in the survival, also in the Moglena, of the descendants of the first Turkish conquerors of Macedonia, the Yuruks, who were themselves nomadic shepherds.[24]

The outlying groups are the last traces of a more recent diaspora. The Vlachs by Lopova and Dzhumaia in Bulgaria were descended from refugees who had fled from the area of Grammus under pressure from the Albanians, and they still preserved in 1912 their nomadic way of life and the same dress as the Gramosteani of Kolonjë in Albania. The Vlachs by Stratus in Acarnania and by Almiros in Thessaly were descendants of migrants from Frasherot Albania; these migrants came originally as nomad shepherds but most of them adopted a settled way of life and other activities. Similarly many Vlachs settled in the Strymon basin by Serres and Nigrita, but once they had adopted a different way of life they lost their distinctive language, dress and customs and became absorbed into the local populations of the towns.

In terms of culture, the Vlachs today stand at various levels. The nomads maintain the primitive traditions. As pastoralists, warriors and hunters, they scorn the agriculturalists, as the Thracian pastoralists did in the time of Herodotus. They work generally in wood alone, making bowls, dishes, cutlery, saddles, and machinery of wood. Because they scorn the idea of working in stone, they hire Greeks to build houses in stone when they make summer villages. These nomad Vlachs have no musical instruments of their own, their arts are song and dance in accompaniment to song, and they have their own traditional dances.

Next in development are the Vlachs of the early villages in the mountains, such as Shipiska, Muskopole, Metsovo, Sirrakou and Kalarritai. They have long engaged in trade in wares such as wool, homespun cloth, rugs, cheese and timber, which come from their traditional activities. In the course of time they have developed new crafts—the Metsovites, for instance, becoming masons and woodcarvers in the decoration of churches—and they have adopted dances from their neighbours, such as the 'Tsamb' dance of 'Tsamouria', an Albanian-speaking region in southern Epirus.

Next are the Vlachs who adopted a settled life, some in the hills, like the Kupatshari, and most in the plains of Macedonia, Thessaly, Epirus or Acarnania, or farther afield. They have become naturalised to their surroundings rapidly. Most of them have been absorbed into the mixed populations of market towns such as Trikkala or Serres or Siatista, and of cities such as Niš, Sofia, Salonica and Athens. All these stages of development run concurrently and will continue to do so until the source of Vlachism—the nomadic life of transhumance—dries up, and this may well happen in the last decade of the twentieth century.

The Sarakatsani

(See Map 10)

Entirely distinct from the Vlachs are the Sarakatsani. They also practise the transhumance of sheep, but they speak Greek as their native language. They do not have access to the pastures of the central range which are in the ownership of Vlach communities. They have to go to the next best pastures, which are on ranges adjacent to the central range or on separate mountains, and they have to rent these pastures from the local villages, which are situated, for instance, high up on West Pindus or Mt Othrys or Mt Parnassus. Until recently the Sarakatsani were entirely nomadic; they had no villages of their own nor access to any villages. Then in 1938 the Metaxas regime passed a law giving them the right to claim citizenship of the hill villages from which they had been renting summer pastures; not all of them did so. Under these conditions the groups of Sarakatsani meet each other only rarely, whereas the Vlachs congregate together in their villages and on their common pastures on the central range during the summer months.

If the various groups of Sarakatsani were, as some have supposed, Greeks of Epirus, Macedonia, Thessaly and other areas who changed at some time from a settled life to a nomadic life each in their own region, it is certain that they would have continued to speak the distinctive dialect of each region; for instance, the Sarakatsani of Epirus the strong Epirote dialect, and the Sarakatsani of Macedonia the local dialect of their part of Macedonia. However, this is not so; Hoeg has shown conclusively that the dialects of the various groups have a linguistic unity.[25] Moreover, they have a number of customs and decorative techniques in common. It follows that at one period in the past the ancestors of these groups did congregate together for the six months of the summer pasturing each year, and—given the geography of northern Greece—this can have been only on the central range *before* its pastures were usurped by the nomadic Vlachs. I conclude then that the Sarakatsani are the descendants of the Greek pastoralists who herded their sheep on the central range of Grammus and Pindus in the early Byzantine period and were dispossessed of their pastures by the Vlachs at the latest by the twelfth century. Their particular way of life has enabled them to maintain their identity in dialect as in other respects during the centuries since that time.[26]

In these pages I shall concern myself with the Sarakatsani of Greek Epirus. I met them often in the 1930s, either on the coast or on the mountains and particularly on the plateau of Ioannina which is a general meeting place during the seasonal migrations. I used to eat with them the yellow maize bread (*boubōta*), which was the staple diet of the very poor in those days. A special study of the Sarakatsani of Zagori has been written by J. K. Campbell, who lived among them in the 1950s. Being interested in the sociological aspects of these Sarakatsani, Campbell approached the problem of their origin without any political or nationalist bias. He concluded that "in their social values and institutions the Sarakatsani, as they exist today, provide no evidence of a past history that was ever anything but Greek."[27]

Of course they have some things in common with the Vlachs, because they lead the same kind of life. For both of them the basic unit and the centre of loyalty is the family. But the conventions of the family are tighter among the Sarakatsani. The daughters are dowered for marriage, and both the families make presents at the wedding, which is a general Greek custom and not a Vlach one. The position of women is lower than among the Vlachs; they are held to account for original sin, and are thought to be responsible for sexual sensuality and for arousing sensuality in the man. Authority is even more strongly patriarchal than among the Vlachs; and if an unmarried girl has a baby, the honour of the family demands that the father of the family kill her and that the baby

Map 10

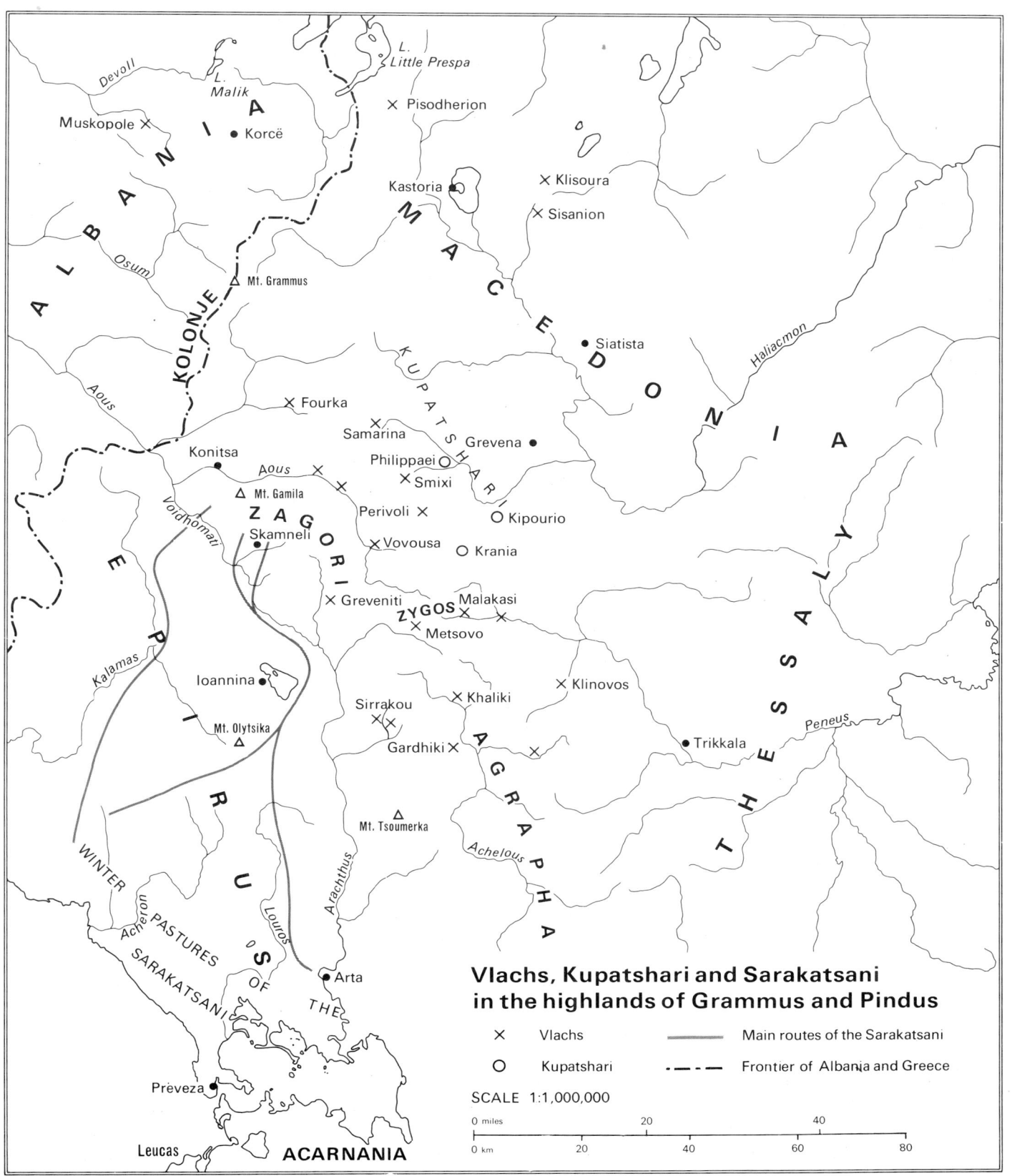

be exposed or destroyed. In their concept of Christianity the Trinity is the replica in heaven of the human family, namely God the Father, the Mother of God, and God the Son. On the other hand the circle of marriage is less restricted than among the Vlachs. Endogamy within a group of kindred or within one or more villages is not practised among the Sarakatsani; indeed there is a religious and social prohibition against marriage within the kindred.

There is no tribal system, but nomadic conditions require the formation of coherent groups. Among the Sarakatsani the groups are formed by related families and/or families associated by marriage. Such a group requires a minimum of fifty persons to be viable and is usually much larger; it is both a company (a *parea*) in the social sense and the personnel of a nomad encampment (a *stani*). The leader of such a group, called the *tselingas* and comparable to the Vlach *tshelniku*, is the head of a leading family which, like a magnet, attracts other families to itself. His powers are very great, because all negotiations and all organisation of the company are in his hands. The tselingas and the tselingas-family are held in honour and hold themselves in honour, and they are usually well-to-do financially. In the troubled times which attended the decline of Turkish rule the tselingas and his henchmen were well-armed and well-mounted, like their Vlach counterparts.

The most numerous of the Sarakatsani in Epirus are those who take their sheep to the mountain pastures of Zagori in the summer, while others go to Mt Olytsika or Mt Tsoumerka or the range between Arta and the Achelous (see Map 10). The Sarakatsani have to hire summer pastures as well as winter pastures, and this makes their lives much harder than those of the Vlachs and it puts their economy close to the subsistence level. Zagori lies between the plateau of Ioannina and the central range of Pindus, and it consists of a large well-watered flysch basin which is surrounded by limestone mountains on three sides and by the volcanic formation of central Pindus on the east side.[28] The best pastures (and the best timber) are on this last side but they are owned by the Vlachs of Vovousa, Flambourari and Greveniti. The Sarakatsani hire the thinner pastures of the limestone ranges, especially those of Mt Gamila, where the lands of five villages—Papingo, Tsepelevo, Kapesovo, Vradeto and Skamneli—afford grazing for some 33,000 sheep and goats. The flysch country has pastures also but mainly for goats. It is for this reason that the Sarakatsani generally have many more goats than the Vlachs. While the lamb and the sheep are associated by the Sarakatsani with Christ and God, the goat is associated with the Devil. On that account the herding of goats is handled by the women, who are looked on to some extent as the embodiment of evil. Among the Vlachs all the herding is done by men and boys.

The Sarakatsani are attracted to Zagori particularly by the lack of competition for grazing from the natives of Zagori, who are great travellers and make their money away from home, whether in Greece or abroad. This has been so over many centuries. After the conquest of Ioannina in 1430 the Turks divided most of Epirus into fiefs, in which the peasants paid a tenth of all produce and some other taxes, and chiftliks, in which the peasants paid up to a half and were little better than serfs. The forty-six villages of Zagori managed to have their lands defined as fiefs, and later on they formed a confederation among themselves which gave them a stronger hand in negotiating with the Turks. In the seventeenth century the Turks granted trading privileges to the Vlachs of Metsovo and neighbouring villages, in connection with the main route through the Pindus range, and soon afterwards they gave to the Zagori villages a high degree of autonomy. This privilege lasted until 1866. It enabled the men to travel freely within the Turkish empire or go abroad, send or bring their money home, and keep their accumulated wealth safe from the depredations of the Turkish government officials. They were able to defend themselves even against the rapacious Ali Pasha, the despot of Ioannina. Thus the Sarakatsani had most of Zagori's pastureland to themselves on paying the rent, and they enjoyed the security from depredation which the natives of Zagori had won.

Prior to 1938 the Sarakatsani lived only in huts (*kalivia*), built by the women with branches, poles and thatch, either circular or rectangular in ground-plan, and floored and plastered inside with mud mixed with dung. There was a central hearth, which was "in fact and in symbol the centre of Sarakatsan family life."[29] When the families migrated, they and their mules had little to carry except the poles, the rugs, wooden or metal vessels, a few pottery cooking pots, and the implements for working wool and making homespun cloth. During the winter they were scattered far and wide along the coast of southern Epirus; an example of winter encampments is given by Campbell in the map at the end of his book.

In the 1920s conditions worsened for the Sarakatsani. As agriculture and arboriculture developed, especially when Greek refugees from Asia Minor were planted in Epirus, there was less pasture land available for the winter months and flocks had to be halved or even quartered, so that the surviving animals could obtain sufficient fodder. After 1938, if they enrolled under the law of Metaxas as citizens of the village where they rented summer pastures, they had the right to graze a certain number of sheep and goats, free of charge, and the few who could afford it were able to own a house in the village of their adoption. But at the same time, Metaxas restricted the number of goats, a measure which hit the Sarakatsani hard. War conditions and post-war conditions have made matters worse, and it doubtful whether their way of life will outlast the present century.[30] But it is a way of life which has been practised in northern Greece not only by the Sarakatsani since Byzantine times, but by their anonymous predecessors for as long into the past as climactic conditions have been favourable to the transhumance of sheep.

Sarakatsani in other parts of Greece speak the same dialect of Greek and have the same idiosyncratic customs. They are found (or were found in the 1930s) in Argolis, Corinthia, Megaris, Attica and central Greece; in the Ionian islands, Euboea, some Cyclades and Sporades, and Crete; also in western Thrace, and before 1922 in Albania and Bulgaria. They spoke no other language than Greek and had no other occupation then shepherding. It is most probable that the origin of their dialect of Greek and their way of life is to be sought in northern Greece very early in the Byzantine period, before the seizure of the pastures of the central range by the Vlachs and the seizure of other pastures, for instance, by the Bulgars and the Koumani (as we know from the documents of Lavra). In other words, we can reconstruct their migration with their flocks on the model of the later migration of the Albanians with their flocks, due in each case to the pressure of other peoples from the north.

One group of Greek-speaking transhumant shepherds stand apart. They are the 'Arcades' or 'Valtetsini' ('men of Valtetsi') of Arcadia, and, unlike the Sarakatsani, they have permanent homes, which are mainly in Mantinea. Their traditional dress consists of red-tasseled *tsaroukhia* (shoes with an upturned toe-piece), *foustanella* (white kilt), and a black or coffee-coloured handkerchief worn as a headband. They rarely marry outside their own society, and they claim to be descended from the ancient Arcades.[31]

The institutions and the outlook of the Sarakatsani, as they have been described by J. K. Campbell, have many similarities with those which were already regarded as traditional by the Greeks of the fifth century B.C. The primitive hut, the sanctity of the hearth, the conventions of hospitality, the strength of the family, the protective value of kindred, the influence of the leading family, the patriarchal authority, the concern with honour and esteem, and the devotion of the women to family obligations were deeply entrenched in the background of the Greek Classical period, especially in northern Greece. The religious ideas of the Sarakatsani, for all their association with Christianity, have much in common with those of that early period. The family bonds, the degree of filial devotion, the sanctity of marriage, the obligations of kinship—all were instituted by gods. The period of life most favourable to the growth of moral excellence was that of the young man in a good family[32]—a Neoptolemus or a Hyllus in plays of Sophocles—and advancing years required the compromise and the cunning which were portrayed in an Odysseus. And in Hesiod's story of Prometheus the first woman, Pandora, was endowed with sexual charm, a lying tongue and a deceitful nature.[33] The link between the two sets of institutions and ideas is to be found not in any continuous tradition but in the common background of a particular way of life and the interplay of man and his environment in this part of the southern Balkans.

A link of the same kind in respect of the art of the Sarakatsani has been noted by Angeliki Hadzimichalis.[34] One interesting point is that as in dialect, so also in art, the scattered bands of Sarakatsani throughout Greece have the same sense of decoration, which is described by Mrs. Hadzimichalis as "simple, static and geometric." It is probable that this artistic sense developed when the Sarakatsani met together on the Pindus pastures before the coming of the Vlachs; but it is also striking that since their diaspora the scattered groups have maintained this concept of art, no doubt because it is related to their way of life. Mrs. Hadzimichalis has pointed out the very strong similarity which exists between this concept of art and the so-called Geometric style of archaic Greece, a style itself very closely akin to the so-called 'northwestern geometric style' of vase painting, which predominated in northern Greece and central Albania for several centuries, overlapping the last period of the Late Bronze Age and the Early Iron Age.

NOTES

1. The best books on the Vlachs are those of Weigand, *Die Aromunen* and Wace and Thompson, *The Nomads of the Balkans*. I owe most to the latter.

2. See *Macedonia*, pp. 89 f.

3. I disagree here with Wace and Thompson, p. 272, who concluded as follows: "The Balkan Vlachs are for the most part the Romanised tribes of the Balkan peninsula, reinforced perhaps at times by tribes from over the Danube. Thus the Vlachs in the west would be for the most part Romano-Illyrians, in the south they might be Athamanians or other hill tribes mentioned by Strabo, but in the east and along the central mountain range there would be a large Thracian and Bessian element." Their view bristles with difficulties. For example, it assumes that tribes speaking Greek, Illyrian and Thracian respectively in different parts of the Balkans *all* adopted Latin as their speech *independently*, but yet they all spoke a peculiar dialect of Latin related to the Rumanian language; such a coincidence is surely incredible. If these Balkan peoples were adopting Latin so widely, why did the nomad shepherds alone retain it? In what follows I give some reasons for my view.

4. Procopius, *De Aedificiis* 4.4.3; 4.11.20; Theophanes as cited by Wace and Thompson, p. 257.

5. Wace and Thompson, pp. 270 f.; although they do not adopt the view as the correct one.

6. Weigand (*A*), pp. 132 f.

7. Cecaumenus, *Strategikon* 244. *Mélanges Iorga* (1933), pp. 779-786, citing S. Eustratiades in *Hellenika* 2 (1929) 383 and Ph. Meyer, *Die Haupturkunden für d. Gesch. d. Athoskloster* (Leipzig, 1894), p. 166. Pastoralists were exempt from the taxes and services imposed on the agriculturists, but they paid fees for both summer and winter pastures (*ennomion*), for pasture in the course of the seasonal migration (*poriatikon*), a tax of one-tenth on each animal excluding draught animals (probably the *mandriatikou dekatia* of Alexius' order) and a 'gift of sheep' (*dosis probatōn*).

8. For the evidence that they were Vlachs, see E. Gibbon, *The Decline and Fall of the Roman Empire* (ed. Bury), 6, p. 391, n. 25.

9. So Weigand (*A*), p. 276; Wace and Thompson, p. 264 and others. It was argued by G. C. Soulis in *Epeteris Byzantinon Spoudon* 23 (1953) 213 that the Malakasii, etc. were Albanians and not Vlachs, but the fact that the modern Malakasii and Bouii are Vlachs is surely decisive.

10. See *Macedonia*, p. 64.

11. So Weigand (*EvM*), p. 52.

12. See *Megale Ellenike Enkyklopaedia*² 7, p. 417.

13. Belt ornaments are shown in Weigand (*A*) in the illustration facing p. 112.

14. See Wace and Thompson, p. 146; the top number given by Weigand (*EvM*), p. 49, was 200 families.

15. For these examples of *synoikismos* and their dates see Wace and Thompson, pp. 145 f., 173 f., and 175 f. The dates given for the earliest villages by E. Kirsten in *DgL*, 1, 1, p. 225 seem to me far too early.

16. Wace and Thompson, pp. 209-210. The distance from southern Thessaly to Pliasa is very great; one may compare the annual mission of the Aenianes to Cassopaea in southern Epirus (Plutarch, *Quaestiones Graecae* 13 and 26).

17. The presence of nomad Vlachs in the southern part of central Greece may be inferred from the occurrence of such Vlachic names as Malakasa on the borders of Attica and Boeotia and from references to Vlachs seen there by early travellers (e.g. J. Spon, *Voyage d'Italie, de Dalmatie, de Grèce* [Amsterdam, 1679] 2, p. 93, and E. D. Clarke, *Travels in Various Countries of Europe* [1816], 2, 3, p. 40). The inference is supported by statements in Byzantine authors that nomadic Albanians and Vlachs came to those areas.

18. Weigand (*A*), p. 87.

19. Wace and Thompson, pp. 206-225 with a map, on which my map is based. They used Weigand for areas they did not know themselves, e.g. for Albania, Epirus and the Aspropotamos valley. They show much too large an area of Vlach settlement between Berat and the coast. Weigand has a useful map at the end of his book.

20. Wace and Thompson, pp. 218 f.

21. Weigand (*A*), p. 59, gave the name as Langa.

22. Weigand (*A*), p. 87 mentioned that Bulgarian shepherds from Dibra pastured their flocks also in the plain of Muzeqijë.

23. So Wace and Thompson, p. 31; their view is supported by the fact that a group of villages to the north of the Kupatshari are named after the sweet chestnut trees of

their terrain. They show the Kupatshari villages on their map 1 facing p. 160. Weigand (*A*), p. 130, derived their name from a Slavonic word for a digger or agriculturalist; this seems less likely. I visited many of these villages in 1943, when I was based for a time on Grevena.

24. Wace and Thompson, pp. 219 f. See also C. J. Jireček, "Die Wlachen und Maurowlachen in den Denkmälern von Ragusa," *Sitzungsber. d. k. böhm. Gesellschaft d. Wissenschaften*, 1879. G. Weigand described the Yuruk Turks as "wanderhirten."

25. C. Hoeg, *Les Saracatsans* (Paris and Copenhagen, 1925–26), 1, viii.

26. Another view is that of T. Capidan in *Dacoromania* 4 (1924–26) 923 f., that the Sarakatsani are Vlachs who remained nomadic but abandoned the Vlach customs and language and adopted in their place the Greek language and a particular variety of Greek customs and ideas. This view is disproved by the case of the Kupatshari, who illustrate what happens when Vlachs do adopt Greek ways; for their Greek has a strong admixture of Vlachic elements, and they retain Vlachic dress. But the Sarakatsani have no trace at all of Vlachic influence.

27. J. K. Campbell, *Honour, Family and Patronage. A study of institutions and moral values in a Greek mountain community* (Oxford, 1964), p. 6. I am drawing upon this book for my description. For Sarakatsani in Acarnania see *DgL* 2, 2, p. 412.

28. For a description of this area see *Epirus*, pp. 258 f.

29. Campbell, p. 151, with an illustration of huts facing p. 208.

30. In the postwar period the number of Sarakatsani in the whole of Greece was reckoned to be about 80,000. See Campbell, p. 1 with note 1.

31. A short account of these peoples is given in *Megale Ellenike Enkyklopaedia*², 7, p. 417.

32. Campbell, p. 329: "The Sarakatsani think of the years of youth as the time of moral excellence. Later come responsibilities and the need for cunning, deceit and lies. There is grudging admiration for the expertise of the shrewd leader but regret that the means to success must be these." In the harsh, exposed life of the Sarakatsani honesty does not always pay in any literal sense.

33. Hesiod, *Works and Days*, 59-89.

34. A Hadzimichalis, *Sarakatsanoi* (Athens, 1957) 1 A, as cited by Campbell; the book is not available to me.

III

The Settled Peoples:
Albanians, Slavs, Bulgars, Turks and Greeks

The Albanians

(See Maps 11-14 and 16)

The Albanians, in the sense of those resident in the modern state of Albania, or Shqiperë as they themselves call it, lived under more primitive conditions than any other Balkan people in the 1930s. This was largely because they had been under Turkish domination from the fourteenth century until 1912–13 and had received thereafter little or no help from the leading powers of Europe. Now the position is entirely different. The country has undergone a double revolution under a single administration, passing through Stalinist communism to Maoist socialism. The population has increased from one million to more than two millions, the standard of living has risen remarkably, and age-old customs have been swept away. Albania today has an economic efficiency and a drab uniformity which make a vivid contrast with the prewar kingdom of Zog.[1]

We are concerned with Albania as it was in the 1930s and with the previous history of its people. Pastoralism and stock-raising were major occupations then, and taxes were paid on 1,424,965 sheep, 773,969 goats, 144,763 cattle and 44,318 horses in 1936–37. Sheep were of the greatest importance, providing milk, cheese, meat and wool for homespun clothing and rugs. Transhumance was widely practised, because the high mountains with their natural forests of pine and beech provided any amount of summer pasture, and the coastal plains, being flooded annually in November and March, were little used for agriculture and therefore afforded excellent grazing for the winter months. Now the floods are under control, the plains are properly irrigated, and rich crops are grown in the coastal plains; and the corollary of this development is that little land is left under grass to give pasturage in winter. As the interior of Albania has one of the highest rainfalls in Europe and the lowlands enjoy an almost Mediterranean mildness in the winter, the country has always been ideally suited to pastoralism of the transhumant variety. In Turkish times, when there were no internal frontiers, Weigand in 1889 saw Albanians moving many flocks for winter pastures through Pelagonia to the coastal plain of Macedonia.[2] Indeed, as long as stock-raising was on a large scale, transhumance was dictated by the climate, the winters in the highlands being too severe and the summers in the plains too hot for the animals to survive.

Most of the Albanian villages were situated then in the elevated country between the mountains and the plains, and the villagers maintained themselves by mixed farming of a primitive kind. The chief crop on the limited arable land was maize, from which a yellow bread (*boubōta*) was made; fuel for men and winter fodder for a small number of animals were provided by the local woods of oak, chestnut, ash and other deciduous trees. In the steep-sided valleys of the Acroceraunian range and in the thickly-wooded hills of the Kurvelesh I stayed with villagers in the 1930s who were on the borderline of starvation, clothed in rags and tatters of homespun, and with no covering for their feet. On the other hand, villages nearer to the coastal plain, such as Dukat at the head of the Gulf of Valona with its 60,000 sheep and goats, were well-to-do and sent a surplus of milk products and wool to the market-towns, which were few and far between. The great majority of the people were illiterate, and there were few schools of any kind, but the standard of home crafts was high in the weaving of rugs and clothing, the carving of wooden implements (Pl. *4a*) and vessels, and sometimes the making of copper pots and gold and silver jewelry (as among the Vlachs).[3] But there were no industries, no railways and only a few dirt roads. Life moved at the pace of a medieval country village.

The Albanian is by habit and instinct a mountaineer, and the heart of Albania has always beaten most strongly in the tangle of very high mountains in the north of the country. That area has been impenetrable to many foreign armies, and its inhabitants have governed themselves and observed their own laws without paying much regard to the rulers of the lowlands, whether Greek, Roman, Turkish or Italian. The laws were traditional, and they were not written down until recently. The Albanians themselves say that their laws were codified, if one may use that word of oral composition, in the fifteenth century by Lek Dukagjini, and that he was an older contemporary and friend of George Skanderbeg (1403–67), the leader of the heroic resistance against the all-conquering Turks. The achievement of Lek Dukagjini was not to invent laws but to organise the traditional ones of the numerous tribes of the northern part of the country—his own home—into a consistent system of law, and to persuade the tribes to adopt it. Since that time the laws have been handed down separately in tribes and in families by oral tradition; and the fact that they still belong recognisably to a codified system is a testimony to the accuracy and strength of an oral transmission, which continued until the mid-twentieth century, when ideological revolutions replaced the code of Lek Dukagjini with that of Enver Hoxha and his colleagues.

The family, in the extended sense of all generations living together, was very deeply entrenched in Albanian life in the 1930s, and within the family the males had an even greater degree of prestige and privilege than was the case among the Sarakatsani. The head of the family, the patriarch, once elected as such by the adult male kindred, had authority over all members of the family and directed all its affairs, including the betrothal of girls and the provision of dowries. The status of women was correspondingly lower. In the Acroceraunian villages all women, from young girls to grannies, were treated like beasts of burden. Even though they were bent double with the huge bundles of brushwood they carried, they still spun wool on a distaff as they walked. It was they who removed stones from the fields, dug and hoed the ground, and even pulled the wooden stake which served as a plough. They ate only what the men left after any meal.

Related families were the units which made up a tribe, and there were very many small tribes, especially in the mountains where each narrow valley lived a life apart from its neighbour. In their turn the tribes were the units which made up the tribal groups or large tribes, of which there were never more than four in all Albania. Each group spoke a marked dialect and had its own peculiarities of dress and its own customs.[4] These four groups were Gegs in the north, Tosks in the centre and south, Ljaps in the southwest, and Tsams in areas on both sides of the frontier between Albania and Greece in Epirus.[5] Thus society in the 1930s was organised on the concept, indeed almost the ideology, of kinship. One may think of the groups of kindred or 'brotherhoods' as forming a system of concentric circles; indeed this term was used in the district of Çermenikë. There, if the ghastly crime of a host killing a guest was committed, 'circle after circle' was the rule. The guest's 'circle', consisting of his own household, his kinsmen in separate homes, his neighbours and the sons of the married daughters of his family, wherever these last might live, tried to kill the murderer; and failing to find him, or other members of his household, they might kill one of his 'circle' (similarly defined).[6] Or again in Dibër, a tribal law laid down that "the kindred which does not take the lead against such culprits (among its own number) commits a fault against the whole tribe."

A constant feature of Albanian life was vendetta, enacted between family and family, village and village, and tribe and tribe. In a system where the individual is primarily a unit in a family, to kill him is to injure and dishonour the family, and the requital has to be carried out by the family, of which the executive arm is the nearest male relative of the dead man. In some areas the circle above the family is involved; then the 'brotherhood' includes the fellow-tribesmen in a vendetta with the corresponding circle, as each killing demands a killing in return. Village feuds arose readily. A dispute which began in the war of 1912 between two villages in the southern part of the Acroceraunian range, Kudhes and Qeparo, was still being pursued when I passed through them in 1930; it was in the form of a vendetta, each village killing a young man of the other village every six months. Not far away a larger village, Kuç, maintained a vendetta with Himarrë, which dated from the same time, but was itself a revival of earlier vendettas.

Where vendetta was so prevalent, it was regulated by the unwritten laws of the tribes, and many of these laws were designed to safeguard the essential needs of society such as food production. Thus a man might not be killed when ploughing, or when shepherding a flock, and the sheepfold, where milking and shearing were done, was sacrosanct. If a man broke these rules, he was punished by his own kindred in the first place, the fine being laid down in terms of 'purses' or 'rams'. Sometimes a family was entirely destroyed in the course of a vendetta, and a part of a village became derelict and deserted for that reason. A peculiarity of villages in the Kurvelesh is that they consist of small groups of houses at a large distance from one another, each group being a *mahalas* and being inhabited by closely related families. One reason for this is to be found in the prevalence of vendetta. As danger was never far away, every man was armed in the 1930s, and the head of the family marked the coming-of-age of a young man by giving him a rifle for family purposes. When Zog sent police to disarm some villagers in accordance with a general edict of state, the villagers shot the police.

In the 1930s the Albanians of the modern state of Albania were only a portion of those who spoke Albanian. Quite apart from the emigrants in Egypt, America and elsewhere, there were large groups of Albanian-speakers in Greece, Italy and Yugoslavia. The most interesting are those who were indigenous to the country but were included in southwestern Yugoslavia by the drawing of the frontier in 1912–13. They now form a rapidly increasing element in the population of southern Yugoslavia, their birthrate being abnormally high. They have remained completely Albanian in the pre-war sense of the word, retaining their traditional customs and living close to the subsistence level in the hilly country, for instance to the north of Ochrid, where I talked with the peasants of Goricë. On the other hand, the standard of living is much higher in the plains of Metohija and Kossovo, where fine horse-drawn waggons and even decorated cars form processions at the wedding ceremonies. In dress, manners and physique they remain unmistakably Albanian, speaking the Geg dialect. The mountainous frontier between Yugoslavia and Albania was easily crossed in the 1930s, when families or tribes moved to Albania in order to prosecute a vendetta, which the Yugoslavs banned as illegal.

What united this plethora of often warring families and often warring tribes as Albanians was a love of their land, a sense of family unity vis-à-vis Serbs, Bulgars, Greeks and Italians, and a unique language, which belongs, like Greek and Latin, to the Indo-European group of languages but is at a primitive stage of development. This language may be the direct descendant of the Illyrian language, which was spoken by the inhabitants of the northwestern part of the Balkans from early in the second millennium B.C. down to the collapse of the Roman Empire. If so, it provides an analogy to the survival of Greek today as the direct descendant of Mycenaean Greek. But the purely linguistic evidence is scanty, because the Illyrians were illiterate, and there are not enough toponyms and personal names to convince the specialists in the linguistic field. But on a broader consideration, the inaccessibility of the mountains of northern Albania, the extreme conservatism of Albanian life and customs until recently, and the arrested development of the Albanian language are strongly in favour of the view that the Shqiptars, as they call themselves,[7] are the linear descendants of the tribes of the northwest Balkans to which the Greeks and the Romans gave the general name 'Illyrians'.

In the fifth and sixth centuries A.D. 'Illyricum', the Roman province of the northwest Balkans which began in the south with Scodra, was a very important part of the Empire, because it provided good soldiers and leading emperors such as Diocletian and Justinian. The line of division between Illyricum and the Greek area, 'Epirus Nova',[8] in terms of Roman provincial administration ran somewhere between Scodra and Dyrrachium and then eastwards on the north side of the Shkumbi and Lake Ochrid (see Map 11). One reason for this line was that it placed the main road from the west to the east, the Via Egnatia, under the control of one province. Another reason was that it corresponded more or less with the line of demarcation between the Illyrian language and the Greek language. Within the Greek area there were two provinces in the northwest, 'Epirus Nova', which ran from south of Scodra to the northern tip of the Gulf of Valona and included the sea-terminals of the Via Egnatia, Dyrrachium and Aulon, and 'Epirus Vetus', which ran from Cape Glossa or Linguetta, the northern promontory of the Acroceraunian range, to the Gulf of Arta and sometimes to the Gulf of Corinth. There is no doubt that the population of Epirus Nova was then partly of Illyrian and partly of Greek blood, the former probably predominating, but it was cultur-

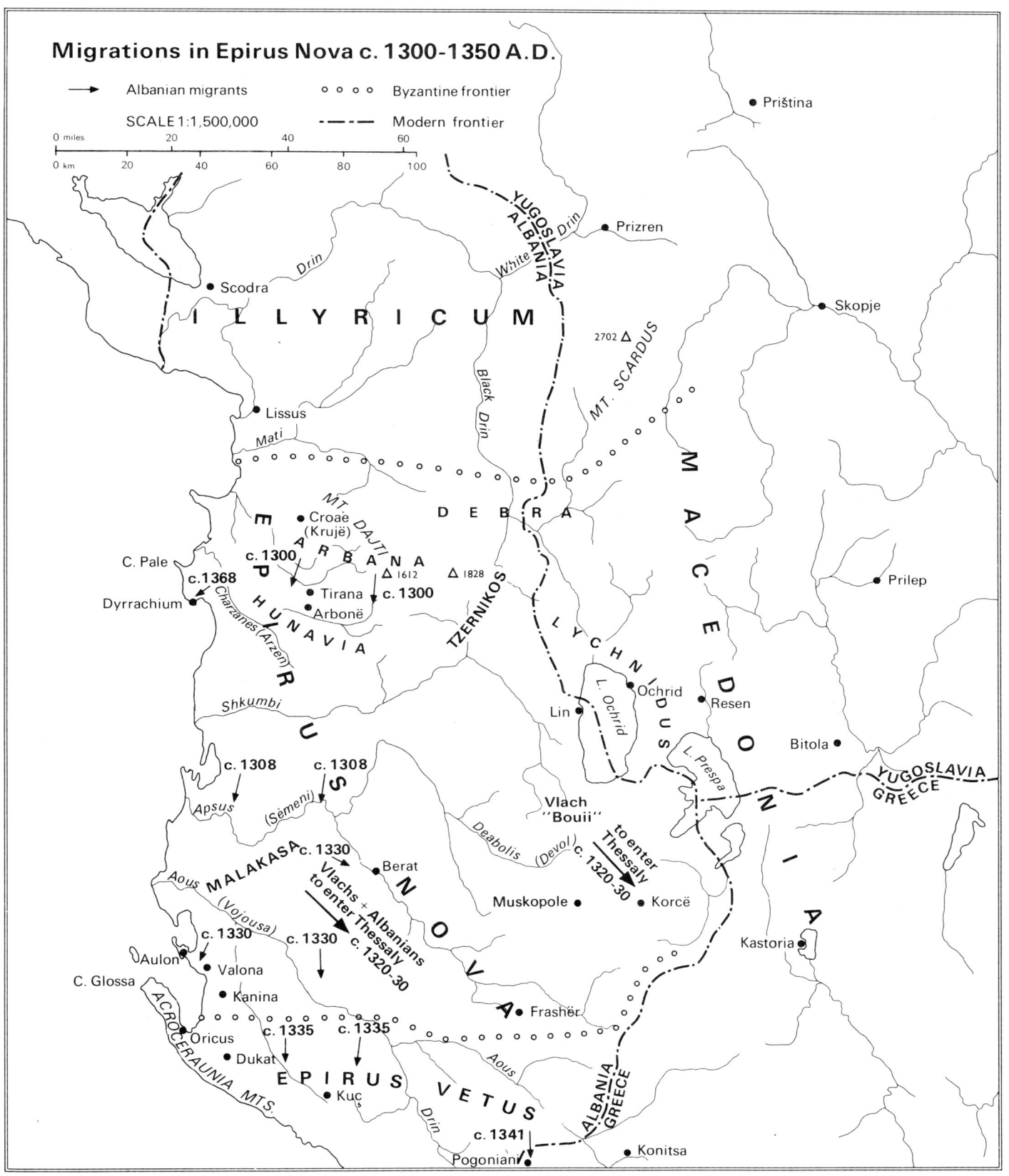

ally Greek and probably considered itself to be Greek or Graeco-Roman. On the other hand the population of Illyricum was Illyrian and thought of itself as Illyrian or Illyro-Roman, using Latin as its adopted language for literary purposes.

For almost half a millennium we know nothing of Epirus Nova except that it suffered from terrible earthquakes and was overrun repeatedly by barbarian invaders who came from north of the Danube. In 1081 even more formidable invaders landed on its coast, the Normans (or the Franks, as the Greeks called them) of the First Crusade, and they conquered and occupied Epirus Nova, while the Byzantine emperor, Alexius, withdrew to concentrate his forces at Ochrid. It was in these circumstances that a region 'Albania' was first mentioned in literature, namely in the Norman French of the great epic, the *Chanson de Roland*, composed c. 1082–84. The place-names of Epirus Nova were reproduced in a French form or in a Biblical form: the river Charzanes (modern Arzen) appeared as Cheriant (line 3208); the river Mati (the modern name) as Val ('river' in the *Chanson*) Marchis, Mari or Morois; the ancient Oricus as Jericho; the modern Kanina as Chanineis and so on. One line of the *Chanson*, 3255, gives what were probably the limits of Epirus Nova on the coast for the Crusaders as 'Baile' (Cape Pale north of Dyrrachium) and 'Glos' (Cape Glossa). Now another manuscript (CV[7]) gives not these names but 'd'Albanie et de Kent' in order to convey the same meaning. Thus it follows that 'Albanie' was inland of Cape Pale; for 'Kent' (Kanina) was inland of Cape Glossa.[9] Again at line 3230 there is mention of Cape Pale, which appears in the best manuscript as 'Baile' and in other manuscripts as Paligea, Baligera, Balie, Balide, Baldise and in V[7], as Albeigne. H. Grégoire and R. de Keyser, who were the first to recognise that names of places in Epirus Nova were mentioned in the *Chanson*,[10] regarded all these readings as corruptions of 'Baile'; and in particular they said "V[7] a corrompu Baile en Albeigne." Yet 'Albeigne' is so unlike the other versions and so remote from 'Baile' that it is most probably not a corruption at all but, precisely as in line 3255, a variant. If it is a variant of Baile (Cape Pale), 'Albeigne' like 'Albanie' is to be sought inland of Cape Pale.

The correct forms in Greek of the place-names in Epirus Nova were given some decades later by the Byzantine writers and among them by Anna Comnena, the daughter of the Emperor Alexius who had fought against the Crusaders. Thus, corresponding to 'Albanie' and 'Albeigne' was the form 'Arbanon' in Anna Comnena's history, which she completed in 1148. This 'Arbanon' was a mountain, since she wrote of passes and paths through it (13.5), and it lay somewhere between Dyrrachium and 'Deurē' (Dibra) in the valley of the Black Drin. The most likely candidate is Mt Dajti, east of Cape Pale (now Rodoni). A plural form in the neuter gender was used by Anna Comnena at 4.8, where "Komiskortes set out from Arbana."[11] As in the case of the 'Acroceraunia' (*sc.* 'orē'), a mountainous area was being named 'Arbana', i.e. Mt Dajti and Mali me Gropë most probably.

From 1166 onwards the suffragan bishops of Dyrrachium included "episcopi Albanenses, Arbanenses, Arbonenses" and even "Arbunenses."[12] As bishops were named not after a race but by a place, these bishops were in charge of a district 'Arbana', or something of the sort. The district was comparatively small, because we hear of suffragan bishops of 'Hunavia' and 'Tzernikos' (Çermenikë), which were situated, like Arbana, on the north side of the Via Egnatia.[13] The seat of the diocese may have been a town called something like 'Arbanos'. We have two mentions of such a town: 'Albanopolis' or in a variant reading 'Albanos polis' in Ptolemy 3.12.20, writing in the second century A.D., and 'Albanos' in the company of the towns Achris (Ochrid), Prilapos (Prilep), and Dyrrachium in G. Acropolites 14, writing in the thirteenth century.[14] The latter author mentioned also a district 'Albanon' as "a little beyond Dyrrachium," and as containing "difficult terrain" (14) and a fort known as 'Kroai' (49), now Krujë, on the western face of Mt Dajti.

The gap between Ptolemy and Acropolites is bridged by the mention of "Ducagini d'Arbania" in a seventh-century document at Ragusa (Dubrovnik). These Ducagini instigated a revolt against Byzantine rule in Bosnia and in particular at Ragusa, but they had to submit after the second unsuccessful intervention at Ragusa, to which they were said to have come "de terra ferma," i.e. overland.[15] The name 'Ducagini' is evidently derived from the Latin 'dux' and the common Albanian name 'Ghin'; indeed an Albanian chieftain in 1281 was referred to as "dux Ginius Tanuschus."[16] Moreover, the leading family of northern Albania from the thirteenth century to the Turkish invasion in the fifteenth century was called 'Dukagjin' (Lek Dukagjini the codifier was one of them), and their properties lay between Lesh (Lissus) and the bend of the Drin. It is here then that we should put the 'Arbania' of the seventh century. The conclusion that 'Albanians' lived there continuously from the second century to the thirteenth century becomes, I think, unavoidable.[17]

'Albanoi' as a people appeared first in Ptolemy 3.12.20. In his description of the Roman world, the southernmost part of the province Illyricum included Scodra, Lissus and Mt Scardus (Šar Planina); and, adjoining it, the northernmost part of 'Macedonia' included the Taulantii (in the region of Tirana) and the Albani, in whose territory Ptolemy recorded one city only, Albanopolis or Albanos polis. Thus the Albani were a tribe in what we now call Central Albania, and they were an Illyrian-speaking tribe, like the more famous Taulantii, in the second century A.D. Men of this tribe appeared next in 1040, alongside some Epirotes (their neighbours on land) and some Italiotes (their neighbours across the sea), in the army of a rebellious general, George Maniakis. Two chieftains of this tribe, Demetrios and Ghin, pursued an independent policy in the early years of the thirteenth century.

In 1204 the Franks of the Fourth Crusade and the Venetians sacked Constantinople and began to divide up the provinces of the Byzantine Empire among themselves. A period of chaos ensued, during which several small principalities were established in the southwest Balkans. The only one which upheld the Greek tradition was that of the Angeli, the rulers of Epirus from 1206 to 1260, and they had to contend with the Albanian principality of Demetrios and Ghin, the Serbian principality of the Nemanja and Uroš families, the kingdom of Thessalonica, and the rival Byzantine principality of Nicaea, quite apart from raids delivered from the west on the coast of Epirus. It was in this period that the flow of immigrants from the northwestern area began (see Maps 11-13). It became a flood in the fourteenth century. They went as mercenaries, raiders and migrants. The great majority of them were speakers of Albanian, but others joined the movement. Whatever their language, they were described by the Greek and Latin writers as 'Albanoi' or 'Arbanitai' or 'Albanenses', and the reason for this collective term can only be that they entered the Byzantine world through the district which the Byzantines knew as 'Albanon'. Thus the Vlach-speaking Malakasii, who invaded Thessaly in 1334 were descirbed as 'Albanoi' by Cantacuzenus 1.474 no less than the evidently Albanian-speaking 'Albanensium gens' which raided Thessaly in 1325.[18] Initially and for a long time all invaders from the northwestern area were simply 'Albanoi'. It was only gradually that distinctions of language were regarded as significant and the concept of an Albanian race in a wider sense developed. The earliest mention of the 'Albanian' language was in 1285: "Audivi unam vocem clamantem in monte in lingua albanesca" ("I heard a voice shouting on the mountainside in the Albanian tongue"). The shouter was in the mountains of Ragusa (Dubrovnik), far to the north of the Byzantine district of Albanon. It is probable that the great mass of Albanian-speaking tribes at the end of the thirteenth century was in what used to be called Montenegro, the most mountainous district of the western Balkans.[19] Here the conditions were most favourable for the survival of the Illyrian language throughout the Dark Age which separated the late Roman Empire from the medieval period.

The southward movement of the tribes was on a very large scale. It was also rapid, because towns and cities were bypassed (Dyrrachium, for instance, being captured only c. 1368). It had two main effects. It took possession of Epirus Nova, the area inland of the coastal strip from Dyrrachium to Valona; and it sent streams of migrants into most parts of the Greek peninsula and some of the Aegean islands. To the settled peoples they were a terror. "Deus misit hanc pestem," wrote the author of the *Gesta Dei per Francos* 2. 293. They came, like a plague of locusts, in huge numbers ("in tanta quantitate numerosa") and in 1325 they ravaged and destroyed everything in Thessaly outside the fortified centres ("omnia quae erant extra castra"). When they wanted to leave Thessaly and go elsewhere, many others appeared with their wives and children ("multi cum uxoribus et filiis") and their combined forces proceeded to wreck other parts of Thessaly. John Cantacuzenus 1. 495 described their raids on the west side of the peninsula in 1335: "The Albanoi who inhabit the area of Balagrita [Berat] and Kanina [inland of Valona], being adaptable to change and by nature revolutionary, ravaged and plundered . . . and oppressed the towns there with their brigandage and open raids" (see Map 13).

The Byzantine rulers had recourse to two methods of treating these raiders. The Emperor Andronicus III gave land to 12,000 Vlach-speaking raiders who submitted to him in Thessaly. 'The Great Domestic', John

Map 12

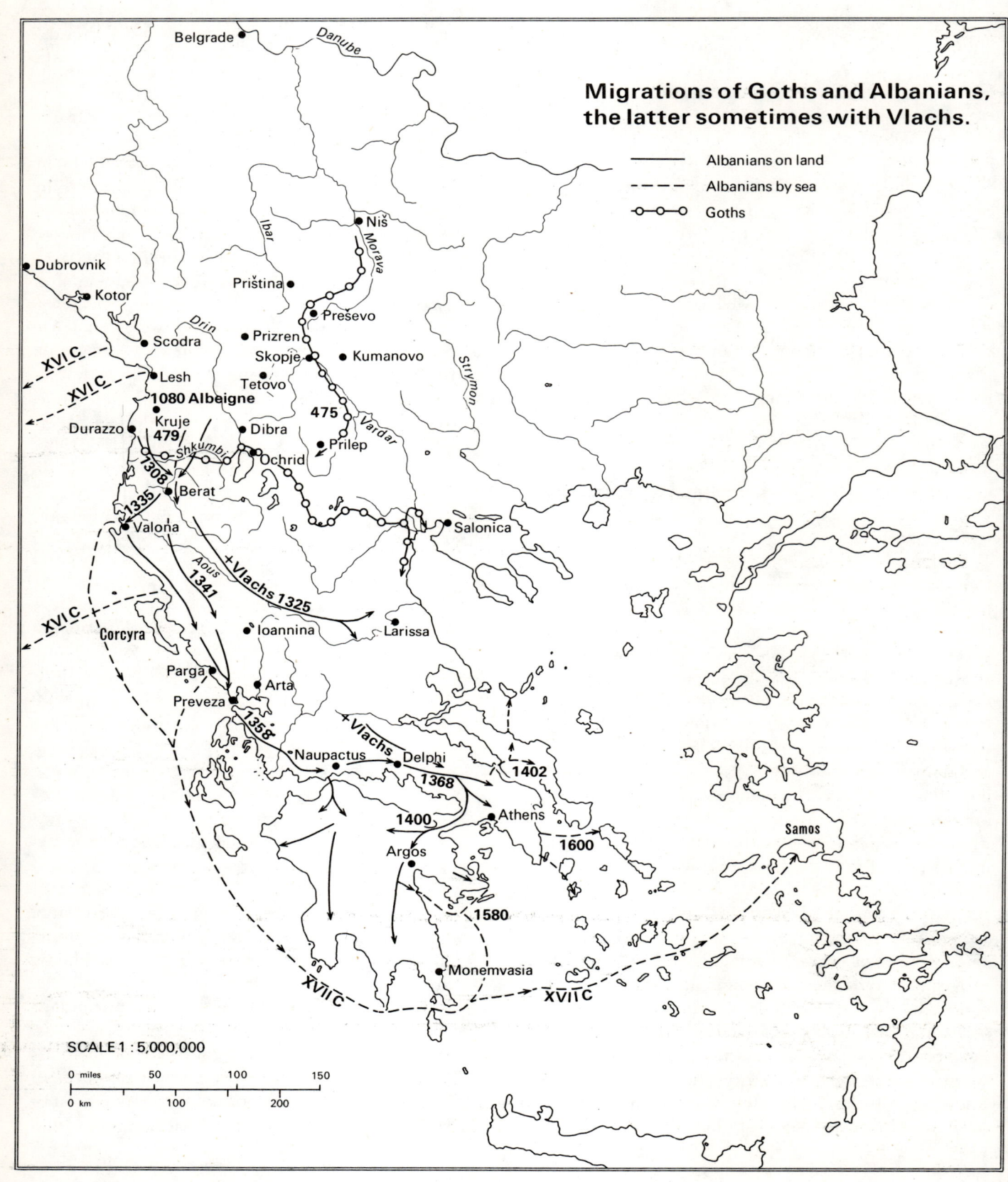

Cantacuzenus, carried out a campaign against the Albanian-speaking tribes in 1335. "As the Albanians inhabited great mountain ranges which were difficult of access and had many retreats and hiding-places, they could not easily be injured by the cavalry." For this reason, light-armed infantry and archers were recruited in Asia and took part in the campaign (Cantacuzenus 1. 495). Even so the Albanians were not destroyed; for they withdrew into the mountains and beat off their attackers from above. However, the Emperor advanced from Thessaly to Dyrrachium and took spoil to the amount of 300,000 cattle, 5,000 horses and 1,200,000 sheep. But the Albanian raids continued and Acarnania was laid waste. In 1341 the Emperor attacked the offending Albanians "around Pogoniane and Libisda" (Lidizda), i.e. in the central part of northern Epirus;[20] and then in 1355 he campaigned from Thessaly as far south as Aetolia and Acarnania and was killed in action (Cantacuzenus 3.319). These campaigns did not stop the flood. Albanians were serving as mercenaries in the Peloponnese c. 1350, and they and their families were given land there to cultivate.

In 1358 the Albanians overran Epirus, Acarnania and Aetolia, and established two principalities under their leaders, John Spatas (*shpatë* in Albanian meaning a sword) and Peter Leosas (*lios* in Albanian meaning a pockmark). Naupactus fell into their control in 1378. The cities which held out against them, especially Ioannina and Arta, were ravaged by a series of plagues, and Thomas, the Serbian Despot of Ioannina, saved himself at first by making marriage alliances with the two Albanian leaders. In the Greek account of the Albanian advance under Peter Leosas we learn that he was accompanied by "Mazarakii and Malakasei of his own race" (*Epeirotica* 2.220; cf. 222 f.).[21] While Mazaraki is in central Epirus by the river Kalamas, Malakasa is the coastal plain of central Albania farther north and the words "of his own race" were used to distinguish the Albanian-speaking Malakasaei from the Vlach-speaking Malakasii. They were accompanied by Bulgars and Vlachs. It is clear that Thomas feared the Albanians above all. Whereas he mutilated the Bulgars and the Vlachs, he allowed most of his Albanian prisoners to be ransomed. Atrocities were committed no doubt by both sides, and Thomas came to be called Albanitoktonos ('Albanian-killer;' *Epeirotica* 2.225). In 1380 Thomas brought in the Turks as allies and passed to the offensive, but he did not advance farther than the basin of the upper Kalamas, where he took Vela (by Vrondismeni), Boursina (Vrousina), and Kretzounista (Dhespotikon).[22] The Albanians and in particular the Mazarakii of the Kalamas valley held firm against him. In 1385 he was assassinated by some of his own bodyguards (*Epeirotica* 2.230).

Other bands of Albanians and Vlachs invaded the Catalan principality of Boeotia and Attica, and a great many Albanians settled there as peasant-farmers in 1368 and later years. Around the end of that century a migrating group of 10,000 Albanians with their families and their animals came from pastures in central Greece to the Isthmus of Corinth and sought entry to the Peloponnese. This was granted by Theodore, who settled them within his own domains, where he used them as tough soldiers and "expert cultivators" (Manuel II, *Funeral Speech*, p. 40). Albanians and others were invited in 1402 to settle on uncultivated but cultivable lands in Euboea, if they were willing to serve as soldiers in defence of the island and work the soil. The proclamation of the Venetian rulers was extended to "quilibet Albanensis vel alia gens, qui non sint nostri subditi, qui cum equis volent venire et venient ad habitandum."[23] By the middle of the fifteenth century the Albanians in the Peloponnese were so numerous that they tried to seize control, led first by one Peter the Lame, and then by a Greek, a member of the Cantacuzenus family, but their attempt failed.

The penetration of the Greek mainland which we have described occurred during the hundred or more years after 1325. The opportunity arose through the decline and disruption of the Byzantine Empire and the wars which followed between the various small principalities of Greeks, Serbs, Catalans, Venetians and others. One of the pressures which set the Albanians and others in motion came from the expanding power of the Serbs which reached its peak under the rule of Stephen Dušan (1331–1355), who subjugated Epirus and Acarnania. A contributory factor seems to have been overpopulation among the Albanians[24]—always a prolific people—and underpopulation in mainland Greece as a result of internal collapse and foreign intervention. The strongest single group of invaders was that of the Vlachs which pressed down into Thessaly and opened the way there for the Albanians. But the most numerous by far were the Albanian-speakers, and their main line of invasion

Map 13

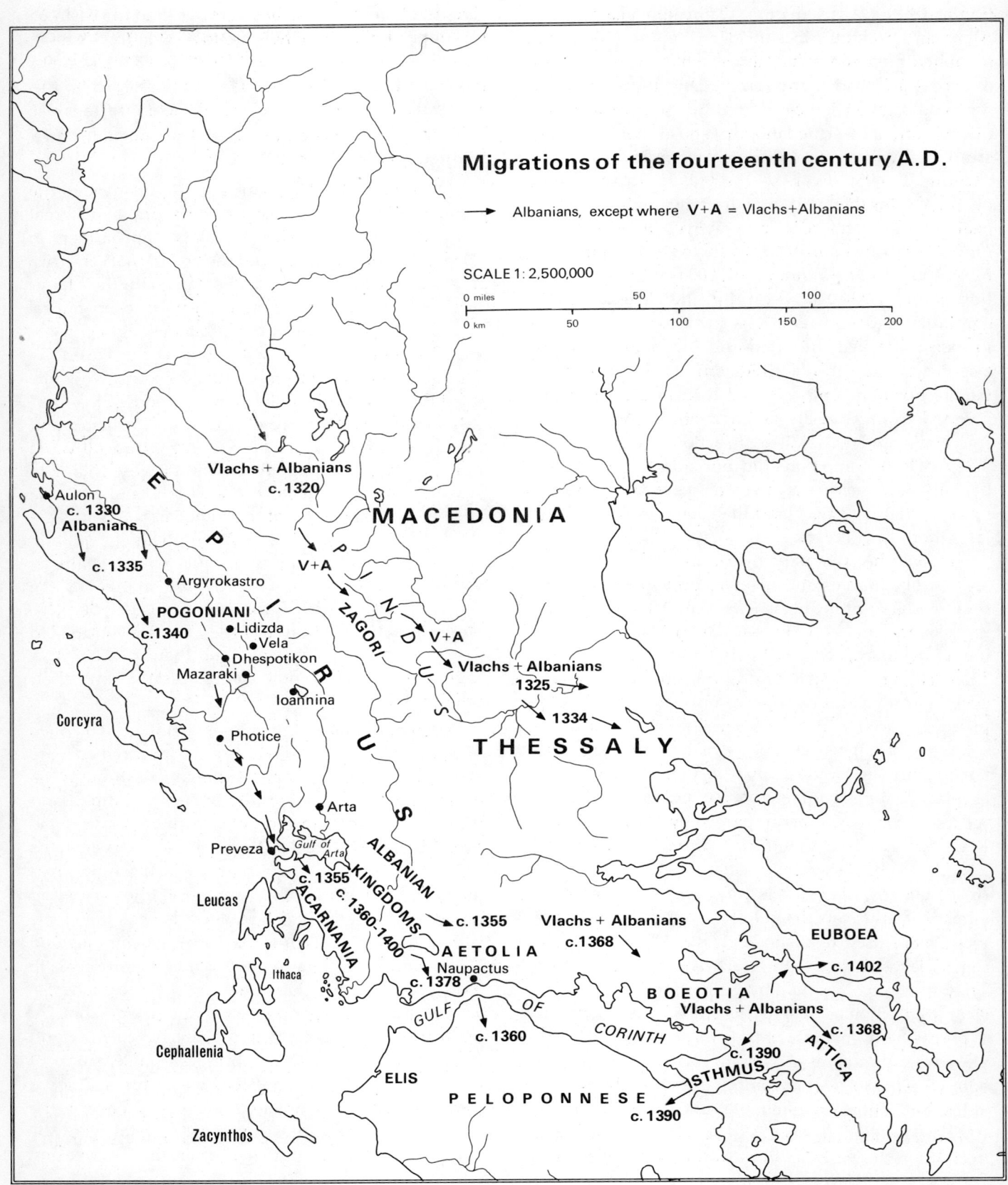

and penetration was down the western side of northern and central Greece[25] (see Maps 11–13).

At first the Albanians came mainly from north of the river Shkumbi. Later, in 1308, 'Albania' was a fairly wide, large region irrigated by four rivers, Ersentha (Arzen), Mathia (Mati), Scumpino (Shkumbi), and Epasa (?Apsus, now Semeni) in the anonymous *Descriptio Europae Orientalis* (ed. Gorka). By 1335 they were in possession also of the area between Berat and the Gulf of Valona, which contains the rich plain of Malakastër. A generation later they held most of northern Epirus and an important group or tribe among them, the Mazarakii, was settled on the western side of the upper Kalamas. The centre of Greek resistance was Ioannina, which controlled its own plateau and shielded Zagori against attack by the Albanians (but not against attack by the Vlachs). As the Albanians overran Acarnania and Aetolia but for many decades were unable to capture Arta, it follows that they advanced and probably settled in southwestern Epirus and crossed the Gulf of Arta at its outlet at Preveza, an Albanian word meaning a crossing.[26] The main stream flowed on and reached Naupactus in 1378.

Once in possession of most of northwestern Greece, the Albanians opened the way for other immigrants. Offshoots of Albanians and Vlachs entered Boeotia, Attica and Euboea, having probably come from summer pastures on Mt Parnassus and from southern Aetolia; and other groups of Albanians forced an entry or gained an invitation of entry into the Peloponnese, sometimes crossing over the western part of the Gulf of Corinth and sometimes coming to the Isthmus of Corinth. In many parts of the mainland co-existence of immigrants and Greeks was practised. But not in Epirus, which bore the main brunt. There the Greek pocket of resistance, which preserved the Greek language even when its ruler was Serb or Italian, was the plateau of Ioannina and its hinterland (primarily Zagori). A typical example of Greek withdrawal into the interior is afforded by the movement of a bishopric from Photice (by Paramythia) to Vela (in the upper Kalamas valley) and finally to Konitsa (in the upper Aous valley).[27] When 'Isaou', the Italian ruler of Ioannina, passed to the offensive in 1399, he had already won over the Mazarakii (Albanians) and the Malakasaei (perhaps Vlach-speakers) and he recruited Greeks evidently from Zagori, Papingo (above Konitsa), and "Druinoupolis with Argyrokastro and the great Zagoria" (probably the high country northeast of Argyrokastro, of which a part is still called Zagorië).[28] He went then to 'Mesopotamo', which I take to have been (like the modern Mesoyefira) below Konitsa at the confluence of the Aous and the Voïdhomati; for he aimed to advance in the direction of Dibra, i.e. via Korcë and Ochrid (*Epeirotica* 2.237). His aim was to join hands with the Greeks who maintained their independence on the frontier of western Macedonia.

Our Greek sources give us an interesting picture of the invaders. Admittedly the Greeks were prejudiced (for in terms of culture they were certainly superior), and they regarded the invaders as a motley lot of barbarians. The author of *Epeirotica* 2.237 described one Boncoes as "Serbalbanitobulgaroblachus" with a disdainful impartiality. In fact the Albanians, the Vlachs and the associated Bulgars were pastoral peoples, mainly nomadic and given to war and hunting, and they were all unlike the cultivated citizens of a Byzantine centre such as Ioannina or Arta.

When John Cantacuzenus plundered Albanian territory as far as Dyrrachium, the spoil consisted of herds among which sheep were the most numerous, being over a million. When 10,000 Albanians came to the Isthmus of Corinth, they brought not only their families but also their flocks of animals. The Albanians in the Peloponnese took their herds in the winter to the coastal plain of Elis, "which was open to the sun, near the sea, had good grazing and was deserted by men (i.e. by the Greeks)"; and these herds consisted of "very many herds of horses, very many of cattle, most of sheep and most of pig."[29] Such Albanians as these—and they were evidently the majority—were described by Laonicus Chalcocondylas (406) as follows: "This race are all nomads, and do not make their stay for long in any one place." They were, then, transhumant pastoralists without fixed abodes or villages. But there were many others who wanted to cultivate the land and were given land by the Venetians and the Greeks, because they were such hard-working and expert cultivators. They had evidently been engaged in agriculture in lands south of the Shkumbi river or in the lakeland and had joined the stream of migrants in the hope of obtaining better land. When Manuel Cantacuzenus, Despot of Mistra in the Peloponnese, took over "all Albania," he deported two groups of Albanians and settled them, one near Constantinople and the other in the

Peloponnese, the latter "a great number."[30] The Albanians were acceptable to the Greek, Catalan or Venetian overlords, as the case might be, because they were capable of reviving agriculture in derelict areas.

In the eyes of the Greeks, the Albanians and those associated with them were fine hunters,[31] excellent horsemen and redoubtable warriors. As has been said by Joseph Campbell, "by and large hunting people are warrior people; and not only that, but many are exhilarated by battle and turn warfare into exercises in bravura."[32] These were the ancestors of the Souliote warriors, whom Byron admired so much in the Greek War of Independence. In the fourteenth century they were feared and hated in northern Greece, but they were hired as mercenaries or attracted as settlers by the rulers of the principalities in the Peloponnese and central Greece and Thessaly. The most warlike of the Albanians were those described by the Greeks as living in great mountainous areas, that is those engaged in pastoralism with the transhumance of sheep. They were certainly illiterate, but they were tightly organised in tribal units with a patriarchal system of leadership. When Manuel Cantacuzenus took over Albania, he expelled "all the men of account" ("tutti li homini di conto"); and John Ducas reported the killing of all the eminent Albanians when the Greeks attempted to gain control of the Albanian settlers in the Peloponnese.[33] The leaders were evidently very capable men, possessing wide powers over their followers, and 'John the Sword', 'Peter the Pockmark' and 'Peter the Lame' led very large armies of Albanian warriors with success. When they were hired as mercenaries, they came not as individuals but as organised bands, sometimes accompanied by their families and animals. The hope of their employers was that the Albanians would "come with their horses" and fulfil their obligations "to maintain their horses, garrison the forts and obey orders."[34] It was these cavalrymen, with their entourage, who were the leaders. The rank and file fought on foot.

With the capture of Ioannina by the Turks in 1430, the role of the Albanians changed very little. The Albanians of Krujë, Mati and Dibra, i.e. of the areas north of the Shkumbi river, fought heroically against the Turks until the death of their leader, Skanderbeg, in 1467 and indeed after it, but unavailingly. The Albanians of the Peloponnese participated in a rising against the Turks in 1459. On the other hand the Turks were soon employing the Albanians as mercenaries and encouraging them to settle in the devastated areas not only of the Greek mainland but also in some of the Aegean islands. So the process of infiltration and expansion continued under Turkish rule. By 1687, for instance, almost all the population of Euboea was Albanian,[35] the Greeks having fled in 1471.

Piracy had led to impoverishment and depopulation in the islands during the late Byzantine period, and Albanians moved in as occasion arose. Thus they were brought to Andros in the Saronic Gulf c. 1600 to cultivate the land; they went from Troezen to Hydra in 1580, and other settlers arrived from Parga, Souli, Valona, Euboea and Cythnos in the seventeenth century. Other groups went to Samos, Psara and Casos, many of the settlers being from western Epirus, Euboea and Thessaly. Yet other groups entered Andros, Ios, Cythnos and Ceos among the Cyclades, and Scopelos in the Northern Sporades. They became excellent seamen, winning distinction in the Greek War of Independence and raising Hydra and Spetsae to a leading position in the carrying trade of the Aegean basin. Groups of soldiers were employed far afield: in Cyprus, for instance, in Byzantine times, and for some 250 years in Crete during the Turkish period.

The conditions which attended the collapse of the Byzantine Empire recurred in the late eighteenth century and thereafter, when the Turks were losing control of their Balkan dependencies more and more, until Albania became free in 1912–13. Throughout this period bands of Albanians raiders pillaged and destroyed the villages of the Vlachs and the Greeks in Epirus, northern Pindus, the lakeland of Prespa and Ochrid, and parts of western Macedonia. One Albanian leader, 'Ali the Lion', emulated the achievements of 'John the Sword' and 'Peter the Pockmark' when he established himself as Ali Pasha, independent ruler of Ioannina. He and his Albanian soldiers, recruited mainly from his homeland in the Kurvelesh and the Drin valley of North Epirus, controlled the whole of Epirus and carried their raids far into western Macedonia and Thessaly. As we have seen, they destroyed the Vlach settlements in the lakeland and weakened those farther south. After the assassination of Ali Pasha in 1822 sporadic raids by bands of

Albanians were a feature of life in northern Greece until the liberation of 1912–13.[36]

Albanian settlements in Greek lands maintained their own language and their own dialect of that language for many centuries. The great majority spoke the Geg dialect which is characteristic of Albania north of the river Shkumbi and of the districts Metohija and Kossovo in southern Yugoslavia; but some settlements, for instance those near Lake Copais in Boeotia, spoke the Tosk dialect, which is native to the area between the Shkumbi and the Aous in general terms (see Map 14). Some scholars regard Ljap and Tsam as sub-dialects of Tosk, but the tribes themselves seem to have been distinct from the Tosks; and their dialects survived in Greek lands in the northwestern area only, as far as I am aware. Within Albania Ljap is spoken in the south and Tsam in the extreme south. There are good grounds for supposing that the different dialects were spoken already in the fourteenth century, when many Albanians came into Greek lands and in particular those who settled in Boeotia and Attica. The fact that most Albanians in Greek lands have spoken the Geg dialect during the last hundred years is an indication of their geographical origin; that is to say, the first settlers came predominantly from north of the Shkumbi river, i.e. from north of 'Arbana', as indeed the literary sources suggest. When they passed through the country south of the Shkumbi, they carried with them only a small number of the Albanians then resident in Epirus Nova, speakers at that time evidently of Tosk, Ljap and Tsam. It was this last group—speakers of Tosk, Ljap and Tsam—which occupied much of Epirus Vetus[37] when the speakers of Geg had leap-frogged beyond them into central Greece and the Peloponnese.

The Albanian language persisted in Greece with full vigour into the 1930s. When Perachora on the Isthmus of Corinth was being excavated, all the workmen spoke Albanian; and I visited Albanian-speaking villages in Boeotia, Attica, Argolis and Epidaurus in the 1930s. Albanian gave way to Greek when the conditions of life changed through the introduction of universal education, military conscription, organised commerce and more mobility of population. In the islands change came sooner; and there Albanian receded in the nineteenth century. It is likely that Albanian will give way to Greek altogether under the conditions of the present half-century. On the other hand, in southern Yugoslavia there has been no weakening of Albanian speech, because the conditions of life have changed relatively little since 1912–13. Even in these days of self-determination the Albanian-speakers in Greek lands have no sense of being anything other than Greek. Their predecessors played a leading part in the heroic fighting which won freedom from the Turks in 1821, and they themselves are fully absorbed into the Greek way of life. When I stayed with Albanian-speaking villagers of Tsamouria (Pl. 4b) in Greek Epirus in the 1930s, they spoke of themselves as Greeks and had no feeling of being a minority.

The Slavs and the Bulgars

During the long Dark Age which followed the decline and then the division of the Roman Empire the Balkan area was the scene of repeated invasions and migrations during which the fortified towns became centres of resistance and the mountain fastnesses provided refuge for some of the indigenous population. Wave after wave of newcomers, flowing from the steppe country of southern Russia, broke through the defences of the eastern part of the Roman Empire and entered the Balkans and the Aegean basin by land and by sea. Each wave was impelled by its eastern neighbour; as soon as one people forced its way into the Balkans, another people began to press against the frontier, which ran along the line of the Danube. Thus in the late fourth century the Ostrogoths in the Ukraine and the Visigoths living between the Dniester and the Danube were impelled southwards by the Alans, themselves under pressure from the Huns, and some groups of Goths defeated the Emperor Valens and destroyed the imperial army at Adrianople in 378 and overran Thrace, Macedonia and Greece, while others sailed out of the Black Sea into the Aegean. But by 477 it was the Huns who were raiding as far south as Thermopylae and threatening Constantinople itself. Meanwhile the most numerous of all the migrant peoples, the Slavs, were on the move from their homelands between the Vistula in Poland and the Dnieper in Russia, and they began to cross the middle part of the Danube before the end of the fifth century. Pressure then was being exerted on the Slavs by the Bulgars, a Hunnic or Turco-Tartarian people, who raided deep into Thrace

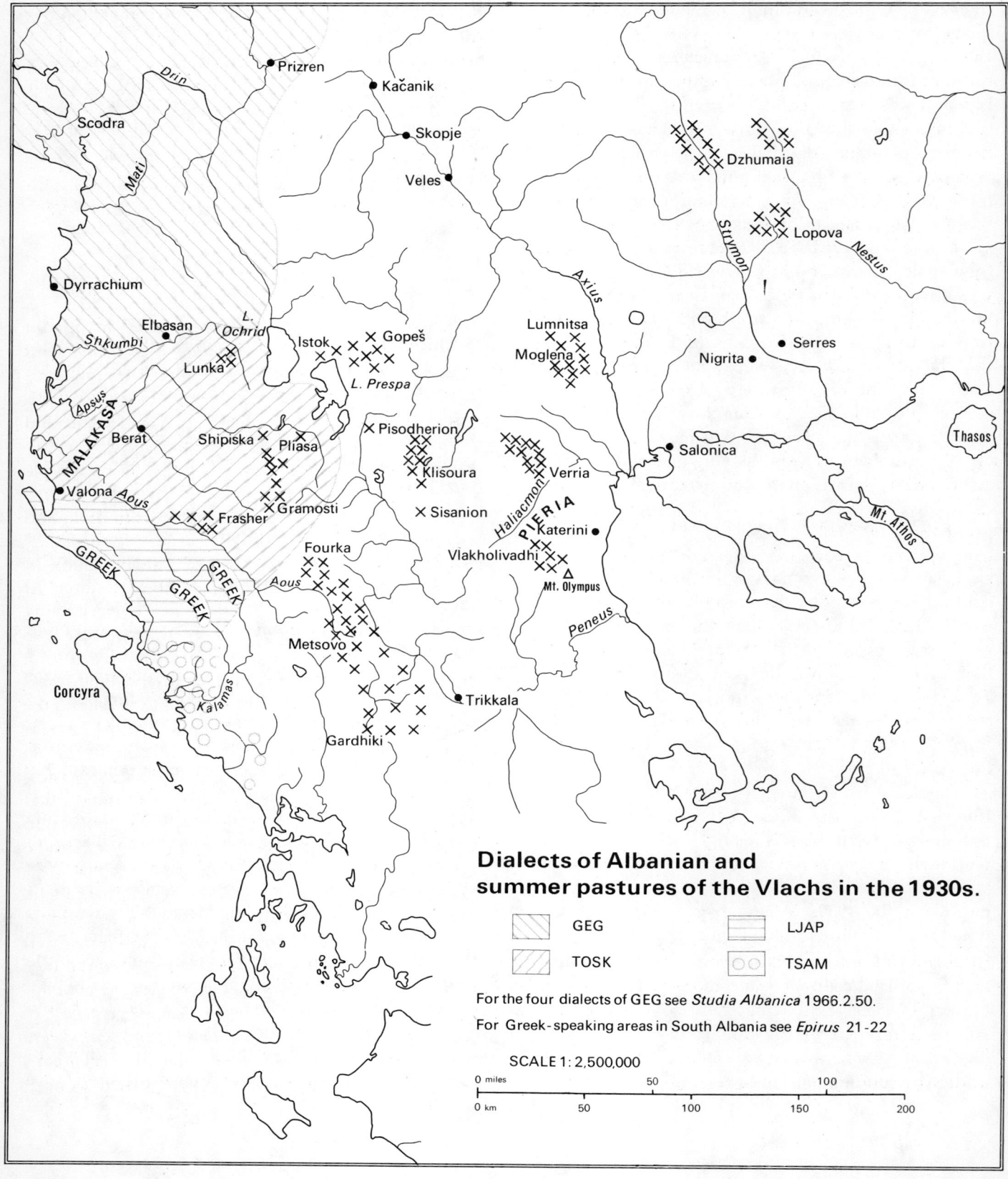

in 493, 499 and 502. Late in the sixth century the Avars, driven on by pressure from the Turks, entered the lands north of the Danube, recruited and organised the forces of the Slavs, and besieged Thessalonica by land and by sea in 597. A century later pressure from the Khazars, situated round the Sea of Azov, caused the Bulgars to join forces with some of the Slavs and establish a new kingdom in the lands between the Danube and the Haemus range, which had been part of the Roman domain for centuries. The Emperor Constantine IV was compelled not only to grant recognition but to pay an annual tribute to the Bulgarian state.[38]

These steppe peoples during the stages of invasion and migration had much in common, whether they were Goths or Turks, and some of their characteristics have been admirably summarised by Gibbon.[39]

> In every age the immense plains of Scythia or Tartary have been inhabited by vagrant tribes of hunters and shepherds, whose indolence refuses to cultivate the earth, and whose restless spirit disdains the confinement of a sedentary life. In every age the Scythians and Tartars have been renowned for their invincible courage and rapid conquests. The thrones of Asia have been repeatedly overturned by the shepherds of the North; and their arms have spread terror and devastation over the most fertile and warlike countries of Europe . . . The flocks and herds which accompany the march of the Tartars afford a sure and increasing supply of flesh and milk; in the far greater part of the uncultivated waste the vegetation of the grass is quick and luxuriant; and there are few places so extremely barren that the hardy cattle of the North cannot find some tolerable pasture. The supply is multiplied and prolonged by the undistinguishing appetite and patient abstinence of the Tartars. They indifferently feed on the flesh of those animals that have been killed for the table or have died of disease. Horse-flesh, which in every age and country has been proscribed by the civilized nations of Europe and Asia, they devour with peculiar greediness; and this singular taste facilitates the success of their military operations. The active cavalry of Scythia is always followed, in their most distant and rapid incursions, by an adequate number of spare horses, who may be occasionally used, either to redouble the speed, or to satisfy the hunger, of the Barbarians . . . As the most honourable shepherds of the Tartar race devolve on their captives the domestic management of the cattle, their own leisure is seldom disturbed by any servile and assiduous cares. But this leisure, instead of being devoted to the soft enjoyments of love and harmony, is usefully spent in the violent and sanguinary exercise of the chase. The plains of Tartary are filled with a strong and serviceable breed of horses, which are easily trained for the purposes of war and hunting. The Scythians of every age have been celebrated as bold and skilful riders; and constant practice had seated them so firmly on horseback that they were supposed by strangers to perform the ordinary duties of civil life, to eat, to drink, and even to sleep, without dismounting from their steeds.

Sometimes the steppe peoples came in pursuit only of booty. Thus in the 540s the Bulgars carried out a raid which threatened Thessalonica and Constantinople and then returned across the Danube with more than 100,000 prisoners, countless cattle and precious loot. The raiders were in the main "cavalrymen, very mobile and lightly armed, using simple tactics; not afraid of the Byzantine forces in open country; but stopped by any walled fortification, and unable therefore to make a complete conquest."[40] Such raids caused demoralisation, depopulation of the countryside and a progressive pauperisation. At other times they came in pursuit of land, moving with their women and children and their possessions, mainly livestock, as we have seen in the case of the Goths. Then they lived off the land, and their numbers were so vast that they were able to undertake major operations of war such as the siege of Thessalonica at the beginning of the seventh century. If an emperor was unable to destroy the migrating hordes, he might give them suitable land on condition that they would serve him in defence of the frontier. So Theodosius made grants of land between the Danube and the Haemus range to the Goths in 382, and Constantine IV was forced to do the same for the Bulgars late in the seventh century. But in between the great raids and the great migrations which were reported in the histories of the period there was a continuous process of lesser raids and migrations and penetrations by smaller bands of these people, especially of the Slavs. When they first obtained land, they were pastoralists and stockbreeders, like the Albanians centuries later, but many of them turned to agriculture and soon became a settled peasant population.

Within the southwest Balkans Slav settlers became more and more numerous in the area which now belongs to Greece, and they went on from the mainland to attack Crete and other islands in 623 and to settle in some of the Cyclades. At the beginning of the ninth century the Slavs in the Peloponnese, who were particularly numerous in Elis, rose against the Byzantine authorities and captured Patras. In Laconia the seaside town of Monemvasia was "in Slav territory" in the early eighth century, and the mountain range of Taygetus was held by two Slav tribes, the Melingi and the Ezeritae, until c. 1250 when the Franks overcame them.[41] North of the Isthmus there is less literary evidence of Slav settlements in large numbers, but they were thick on the ground in parts of Thessaly, where they rose against the Byzantine rulers in 799. The largest concentration of such settlements was on the western side of Pindus, particularly in Epirus; as the tenth century epitomator of Strabo remarked (*Geographici Graeci Minores* 2. p. 574), "the Scytho-Slavs occupy today all Epirus, and almost [all] Hellas [central Greece], Peloponnese and Macedonia"—a statement which is an exaggeration but which indicated the degree of settlement in these areas. The coastal plain of Macedonia and the Strymonian plain had many Slav settlements in the seventh century, and these Slavs lived peacefully until the emperor executed their leader. They then revolted and laid siege to Thessalonica for two years by land and by sea, namely the Sclaveni near the city, the Strymonii from the Strymon basin, and the Runchini and the Sagoudatae from the plain west of the Vardar.[42]

The pattern of Slav settlement is revealed also by the distribution of Slavic place-names in Greece.[43] Much the greatest number is found in the interior of Epirus, in the canton of Ioannina (Vasmer records 334 names); and the next highest number (120) is in western Thessaly in the cantons of Triccala and Kardhitsa. These areas were excellent for the raising of stock, especially sheep. Next come other mountainous areas: Aetolo-Acarnania (98), Achaea (95), Arcadia (94), and Laconia (81), where we know that two large Slavic tribes lived on Mt Taygetus. The smallest numbers of Slavic place-names in relation to considerable areas occur in Attica, Boeotia and Euboea, and within the Peloponnese in the Argolid. Of course, the evidence of the place-names is to some extent vitiated by the fact that warmer areas such as Preveza and Arta in the west and parts of Attica and Boeotia in the east were occupied later by considerable numbers of Albanians who imposed their own names on the countryside.[44] But when we take the literary evidence together with that of the place-names, we may conclude that the earliest bands of Slav immigrants into Greece and perhaps the overall majority of them, came as pastoral semi-nomadic peoples and occupied the higher and wetter areas which were most favourable for stock-raising and for the transhumance of sheep.[45] Other groups settled in the fenlands and the plains of Macedonia, which, being swampy and less parched in summer, were very suitable both for stock-raising and for agriculture—especially at Ochrid, Prilep, Veles and Edessa.[46] Still others went overseas, at first in dug-out tree trunks (*monoxyla*), and then in local craft, to the northern Ionian islands, to Crete and to some Cyclades, where Slavic place-names also testify to their presence.

Farther north the swampy coastal plain of central Albania with the rich city of Dyrrachium attracted the Slavs, as it had the Goths. In 548–9 huge numbers of Slavs crossed the Danube and came south, evidently over the Kačanik pass, into Upper Macedonia from which they entered Albania. "They spread destruction through all Illyricum as far as Epidamnus (Dyrrachium), killing or enslaving all they met" (Procopius, *de Bello Gothico* 3. 29. 1 f.). There is however no indication and indeed no likelihood that they pushed their way into the tangled mountains of north Albania. On the east side of the central range they settled in the upland country of western Macedonia, from which they removed many of the Greek-speaking inhabitants and placed them north of the Danube c. 585. Two generations later, the Greek-speakers came back to at least part of their old territory, 'the Keramesian plain', so named after Ceramiae below Prilep in Pelagonia.[47] We hear of the Slavs also between the Axius and the Strymon in 698. The Slavs of this period migrated as relatively small tribes and seem to have combined into large groups of tribes only when they were led by others, e.g. by the Avars and the Bulgars. Most tribes continued as such after settling down for instance in Laconia, but in some areas the tribes may have dissolved in course of time so that, for instance, the Slavs in the Strymonian plain came to be known not by tribal names but simply as Strymonii. When they settled in the plains, they soon adopted local ways and eventually became Graecised in culture, religion and even language. This development was already noted in the ninth century by the Emperor Leo VI (886–912) in his *Tactica*. He pointed out that the Slavs had refused to serve any leader when they were north of the Danube, but finding it necessary south of the Danube had preferred a leader of their own race to the rule of Byzantium. However, the Emperor Basil I (867–886) 'Graecised' them, converting them to Christianity and the rule of Byzantium and teaching them to fight against the enemies of Byzantium.

However, one important group of Slavic peoples showed themselves capable of united action under a leader of their own, called Samo; for they threw off the rule of the Avars in central Europe c. 623. And another group, called Croats and Serbs, probably at the instigation of the Emperor Heraclius (610–641), defeated and expelled the Avars who had established themselves at Sirmium on the Save (west of Belgrade), and then took over their lands themselves. It was the descendants of these Serbs who set up an independent state in Zeta c. 1040–1100 and then broke away finally from Byzantine control, when they founded a separate state, extending as far south as Prizren, towards the end of the twelfth century.

Whereas the Slavs crossed the Danube mainly in its middle reaches and settled in the western half of the Balkan area, the Bulgars came from farther east and crossed the Danube mainly in its lower reaches. The first tribes of Bulgars to reach the north bank of the Danube were the Utigurs and the Kutrigurs, sometimes at odds with one another, and they made raids into Byzantine territory from c. 490 onwards. Moreover, they became leaders and allies of the Slavs, and their joint forces ranged far and wide, indeed in the phrase of Procopius "from the Ionian Gulf [i.e. our Adriatic Sea] to the suburbs of Byzantium."[48] The Kutrigurs organised a particularly impressive raid in 558-59; when the main forces entered Thrace, they fanned out into three groups which turned respectively against Byzantium, the Thracian Chersonese (Gallipoli) and Greece.

Soon afterwards the Avars arrived and replaced these two tribes of Bulgars in the leadership of the Slavs. During the period of Avar hegemony another tribe of Bulgars, called the Onogurs, was building an empire in the hinterland of the Sea of Azov, an empire which was called by Byzantine writers "Old Great Bulgaria." Their king broke the power of the Avars c. 635–40, but on his death most of his people moved forward to the north bank of the Danube under pressure from the Khazars c. 650.[49]

In many respects the Bulgars were less primitive than the Slavs. They had ceased to be nomadic, combined stock-raising with agriculture and acquired the art of organising other peoples. The Onogurs in particular had shown themselves capable of building an empire, and they proceeded now to defeat the Byzantine armies and occupy the rich lands south of the Danube delta. In 681 their new empire, the so-called First Bulgarian Empire, extending from the Dniester to the Haemus range, was recognised by Constantine IV, who agreed to pay an annual tribute. Despite pressures from all sides this Bulgarian empire maintained itself on the flank of the Byzantine Empire for three and a half centuries, during which the Onogur leaders and their Slav subjects grew together to form the Bulgarian nation. At the height of their power they expanded westwards, obtaining control of Serdica (Sofia) and then of the upper Vardar valley and the lakeland of Prespa and Ochrid; and they took control of central Albania and Dyrrachium early in the tenth century, when Symeon was on the throne. After a period of decline the strength of the Bulgarian Empire was further developed in this western area by Samuel, who made his capital first at Prespa and then at Ochrid, extended his realm southwards to capture Verria and threaten Thessalonica, established garrisons in Thessaly and Epirus, and raided as far as the Isthmus of Corinth. Later he turned north, seized much of Dalmatia and Bosnia and made an alliance with Stephen I, king of Hungary. His empire ran now from the Adriatic to the Black Sea and from the Danube to Thessaly. But he had overstrained his resources.

In a twenty-years war the remarkable Byzantine emperor Basil II demolished the First Bulgarian Empire step by step. Striking at the central part of its system and gaining control of the strategic area round Sofia, he conquered the eastern Bulgarian territories up to the lower Danube and then struck southwest into southwestern Macedonia and Thessaly. The turning point was at Skopje, where Basil's army crossed the river at night and caught the Bulgarians off their guard on the right bank, and the decisive victory was gained at the narrow pass of Klidhi in the

Strumitsa valley. In 1018 the Bulgarians submitted at Ochrid to the rule of the Byzantine Emperor.

A renascence of Bulgarian power commenced in 1185, when Peter and Asan led a revolt of the Bulgars and the Vlachs at Trnovo, north of the Haemus range, and joined forces with the Koumani, then north of the Danube. The growth of the Second Bulgarian Empire, as it is called, followed the same lines as that of the First: for the Bulgars captured Niš and then northern and western Macedonia, and bishops were soon installed at Prizren, Ochrid, Skopje and Verria. John Asan II (1218–41) claimed in an inscription set up at Trnovo: "I occupied all the land from Adrianople to Dyrrachium, Greek, Serbian and Albanian alike." Thereafter the empire dissolved as a result of Mongol and Tartar raids, internal dissension and the rise of rival powers. The Turks took Adrianople in 1363, and the last province of the Empire, the Vidin, fell in 1396.

As Bulgaria began to sink, Serbia rose to power under the leadership of the Uroš dynasty and expanded southwards through the Kossovo gap, annexing Tetovo, Kitsevo and Dibër on the one hand and Skopje, Veles and Štip on the other. The Serbian right to these territories was recognised by the Byzantine Emperor in 1299. Stephen Dušan (1331-55) made further conquests on the western side of the central range, adding Kroai (Krujë), Berat and Valona, and then Epirus, Acarnania and Aetolia to his realm. On the eastern side his authority ran from Kastoria to Kjustendil and from Thessaly to the Strumitsa valley and to Serres with the exception of Thessalonica, which was still held by the Byzantines. After his death decline was rapid.[50]

The Turks and the Greeks

The Turks by-passed Constantinople in their invasion of Europe (Map 15). They proceeded up the so-called Royal Road to capture Adrianople in 1361 and Philippoupolis (Plovdiv) in 1363–64. A counterattack by the Serbian kingdom was severely defeated at Črnomen on the Marica (anc. Hebrus) in 1371. The main advance, commanded by the Sultan Murad, was on the line of the Royal Road, first to Sofia, captured c. 1385, and then to Niš in the following year. A detachment turned southwest to capture Štip, Prilep, Monastir and Ochrid by 1385. At the same time another army was advancing along the Via Egnatia, capturing Drama c. 1375, Serres in 1387 and Thessalonica in the same year, after a long siege. The decisive battle was fought at Kossovo Polje, the nerve-centre of Dušan's greater Serbian kingdom, in 1389 as the climax of a campaign in which the Turks defeated a coalition of Serbs, Bulgars and Bosnians, and five years later their forces in the south reached the Peloponnese. Thus the foundations were laid for the rule of the Turks in the Balkans which was to last until 1912–13.

The most amazing phenomenon in almost a millennium of migrations and invasions, extending from the Goths to the Turks, was the survival of the Greeks. By any normal calculation their empire, which we call the Byzantine Empire, seemed certain to fall time and time again, and even when the Turks came the capital did not lose its independence until 1453. Their capacity for survival, reconquest and resistance was due to that combination of intelligence and courage which has distinguished them from all other peoples. But on the Greek mainland how did Greeks survive in the darkest days of invasion by Slavs and Albanians? The cities, as we have seen, were centres of resistance, and even when they were captured and looted the population survived and rebuilt its prosperity in course of time. But in addition the cities were the centres of culture, and it was through the spread of culture within the cities and then outwards from the cities that Slavs and Albanians and other immigrants were eventually 'Graecised'. It was the process which Alexander the Great had deliberately promoted in the cities he founded in Asia, and it was a process which some Byzantine Emperors recognised at the time. Thus the Emperor Leo the Wise observed that his predecessor, Basil I, (867–86), prevailed upon the Slavs to abandon their traditional ways and made them into Greeks (*graikōsas*).[51] Besides the cities, there were other channels of continuity: the Greek church, the Greek monasteries with their scholastic tradition, the Greek shepherds practising transhumance, and the Greek mountain villages. These preserved the Greek language for all varieties of spiritual and secular use.

No part of Greece suffered more than Epirus in terms of invasions, occupations and migrations.[52] The phrase which Porphyrogennitus used of the Peloponnese may be applied more emphatically still to Epirus: "the whole land was Slavised and became barbarian [i.e. non-Greek]." But the Slavs were only the beginning. The Vlachs took the best summer pastures and the finest forests, and the Albanians took most of the cultivable land. At the lowest ebb Ioannina and Zagori alone survived as Greek-speaking areas, pinched between Vlachs and Albanians, and there were clergy and monks and Sarakatsani and no doubt pockets of Greek speech in remote villages in the mountains. Even this small amount of leaven was enough. It brought the Slavs to the adoption not only of Greek ways but also of Greek speech. It brought the Vlachs and the Albanians into common revolt against any occupying power and into acceptance of Greek nationality. In course of time they will adopt Greek speech, as so many of their kindred have done in central and southern Greece, and they will become Greeks in the sense in which Isocrates used the term c. 380 B.C. "The name has become a mark no longer of race but of outlook, and it is applicable to those who share our culture rather than to those who are of our blood."[53]

There was, however, one people the Greeks were never able to assimilate into their own culture—the Turks. Perhaps political oppression and religious fanaticism created too wide a gap between rulers and subjects—certainly much wider than that between Romans and Greeks—and the Turks themselves had a long-lasting pride in their institutions and their achievements. Their conservatism and with it their exclusiveness lasted until the time of Kemal Attaturk.

The Pattern of Historical Invasions and Migrations.

The Adriatic Sea has often produced its own seafarers, who have practised trade and/or piracy, founded colonial bases and occasionally engaged in migration. For instance, the Liburnians—an Illyrian tribe of the northeastern shore of the Adriatic—preceded the Greeks in the colonisation of Dyrrachium and Corcyra during the eighth and seventh centuries B.C.,[54] and the Ardiaei who held the central part of the eastern Adriatic coast as far south as Lissus in the Hellenistic period raided far into the Sicilian Sea and the Aegean. The Venetians did likewise. We hear of movements of peoples only in one direction, from the Balkans and not to the Balkans: Albanians in large numbers and Greek-speaking inhabitants of the canton of Himarrë in what is now southern Albania emigrated to Italy, especially Calabria, early in the period of Turkish occupation, and Albanians sailed from Valona and Parga (some coming from Souli) to join in the colonisation of Hydra and other islands in the Aegean. All invading forces, which have started from Italy, have aimed at the capture of Dyrrachium, to which the crossing of the Southern Adriatic is most safely made: for example, the Romans, the Normans of the First Crusade, and the Italians in 1939. Their next objective by sea has been the capture of Corcyra.[55]

In the history of Aegean seafaring, the peoples of the Vardar basin and the Strymon basin have played no part. Macedonians, Paeonians and Thracians figured always as soldiers, not sailors, and others have exploited their coasts. Nor have there been examples of sea-borne invasions being successfully conducted against these coasts. On the other hand, the east coast of peninsular Greece has given off waves of migrants at various times and has mounted sea-borne attacks on others. Self-standing sea-borne attacks upon the east coast of Greece were made by the Persians in 490 B.C. and Mithridates' fleets in 88 B.C., but in most cases a navy was auxiliary to a main invasion by land, as in the expedition of Xerxes. As far as I am aware, there has not been a sea-borne immigration into the eastern side of the Greek peninsula in historical times.

Movements overland from peninsular Greece northwards into the central Balkans seem to be unknown. One reason is to be found in climate: people reared in the Mediterranean climate will go anywhere in the Mediterranean rather than settle in the continental climate of the hinterlands of Albania, Macedonia and Thrace. Movements overland from Albania and Macedonia were not so limited. Peoples from these areas moved freely into zones either of continental or of Mediterranean climate, because they themselves lived in a transitional zone. Yet the greatest bulk of movement by far has been from the north and the east overland through Albania, Macedonia and Thrace into the Greek peninsula and islands. When we consider those movements, we can see that they conform very closely to a set pattern.

The first problem for migrating peoples from the north is to break into the southwestern Balkans through one or more of the very few gates of entry. Early in the third century B.C. the Gauls invaded Italy and the Balkans, having become so numerous that they could not be supported by the produce of their homelands in central Europe (Justin 24.4: "Galli, abundanti multitudine, quum eos non caperent terrae quae genuerant"). In the Balkans one group of Gauls, led by Bolgius, moved towards the Kačanik pass. Although the Dardanian king, who ruled on the Danubian side of the watershed, offered to contribute 20,000 warriors to a joint defence force, the Macedonian king spurned the offer and tried to hold his northern frontier unaided.[56] The result was a military disaster, in which the Macedonian king lost his life, and the Gauls poured into northern Macedonia, where the people took refuge in the walled towns. At this point the Gauls turned westwards into central Albania (as the Goths did later),[57] presumably because they regarded the forcing of the Demir Kapu pass or of the passes from the west at Kirli Dirven and between Ostrovo and Edessa as too difficult. Meanwhile two other groups were in action, one operating against "the Thracians and the Triballians" (i.e. between the Danube and the line Sofia-Plovdiv), and the other, commanded by Brennus and Acichorius, entering Paeonia (i.e. via either the Preševo pass or the Sofia-Radomir-Kjustendil route into the basins of the Pecinj and Bregalnitsa rivers, eastern tributaries of the Vardar; see Maps 1–3).

During these initial operations the Gauls did not penetrate into the lower plain of Macedonia or enter Greek soil in the west. Later Brennus persuaded them all to serve together under his leadership and to seek plunder in Greece. In 279 B.C. he led an army of 152,000 infantry, 20,400 cavalry, and a train of 2,000 waggons, accompanied by many camp-followers,[58] and he fought his way into Lower Macedonia, suffering considerable losses but inflicting a severe defeat of the Macedonian field-army, now commanded by Sosthenes (see Maps 2 and 5). Once again the Macedonians withdrew into their walled cities, and the Gauls passed south into Thessaly, where they committed atrocities in the countryside. Taking the coastal route by Halus, they crossed the Spercheus at a point below that held by the Greek defence force and advanced to Thermopylae, where an army of some 28,000 troops from central Greece was already in position. Unable to force the pass, Brennus divided his greatly superior numbers. He sent one army of some 800 cavalry and 40,000 infantry over a high pass into the upper valley of the Mornos (anc. Daphnus) in Aetolia,[59] which had the effect of drawing off the Aetolian contingent from the army at Thermopylae. Brennus himself with 40,000 infantry turned the pass of Thermopylae by following a mountain track, as the Persians had done in 480 B.C., and on the dispersal of the Greek forces he hastened on to Delphi without waiting for the main force under Acichorius. Meanwhile the Aetolians had destroyed most of the Gauls in Aetolia, and they then switched their attack onto Acichorius, who was encumbered by the baggage train. Brennus was defeated at Delphi and later committed suicide. Only a fraction of the whole escaped; for as the survivors withdrew northeastwards, they were harassed by the Greeks and the Macedonians at the narrow passes.

From the experience of the Gauls we can see that any large-scale invasion by peoples who were bent on plunder but were prepared to settle as migrants had to go through four phases of operations. The first was to break a way into Upper Macedonia. The second phase consisted of the occupation of Upper Macedonia west of the Vardar and the extension of the conquest through the lakeland as far as Durazzo (Dyrrachium). The third phase was to force a way into Lower Macedonia and ideally to capture the coastal plain east as well as west of the Vardar. And the last phase was to press down southwards into Greece, whether by the western route via Epirus or by the eastern route via Tempe, Thermopylae and the Isthmus. The first three of these phases were implemented not only by the Gauls but also by the Goths of Theodoric and Thiudimer, by the Slavs in 548–49, and by the Bulgars in the expansion of their First Empire and again in the Second Empire. It is to be noted that the districts to the east of the Vardar, the ancient Paeonia, were left to a different group of Gauls, which entered Paeonia from the northeast. The reason for this was the river itself; for it was very difficult indeed for an army with a train of waggons and camp-followers, often including women and children, to cross the Vardar at any season of the year unless bridges were left standing. A much smaller river, the Spercheus, was a serious obstacle to Brennus, and when a detachment of his troops succeeded in swimming and wading across its swampy delta at night and driving the Greek defenders away from the river bank, he still had to make the local population build bridges so that his baggage train could be taken over.[60]

The fourth phase, pressing down southwards into Greece, presented problems of its own. On the east side of the peninsula the entry from Macedonia was known to be so difficult that Brennus had to persuade the Gauls to unite all their forces for the attempt. In fact the Greeks did not defend any of the points of entry from Macedonia, and it is probable that the Gauls crossed the Peneus near its mouth, because their march was through Magnesia.[61] The next barrier was the Spercheus; for the Gauls were crossing and not following the lines of drainage. The Greek defence of the Thermopylae Pass succeeded in that it compelled Brennus to divide his forces, and it was through this division that the Gauls incurred their failure. Had they succeeded, they would still have had to cross the Cephissus, force an entry at Parapotamii and Chaeronea into Boeotia, and then carry the passes over Cithaeron, Karidhi and Gerania in order to reach the Peloponnese. Once in retreat the Gauls were set upon by the victorious Greeks and their lines of communication were cut by the Greeks in their rear who issued from the walled cities. Thus the experience of the Gauls illustrates the point that the eastern side of the peninsula is particularly hard to conquer, not only because of its geographical structure, but also because the settled population was very large and well organised and their cities were walled.

The western side of the peninsula offered less difficulty (see Maps 1, 4 and 6). The lines of drainage could be followed and indeed there were several parallel valleys running NNW by SSE to choose between. If the Vijosë (Aous) was crossed near its mouth, the way from the Gulf of Valona to the Gulf of Arta (via the Vijosë valley, the Drin valley, two subsidiary valleys of the Kalamas, Dodona and down to the Gulf) could be made without the crossing of any large river or any high pass. Proceeding south from Preveza to Actium at the mouth of the Gulf, so avoiding the crossing of the Arachthus, the pass of Arta and the narrows by Mt Makrinoros and Karavassara, an invading force could follow the coast and the lowlands to the Gulf of Corinth or force the pass of Klisura to reach Antirrhium, from which there is the shortest crossing by sea to the Peloponnese. The chief centres of population on this side of the peninsula were in the valley of the Drin, the plateau of Dodona (by Ioannina), and the plain of Arta. Powerful invaders, such as the Normans of the First Crusade or the Romans of Flamininus in 198 B.C., were able to occupy these areas, but less powerful forces, such as those of the Albanians, followed the more westerly valleys and used the Preveza-Actium crossing, so that they cut off the most populated areas from the sea and hoped to wear them down. Moreover, the total population on the western side of Greece north of the Gulf of Corinth, has always been far smaller than that on the eastern side, and in general it has been less progressive and less well organised. Thus there is no doubt that it was much easier for an ancient army of invasion to push down the western side of Greece than down the eastern side.

Invaders from the northeast who entered ancient Paeonia, as the group of Gauls under Brennus and Acichorius did at the start of their operations, may have been content to settle in the fertile and rich basins of the Pecinj and Bregalnitsa rivers; but if they pressed on southwards, they had to leave the Vardar valley at Demir Kapu and make the detour eastwards via the Strumitsa valley and Valandovo, in order to break into Lower Macedonia on the east side of the great river. We have seen that this route was used, for example, by Sitalces in 429 B.C. (see Map 15), the Scythians in 268 A.D. and the Germans in 1941.[62] Again, powerful forces were needed because the eastern side of the coastal plain and the adjacent Langadha basin have always been heavily populated, and the great city of Thessalonica was strongly fortified for many centuries. Here too the Vardar was a formidable barrier. There have been several periods when one power ruled west of the Vardar and another east of it, and a decisive step in the growth of the ancient Macedonian kingdom was the acquisition of territory east of the river through the favour of Persia.[63]

The pattern of invasions on a large scale from the east may be seen from the Persian and Turkish irruptions into southeastern Europe (see Map 15). The first objective of Darius and Murad alike was the securing of eastern Thrace from the Aegean coast to the Danube or at least to the Haemus range and as far inland as the plain of Plovdiv; for this part of Thrace faces the Black Sea rather than the Aegean basin. Progress eastwards was then barred by the massive ranges of Rila and Pirin, the ancient Rhodope. Next, the Persians advanced along the southern route only, conquering the hinterland up to Mt Belasitsa (anc. Orbelus); the Turks advanced at both ends of Mt Rhodope,

Map 15

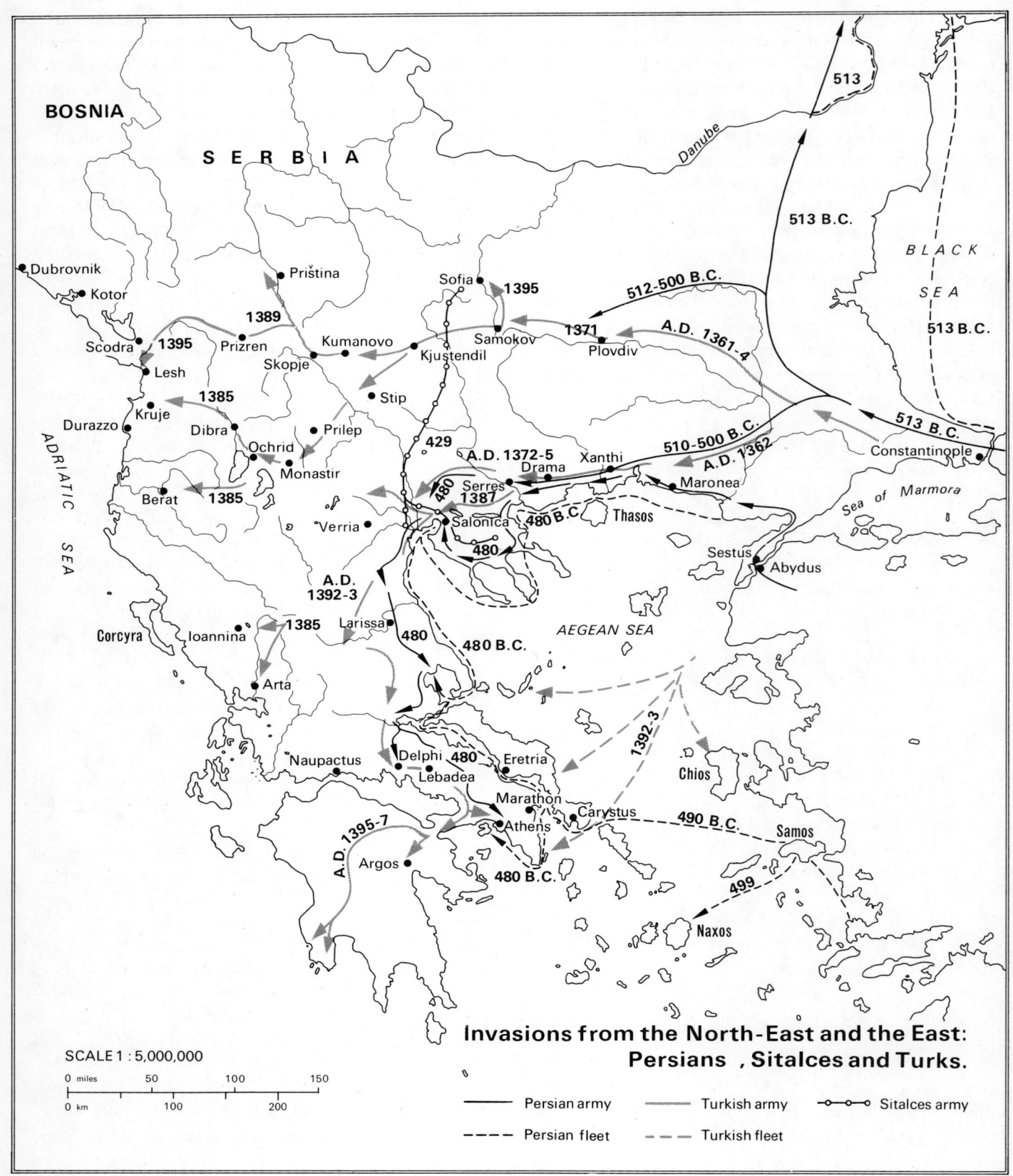

Invasions from the North-East and the East: Persians, Sitalces and Turks.

capturing Samokov on the route between the plain of Plovdiv and the source of the Golemiskr river on which Sofia is situated, and occupying Serres and the eastern side of the Strymon basin. The next stage was the advance of Persian influence to the Vardar, and then through a marriage alliance with the house of Amyntas, king of Macedon, to the western part of Lower Macedonia and finally, through the agency of Alexander I, king of Macedon, into Upper Macedonia.[64] The Turks advanced again in both sectors, one force from Samokov via Štip and Prilep to Ochrid, and another into the plain of Lower Macedonia up to Edessa, so that the whole of northern and central Macedonia, together with the lakeland area of Ochrid-Prespa-Little Prespa fell under their control. On the coastal sector the Persians and the Turks used the route up the Kumli valley by the Stena Dov Tepe Pass into the Vardar valley near Gevgheli as well as the route through the Langadha basin.

The next advance in each case was carried out by the original conqueror's successor, namely Xerxes and Bayezid. From Pieria they penetrated into north-eastern Thessaly. The Persians then followed the coastal route, as we have seen that the Gauls did, as far as Thermopylae; but the Turks passed through the central part of Thessaly via Pharsalus and Thaumaci into the Spercheus valley. When the Persians had forced the Pass of Thermopylae, they advanced through Doris and then split so that one detachment took the Pass of Gravia to attack Delphi (as Brennus did) and the main army passed down the valley of the Cephissus into Boeotia and then Attica. The Turks went through Doris to Delphi and from there by Arachova and Lebadea into the Boeotian plain. The Persians of Xerxes and the Turks of Bayezid alike occupied Athens and reached the narrow neck of the Isthmus; but it was only the Turks who succeeded in capturing the Peloponnese. From these campaigns it is clear that if one starts from Pieria in southern Macedonia one is certain to continue one's progress down the eastern side of central Greece towards the Isthmus.

However, to conquer and settle on one side only of the peninsula is insecure. While the greatest number of Slavs settled on the western side of central Greece, others occupied the western side of the Thessalian plain, the Spercheus valley and Aetolia, regions which were also suitable for their practice of stock-raising. The Serbs expanded down the western side of Greece, incorporating Epirus, Acarnania and Aetolia in their empire, but they also seized Thessaly. And the Albanians made their main migration down the western side, but branches of them entered the southern parts of the eastern side of central Greece. So too the Turks, having conquered the eastern side, went on to attack the western side, concentrating their attacks upon Arta and Ioannina. Similarly farther north they delivered attacks on Berat and Krujë from their base in the lakeland area; and they advanced via Kjustendil and Kumanovo to Prizren, Scodra, and the Adriatic coast. A large army crossed the Kačanik Pass and defeated the Serbs at the battle of Kossovo on the Danubian side of the watershed in 1389.[65]

Large groups of migrating peoples, such as the Goths, the Slavs (whether led by the Avars or the Bulgars) and the Albanians, followed the same routes and conformed more or less to the pattern of military invasions. But there was also small-scale migration or infiltration, especially by nomadic and semi-nomadic peoples, such as the Vlachs and many of the Slavs and Albanians, who lived by the transhumance of sheep. Their need to use summer and winter pastures brought them into the mountains and down to the coast, so that they covered a much wider front than an invading army. At the same time they were able to infiltrate a district without disrupting the life of the settled population to any marked degree, and we must allow for a considerable amount of peaceful penetration and sometimes invited infiltration into the Peloponnese, for instance, in the period before the Albanian rising in the latter part of the fifteenth century. For the Vlachs in particular the division between the western side and the eastern side of Central Greece was less rigid than it was for invading armies, because the Vlachs were able to move freely in high mountainous areas during the summer months and could appear at unexpected places on the edge of the plains on either side of the central range. This added a further dimension to their moves, but when they migrated, for instance under pressure from the Albanians, they used the same routes as other migrating bands.

Our knowledge of the campaigns, invasions and migrations which we have been describing is derived entirely from written texts, except in some matters concerning the Vlachs and the Albanians, where the source is an oral tradition or a traditional practice.

The texts are on the whole dependable, and the geographical identifications are rarely in doubt, so that a strong web of historical reconstruction can be established for the southwest Balkans. When the threads of oral tradition, on such matters as the origins of a Vlach village or an unwritten law of vendetta several centuries old, are woven into this web, it is clear that they are of a piece and record historical facts.

The part which archaeology plays in this reconstruction is small at present, but its importance is beginning to emerge. For example, in the period when we hear least of the Albanians in literary sources, that is in the seventh and eighth centuries A.D., it so happens that a distinctive culture has been found through excavation to have flourished at Dalmace, Shurdhah (medieval Sarda), Krujë, Lesh, and other places (see Map 16). This culture reached its height in those centuries but continued into the tenth and eleventh centuries, so that its life overlapped the mention of 'Ducagini d'Arbania' in a seventh-century document and that of 'Albeigne' in the Chanson de Roland (see the discussion in the first section of this chapter). An interesting feature of this culture is that it has been found only to the north of the Shkumbi valley; that it is concentrated within the cantons of Mirditë and Mati (between Shtish-Tufina near Tirana and Dalmace in the north); and that it has outlying pockets at the north end of Lake Ochrid, at Golaj in Albanian Kosovë, and at Mijele at the northern end of Lake Scodra. Thus the ambit of this culture is precisely in the region which we have identified on literary grounds as that of 'Arbana' and 'Albeigne'. The conclusion seems to be clear that the people of this region—known no doubt as Arbanoi and Albanoi—developed in this mountainous terrain, with many peaks of five and six thousand feet, a culture of their own which was distinct from those of the Serbian state in Zeta to the north, the First Bulgarian Empire in the lakeland area, and the Byzantine province of Epirus Nova.

The salient features of this culture have been described by Hena Spahiu and Skendër Animali.[66] The discoveries are from burials, the men having been inhumed with weapons of iron (axes, arrowheads and knives) and the women with jewelry (earrings, fibulae, necklaces and bracelets), while pottery, small knives and fibulae were common to both sexes. The axes were descended from the Roman type of axe; similar ones were used in central Europe in medieval times and were adopted, for instance, by the Avars. The knives and arrowheads are of types found throughout the Balkans. The jewelry has technical peculiarities which are attributed to local craftsmen working with silver, copper and iron of which the two last are still mined today in this region (see Map 16). There are some features which are related to the jewelry of western Yugoslavia and Hungary, e.g. pendants attached to a belt and to clothing. The influence of Byzantine jewelry was strong, and there were imported pieces, some with Greek script, at Krujë, which is the largest site with this culture in the vicinity of Dyrrachium. Some belt-buckles of "the human mask" shape (in which the apertures resemble a human skull) have been found throughout the Byzantine world and even beyond it.[67] Thus the Mirditë-Mati culture, if we may so call it, was a fusion of central European elements at a time of many migratory movements and of Byzantine elements which stemmed from a long tradition of settled civilisation.

The most important cemeteries were situated close to the strong citadels of Dalmace, Shurdhah, Lesh and Krujë, and there is no doubt that the men and the women buried there belonged to the ruling family in each case. The other cemeteries, mainly in mountain fastnesses, for instance at Rremull and Dukagjin in eastern Mati, belonged to similar families; indeed one may have been that of the 'Ducagini d'Arbania' mentioned in the seventh century document at Dubrovnik (Ragusa). The number of cemeteries in the cantons of Mirditë and Mati have been reported as twelve, and we may deduce that society was organised in small tribes, exactly as in the 1930s when Mrs. Hasluck gave the number of tribes in the area as ten (see Map 16).[68] Given this type of social organisation and the geographical conditions of the region, it is evident that some of the population was settled in towns such as Lesh and in villages in the mountains, and that others were pastoralists practising a good deal of transhumance.[69] The tribal leaders were relatively rich and they employed local craftsmen in the making of jewelry. They were well-armed (fighting probably on horseback rather than on foot) and exercised their rule from citadels or mountain fastnesses. There is no indication of artistic orginality in this culture, apart perhaps from some technical skill in metallurgy. Pottery seems to have been restricted to large jugs and water-containers,[70] and it is evident that other vessels were made of wood, as among the Vlachs today.

Map 16

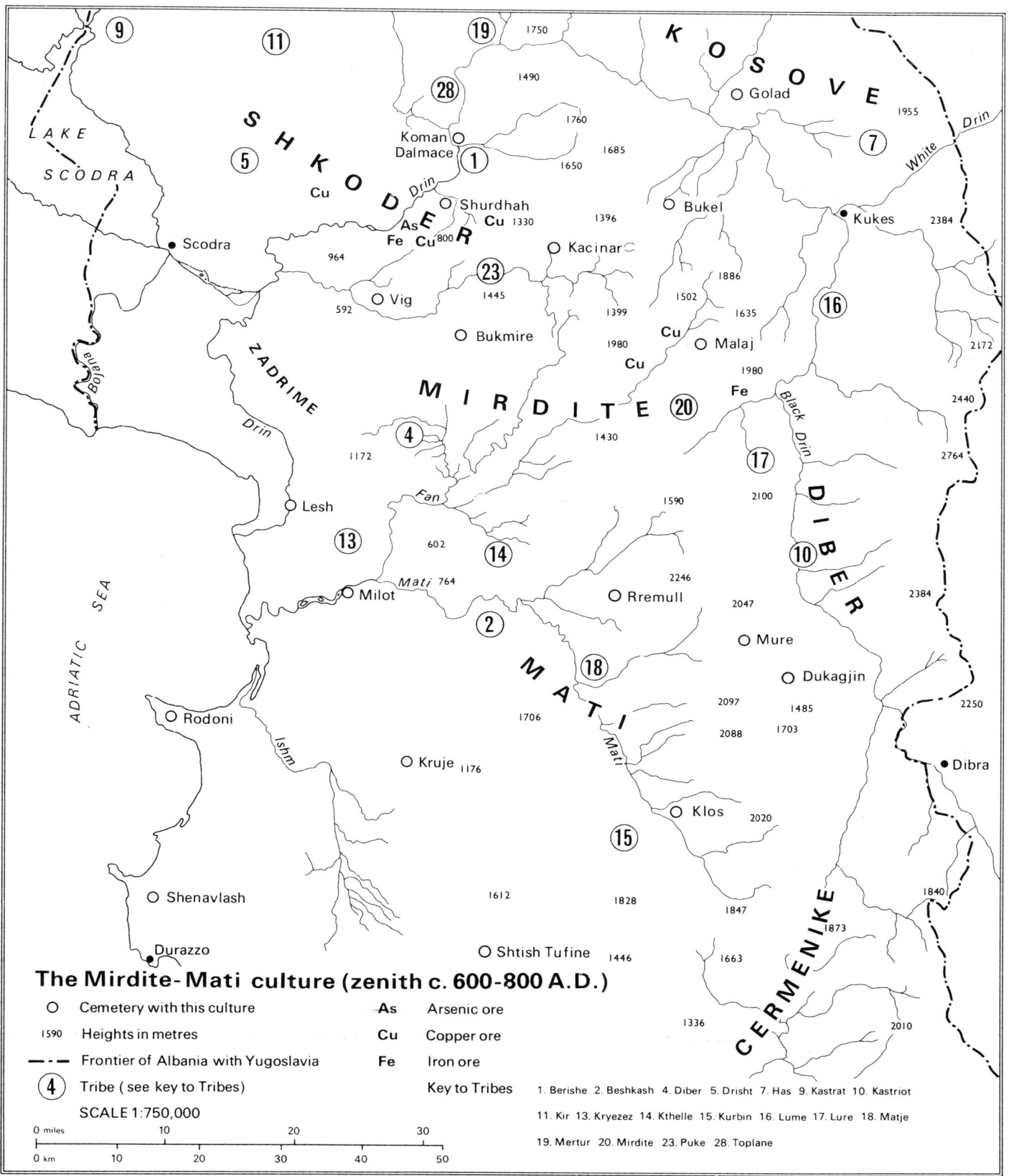

The bearers of the Mirditë-Mati culture in what may be called the Dark Age of European history lived on the fringe of the Byzantine Empire, and they were influenced by its civilisation, but only superficially. Their social organisation, their way of life, and no doubt their outlook were entirely alien to those of the settled Byzantine peoples. This same region produced the heroic resistance to the Turks which was led by Skanderbeg and his friend Lek Dukagjini who codified in the fifteenth century the traditional law of the preceding centuries. This area too is the home of the epic lays,[71] recited to the accompaniment of the *lahute*, which are believed by some scholars to have originated in the sixth and seventh centuries A.D., i.e. with our Mirditë-Mati culture. We may bear this region and its culture in mind during the second part of this book, when we shall be dealing with cultures which are known primarily through archaeology and are connected in some way with the epic lays which preceded the work of Homer.

NOTES

1. I travelled extensively in Albania from 1930 to 1939 and returned there in September 1972.

2. Weigand (*EvM*), p. 52.

3. These crafts, now becoming less common, are illustrated in *Popular Art in Albania* (University of Tirana, 1959).

4. The pattern of dialects today is shown in a map in *SA* 1966, 2, 50; for dress see *Popular Art in Albania* and for architecture *Monumentë të Arkitekturës në Shqipëri* (Tirana, 1973).

5. As observed by W. M. Leake, *Travels in Northern Greece* (London, 1885) 1, p. 61. The Italians accused the Greeks of maltreating the Tsams in Greek Epirus before the Italians invaded Greece; the accusation was groundless.

6. Described by Margaret Hasluck, the widow of F. W. Hasluck, in her fascinating book *The Unwritten Law in Albania*, p. 225. from which I am quoting. In the 1930s she was living in Albania where I had the pleasure of meeting her.

7. See Eqrem Çabej, "L'ancien nom national des Albanais," *SA* 1972, 1, 35; he dated the adoption of the name Shqiptar to a time after the Turkish conquest. An interesting analogy is provided by the Vlachs who now call themselves Arumani, just as the Albani call themselves Shqiptar.

8. Known by the Greek authors also as "the Greek Illyris."

9. I disagree here with Kolë Luka, "Le nom d'Albeigne-Albanie et l'extension de l'Arbanon durant les XIe-commencement du XIIe siècles," *Deuxième Conférence des études Albanologiques* (Tirana, 1970), pp. 199 f. He assumed that "Albanie" meant for the Crusaders the whole of Epirus Nova. In any event his argument overlooks the fact that the *Chanson* 3995 spoke of "the land of Ébire" (Epirus), meaning precisely Epirus Nova.

10. "La Chanson de Roland et Byzance," *Byzantion* 14 (1939) 273 f.

11. Kolë Luka (loc. cit.) seems to mistranslate the passage when he writes "Komiskortès à la tête de ses Albanais" (p. 201); see also *SA* 1964, 2, 143 on the views of E. L. Vranouse, *Komiskortes ho ex Arbanon* (Ioannina, 1962).

12. D. Farlatus, *Illyricum Sacrum* 7, pp. 191 f.

13. Thalloczy, Jireček and Sufflay, *Acta et Diplomata res Albaniae mediae aetatis illustrantia* 1 (1913), nos. 59 and 199; G. Acropolites 67.

14. The identification of Albanopolis is uncertain. D. M. Nicol, *The Despotate of Epiros* (1957), p. 223, assumed it to be Elbasan, but Elbasan is too far south in relation to Krujë. Most Albanian scholars, following a lead given in *Acta et Diplomata* etc. no. 48, think it was Krujë; but we have "Kroia" as the ancient name of Krujë, and it is difficult to see why it changed from Kroia to Albanos and back to Krujë. A village called Arbonë to the south of Tirana may be closer to the original Albanos. For the wide distribution of various forms of this name in modern Albania see Eqrem Çabej (op. cit., note 7).

15. Published by V. Makusev, *Pamiatniki Dubrovnika* (Petrograd, 1867), pp. 307 and 373.

16. Sufflay, *Servët dhe Shqyptarët*, p. 197. For this family see A. Gegaj, *L'Albanie et l'invasion turque* (Louvain, 1937), pp. 12 f.

17. I see no merit in the often repeated view of Weigand (*EvM*), p. 15 that the Albanians are the descendants of non-slavised Thracians. As the Slavs came into the western part of the Balkans, a migration from Thrace would have run against the stream; there is no sign of Albanians surviving in Thrace; and the evidence of Ptolemy shows the name existed not in Thrace but in the neighbourhood of Dyrrachium before the Slavs appeared on the scene.

18. E. Kirsten, in *DgL* 1, 2 (1951), p. 720, n. 111 made the same point in connection with the name Malakasa in Attica.

19. There is much to be learnt about the medieval Albanians from *Acta et Diplomata* etc.; for example the extension of the name "Albania" to include the district of Prizren in 1198 (no. 113 with note on "pulatum"), the evidently numerous and small tribes in 1304 (no. 563), the "nobiliores Albani" in the social structure (no. 482), and the "pastores" and "vicus pastoralis Albanensium" near Scodra in 1335 (no. 798; cf. no 746, "regiones pastorias Vlachorum et Albanorum"). No. 245 is wrongly punctuated; one should read a comma between "Albania" and "Dyrrachium."

20. For descriptions of these places see *Epirus,* pp. 268 and 90.

21. This work, sometimes called *The Chronicle of Epirus,* is published in the *CSHB.*

22. For these places and their strategic importance see *Epirus,* p. 194 (Vela); p. 186 (Vrousina); pp. 197 f. and 695 (Dhespotikon); with maps 7 and 18.

23. C. N. Sathas, *Documents inédits relatifs à l'histoire grecque au Moyen Age* 2, p. 79 (no. 298).

24. Ducas 23, 8 (*CSHB*) called them "a race beyond number."

25. E. Kirsten (loc. cit., note 18) is of this opinion, n. 110, "die Geschichte der albanischen Landnahme in Aetolien, Akarnanien, dann bei Korinth . . . zeigt, dass die Bewegung auf der Westseite Griechenlands verlief und Mittelgriechenland von SW her erreichte."

26. Another indication is provided by the distribution of Slavonic place-names. These were (before the rule of Metaxas) frequent in the canton of Ioannina, rare in that of Arta, and rarer still in that of Preveza, being displaced predominantly by Albanian place-names such as Toskesi and Ljapokhori. See *Epirus,* p. 27, n. 2.

27. See *Epirus,* p. 195.

28. For these places see *Epirus,* p. 20, map 2, and p. 31, where I suggested that Zagorië included at one time the valley of the middle Aous from Permet to Konitsa and so linked up with Zagori. This may have been so in 1399.

29. The document is cited in Sp. Lambros, *Palaiologeia kai Peloponnesiaka* 3, p. 195.

30. C. N. Sathas (op. cit., note 23) 9, p. 144.

31. So described in a letter of Luc Notaras in Sp. Lambros, *Onomatologia tes Attikes,* p. 13.

32. Joseph Campbell, *Myths to Live by* (New York, 1972) p. 176.

33. Sathas (op. cit., note 23) 9, p. 144; Ducas 45.12 (*CSHB*).

34. Sathas (op. cit., note 23) 2, p. 79, qui cum equis volent venire; and Ljubić, *Listine* 10 no. 467, p. 445, ut equitent et stent in castris apud te ad obedentiam tuam.

35. So B. Randolph, an early traveller, cited by F. W. Hasluck in "Albanian Settlements in the Aegean Islands," *BSA* 15 (1908–9). I am indebted to this article in what follows.

36. For such latter-day raids see *Praktika* 1934, 86.

37. See *Epirus* p. 20, map 2 for the distribution of Greek-speaking villages in Albania, Albanian-speaking villages in Greece, and Vlach-speaking villages in Pindus on both sides of the modern frontier between Albania and Greece. It shows the situation as it was c. 1930.

38. For a general account and full bibliography see *The Cambridge Medieval History* 4, 1 (1966), pp. 473 f. and 952 f.

39. E. Gibbon, *The Decline and Fall of the Roman Empire* (ed. Bury) 2, pp. 74 f.

40. P. Lemerle, "Invasions et migrations dans les Balkans depuis la fin de l'époque romaine jusqu'au VIIIe siècle," *Revue Historique* 211 (1954) 287.

41. For these tribes see M. Vasmer, "Die Slaven in Griechenland," *Abhandl. Preuss. Akad. Wiss.* 1941 Phil-Hist. Kl. no. 12, p. 14.

42. See P. Lemerle (op. cit) p. 301, citing *Miracula S. Demetrii Martyris* 2.4. When the siege was raised, the people of Thessalonica destroyed the villages of the Slavs.

43. See M. Vasmer (op. cit.).

44. Vasmer argued that the small number of Slav place-names near the coast was due to early recapture of coastal areas by Byzantine forces which landed from the sea; but there is little evidence that this actually happened.

45. Hesiod, *Eoiai* fr. 97 wrote of "men rich in sheep and rich in cattle, men beyond number" in Ellopie, the name then of the plateau of Ioannina. See *Epirus,* p. 41 for the unusually large sheep and cattle of Epirus in ancient times.

46. The cattle of the Paeonians were particularly famous. See *Macedonia,* p. 14 for the cattle and sheep raised in Macedonia in 1959.

47. The account is given in *Miracula S. Demetrii Martyris* 2.5.195-6. For Ceramie in the Roman Itineraries see *Macedonia,* p. 67. For the nationality of the leader of the returning people, which is in dispute, see Lemerle p. 297; K. N. Setton, "The Bulgars in the Balkans and the Occupation of Corinth in the Seventh Century," *Speculum* 25 (1950) 510; and P. Charanis in *Studies on the Demography of the Byzantine Empire* (reprint, 1972) pp. 230 f.

48. Procopius, *de Bello Persico* 2.4.4-5; *Historia Arcana* 18.20. Weigand (*EvM*) p. 16, described them as a "Reitervolk."

49. For a brief account see the article of K. N. Setton cited in note 47 and *The Cambridge Medieval History* 4, 1, ch. xi by D. Obolensky.

50. For Serbia see *The Cambridge Medieval History* 4, 1, ch. xii by M. Dinić.

51. Leo, *Tactica,* const. 18.99-101.

52. During the German occupation the tenacity of the villages of southwest Macedonia and northeast Epirus, which are interrelated, and their ability to survive on their own slender resources were very impressive.

53. Isocrates, *Panegyricus* 50.

54. See *Epirus,* pp. 414 f. for the evidence.

55. Similarly an invasion of Italy or Sicily mounted from northwest Greece, e.g. by Alexander the Molossian and by Pyrrhus, was possible only if the invaders had the control or the co-operation of Corcyra and Apollonia or Dyrrachium.

56. The chief sources for the Gallic invasions are Pausanias 10.19.5–23.14, Diodorus Siculus 22.9 and Justin 24.4–25.2. It appears from Justin 24.4 that the battle occurred at or near the Kačanik pass because the Macedonian king had a hastily gathered force—not the field army—and was in close proximity to the king of Dardania, with whom he had a chance of making a joint defence.

57. Pausanias 10.19.7 gives the objectives of Bolgius as "Makedones and Illyrioi." I see no likelihood in the view that Bolgius entered Macedonia "by the Aous pass," as stated by W. W. Tarn in *CAH* 7, p. 101; for Bolgius could have reached that pass only by following the coastal route in Albania and he would have still been west of the Pindus range in going through the Aoi Stena.

58. Numbers of this order are given by Pausanias 10.19.9, who added the point that each cavalryman had three mounts and two grooms; Diodorus Siculus 22.9; and Justin 24.6. Tarn (loc. cit.) gaily reduced the number of Brennus' "fighting men" to 30,000 at the outside, but he does not explain how Brennus, facing some 28,000 Greek troops at Thermopylae, came to divide his force into three separate bodies.

59. See W. J. Woodhouse, *Aetolia* (Oxford, 1897), pp. 67 and 373 for the route, which brings one down the valley to Lidhoriki; I used it in 1944, when going to investigate the destruction of EKKA by ELAS.

60. Pausanias 10.20.6-9.

61. Pausanias 10.20.6, saying that when the Greeks mustered at Thermopylae they heard that the Gallic army was already "around Magnesia and Phthiotis."

62. Justin 25.1-2 reports that after the failure of Brennus' army another force of Gauls defeated the Getae and the Triballi (north of Sofia) and then threatened Macedonia, where they camped within a day's march of the king's camp on the coast; it seems that they came into Macedonia via Valandovo and were not far from Thessalonica. The affair is placed at Lysimachea by W. W. Tarn in *CAH* 7, pp. 106 f.

63. See *Macedonia* II, which is in press, for the growth of the kingdom.

64. Justin 7.4, discussed in *Macedonia* II.

65. I am following the account of D. E. Pitcher, *An Historical Geography of the Ottoman Empire* (Leiden, 1972).

66. The first discovery was made at Dalmace near Koman and was reported by Th. Ippen in *WMBH* 10 (1907) 20 ff. Many sites have been excavated since the last war. See *SA* 1964, 1, 149-181 (on Krujë, in French); 1966, 1, 199-211 (a general study of the problems, in French); *StH* 1969, 1, 179-88 (on contacts with the Avars, in Albanian with a summary in French); 1969, 2, 155-69 (a general article, in Albanian with a summary in French). The controversial issues have been whether this culture was Slavic, Avaric, Hungarian, Albanian, Illyrian, and so on, and the Albanian archaeologists claim that this culture (and indeed all cultures in modern Albania) was indigenous and created by Illyrio-Albanians.

67. See *SA* 1964, 1, 165 f., plates I-IX and the descriptions in the text. Only one sword was found; this was at Krujë and is of the type carried by the Gauls. Another of the same kind is known from Elbasan in the Shkumbi valley. There are no Avaric pieces in Mirditë-Mati, but gold belt-fittings and a gold and silver vessel have been found at Vrap near Pekinj in the Shkumbi valley (*SA* 1966, 1, 209). These finds were on the route of the Via Egnatia, leading to Dyrrachium, and it was this route which was used by Gauls, Goths, Avars and others.

68. See the map of sites in *StH* 1969, 2, 161, and that of Mrs Hasluck in *The Unwritten Law in Albania*, end-pages.

69. Apart from Lesh the cemeteries and the citadels were not accompanied by the remains of built sites, and it is probable that huts were made of perishable materials, such as timber, thatch and clay. The sites outside Mirditë-Mati suit this interpretation; for the swampy ground by the Lakes of Scodra and Ochrid provided pastures for sheep, the former in the winter and the latter in transit to the coastal plain of Macedonia, and the site at Golaj marks an extension of summer pastures.

70. *SA* 1964, 1, 151 and pl. IV; they were locally made and of shapes common elsewhere in the Balkans.

71. See Qemal Haxhihasani, "Les recherches sur le cycle des Kreshnik (Preux)" *SA* 1964, 215-221; he reports the recording of some 400 epic songs since the last war. From medieval times onwards these epic songs have been handed down and developed in a pastoral society. To quote Qemal Haxhihasani, p. 219: "Tout comme les matériaux anterieurs, même les nouveaux matériaux contiennent, dans une large mesure, des éléments de la vie pastorale. Depuis l'origine des protagonistes jusqu'à leurs gestes et aventures, on ressent partout le souffle d'un milieu pastoral, d'une vie reflétant avec des notes très naturelles, les traits de nos tribus septentrionales, porteurs de ces chants. Le milieu agricole est quasiment absent dans les chants de ce cycle. Et cela n'est pas sans avoir son importance, car il marque un *terminus ad quem* pour la vie même du cycle."

Part Two

The Prehistoric Period

COMPARATIVE CHRONOLOGIES c. 4000–1500 B.C.

B.C.	S. Greece	E. Thessaly	Albania	Macedonia	Pelagonia	Paeonia	Russia
4000	L.N.A.	L.N.A.	↑ Dunavec - Cakran	↑ Servia IIa	↑ Starčevo	Vršnik	Kurgan I
3000		Arapi			Porodin		
2900			Velcë				Kurgan II
2800	E.H. I	Dimini	Kamnik Malik I			Anza IV	
2700		"Classical"	Malik IIa 1	Servia IIb		Anza ends	
2600			Malik IIa 2				
2500	E.H. II	Larissa					Kurgan III
2400	Leucas R						
2300	Graves	Rakhmani	Malik IIb		Crnobuki	Bubanj-Hum Ia	Kurgan IV
2200	E.H. III			Servia ends			
2100		E.B.A.	Malik IIIa	Armenokhori			
2000	M.H.						
1900	Leucas F+S	M.B.A.	Malik IIIb	Armenokhori ends	Bukri and Kravari	Bubanj-Hum II	
1800	Graves		and c				
1700	L.H. I	L.B.A.					
1600	end of L.H. I		Malik IIId	L.B.A.			
1500			Malik abandoned		sites abandoned		
1400			after 1400				

A continuous line below a site indicates that it continues until the line ends.
An arrow above a name means that the site had an earlier history.

IV

The First Impressions Made by Man on the Southwest Balkans

Movements in Pursuit of Animals

In the Middle Palaeolithic period (c. 50,000–30,000 years ago), when the first considerable numbers of men[1] settled in the southwestern Balkans, the land masses were more extensive than they are today, because, with so much water conserved in ice-caps, the level of the sea was about 100 metres lower. Thus Corcyra was joined to Epirus, and Chalcidice to Pieria, and there was no sea water to separate central Greece from the Peloponnese. The snow line was lower, being for instance at the 800 m altitude in Epirus, and animals and men had to descend to lower levels of country in order to live through the winter than they do today. But there were some compensating advantages. What is now a relatively narrow belt of coastal plain was then a large shelf of low-lying and often marshy land extending far into the Adriatic Sea and covering what is now the Thermaic Gulf. The significance of the change may be seen from a remark made by Mrs. Hasluck in a different context.[2] "If only the coastal plain [of central Albania] were more spacious, it would be a perfect complement to the mountains for pastoralism on the grand scale." Then it was so, not only on the Albanian coast between what are now the Gulf of the Drin and the Gulf of Valona, but also off Epirus, Acarnania and Elis, and on the eastern side of the peninsula between Pieria and Chalcidice (see Map 17).

The analysis of pollen from borings made to the northwest of Ioannina in central Epirus has shown that in the Middle Palaeolithic period there were continuous forests of oak, fir, beech and pine at that altitude, and that the types of vegetation were fundamentally the same as today. The difference is that in our warmer age beech and pine grow only at higher altitudes and undisturbed natural forests are found only in the remote parts of the Pindus and Grammus ranges and in the high areas of Albania and southern Yugoslavia; but then the forest cover extended to lower levels and the alpine pastures above the tree line were correspondingly larger in area. The western side of the peninsula is and always has been much wetter than the eastern side, the rainfall at Ioannina for instance being double that of Larissa and treble that of Athens,[3] and the pastures of the western side have always been richer and more abundant. It was here then that ideal conditions existed for ruminant animals in the Middle Palaeolithic period. We derive independent evidence that this was so from the settlements of Palaeolithic men, who being hunters chose the areas in which game was most plentiful. The pattern of their settlements within this area, being uncomplicated by any concern for agriculture, shows where certain types of animal bred most successfully and where in any period a hunting people, and also a pastoral people rearing this type of animal, will wish to settle.

Much the largest concentrations of men using tools of Mousterian types in the Middle Palaeolithic period were located in the lowlands of southern Epirus and northwestern Thessaly, from Larissa westwards. Other settlements or tools indicative of camps have been found in the lowlands of central Albania near Apollonia, in the plain of Butrinto in south Albania, in Corcyra and in Elis; and on the eastern side in

Map 17

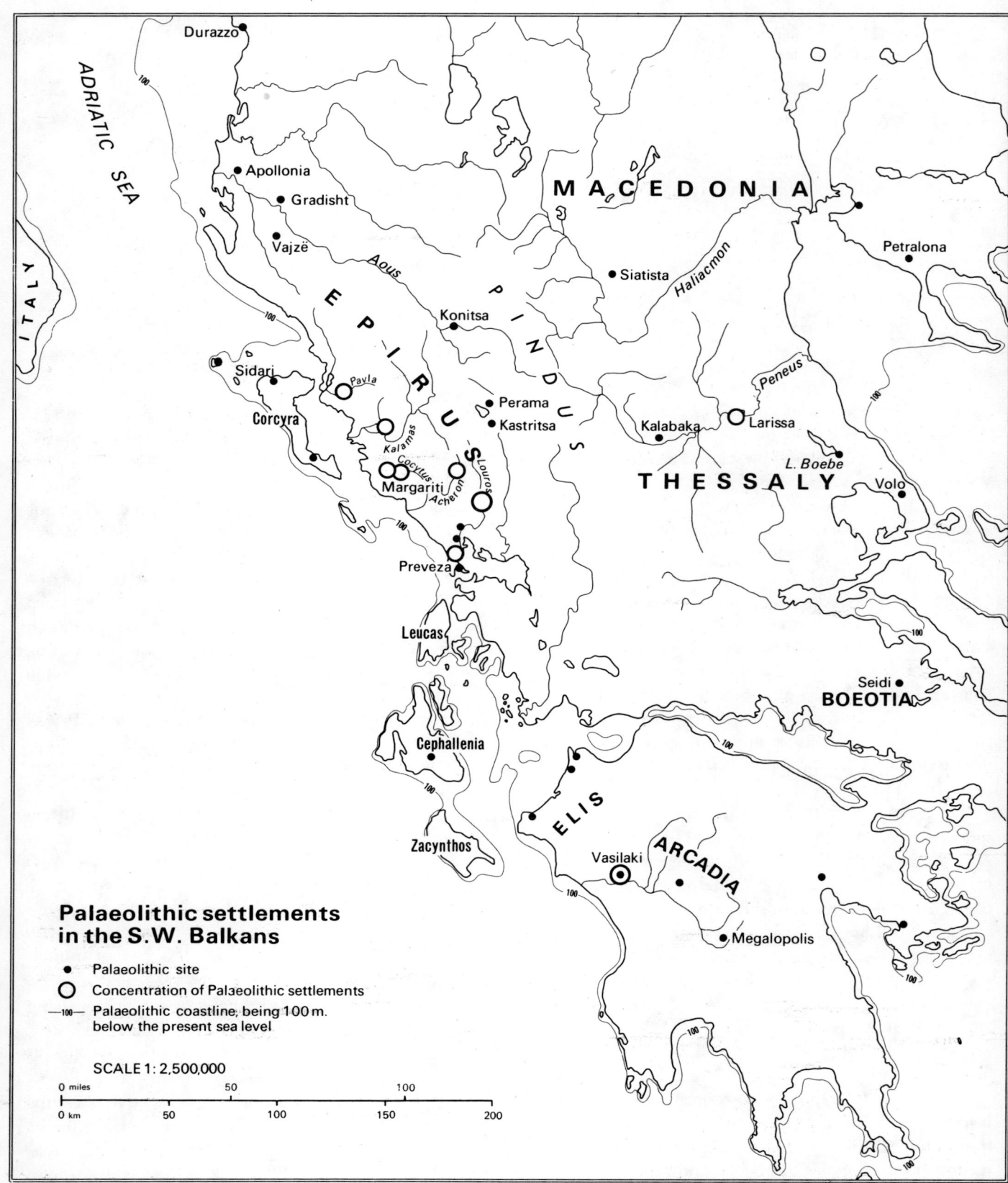

southwest Macedonia by Siatista and in Chalcidice facing what is now the Thermaic Gulf at Petralona, where the fossilized skull of a woman proves that the first layer of men there were of the Neanderthal type. The general pattern of settlement coincides with the habitats of the main groups of transhumant pastoralists of modern times—Albanians, Vlachs, Sarakatsani and Arcades—when they are pasturing their herds during the winter months. This is not surprising; for the chief difference between Palaeolithic men and the modern nomadic pastoralists is that the former followed the animals and the latter lead them.

The chief target of the Palaeolithic man's throwing-spear or javelin was the large red deer and its smaller cousins, the fallow deer and the roebuck. In the Asprokhaliko rock-shelter in the lower Louros valley of southern Epirus much the most numerous bones were those of these kinds of deer. Next in number came those of sheep or goats,[4] then horses and cattle (*bos primigenius*), then a now extinct kind of rhinoceros. Of these animals the red deer and the sheep or goats were transhumant and therefore moved to the alpine pastures of the Pindus range for the summer months, and the hunters moved with them. Evidence of their movement has been found on the western side of the peninsula at Konitsa on the upper Aous, and at Kastritsa and Perama in the plain of Ioannina, which are important staging areas in the modern migrations of sheep from winter to summer pastures (Pl. 3a). Farther north in a cave and in deposits in the plain of Butrinto there were also bones of bear (found now only in the central range) and of a large chamois (*Capra ibex*), which was extant in the central range at the end of last century when Heuzey hunted it.[5] In Corcyra which was close to the coast and had a more temperate climate, there were bones also of buffalo, pig and hyena.[6]

Human settlements, whether in caves, rock-shelters or open camps, have been found so far in the following areas on the western side of the peninsula. (1) Near Apollonia on the edge of the Malakastër plain; (2) at Gradisht in the lower Aous valley; (3) at Vajzë between the Shushicë valley and the Aous valley; (4) at two sites in the Butrinto plain;[7] (5) at Konitsa on the upper Aous; (6) near Gumani and Igoumenitsa on the lower Kalamas; (7) in the plains of Margariti and Paramythia;[8] (8) in the district of Preveza, (9) in the lower valley of the Louros before it enters the plain of Arta; (10) in Lakkasouli, the catchment area of the Acheron; and (11) at Kastritsa and Perama near Ioannina. The settlements were close to lakes,[9] marshes, head-springs (*kefalovrisia*) and rivers, to which the game came for water. Apart from those at Vajzë, Konitsa, Kastritsa, Perama, and Lakkasouli, all the sites were on the *last* foothills on the inland side of the extensive low-lying plains into which the Aous, the Pavla, the Kalamas, the Cocytus, and the Louros flow. In Palaeolithic times these places were a considerable distance inland, and from them one looked out over great areas of marshy plain. They were chosen because they were particularly appropriate for the hunting of transhumant animals during the winter period. The other sites were in staging areas during the migrations to the summer pastures.[10] Dr. E. S. Higgs has remarked of the Palaeolithic sites which he excavated in Epirus:[11] "Of particular interest has been the remarkable similarity observed between the movements of Palaeolithic hunters and the present day transhumant pastoralists, the Zagori Sarakatsani."

On the eastern side of the peninsula the greatest concentration of open camp settlements was close to the river Peneus, extending eastwards to Larissa[12] (then far inland). As much of the Thessalian plain was inundated, these settlements corresponded in position to those of the Louros valley. Here too there were many bones of ruminant animals and (as the rainfall was less heavy and the climate warmer than in Epirus) bones also of elephant, hippopotamus, rhinoceros and horse. No doubt the hunters followed the ruminant animals to their summer pastures on the Pindus range, even as the Vlachs lead their flocks thither nowadays. Indeed there is evidence of it. Whereas Palaeolithic men in Epirus made their tools at the sites of the flint-beds which are very widespread in Epirus but particularly rich in Lakkasouli,[13] the settlements of the Peneus valley were far removed from the carnelian-beds from which their tools were derived. These beds of a dark red-brown carnelian are situated northwest of Kalabaka in the upper Peneus valley, some fifty miles away from the nearest known camp settlement. As no cores of carnelian have been found in the settlements, it is evident that the flakes of carnelian were struck and fashioned at or near the carnelian-beds, which lay on the route towards north Pindus. Indeed there is a Middle Palaeolithic site there at Theopetra near Kalabaka. Thus the Palaeolithic hunters of Thessaly were following the same kind of life and no doubt taking the same routes as the Vlachs of today who move their sheep from the Larissa area to Samarina and other high villages of north Pindus. In the winter months they lived in the lowlands, where their prey were pasturing. Indeed, open camps of the Middle Palaeolithic period, together with some remarkable rock-paintings of mammoth, have been found as far to the east as Halonnesus, now an island, but then part of Thessaly.

The rich pastures of the plain of Elis extended then over what is now the mouth of the Gulf of Corinth, and summer pastures were provided by the highlands of Arcadia. Settlements or signs of settlement have been found near the present coast, and many tools of the Palaeolithic period in the region of Megalopolis, but the largest concentration of settlements was at Vasilaki on the Elis-Arcadia border by the Alpheus, just before it enters the plain.[14] It seems then that here too the hunters followed the movements of transhumant animals, for the pattern of settlements resembles that farther north (e.g. of Apollonia–Vajzë–Konitsa; Preveza–Louros valley–plain of Ioannina; and Lake Boebe–Peneus valley–carnelian-beds) with the heaviest concentration at Vasilaki corresponding to those in the Louros valley and the Peneus valley. This pattern conforms with the movements of the transhumant pastoralists of modern times, the 'Arcades' or 'Valtetsini'. Towards the end of the Upper Palaeolithic period, when the Louros valley sites were drawing to an end, a similar culture appeared in the Seidi Cave by Lake Copaïs in Boeotia. There may have been contacts too with Apulia, where the Romanelli Cave had a very similar microlithic industry to that of the last phase in the Louros valley; if so, the passage of the Adriatic Sea was probably made at the latitude of Durazzo or Lesh, where the seas are less dangerous.[15]

The settlements on the western side of the peninsula were not only the most numerous but also the most long-lasting. While those of northwestern Thessaly came to an end in the early part of the Upper Palaeolithic period, those of Epirus and Elis were active down to the end of that period, i.e. down to c. 9000. Thus transhumant pasturing of ruminant animals and hunting of these animals had a life of over 40,000 years, but only in this highly specialised area of central Albania and western Greece, from the Malakastër plain to the Alpheus valley.

Whence did the hunters of the Middle Palaeolithic period come into the area bounded roughly by Apollonia-Larissa-Louros valley-Elis? There are some traces of Mousterian industries in Bulgaria, but the general lack of Palaeolithic objects in Macedonia except by Siatista and at Petralona[16] makes it very unlikely that they came through Macedonia from the east or northeast. When we turn to the north and the northwest, the present evidence is distinctly favourable; for the rock-shelter of Crvena Stijena in Montenegro near Nikšić at the head of the Zeta valley contained tools of Mousterian type like those in Epirus and Corcyra, and these too are dated to the Middle Palaeolithic period. There, too, the settlement was long-lasting; its last phase resembled the last phase at Asprokhaliko in Epirus and at the Seidi Cave in Boeotia.[17] We may conjecture, then, that the hunters moved in pursuit of game very gradually down the coastal region of the eastern Adriatic, entering our area perhaps at the Zeta valley and moving south until they found the huntsman's paradise in what is now southern Albania, Corcyra and Epirus, from which some of them crossed Pindus into northwestern Thessaly and others penetrated as far south as Elis. Such a movement from Montenegro to Elis may have taken some centuries or even millennia, and there is still a geographical gap in the evidence between Montenegro and Apollonia, except that a Palaeolithic deposit was reported before the war as having been found near Tirana. But the clear and relatively firm picture of the Middle Palaeolithic period which emerges has great importance, for it reveals a way of life fitted particularly well to the geographical conditions, a way of life which has persisted—not necessarily without breaks and intermissions—down to the 1930s and even on a diminished scale until today in the same area.[18]

Movements in Pursuit of Lands

We move next to the period in which man ceased to be only a hunter and became also a breeder of domesticated animals and a sower of seeds, a farmer in the modern sense of the word. This development came in the post-glacial period when the ice-caps shrank and the seas attained more or less their present level. Perhaps with the tremendous change in climate conditions worsened for animals and men, hunting became less productive and new methods of acquiring food became necessary for survival. It is generally agreed on present evidence that men first became farmers in the Near East, and that their new way of life soon spread from there to the Balkan area; reaching it around the end of the eighth millennium and initiating what is known as the Neolithic Period[19] (see Map 18).

The earliest phase is known as Preceramic Neolithic, because pottery was not in use. Containers were no doubt made of skin, wicker and wood, the last being used evidently for some agricultural instruments. The earliest known settlements in the southwest Balkans are all in the plain of Thessaly, an area particularly favourable for agriculture. Two of the excavated settlements, Argissa and Souphli Magoula, are by the Peneus in the vicinity of Larissa; another is near the coast at Sesklo (between Lake Boebe and Pagasae); and other settlements have been inferred from surface finds at sites in northern Thessaly and in southern and southwestern Thessaly. The settlements were no longer open camps but closely built villages of small huts. It has been possible to reconstruct their way of life from charred remains and animal bones. They grew crops of wheat, barley, millet, lentils and other vegetables, and they perhaps cultivated the olive. Their favourite animals were sheep but they also kept goats, pigs and cattle; they hunted deer, hares and birds, but only to a limited extent; and they collected shellfish and engaged in fishing. That they or their contemporaries in the Aegean practised seafaring is clear from the fact that about half of their blades for tools were of obsidian, a vitreous lava, found not on the Greek mainland but in Melos and elsewhere overseas. Some blades were of carnelian, as in the Palaeolithic period; the occurrence of these and the use of serpentine (greenstone) for what were apparently amulets (known from their shape as 'ear-plugs') show that the settlers travelled into the high parts of the Pindus range. They did so no doubt in the practice of transhumance, when they took their herds of sheep to the summer pastures of the Pindus range.

That the first settlers came to Thessaly from the Near East seems to be most probable. The earliest layers of the three excavated sites at Argissa, Souphli and Sesklo show a fully-fledged civilisation and no preliminary stages to it, and the appropriate precedents are to be seen in the Near East, especially in Anatolia.[20] It is possible that the first explorers came by boat, but it is probable that the majority of the settlers came by land, bringing some domesticated animals with them and moving gradually along the Thracian coast, rather than that they all came by sea and had to begin again with the domesticating of the wild animals of Thessaly. If they came both by sea and by land, they resembled the Slavs in this respect. It was, however, easier then, because they did not have to contend with any existing inhabitants, as far as we can see.[21]

Far away to the northwest, a Preceramic level was found in the rock shelter at Crvena Stijena at the head of the Zeta valley. The artefacts were closely related to those found in Thessaly, but the relationship may have been due rather to a common source than to any direct contact.[22] Late in the Preceramic Neolithic period the site of Sidari in Corcyra was occupied by a seafaring people of similar culture. It is impossible to say whether they came to the island from the north or from the south. In the northeastern Peloponnese near Hermione a Preceramic layer has probably been identified at the Franchthi Cave.[23] In the long history of this cave two new phenomena appeared c. 6000 B.C.: the bones of domesticated caprines and the seeds of cereals. It is evident that the farmers responsible for these phenomena came into the Peloponnese, perhaps from central Greece.

Entirely new phenomena marked the start of the Early Neolithic period. A well-made, if simple, pottery appeared at a number of sites without any sign of the preliminary stages in pottery-making which we should expect. As S. S. Weinberg has expressed it, "clearly the first pottery made in Greece was in a tradition already long established and was the product of experienced potters." Figurines, seals and whorls of clay appeared also in an advanced form of development. Stone was used for the making of vessels, tools (such as axes, chisels and pestles) and figurines, and many of these were exquisitely made and beautifully polished. Such arts had not been known before in Greece. Of some forty settlements which have been identified for this period, five were at Preceramic sites, where the change to well-made objects was marked and abrupt.[24] Thus much points to the intrusion of newcomers with an already established civilisation, which superseded that of their predecessors. But there were also some features suggestive of continuity; thus 'ear-plugs' and clay sling-bullets were common to the Preceramic period and the start of the Early Neolithic period, and people lived in closely-built villages of small huts in both periods. Indeed D. R. Theochares has argued from the case of Sesklo, where he found some very early experiments in the making of pottery, that there was direct continuity not only at Sesklo but at other sites where early experiments in making pottery were conducted (he maintained) outside the settlements and so have escaped notice; but this seems most unlikely, since early experiments *were* made *inside* the settlement at Sesklo. The theory which fits the evidence best is that there was physical continuity between the two periods at five sites, where the Preceramic population merged with the newcomers; that the novelties in pottery, figurines etc. were introduced by the newcomers who not only came to Preceramic sites but established new sites of their own; and that the common features of the two periods were due to a similar background in the Near East, from which the first Preceramic settlers and the first Early Neolithic settlers came.

Most of the Early Neolithic sites were close to the sea or within easy reach of the sea on the eastern side of the Greek peninsula, and one has recently been found at Ayios Petros in the Northern Sporades. This pattern of settlement suggests, in the words of S. S. Weinberg, "both an eastward and a seaward orientation for the Early Neolithic culture."[25] This suggestion is put beyond reasonable doubt by the close similarity between the Greek sites and Çatal Hüyük in the Konya plain of Turkey (in the ancient province of Lycaonia) in respect of the earliest Greek pottery, figurines, seals and blades. In particular, the earliest pottery on the Greek sites was marked by a general uniformity; since this uniformity disappeared later, it is to be attributed to a common background. As pottery of the same type as the earliest Greek pottery occurred at the same period at Çatal Hüyük, we may conclude that the earliest settlers in Greece came from the orbit of the Çatal Hüyük culture. One interesting link may be seen at Prodromos in western Thessaly, where a secondary burial of skulls was made as at Çatal Hüyük. Contact between the coasts of the Aegean was maintained later in the period, because an unusual incised pottery with white filling at Nea Makri on the east coast of Attica has much in common with pottery of the same period at Mersin on the south coast of Turkey (in ancient Cilicia).[26] The trade in obsidian from Melos was another indication of regular seafaring.

The largest concentration of sites was in Thessaly, and much the largest site was that at Sesklo, just inland of the Gulf of Pagasae and well placed for commerce by land and by sea. While Çatal Hüyük may be called a city, and Sesklo was a large town, most of the other settlements in Greece were villages of some twenty or thirty small houses.[27] Expansion by sea led to the planting of settlements off the west coast of the peninsula at Choirospilia ('Pigs-cave') in Leucas and at Sidari in Corcyra. There was also expansion by land from Thessaly. Settlements have been found at Asphaka, north of Ioannina, and at Varytimidhes by Servia on the river Haliacmon in southern Macedonia. These places, being far inland, were no doubt reached by the passes of the Zygos and Volustana respectively, and it is probable that we may see in the settlements some evidence of the transhumance of sheep on the highlands of Pindus and Olympus. A sample of the animal bones found at Sesklo in Early Neolithic levels shows that 62.7% of the total were of sheep and goats, and such a high proportion means that very considerable flocks were being maintained.[28] In that case transhumance was necessary, and the alpine pastures of the Pindus range were better and larger than those of the coastal range of Thessaly on Mt Ossa and Mt Pelion.

An important offshoot to the north was at Nea Nikomedeia, then on the edge of a marshy lake or an inlet of the Thermaic Gulf, in southern Macedonia; it was probably reached mainly by sea, and the settlement may have been planted late in the Early Neolithic period.[29] It was defended by a ditch against marauders, presumably of the Starčevo culture which was centered in Pelagonia. In its lay-out and its architecture it rivalled Sesklo and may be regarded as a comparable but smaller centre of commerce. Here too the important animals were sheep and goats, and it is evident that transhumance was practised, summer pastures being found on Mt Olympus and Mt Bermion. Flint and not obsidian was used, and the settlers made cult images of frogs from a beautiful green serpentine, which came from the central range of northern Pindus. We may infer from this that some transhumant shepherds from Lower Macedonia took their flocks to northern Pindus for summer pastures.[30]

A completely separate culture developed in the

Map 18

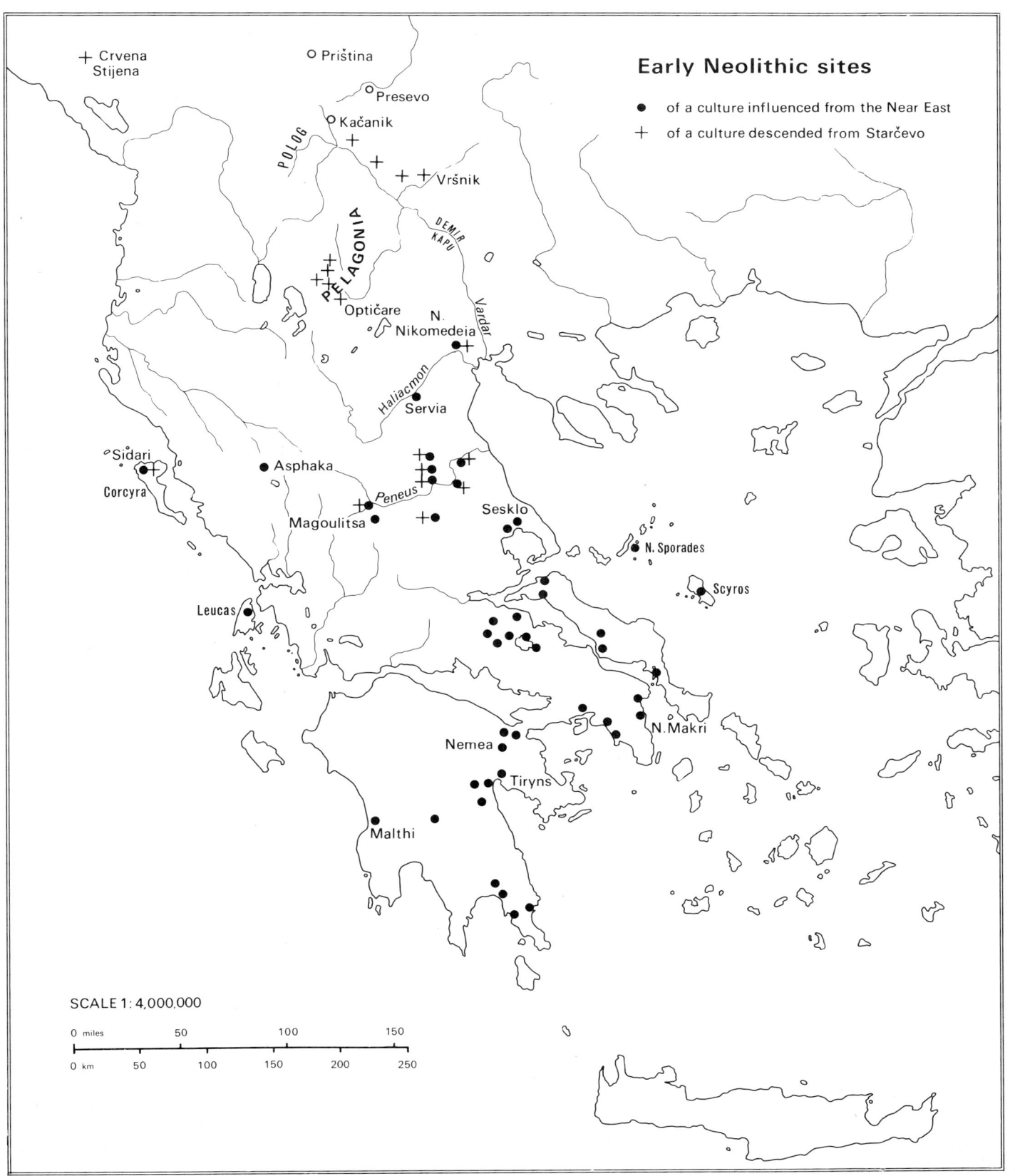

basin of the middle Danube in the vicinity of Belgrade, and this culture spread southwards into our area in the course of the Early Neolithic period. Synchronisations based on carbon 14 analysis, especially when samples are very few, are not foolproof; indeed differences of opinion on the date of the first layer at Nea Nikomedeia fall within a bracket of almost 1000 years.[31] But where many samples are taken, synchronisations become more stable, even if absolute dates remain somewhat uncertain. Thus the first potteries of sites in Thessaly, of Elatea in Phocis and of Sidari in Corcyra, all belong to the first half of the sixth millenium in radio carbon dating, and the first of Starčevo and Lepenski Vir III in the Danube basin has been placed within a bracket of 6500 to 5300 B.C.[32]

Within our area one group of settlements with the Starčevo culture lay mainly on the eastern side of the upper Vardar valley and on its eastern tributaries; the earliest of them were at Anza and Vršnik, both near Štip in the Bregalnitsa valley. It is likely that the settlers came via the Kačanik and Preševo Passes and moved on the eastern side of the great river. The other group of settlements with the same culture appeared in Pelagonia, the most southerly being at Mogila and Optičare near Monastir. As the plateau of Pelagonia, being about 600 m above sea level, is very much higher than the valleys of the upper Vardar and its eastern tributaries, it is probable that the settlers came via the similar high plateaus of Priština and Polog, keeping west of the Kačanik Pass and also west of the great river. The whole area—both the plateaus and the valleys—was heavily wooded, but the forests seem to have been no deterrent to movement. On the other hand, the large rivers were often impassable, and the two groups of settlements west and east of the Vardar developed thereafter on separate lines,[33] presumably because communication across the middle reaches of the Vardar was rarely achieved.

In any southwards expansion of these two groups, the Vardar and the mountains on either side of the Demir Kapu formed a hard and fast line of division. Thus when we find a northern influence at Nea Nikomedeia in Lower Macedonia west of the Vardar, we may surmise that it came from or via Pelagonia and not from east of the Vardar.

In the last phase of the Early Neolithic period there were interesting developments in Thessaly. There was a flow of influence into Thessaly which came from the south, from the strong group of sites in Phocis and Boeotia, but it was a passing influence.[34] A much stronger impact followed in the form of a crude monochrome pottery, on which jags or ridges were 'impressed' by special techniques, the earlier being called 'Barbotine' (with the imprint of fingernails or small bones) and the later 'Cardium' (with the imprint probably of a cardium shell). Together with this 'impressed' ware, crude 'pear-shaped' figurines made an appearance in place of the fine naturalistic figurines of earlier times. The bearers of this culture were certainly dominant in northern Thessaly and in western Thessaly, where their leading site was at Magoulitsa, west of Kardhitsa. On the other hand, their influence was small in southern Thessaly, and it had practically no effect on the coastal sites, Sesklo and Pyrasos.[35] It is clear then that they did not come from the south where the tradition of painted pottery continued unbroken, nor by sea from the east as the coastal sites were unaffected. Moreover, the pattern of settlement suggests not only that they had come from the north, but also that, like the Vlachs in the medieval period, they occupied northern and western Thessaly because these districts were closest to their summer pastures. They were agriculturalists but also pastoralists and hunters; for it has been noted at Prodromos near Kardhitsa that hunting and stock-raising were more important there than agriculture in the Early Neolithic period.[36]

In this instance we do not rely only on the inferences which can be drawn from the pattern of settlement and geographical conditions. For the 'impressed' ware was characteristic of the Starčevo culture and later of its direct descendant, the Vinča culture.[37] The Barbotine form has been found in abundance at Crvena Stijena at the head of the Zeta valley, the natural route of entry into the coastal plains of Albania; but there is as yet no evidence of its presence at this time in central Albania.[38] The site of Sidari in Corcyra was taken over by people with impressed ware,[39] and they may have come from the Dalmatian coast of the Adriatic Sea. The chief centre of Starčevo culture within our area was, as we have seen, Pelagonia, where there had been a long undisturbed period of growth. No doubt the people who entered northern and western Thessaly came either from Pelagonia and its environs or from farther north via Pelagonia. One sign of their expansion may be seen at Nea Nikomedeia, where the last phase of the Early Neolithic settlement was marked by the appearance of impressed ware of both kinds.[40] The movement into Thessaly is likely to have been made down the Haliacmon valley and then through the Khasia region and/or by the Volustana Pass above Servia through Perrhaebia; for Tempe was probably impassable for anything more than a few men, and certainly impassable for herds of animals.

The transhumance of sheep was doubtless practised in Pelagonia, as we have seen it was at Nea Nikomedeia and in Thessaly generally. There was, however, the difference that the sheep had to descend from Pelagonia and its hard winter to a low-lying plain, whether in Albania or more conveniently in Macedonia or northern Thessaly. Thus the Starčevo people of Pelagonia may well have known the region of Nea Nikomedeia and the plain of Thessaly for several centuries before they seized control. Indeed there is interesting evidence which shows that this was so. At Prodromos, impressed ware was found in *all* strata, i.e. it first appeared at a much earlier date there than elsewhere in Thessaly; and the pear-shaped figurines were again earlier there than elsewhere. Two were quite unparalleled, one showing a woman carrying a bag (for a baby?) on her back, and another showing a woman in childbirth. There were two settlements at Prodromos, some 500 m apart. Prodromos II had suffered ten disastrous conflagrations by the end of the Early Neolithic period; a remarkable roof of trunks and branches, some of which were unworked and others of which were worked into planks (perhaps for a temporary structure), was found on the site of a rectangular house, ten metres square.

As we have noted already, hunting and stock-raising were the main pursuits of the settlers at Prodromos. All these features are best explained by the hypothesis that transhumant shepherds of the Starčevo culture and hunters and shepherds of the local culture used these settlements mainly as winter camps, and their settled neighbours sometimes attacked them and burnt their huts. In the opinion of the excavator, G. Hourmouziadis, the life of the settlement at Prodromos II covered some 500 years;[41] and if the link between Prodromos and Çatal Hüyük in regard to secondary burial of skulls goes back to the earliest period of Early Neolithic, its life was considerably longer. In any case it is clear that people of the Starčevo culture were practising transhumance alongside the people of Thessaly and Nea Nikomedeia for a half-millennium or more before they actually seized power. We shall not be surprised to find similarly long periods of coexistence before invasion in the case of the Kurgan people, the so-called Dorians, and the Vlachs and Albanians in historical times.[42] Nor was transhumance limited only to the east side of the peninsula; for a few sherds of impressed ware, both of the Barbotine and the Cardium techniques, have been found at Kastritsa in the plateau of Ioannina.[43] It is uncertain whether they belong to this period or to the Middle Neolithic period.

When the people of the Starčevo culture gained control of northern Thessaly and western Thessaly—the latter probably much forested—they occupied the existing settlements, as at Nea Nikomedeia, and engaged in stock-raising and agriculture, as in Pelagonia. As time passed, their influence and perhaps their control began to decline; for they were less advanced in the making of pottery and of figurines, and the older culture, emanating particularly from Sesklo, was already regaining lost ground when the Early Neolithic period came to an abrupt end.[44]

Migrations and Invasions Leading to the First Population Overlappings

The settlements of the Middle Neolithic period in Greece were concentrated to a remarkable degree on the eastern side of the peninsula, near the coast and in particular areas—southeastern Thessaly, the Copaïs region, eastern Attica, the Attic side of Euboea, Corinthia-Argolis and Laconia. Of sixty-seven sites recorded by S. S. Weinberg, only four were situated on the western side of the peninsula. These are shown on Map 19. Once again we see a pattern of settlements which looked eastward and seaward, and the presumption is very strong that it was due to migrations of people who came from the east to the Greek peninsula at various times in this period of a thousand years or so.

Thessaly is again a very important area, so much so that the period has been labelled that of the 'Sesklo-kultur' (Sesklo being an important site in Thessaly). The period opened with the destruction by fire of two settlements in western Thessaly: Magoulitsa and Prodromos, and thereafter the intrusive Starčevo

Map 19

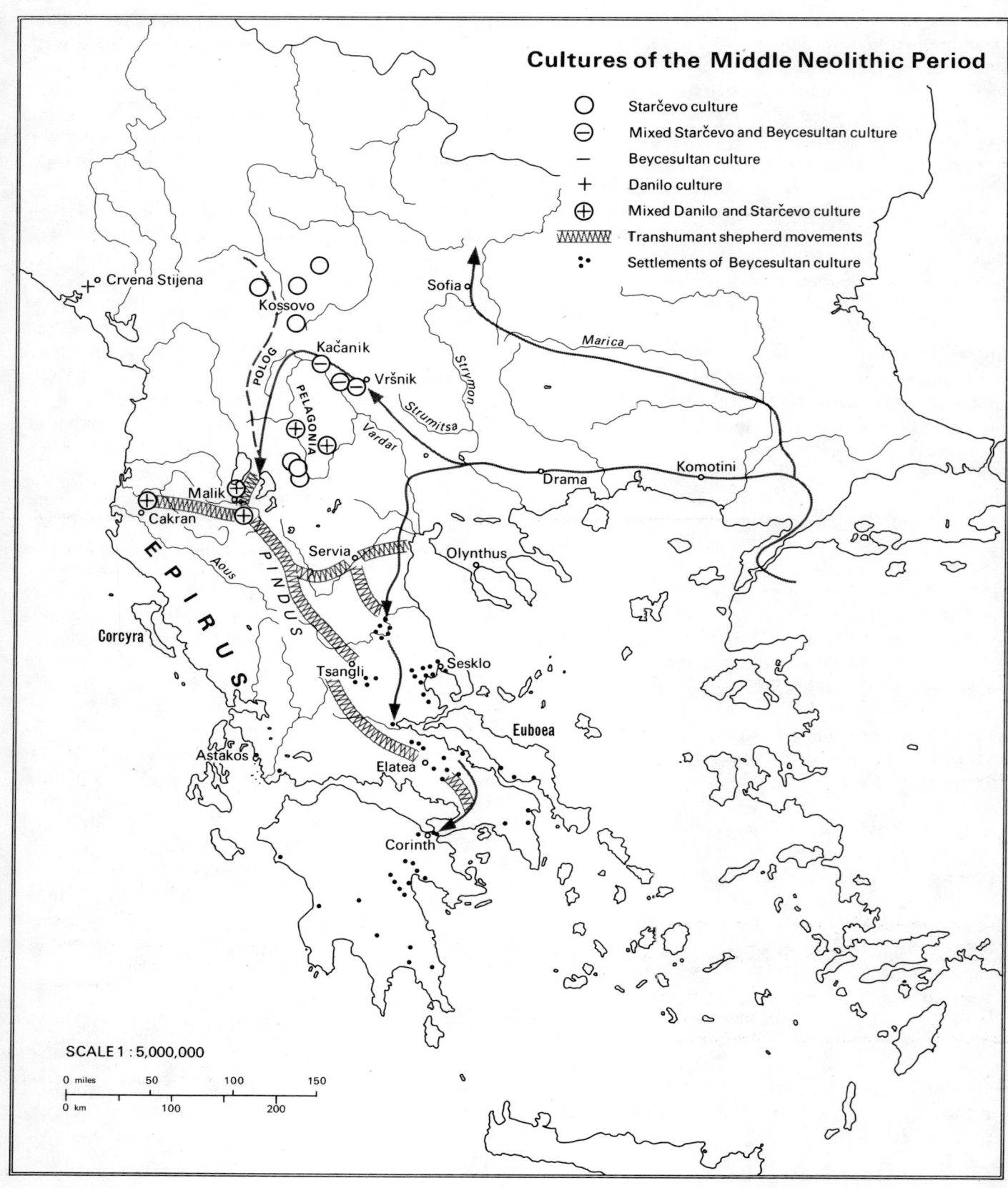

element there and elsewhere disappeared from our view, whether by elimination or absorption is unknown.[45] Farther north, Varytimidhes by Servia and Nea Nikomedeia, the latter marked by the Starčevo phase, were abandoned. New phenomena appeared: a painted pottery with some new motives (replacing the earlier monochrome wares), which was at first common to all settlements in Thessaly, and the construction of houses with stone foundations and (at Otzaki and Tsangli) internal buttresses and interior partitions. The origin of the painted pottery is uncertain, but one striking ornament known as the whirl pattern on the inside of bowls, which appeared later on, has been found also at Samarra on the Tigris. Houses with the peculiarities of those at Otzaki and Tsangli have been found at the same period at Can Hasan in the Konya plain of Asia Minor. The rational interpretation seems to be that a new element of population reached the coast of southern Macedonia and occupied Thessaly, expelling or subjugating the bearers of Starčevo culture and introducing their own way of life which was based on agriculture and seafaring. They came at the beginning of the Middle Neolithic period from the Near East, and thereafter they maintained contact with the world of the Near East.[46]

In the latter part of the period a new type of house appeared at Sesklo and Otzaki; it has been accorded the Greek name which was applied in the Homeric poems to the hall of a Mycenaean palace, 'megaron'. Relatively narrow in relation to its length, it had a porch, usually supported on wooden pillars, and an indoor hearth set towards one side. Early examples of it have been found at Jericho and at Beycesultan. Another novelty towards the end of the period was the arrow of obsidian or flint, and it was suggested by Gordon Childe that the bow and arrow, so much superior to the sling and clay bullet, were associated with the spread of the grey-black burnished wares,[47] to which we shall come shortly.

It was probably in the latter part of the period that a settlement was made on the south bank of the Haliacmon river at Servia, quite close to the abandoned Early Neolithic site. Its position on that bank and its pottery indicate that it was "a northern outpost of the Sesklo culture" of Thessaly.[48] It was defended by a ditch, 2.35 m deep with one side vertical and the other sloping steeply, and the enemies against whom it was built were evidently people north of the river with the Starčevo culture which is known farther north in Pelagonia. Subsequent building levels had no defences, either because a modus vivendi was established locally or because the Servia settlers became stronger. Perhaps the former was the reason, for it is noteworthy that the houses were made in the Macedonian style (as at Nea Nikomedeia and elsewhere) with wooden frames of chestnut, oak and pine, and with wooden floors, and that they had hearths inside which were needed in the harsh winters, so much colder that those of central Thessaly. The site commands the route which runs from the crossing of the river to the Volustana Pass and then into the upland area of Perrhaebia, the valley of the river Titaresius and the northern edge of the Thessalian plain. From the point of view of Thessaly, the planting of an outpost at Servia meant that Perrhaebia was included in her territory, and this is of interest because the area has always been of the greatest importance to transhumant pastoralists, who pasture their flocks in winter by the Titaresius and the Peneus and in summer on Olympus, Pieria and Pindus.[49] No doubt this was so in the Middle Neolithic period too, although we do not know whether the Thessalian peoples of the plain practised transhumance themselves or encouraged its practice in others.

The new regime in Thessaly was already long established when changes came about in Boeotia-Euboea-Attica and the eastern Peloponnese. There, too, stone foundations for houses came into general use and some rooms (e.g. at Lerna) had internal buttresses; a new form of pottery was made, 'Neolithic Urfirnis', so called from its lustrous glaze; and slender small-breasted female figurines took the place of the steatopygous type. There were certainly close links with Syria and Cilicia, where such pottery and figurines were made, and one type of glazed vessel, a 'husking tray', had its closest analogy at Hassunah on the Tigris. It looks as if another wave of migration, coming perhaps via Thessaly, entered these areas, overlaid the earlier population and maintained contact with the world of the Near East.

The area which lies between Thessaly and Boeotia–Euboea–Attica, namely the Cephissus valley in Phocis, proved to be the most conservative of all areas. There the Early Neolithic tradition, as instanced by the so-called 'Chaeronea ware', lived long into the Middle Neolithic period, and it was only in the second half of the period that the influences of painted pottery in Thessaly and of Urfirnis ware in Boeotia-Euboea-Attica began to make themselves felt. It seems then that this part of Phocis, being relatively remote from the sea and colder in climate, appealed less than other parts of east Greece to the settlers who came from the Near East.

Towards the very end of the Middle Neolithic period the areas of east Greece as far south as the Isthmus of Corinth were affected by a new development, the arrival of grey-to-black burnished wares of pottery. These have been noted particularly at Sesklo and at Kouphovouno by Iolcus in Thessaly, at Elatea in the Cephissus valley and at Corinth itself.[50] This pottery is marked sometimes by a "shallow grooving to produce a rippled surface," and there are a few four-legged cult vessels, to which we shall refer later. That the innovation was due to invaders is generally agreed, but there is doubt whether these invaders came from the central Balkans or from Beycesultan in Asia Minor (in the ancient province of Phrygia), as both areas provide close analogies of the correct period.[51]

Turning to the northeastern part of our area, we find similar grey-to-black burnished wares, sometimes with the rippled surface, which have been separately interpreted as evidence of a stream of invasion travelling along the Thracian coast via Komotini and Drama and then via the Strumitsa valley into the Bregalnitsa valley, on the eastern side of the Vardar valley.[52] There the new influences were entering a zone of well-established Starčevo culture in the Ovče Polje basin, and they brought about at Vršnik (near Štip in the Bregalnitsa valley) a mixed culture, representing the Starčevo aspect on the one hand and the new influences on the other hand, which were held to have come ultimately from Beycesultan.[53] The bearers of this Vršnik culture expanded northwards but did not establish themselves beyond the passes over the main watershed (at Kačanik and Preševo). In the areas farther north, Kossovo and Metohija, the Starčevo traditions held firm. The communities of the Bregalnitsa area (Vršnik, Anza and Zelenikovo, for instance) were primarily agriculturalist and raised cattle and pigs more than sheep and goats. They traded southwards to the Aegean basin, as we know from the occurrence of ornaments made from an Aegean shell, the *spondylus gaederopus*, and it is probable that the black burnished ware in the lowest level at Olynthus in the Late Neolithic period belongs to this complex east of the Vardar.[54]

It has been shown by D. Srejović that a second and larger stream of invasion of similar origin and at the same period went up the valley of the Marica (ancient Hebrus) into the fertile eastwards-facing plain and occupied the leading site there, Karanovo. The next advance from there was into the plateau of Sofia and then northwards to the Danube, where the invaders split into two arms, one going downstream and the other upstream into Yugoslavia.[55] We have in the movements of these two streams a close parallel to the Turkish invasion of the Balkans (see Map 15). It may have taken several generations to reach the Vardar and the Danube respectively.

In the northwestern part of our area the rockshelter of Crvena Stijena near the head of the Zeta valley was used during the Middle Neolithic period by people who were mainly hunters of deer, pigs, oxen and perhaps goats. Unlike their predecessors of the Early Neolithic period they did not have impressed wares of pottery, and it is clear that their affinities were with the cultural complex of Danilo (inland of Šibenik on the Dalmatian coast) and Kakanj (north of Sarajevo in Bosnia).[56]

Evidence of Middle Neolithic settlements in Albania—the earliest yet known in that country—has been discovered only recently. One site is Dunavec, south of Malik, in the high lakeland area, and there are surface finds of the period from Pogradec at the southwest corner of Lake Ochrid and at Vashtemi, south of Malik.[57] At that time the lakeland plains were covered in forest, as the hills northeast of Lake Ochrid are today, and the attraction of the area for these first settlers lay primarily in its magnificent summer pastures. When the Vlachs were at their most prosperous, they had their chief centres in this very area, at Muskopole and Shipiska to the southwest of Malik. For winter pastures the Middle Neolithic peoples had to go, like the Vlachs, to the coastal plains of central Albania and/or to enter the Haliacmon valley and proceed to the coastal plain near Nea Nikomedeia or to the Thessalian plain; for the winter is severe in the lakeland, the plains being more than 800 m above sea level. As we have seen, the easiest access to the lakeland is from the north via Kitsevo and the similar terrain of Polog. It is in the north too that similar areas with basins of fertile land and fine pastures at high altitudes are to be found, in Metohija and Kossovo and farther north in Bosnia.

The excavator of the settlement at Dunavec, Muzafer Korkuti, has published only preliminary reports so far, but he and his colleague, Zhaneta Andrea, have published a full report of another excavated site, Cakran, which is intimately related to Dunavec. Indeed the two sites are said to be of one and the same civilisation. Let us turn therefore to Cakran. It is situated on low-lying land between the lower Aous valley and the plain of Malakastër, which has the richest pastures in Albania. This was the place of which Herodotus told a story about a flock of sheep sacred to the sun-god (9.93). These sheep pastured by day on the banks of the river (the Aous) and were kept at night in a cave for fear of the wolves, and they were entrusted to the charge of the richest of the citizens.[58] One of them, Euenius by name, fell asleep, and the wolves entered the cave and killed sixty sheep. The people of Apollonia (for this was the name of the Greek colony founded near Cakran many centuries later) put out the eyes of Euenius, and thereafter the ewes and the land were stricken with barrenness. No doubt Cakran was a winter station for transhumant shepherds who brought their flocks down from the lakeland to these famous pastures for the winter months. The close relationship of the two sites, Cakran and Dunavec, is thus most readily explained.

The settlement at Cakran has some peculiar features. The subsoil under the deposit, which is seldom deeper than some three metres, is a tight-packed clay, and this clay was found to have had wide trenches cut deep into it. The excavators inferred that the houses of the settlement had been sunk in this way into the subsoil, so that the roofs (they estimated) were more or less at ground level. They found evidence of hearths, sometimes in a fixed position and sometimes moveable, but otherwise no sign of the supposed houses, which must have been made of perishable material, such as is employed today in Vlach winter encampments. When later houses were built on top of the debris of their predecessors, the roofs would have been at a higher level and would have shown above the ground. The whole deposit occupied "a large cul-de-sac with a diameter of 20 to 30 m."[59] The labour of digging these pits out of clay with the tools of bone and stone which the men of the time had must have been very great, and I suggest that the excavated areas may have been used in lieu of the cave mentioned by Herodotus for the protection of flocks of sheep at night as well as for the humans.[60]

The pottery may be put into five categories: (1) coarse impressed ware of Barbotine type (there was none of Cardium type) in the Starčevo tradition; (2) incised grey-to-black burnished ware of excellent quality, the incisions being sometimes encrusted with white paint; (3) plastically ornamented grey-to-black burnished ware; (4) a special form of incision made with a tool ('ornement à gaufrage' or 'stamp-decorated'), again on the grey-to-black burnished ware; and (5) a very rare painted pottery of which only eleven sherds were found.[61] Pottery of these categories was found in every layer of the deposit which was excavated, and the conclusion of the excavators was that they were dealing with a single deposit within which these categories of pottery were in use.[62] No doubt the depositing of contemporary material sometimes in a sunken house and sometimes on the ground level outside (some two metres higher) has contributed to the mixture; but we are told in a preliminary report that there was an identical mixture of pottery of different categories at Dunavec. It is certain then that the coarse Starčevo-type ware, the fine grey-to-black burnished ware with various forms of ornamentation, and the rare painted pottery were in contemporaneous use for some time at least within the span of the settlement's occupation.

The most remarkable vessels of the grey-to-black burnished ware were four-legged vessels with a round aperture at the front, the legs being ornamented with plastic decoration and with incisions; white paint was used to fill incisions and red paint sometimes covered the legs or parts of them. Examples from Elatea and Cakran are illustrated in Plate 5b. Fifty-one legs or pieces of legs were found at Cakran, and seventy fragments of these vessels at Dunavec, but there were no whole vessels.[63] Such vessels were much used at Danilo in Dalmatia and Kakanj and other sites in Bosnia in the Middle Neolithic period of the West Balkans. Examples have been found also at Novi Pazar on the Ibar, Priština in Kossovo, Tsiplevets near Prilep in Pelagonia, Kamnik in Ersekë (L. N.), Olynthus on the coast of Chalcidice (L. N.), Servia on the Haliacmon (L. N.), Tsangli in western Thessaly (L. N.), Elatea in Phocis (M. N.), Chaeronea by Lake Copaïs (M. N.) and Corinth (M. N.).[64] It has been conjectured that these vessels represented the female element in a fertility cult and that clay phalli, sometimes painted red, represented the male element. Such phalli have been found at Malik, Servia, Tsangli and Elatea within our area.[65] It seems to have been tacitly assumed that the cult was concerned with human fertility, but the fact that the vessels are always four-legged suggests rather that the cult was concerned with the insemination and conception of quadruped animals, on which the livelihood of the human society depended.

A feature of one four-legged vessel from Cakran is a prune-shaped plastic protuberance, and such protuberances were a feature also of the pottery at Dunavec.[66] Heavy grooving on sherds from Dunavec was also illustrated. Both the protuberance and the heavy grooving were characteristic of pottery at Kakanj.[67]

When we endeavour to date the deposit at Cakran, the relationships of the categories of pottery are important. Category (1) may belong to any of the Neolithic periods, appearing for instance in similar idioms in the L. N. settlement of Porodin.[68] Categories (2) to (5), being the grey-to-black burnished wares, first appeared in Greece near the end of the M. N. period and continued into L. N.[69] Close analogies for (2) are provided at Elatea (M. N.);[70] for (3) at Porodin (L. N.), Servia (L. N.) and at Elatea (M. N.);[71] for (4) at Servia (L. N.);[72] and for (5) at Velcë (L. N.), just on the other side of the Aous valley from Cakran.[73] My conclusion is that the settlement at Cakran began at the earliest towards the end of the Middle Neolithic period and ended in the latter part of the Greek Late Neolithic period when Velcë was starting. Here I am at variance with the excavators, who have dated the deposit to the *early* part of the Middle Neolithic period and have claimed that the four-legged vessels of Cakran and Dunavec antedated the similar ones of the Danilo-Kakanj cultures. They recognised "la ressemblance totale" of category (4) sherds with those of Servia IIa, which Heurtley dated to the start of the Macedonian Late Neolithic period, but they think they are nearer to the truth in making this pottery "remonter au néolithique moyen" and the early part of Middle Neolithic at that.[74]

If we are correct in our dating, it seems that the Starčevo group, represented by category (1), came originally from the north into the lakeland area and that it was engaged in transhumant pastoralism and to a lesser extent in agriculture.[75] The second element, represented by categories (2) to (4), which are much finer wares, was ultimately of eastern derivation. This element appeared towards the end of the Middle Neolithic period in southern Thrace, the eastern side of the Middle Vardar valley, parts of Thessaly,[76] Phocis and Corinth—and it continued with a widening distribution in the Late Neolithic period. It probably reached the lakeland and so Cakran via the bend of the upper Vardar, Polog and Kitsevo; for as we have noted already, the bearers of the grey-to-black burnished wares failed to break their way northwards into Kossovo. It seems that in the lakeland the two elements combined in the practice of transhumant pastoralism, presumably under the leadership of the second element, and it was through this way of life that the cult vessel with four legs for the propagation of the flocks spread to Tsangli, Elatea, Chaeronea and Corinth as winter stations.[77] The use of 'encrusted' or, as it is sometimes called, 'fugitive' white paint on these vessels should also be noted as an indication of influence from the north at a very early date. Lastly we have to notice the developments at Servia. The Middle Neolithic period ended with the destruction of the fifth settlement by fire, and the sixth settlement known as Servia IIa followed immediately upon it.[78] Four new kinds of pottery appeared in the sixth settlement, and three of these were there at the start. As Heurtley put it, "the first of these [viz. the two phases of pottery in the Late Neolithic period in Macedonia] is represented only at Servia, and is characterised by stroke-incision, black-polished ware and its varieties, grey-on-grey, and by an absence of bases and of handles." Encrusted paint was in use also.[79] A simple painted style developed later at Servia. It was from Servia that these four kinds of pottery spread into other parts of Macedonia. Heurtley stated with confidence that these events and these innovations at Servia were due to invaders who came from the north (he thought probably from the Middle Danube ultimately),[80] who brought new ideas into this part of the Haliacmon valley. Recent discoveries, and especially those at Cakran and Dunavec and in the Bregalnitsa valley, have enabled us to place the invasion and destruction of Servia within a wider setting. But Servia still remains a particularly important site because it occupies such a strategic position, not only in the seasonal migrations of pastoralists, but also on the main route of invasion for peoples of the north who seek entry into the eastern part of the Greek peninsula.

When we review the assembled evidence for the

last phase of the Middle Neolithic period, we can see the broad outlines of a very large movement of peoples who brought with them the grey-to-black burnished wares. As between district and district the chronology of their movements may be blurred and indistinct,[81] but the general direction of their movements westwards and southwards is not in doubt. An outline of these movements is suggested on Map 19. Two types of movement may be distinguished. The first consisted of people who settled as agriculturalists, whether in the Bregalnitsa valley or in the Thessalian plain near the coast; and the second consisted of pastoralists who infiltrated pastoralist communities of Starčevo culture and led some of them gradually southwards into the eastern part of central Greece in search of winter pastures. The analogy between the first type of movement and the Turkish invasion of the Balkans is very close in its geographical pattern, if we compare Map 19 and Map 15. The second type of movement finds a close analogy with the combination of Vlachs and Albanians which in the fourteenth century A.D. gained access to Thessaly and to Boeotia-Euboea-Attica and the Isthmus of Corinth, if we compare Map 19 and Map 13.[82]

Summary of Developments

During the long period which we have been considering, man's struggle was with his physical environment rather than with his fellow man. He evolved different ways of obtaining a subsistence. One was the hunting or the raising of ruminant animals in those parts of the southwest Balkans which provided the best conditions for the animals. In the Palaeolithic period these parts were principally Greek Epirus—Pindus range—western Thessaly (when Epirus included Corcyra, and Thessaly included what are now the Northern Sporades); secondarily some areas west of the Adriatic-Aegean watershed and some areas in the western Peloponnese; and lastly a few isolated places in Boeotia and Argolis. In the Early and Middle Neolithic periods the pattern was somewhat different. Central Albania, the lakeland, Grammus and Pindus, the Haliacmon valley down to Servia, Perrhaebia and western Thessaly were mainly the preserves of nomadic pastoralists, although some semi-permanent and permanent settlements with agricultural production were established within the area, e.g. at Cakran, Dunavec, Servia, Prodromos and Magoulitsa. Nomadic pastoralism was practised also farther north, probably in the Zeta valley and the Peć basin for instance, and farther south in southern Pindus, Parnassus, Cithaeron and Gerania with offshoot settlements in the Cephissus valley and winter encampments as far south as Corinth.

There is an interesting difference between the Palaeolithic pattern and the Neolithic pattern: the areas of western Greece from Greek Epirus to Elis, which had been the chief hunting grounds of Palaeolithic man, were used either very little or not at all by men of the Early and Middle Neolithic periods. One reason may have been that the western areas were more heavily forested and harboured more wild animals, especially wolves, which were dangerous to domesticated ruminant animals, than the eastern areas of Greece. Changes in climatic conditions may have played a part, too. But the chief reason was that men who practised this way of life were still thin on the ground, and they were under no pressure to go outside the most suitable areas.

The other chief way of obtaining one's subsistence was a combination of agriculture and stock-raising with the emphasis on cattle and pigs rather than on sheep and goats. The best areas for this purpose were ancient lacustrine basins where soil was peaty and water was abundant: for instance, the Ovče Polje basin by the Bregalnitsa; the plain by the upper Cerna Reka (anc. Erigon) in Pelagonia; the lakeland plain near Malik; the coastal plain by Nea Nikomedeia; the rich Thessalian plain, especially by Lake Boebe; and the equally fertile plain by Lake Copaïs. There were also suitable areas in eastern Attica, Corinth, Argolis and Laconia. As agriculturalist communities were relatively thinly spread, they were under no particular pressure to go outside the best areas, and in consequence little attempt was made to develop lands of a similar character on the western side of the peninsula.

The areas which we have enumerated were at varying altitudes and at varying distances from the sea. In consequence they attracted different types of people. The lakeland, being over 800 m high and very far from the sea, appealed to an inland people from similar sub-alpine regions; Pelagonia and Ovče Polje were attractive to inland peoples of the Danubian region, and the latter (being lower and nearer the sea) also to people from Anatolia; and the rich coastal plains seemed good to people conversant with the sea or accustomed to living not far from the sea. Because of these different appeals few areas became centres of competition: Ovče Polje and Thessaly were perhaps the only ones.

When population was so sparse and land so plentiful, these two ways of life could coexist peacefully, as they seem to have done during most of the Early Neolithic period in Thessaly. Indeed they were mutually beneficial in that animal-products could be exchanged for cereals and fruits.[83] The areas of overlapping interest were very few: they might arise at Nea Nikomedeia and Servia, and in the western Thessalian plain, the Cephissus valley and the Lake Copaïs region—that was in areas where winter pasturing might compete with agricultural development or where a migrant route and a trade route passed through a single strategic point. Evidence of the destruction of a settlement by fire, probably through human agency, has been found mainly in these very areas.

Men may have crossed the Adriatic Sea late in the Upper Palaeolithic period, and seafaring in the Aegean basin was practised throughout the Neolithic period, as we know from the distribution of obsidian. When much of the mainland was uninhabited by man and the forests and the swamps harboured dangerous animals, it was less arduous and usually safer to proceed, say, from Nea Makri in Attica to Astakos in Acarnania, for instance, by sea than by land. Trade certainly existed in a simple form. But it was limited by the lack of the domesticated horse and of the freight-carrier, however rudimentary. Yet by the end of the Middle Neolithic period the foundations for man's progress had been well laid in the southwest Balkans, and there was plenty of virgin land available for any increase of population.

NOTES

1. The numbers were of course tiny by our standards; a settlement such as that at the Kastritsa cave might have numbered only twenty-five persons. For general accounts see CAH^3 I, i (1970) pp. 557 f. and ITEE 1, pp. 32 f.

2. M. Hasluck, *The Unwritten Law in Albania*, p. 6.

3. See *Epirus*, p. 17, n. 3 for rainfall figures. Pasture for many ruminants includes the leaves of the oak trees and oak scrub which cover many parts of Albania and Epirus and the entire district of Khasia in northwestern Thessaly.

4. These were of course wild; the first animal to be domesticated was the sheep but probably not before 10,000 B.C., so CAH^3 I, i, p. 249.

5. For chamois see *Epirus*, pp. 98, 130, 214, 289; extant also above the head of the Bay of Valona.

6. Reports on Corcyra in *Kerkyraika Khronika* 11 (1966) 141 f.; 14 (1968) 77 f.; and 15 (1969) 124 f.; and *Balkan Studies* 10 (1969) 393 f., all by A. Sordinas, to whom I am most grateful for sending me offprints.

7. For references see *Epirus*, p. 289.

8. For description of these areas see *Epirus*, p. 80. The individual sites are listed and described by S. I. Dakaris, *Cassopaia and the Elean Colonies* (1971), pp. 21 f. and *Thesprotia* (Athens 1972), pp. 44 f.

9. The Lake of Ioannina was higher then than today. Lakes now draining into the sea were larger then, being landlocked (e.g. Lake Vivari by Butrinto and the Acherusian Lake), and others were very large (e.g. the basin now containing the Gulf of Arta). As a much greater area of snow was melted each year, the lakes were no doubt larger on the average.

10. Vajzë is on the route from the Gulf of Valona across the Shushicë valley to the Aous valley, leading eventually to the pastures by Malik and Muskopole. Konitsa is on the way to Samarina and also to Briaza and Vovousa. Kastritsa and Perama are on the way to Greveniti and Vovousa, Metsovo and the Zygos. Lakkasouli is on the way from the Preveza district via Gourana (Trikastron) to Dodona and the Ioannina plain.

11. *AD* 23 (1968) 296.

12. For references see CAH^3 I, i, pp. 557 f. and 665 f.

13. In *Epirus*, p. 165 I commented on the "masses of unworked flints" at Sistrounion which I visited in 1933. Worked flints have been found nearby at Romano.

14. For references see CAH^3 I, i, pp. 559 f. and 667 f.

15. Ibid., pp. 561 f. Perhaps migrants from east to west, as in later times.

16. There were more dangerous animals in Macedonia; for the cave of Petralona had bones of lions, cave panthers and wolves among the thirty-four kinds of animal bones.

17. Ibid., pp. 562 f. and 669. For Crvena Stijena see *Glasnik zem. muz. Sarajevo Arh.* 13 (1958) 21 f. and the comments of V. Milojčić in *Germania* 38 (1960) 325.

18. In the words of S. I. Dakaris "the character of Epirus is such that some form of nomadic economy has always been necessary for the full exploitation of the natural resources" (*Cassopaia and the Elean Colonies*, p. 20, n. 71).

19. I am following S. S. Weinberg in *CAH*³ I, i, p. 570; but scholars vary in their dating by as much as a millennium for the mainland and by a millennium and a half for Crete (ibid., p. 616).

20. So V. Milojčić, *Otzaki-Magula* I (Bonn, 1971), p. 138.

21. Argissa had been a Palaeolithic and Mesolithic site, but a deep layer of silt—a legacy of the flooding of the plain—separated the Mesolithic level from that of the Preceramic Neolithic period. The Palaeolithic hunters had used javelins and the Mesolithic hunters bows and arrows, but the Preceramic Neolithic farmers had a much inferior weapon, the sling, as we can infer from the clay bullets which have survived. This suggests that there was an interval between the two cultures.

22. For the relationship see V. Milojčić in *Germania* 38 (1960) 332.

23. See A. Sordinas in *Kerkyraika Khronika* 11 (1966) 141 f. for Sidari, and *AR* 1973–74, 13 for the Franchthi Cave.

24. A possible exception is Sesklo, where Theochares has argued in favour of some continuity; see *Ergon* 1965, 5 f. and *Thessalika Meletemata* 1 (1967) 104 f. His argument is reviewed by V. Milojčić in *Otzaki-Magula* 1, 140 f. The Franchthi Cave may be a sixth such site.

25. *CAH*³ I, i, p. 575, and *AR* 1973–74, 33.

26. *AAA* 1971, 2, 167 (Prodromos); D. R. Theochares in *AM* 71 (1956) 10 f.

27. See *AR* 1973–74, 23 for a report on the current excavations by D. R. Theochares at Sesklo, and his remarks on village settlements in *ITEE* 1, p. 57.

28. *Ergon* 1973, 14 f. For Aspha<i>k</i>a see *PPS* 32 (1966) 22 f. and for Servia *AR* 1973–74, 26. At Sesklo pigs were about 20%, cattle 10%, and deer—the chief wild game—only 4%, hunted probably on Pelion and Ossa.

29. The full report on Nea Nikomedeia is not yet published, but see *CAH*³ I, i, pp. 577 f. and *Macedonia*, p. 219 with references. Clay figurines of sheep and goats were found. Pigs and cattle were of less importance, as at Sesklo.

30. They may well have used Servia as an intermediary station. I do not subscribe to the view of S. I. Dakaris in *Thesprotia* p. 48, para. 125, that the culture of Thessaly spread through the agency of nomad shepherds via Epirus into Corcyra and Leucas. As we are dealing with areas which were either unpopulated or very thinly populated, we should not seek to convert the nomad shepherds into seafarers but leave them, like the Vlachs, to continue with their own way of life.

31. See S. S. Weinberg in *CAH*³ I, i, pp. 572 f., 577 and 587.

32. M. Gimbutas, "Anza, ca. 6500–5000 B.C." *Journal of Field Archaeology* 1 (1974) 33; and *CAH*³ I, i, p. 295.

33. See now the interesting preliminary report on Anza I, which shows that the basin of the Bregalnitsa valley or Ovče Polje (see *Macedonia*, p. 9) was then heavily forested, sheep and goats were chief among the domesticated animals by far, and hunting except of the aurochs was on a very small scale (see table on p. 47). A wider range of cereals was grown there than in Pelagonia.

34. Represented by Milojčić's "buntpolierte Keramik" in *Otzaki-Magula*, p. 146.

35. Ibid., pp. 146 f. For Magoulitsa see *Thessalika* I (1958) 37 f.

36. *AAA* 1971, 2, 164 f.

37. V. Milojčić in *Jahrb. d. röm-german. Zentralmuseum* 6 (1959) 1 f.; *CAH*³ I, i, p. 586 "wares . . . which can be traced northward through Macedonia into Yugoslavia, whence they most likely came."

38. A. Sordinas, *Stone Implements from Northwestern Corfu, Greece* (Memphis, 1970), pp. 6 and 16 f.

39. A. Benac in *Glasnik zem. muz. Sarajevo Arh.* 12 (1957) 19 f.; *Germania* 38 (1960) 33 f.

40. *CAH*³ I, i, pp. 585 f. and 589; *Macedonia*, p. 219.

41. *AAA* 1971, 2, 164 f. See *AR* 1973–74, 26 for the use of branches, trunks and planks in houses at the Early Neolithic site by Servia.

42. Such long periods are in fact the norm; and not as surprising as e.g. A. M. Snodgrass supposed in his review of *Macedonia* (*JHS* 94 [1974] 230).

43. *Epirus*, p. 292 and figs. 7, 2 and 3, *PAE* 1951, 177.

44. See V. Milojčić, *Otzaki-Magula*, pp. 148-50 and 108 for the revival of the naturalistic figurine.

45. Ibid., p. 150 and *AAA* 1971, 2, 164 f.

46. Compare the inference made by S. S. Weinberg in *CAH*³ I, i, p. 593: "Together they suggest some reinforcement of the population of Thessaly by elements from Anatolia or northern Mesopotamia, or both, during the Samarra period, which is now dated in the latter part of the sixth millennium B.C. The megaron arrived later, but probably by the mid-fifth millennium it had been introduced into Greece from Anatolia."

47. Ibid., pp. 591 and 599 f.

48. *PM*, pp. 113 f.; the quotation is from *AAA* 5 (1972) 27, the report by C. Ridley and K. Rhomiopoulou on their current excavations at Servia (see also *AAA* 6, 423 f. for the houses there especially).

49. Gatherings of Vlachs at Tirnavos on the Titaresius and at Elassona in central Perrhaebia were described by Wace and Thompson, pp. 11 f., 142 and 174; at that time the Vlachs of Perrhaebia moved their flocks to summer pas-

tures mainly round Samarina in northern Pindus. It is interesting that Heurtley noted in *PM*, p. 64 that the closest links of the Servia pottery with Thessalian pottery were at Tsangli and at settlements near Larissa. This would accord with the practice of transhumance very well.

50. *Thessalika* 1 (1958) 3-15 with figs. 5 and 6; *Hesp.* 31 (1962) 158 f.; 6 (1937) 487 f.

51. See S. S. Weinberg in *CAH*³ I, i, pp. 597 f.

52. D. Srejovic, in *AI* 4 (1963) 7 f.

53. So M. Garašanin in *Glasnik zem. muz. Sarajevo Arh.* 9 (1954) 5 f.

54. For the *spondylus* see M. Gimbutas' report on the excavations at Anza in *Journal of Field Archaeology* 1 (1974) 60. I am very grateful to Dr Barbara Wittman for sending me an offprint of this article. For Olynthus see the comments of Heurtley in *PM*, p. 109 at a time when he did not know of the discoveries in the Bregalnitsa valley.

55. In *AI* 4 (1963) 7, citing the words of B. Jovanović: "die kleinasiatische Welle wäre demnach im Sinne einer Stufenmässigen Wanderung zu werten, die den grössten Teil des Balkans eingenommen hätte."

56. The report is in *Glasnik zem. muz. Sarajevo Arh.* 12 (1957) 46 f.

57. For Dunavec see *Buletin Arkeologjik* (Tirana) 1971, 5-21. When I was in Albania in 1972, some of the material from Dunavec and Cakran was exhibited in the Museum of Tirana, and I was able to see other material in the local museums of Poyan (Apollonia), Pogradec and Korcë, which included some large celts of greenstone, almost round in section and shaped like a truncated canine tooth.

58. Two details—the pasturing by day and the fear of wolves—show that the story is of the winter period; for in summer any sheep near Apollonia pasture by night and the wolves do not descend to the lowlands.

59. So *Bulletin d'archéologie sud-est européenne* (Bucarest) 2 (1971) 12. The first reports by M. Korkuti and Zh. Andrea were in *Buletin Arkeologjik* (Tirana) 1969, 14-26 and *Iliria* I (1971) 343 f., and the full report in *SA* 1972, 1, 15-30 with 12 plates. I am most grateful to Frano Prendi and other friends in Albania for sending me copies of these periodicals.

60. A shepherd near Spilio on Mt Kissavos (Ossa) with whom I spent some weeks in early 1943, slept alongside his pen (*stani*) in order to be woken up by the alarm of the sheep if wolves were in the vicinity. On such occasions he uttered terrific shouts, which (he claimed) frightened the wolves away. A cul-de-sac or narrow coombe is still much used for winter pens, and if the pen was underground it would be sheltered from the piercing 'bora' or north wind.

61. *SA* 1972, 1, 22-25, giving six categories, but I have combined "la ceramique à impression" with "la ceramique grossière barbotine" for the purpose of the present study (these two being shown on plate V, the coarse ware on V, 16-17). The term 'stamp-decorated' has been used by C. Ridley and K. Rhomiopoulou for similar pottery at Servia (*AAA* 6 [1973] 423).

62. *SA* 1972, 1, 28 "ces trois catégories de ceramique se sont mélangées et se retrouvent indistinctement, soit au fond, soit au commencement de la couche de civilisation dans tous les points fouillés . . . . On est donc en présence d'une agglomération néolithique d'une seule couche."

63. Described in *Bulletin d'archéologie sud-est européenne* 2 (1971) 13 with fig. 1; *SA* 1972, 1, 25-27 with plates 10 and 11; and *Buletin Arkeologjik* 1971, 14.

64. See S. S. Weinberg in *CAH*³ I, i, pp. 598 f. with bibliography and *SA* 1972, 1, 26 with bibliography. The specimen from Tsiplevets is in the Museum of Monastir, where I saw it in 1968; it is unpublished. For Kamnik see *SA* 1972, 1, 9 with plate VIII, 1 and 6; Olynthus *PM*, p. 162 no. 160; Servia, *PM*, p. 140 fig. 9 i; Tsangli *PTh*, fig. 56 a; Elatea *PTh*, fig. 142 f. and *Hesp.* 31, 190 f.; Chaeronea *PTh*, p. 199 and *AM* 30, 123, fig. 2 c and p. 137, fig. 9. See also *Macedonia* pp. 231-32 and 244 with n. 3.

65. References are given in *Macedonia*, p. 244 n. 3 fin. They occur both with and without testicles. See *SA* 1966, 1, plate X b; *PTh*, p. 123 with fig. 76 j; *Hesp.* 31, 202 with pl. 68, 2. E. Vermeule comments on these cult vessels in *Greece in the Bronze Age* (Chicago, 1964), p. 21.

66. *Buletin Arkeologjik* 1971, 20-21, pls. 2, 3.

67. A. Benac, *Studije o kamenon i bakarnom dobu u sjeverozapadnom balkanu* (Sarajevo, 1964), pl. 10, 2 and 3.

68. Compare *SA* 1972, 1, pl. V with Grbić, *Porodin* (Bitolj, 1960), pl. XV, 1-4 and pl. XXXV. M. Korkuti and Zh. Andrea make comparisons with Smilčić in Dalmatia near Split, but Porodin is much nearer.

69. S. S. Weinberg in *CAH*³ I, i, pp. 597 f.: "Their arrival in Greece probably occurred only shortly before the end of the Middle Neolithic Period."

70. *SA* 1972, 1, pl. VI and *Hesp.* 31, pl. 62 d and 186 f.

71. *SA* 1972, 1, pl. VII, 1, 2, 4-5 and *Porodin* pl. XXII, 1, 2, 6, 8; *SA* pl. VII, 3 and *Porodin*, pl. XXIII, 2; *SA*, pl. VII, 10-11 and *Porodin* pl. XVI, 2; pl. XXXV, 4 and pl. XXXVI, 2. At Servia *SA* 1972, 1, pl. VII, 15 and *PM*, fig. 11 j, pl. VII, 14 and 11 b; Pl. VII, 16 and 11 l; Heurtley's "rippled and grooved ware" is called "gerillte" in Ovče Polje by Sjerovic and "kanelyrat" at Dunavec by Korkuti (*Buletin Arkeologjik* 1971, 12 with pl. II, 1-2). At Elatea *SA* 1972, 1, pl. VII, 14-16 and *Hesp.* 31, 189 f.

72. *SA* 1972, 1, pl. VIII and *PM*, p. 66 with figs. 8 and 9; the similarity has been noted in *AAA* 1973, 423.

73. *SA* 1972, 1, pl. IX and *Epirus*, p. 291 with fig. 6 (Velcë 2a in Mustilli's categories of pottery) and p. 293 with fig. 9 showing similar ware from Astakos (H. Nikolaos) in Acarnania.

74. In this case as in others it is not possible, at least if one is attempting a historical interpretation, to accept the views of "seasoned excavators," as A. M. Snodgrass wishes in *JHS* 94 (1974) 230 (reviewing *Macedonia*), when they give dates around a thousand years apart for the same classes of pottery in areas not far from one another but in different national territories. As the pottery at Servia is securely tied

into Aegean chronology through its affinities with wares in Thessaly and as the stratification is more firm, I have no hesitation in preferring the date given by Heurtley.

75. Stone artefacts at Cakran include some milling-querns (*Bulletin d'archéologie sud-est européenne* 2 [1971] 12).

76. *Thessalika* 1 (1958) 3 f. at Kouphovouno by Iolcus at the end of the period 'Thessaly A'; with figs. 5 and 6.

77. Usually these vessels were made of black burnished ware, but their distribution is very much more limited than that of this ware.

78. *PM*, pp. 52 f.

79. *PM*, pp. 77 and 114.

80. *PM*, pp. 113 f. and 128. At that time it was believed that the black burnished ware was of Danubian origin; but recent opinion has favoured an Anatolian origin (*CAH*³ I, i, p. 599).

81. This is partly because the establishment of local regional chronologies has inevitably taken place piecemeal as a result of increasing discoveries. Thus there is a Middle Neolithic period of the west Balkans, another of the central Balkans, another (emerging) of Albania, another of Macedonia, and another of the Greek peninsula. Correlation is difficult and, in the early stages, sometimes it may appear to have been arbitrary. Thus Heurtley divided Middle Neolithic from Late Neolithic by the destruction layer of the fifth settlement at Servia, but a preliminary report by his successors at the site of "MN structures . . . which post-date the destruction" indicates a different point of division, presumably by closer correlation with the chronology of the Greek peninsula (*Arch. Reports* 1973–74, 26).

82. The Turkish invaders were mainly of pastoralist origins and habits, and the Yuruks in particular continued to be pastoralists in Macedonia.

83. This has always been so, indeed even in the last war, when both the resistance forces in the mountains and the occupying power in the lowlands were happy to protect and encourage the transhumant pastoralists for their own food supply.

V

Trade, Power and Conquests

The Late Neolithic Period

The movements which were initiated towards the end of the Middle Neolithic period affected the Greek peninsula during the Late Neolithic period. Then the continued and widespread use of the grey-to-black wares showed that the people who introduced these wares and their descendants formed an important element in the mixed populations which held the eastern side of Greece. The distinguishing marks of the new period were a quickening and an expansion of trade and an enrichment of culture which flourished under settled conditions in the peninsula and benefited from wider contacts abroad. As populations increased, new settlements were founded. They were particularly numerous in Euboea, the forecourt of the island world; and some islands of the Aegean were occupied now for the first time. On the other hand there was practically no development on the western side of the Peloponnese and central Greece. The country set its face towards the east (see Map 20).

With the growth of seafaring in the Aegean the influences of the Near East, emanating particularly from Cilicia and Syria, made themselves visible in the polychrome and matt-painted potteries which developed alongside the grey-to-black wares in eastern Greece. There was no indication of any population moving from the Near East to Greek lands. Rather, as in the 'orientalising' period of Classical Greece, the peoples of the Greek mainland were absorbing the more sophisticated ideas of the Near East as they increased in prosperity. The pattern of settlements south of Thessaly in the Late Neolithic period showed large concentrations by the Isthmus of Corinth and in the plain of the Argolic Gulf, both well placed for sailing into the Aegean basin. Trade began to grow also in the western seas. Ships did not circumnavigate the Peloponnese at that time, but they set out from Corinth and used the harbours of the Ionian islands. As trade developed, polychrome and matt-painted wares appeared at Astakos (H. Nikolaos) in Acarnania, at the island Meganisi in the Leucas Channel and at Choirospilia ('Pig-cave') on Leucas. In the latter part of the period we shall see evidence of trade proceeding via Corcyra to the Bay of Valona and the heel of Italy.

For a long time Thessaly shared in the general trends of the period. Then a clear-cut line of division arose between eastern Thessaly and the regions to the west and south. Thereafter eastern Thessaly belonged rather with the north and developed its own orbit of trade there both by land and by sea, exploiting its fine harbours in the Gulf of Pagasae. The change came about with the rise of the remarkable culture called the 'Dimini culture' after Dimini, a village near the head of the Gulf of Pagasae. A settlement on a low hill there was found to be defended by five concentric circles of stone walls with passages and open yards, and the central yard of all contained the only buildings, namely a house of the 'megaron' type, some 11 by 6 m, and some smaller structures. A similar set-up was found to exist at Sesklo, where the megaron was some 20 by 8 m; and a larger megaron, almost 30 m long, has been excavated recently near Velestino, some ten miles northwest of Dimini. These fortified citadels and megara were not fortified towns

Map 20

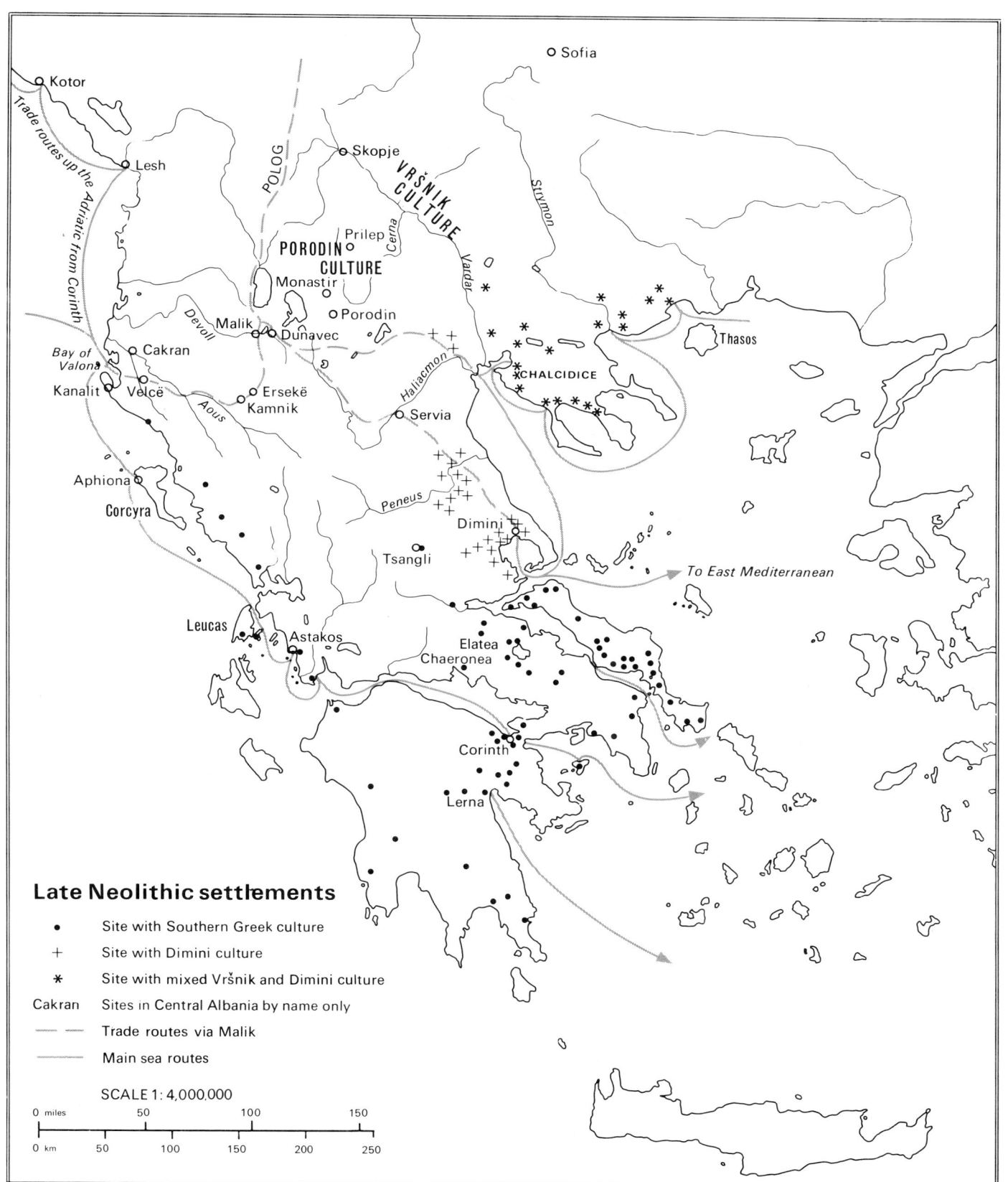

but capitals and palaces of the ruling dynasts of the district. They may seem small to us; but when compared with the small open villages and the wattle-and-daub huts of the rest of Greece they were centres of affluence and power. The wealth of the dynasts was not due to any exploitation of regions to the west; for western Thessaly stayed aloof from the 'Dimini culture' and Epirus was still almost uninhabited. Rather it grew from the profits of a trade which reached overland northwards through Servia in the Haliacmon valley into the lakeland area, as we shall see later, and by sea into the Thermaic Gulf and the Aegean. Thus at this time, after 2800 B.C. or so, the Gulf of Pagasae became a richer centre of exchange than the Isthmus of Corinth. The dynasts were a new type of man, unparalleled then and earlier in southern Greece. It seems that they had come not from the south but from the north, probably via Servia where an unusually vigorous population had established itself at the end of the Middle Neolithic period. The dynasts were quick to develop and exploit the intercultural trade which began to pass through their domains.[1]

In southern Epirus the situation was very different. A small amount of coarse pottery has been found in caves at Filiates near the Kalamas and at Nounesation in the Cocytus valley, and on an open site at Louro near Preveza, which seems to have been of this period; and flint tools of neolithic types have been found at a number of open sites in the coastal plains, particularly between Paramythia and Preveza.[2] These objects belonged no doubt to small groups of transhumant pastoralists who brought their herds down to the caves and the plains for the winter. For the district is precisely that used by the Sarakatsani of modern times (see Map 10). We may assume that the shepherds of the Neolithic period, like the Sarakatsani today, went to the pastures of Zagori and to the western side of Pindus for the summer months. As the coarse pottery in these caves resembled that made in southern Greece, it is evident that these shepherds had southern affiliations with shepherd communities of Acarnania and Aetolia and had no connection with the shepherds farther north, for instance at Cakran.

In southern Albania similar groups of transhumant shepherds used caves by the river Pavla (south of Delvino) and at Spilë below Himarrë. The former cave yielded bones of sheep, pig and birds, and the latter of sheep, pig, goat, and cattle. The sheep and the goats were probably domesticated, and the rest were hunted. Farther north at the head of the Bay of Valona a rock-shelter at Kanalit contained traces of hearths, sherds of pottery and bones of domesticated animals, and many artefacts of a neolithic type were found on open sites. The Italian Mission which made the discoveries described the coarse pottery as hand-polished, sometimes yellowish in colour and sometimes with a slip of clay, and dated the objects to Neolithic and Sub-Neolithic.[3] Nothing more precise has been reported.

In contrast a wide variety of tools and six classes of pottery were found farther inland at Velcë by the same Italian Mission. The painted pottery was closely related to the pottery at Astakos which was of southern Greek style, and some of the coarse ware likewise;[4] but other forms of coarse ware, e.g. with incised spiralling grooves and with punched holes in parallel lines, were connected rather with the northern styles of Cakran and Servia.[5] Thus Velcë was an intercultural site, mediating between the coastal traffic and the peoples of the interior. It lay some twenty miles inland on the route from the Bay of Valona to the Aous valley, which gave access to the interior. It had its own assets too; for it lay close to the open-cast asphalt mines of Selenicë, the asphalt being a material of great value for caulking boats and for other uses. The settlement of Velcë had an unusually rich armament of weapons (including arrow-heads) and tools of flint. These may have been made for export to flintless areas.[6]

On the route inland from Velcë to the lakeland area, a site has recently been excavated at Kamnik near Ersekë in the district of Kolonjë; it stands at a height of about 1200 m above sea level, on the side of Mt Grammus (see Map 4). The finds there were various flint tools and weapons (including arrow-heads), sling-bullets, hoes, querns and spindle-weights; several classes of pottery, mostly painted; and hearths and pottery-kilns, e.g. a circular one two metres in diameter. Kamnik had close links with Velcë, some of the pottery at the two sites being indistinguishable. Kamnik was unique in some respects, e.g. in coating some pottery with bitumen (presumably from Selenicë); and it had close links in other respects with Malik I, to which we shall turn shortly.[7] The community at Kamnik practised agriculture and stock-raising, and derived its wool and milk-products from transhumant pastoralism, sending the sheep down to the plain of the river Pavla, for instance, as the Vlachs of Kolonjë did in the 1930s.[8] As the people of Kamnik were engaged in trade on the trans-Balkan route, they imported some pottery, which included pieces of Dimini ware. In consequence, the founding of the settlement can be dated to some time within the Dimini 'classic' phase, i.e. within 2800 to 2700 B.C.[9]

Malik stands some 850 m above sea level. It is on the edge of the lakeland plain at a strategic point, where the Devoll leaves the plain and enters the wild countryside of Gramsh.[10] The first settlement was of moderate size and had only two levels of habitation. Its pottery had close links with that of the Dimini culture from the start. There was also an indication of influence from the north in the presence of 'crusted' ware in which red and/or white paste had been applied after the firing of the vessel and was apt therefore to flake off; for crusted ware was not found in Thessaly in the 'classic' Dimini period.[11] We have noted examples at Cakran and Dunavec, both sites being earlier than Malik, and it was found a little later at Kamnik.[12] The connection of Malik with Thessaly was maintained evidently along the natural route via Bilisht into the upper Haliacmon valley and thence via Servia and Perrhaebia into the Peneus valley (see Map 5). The connection of Malik with the north ran most easily through the lakeland to Kitsevo and thence through Polog to Kossovo, a route used as late as A.D. 1800 for pack-animals carrying goods from western Macedonia to Hungary.[13] For these routes see Map 2.

In the first layer at Malik there were the remains of a two-roomed rectangular house, with a hearth in each room; the walls were of wattle and daub, the floors were of beaten or baked earth, and the building stood on a platform of oak beams. Such a house was built for permanent occupation and not for summer use only. The beginning of Malik I was dated by F. Prendi, on the evidence of imported Dimini-type pottery, to the end of the Dimini 'classic' phase, i.e. "aux environs des années 2700." This was approximately when Servia IIb began. Malik and Kamnik were founded at about the same time, but Malik I ended with its second level of habitation. Kamnik had five levels of habitation and may therefore have lasted until 2600 or even later.[14] It was Prendi's opinion that the culture of Kamnik was to a very great extent concomitant and then continuing with that of Malik I. What then was the relationship of the Malik-Kamnik culture to its neighbours? The adjacent site at Dunavec may have ended before or been displaced by Malik I, if I am correct in dating the Cakran-Dunavec complex within the bracket of the end of Middle Neolithic and the early part of Late Neolithic, so that it was in part at least contemporary with Servia IIa but not with Servia IIb. The settlers of Malik I were not, as the settlers of Dunavec had been, engaged in transhumant pastoralism, although they may have practised or encouraged it as a subsidiary source of food supply (as we have supposed the inhabitants of Kamnik did). Rather they were agriculturalists, stockbreeders and traders. They had very much in common with Servia, but their houses were differently constructed, and they chose to live at a much higher altitude and in a colder climate. Moreover, when they left Malik, they went to an even higher site at Kamnik. Their relations with Thessaly were clearly those of trade. It is certain that the settlers of Malik and Kamnik did not come from northeastern Thessaly, where the coastal plain enjoys a mild winter; for men acclimatised to eastern Thessaly since the beginning of the Dimini phase would never have chosen to live so far inland at altitudes of 850 and 1200 m in the midst of snowbound mountains.

If we think in geographical terms, it is likely that the settlers of Malik I were accustomed to some high terrain of similar character and came into the lakeland by moving through terrains of the same kind, i.e. from the north via Kossovo, and perhaps ultimately from Bosnia, like their predecessors the founders of Dunavec and Cakran. There is indeed some evidence that this was so. We have already mentioned crusted ware as common to Cakran, Dunavec, Malik, Kamnik and Servia, and it is generally agreed that this form of paint was brought from the Danubian region. Dunavec, Cakran, Kamnik and Servia had the four-legged cult vessels which seem to have originated in Bosnia (at Danilo and Kakanj). Cakran, Kamnik, Servia IIb and Velcë had pottery incised with continuous spiralling grooves, a technique which has been held to be of northern origin; and it occurred in paint on pottery of Malik I and Kamnik. Clay hearths at Malik I were decorated with deep spiralling designs, perhaps for some religious cult.[15] These features lead me to suppose that the wedge of country beginning with the lakeland and widening southwards to include the middle Haliacmon valley on the east and the slopes of Grammus and Velcë on the west was being peopled by migrants mainly from Bosnia who came in successive waves from the end of the Middle Neolithic period until c. 2700 B.C.

After the abandonment of Malik I an interval of time elapsed, and then a much larger settlement of a different kind was planted on the site, Malik IIa1. Rectangular houses of reed-and-daub walls were set on a wooden platform of beams, itself supported on great numbers of stakes, mostly of oak, deeply embedded in the muddy clay of the outflow from the lake, which formed the waters of the Devoll. The stakes of these pile-dwellings had been sharpened with flat celts of copper, fixed to a wooden haft like an adze, and the village was surrounded with a double palisade of sharpened stakes. Copper fish-hooks were found, and this lake and others were no doubt as rich in fish then as they were in Hellenistic times. Pile-settlements have been reported at other lakes in the area—Ochrid, Prespa, Rudnik and Kastoria—but only that at Kastoria has been investigated. There Keramopoullos counted 500 cedar stakes planted in clay to serve as piles, grey and red obsidian blades, a nucleus of black obsidian, and signs that a metal blade had been used to work a piece of hardstone. He thought the settlement to be of neolithic date but was surprised to see signs of a metal tool.[16] The discoveries at Malik make it very probable that all these settlements were contemporary with Malik IIa1 and the presence of a nucleus of obsidian supports the belief that trade was passing up the Haliacmon valley via Kastoria to Malik, the only pieces of obsidian in the Late Neolithic period recorded in Heurtley's *Prehistoric Macedonia* being from Servia.[17]

Malik IIa1 was destroyed by fire; so too was the pile-settlement at Kastoria. The next settlement rose at once on the debris of Malik IIa1. It was not on piles, and copper seems to have become rather scarce. It is perhaps more likely that the destruction of Malik IIa1 was due to an invasion than that it was due to an accident, as Prendi supposed; but in any case there was a continuity of culture between Malik IIa1 and Malik IIa2. If there were invaders, they came from the same background. What was that background? Pile-settlements of the Neolithic Age have been found in the Mondsee in Austria, with flat celts and fish-hooks of copper, which was smelted in that region, and at Ljubljana (formerly Laibach) near the head of the Adriatic Sea, with flat celts of copper.

Moreover, copper was being mined in Metohija in the Eneolithic period, to which Prendi attributed Malik II in terms of Balkan chronology.[18] The evidence then is fairly strong for supposing that the settlers of Malik IIa (both 1 and 2 if due to different people) came from northwest Yugoslavia via Bosnia and Metohija to the lakeland area. The supply of copper declined later, perhaps through worsening relations with the people of the Metohija basin.

Malik IIa2 had extraordinarily wide contacts. Objects found there were either imported from or copied from the following areas: northeastern Thessaly, Servia, Porodin in Pelagonia, Butmir and Kakanj in Bosnia, Lengyel in Hungary, the Lipari islands, Dikili Tash near Drama in Greek Thrace, Karanovo in central Thrace, Krivodol in Bulgaria, and Salcuta in west Rumania. Pottery of Malik II types and a flat celt of copper were found also at Kamnik in the uppermost layer. There is only one explanation for this, that Malik stood at the crossroads of trans-Balkan trade between the countries of the northwestern Aegean area and the Danube basin. Routes from the Pagasaean Gulf via Servia and Kastoria and from the Thermaic Gulf via Verria or Edessa met in the lakeland at Malik. From there traffic went either overland via Polog to Peć and Priština and so to the Danube valley, or overland via Kamnik and Velcë to the Gulf of Valona and by sea to the head of the Adriatic and central Europe. As we have already mentioned, the overland route from western Macedonia via Kitsevo and Polog was used by Vlach traders with pack-animals for traffic with central Europe as late as the turn of the nineteenth century. The traffic by sea in the Dimini period has been demonstrated by the excavation of the cave of Grabak on the island of Hvar off the Dalmatian coast. Together with objects which derived directly or indirectly from the coasts of the Mediterranean, Ionian and Etruscan seas, there was painted pottery from Chalcidice and Macedonia. As this pottery is unlikely to have been carried round the Peloponnese and in any case has left no traces there, we may conclude that it and many other goods reached Hvar via Malik, passing through the lakeland area.[19] For these routes see Maps 1 and 4.

Within its own area the contacts of Malik IIa2 were strongest with Servia IIb both in pottery and in pintaderas (clay stamps), phalli, figurines and stone celts, so much so that we may conclude that the settlers were of the same stock. There were offshoots of this group at Nea Nikomedeia in the coastal plain where the old mound was reoccupied and defended with a ditch and a new site was also developed. Crusted ware was in use there. It has been found also at Kapoutzedhes near Salonica and at Kritsana in Chalcidice, whither it came probably through trade.[20] If transhumance was practised on a large scale when Malik IIa2 was so prosperous, then its winter pastures were obtained mainly in the coastal plain by Nea Nikomedeia.

The events which we have been describing had little effect on Pelagonia. There the very long Starčevo tradition came to flower in the remarkable Porodin culture at the beginning of the Late Neolithic period.[21] There were many settlements in the form of closely-built villages of some thirty houses with two or more rooms, all situated on low rises in the marshy plain by the river Cerna and its tributaries. The rooms had hearths, and the floors of clay rested on wooden beams. The people grew wheat and other cereals, wove cloth, raised sheep, horses, pigs and cattle, and made figurines of these animals and also of birds, bears and lynxes, the last giving their name to the area 'Lyncus' (Pl. 5a). There sheep pastured during the summer on the neighbouring mountains and in the winter in the lowlands of Macedonia or Thessaly.[22] Equipped with stone celts and arrow-heads, flint blades and clay sling-bullets, they defended their land successfully through the Late Neolithic period. Their tradition was carried on in the so-called Crnobuki culture, which was contemporary with the Rakhmani phase in Thessaly.

On the east side of the Vardar the mixed culture of Vršnik developed uninterruptedly during the Late Neolithic period and the transition from the earlier phases to that of the later phase (e.g. to that of Anza IV corresponding to the Dimini phase in Thessaly) was marked by modification rather than change.[23] Here, too, copper made its appearance for the first time. That the contacts of the sites in the Ovče Polje with the Aegean world increased is clear from the number of new sites on the eastern side of the lower Vardar, which were occupied for the first time in this period (see Map 20). These sites were strongly influenced by eastern Thessaly with which they were brought into close relationship by maritime trade; but they were primarily outlets of trade for Macedonia east of the Vardar and for parts of Thrace. Another strong influence was that of Karanovo III, in the plain of central Thrace.[24] At the end of the period a new type of pottery, the 'graphite painted wares', appeared in the area to the east of the lower Vardar (i.e. at Paradimi and Strumsko).

In this section we have rarely gone beyond the points of ingress into our area, but we must now turn back and give a brief picture of the semi-nomadic pastoral peoples of the Russian steppes during this part of the Late Neolithic and Eneolithic periods. Occupying the vast area from the eastern Ukraine to southern Siberia, they learned to domesticate and ride the horse, make flint arrows for bows, and work copper earlier than their contemporaries in the southwest Balkans. Stock-raising was their main pursuit, and fishing and agriculture were ancillary to it. They lived either in small open villages of lightly constructed, rectangular, semi-subterranean houses or on hill-sites fortified with massive stone walls and containing timber-built houses of a considerable size, e.g. with two or more rooms of large dimensions, laid on stone foundations. The occupants of the latter were evidently members of the ruling class. When important rulers died, they were buried with their precious possessions in graves which were covered by large tumuli of soil or stones. As the Russian word for tumulus is *kurgan*, the culture of these peoples has been called the Kurgan Culture by M. Gimbutas.[25]

The Kurgan peoples flowed into both Europe and Asia in a series of waves during a period of more than a thousand years. In the same way the peoples of the steppes flowed into Europe in the thousand years between the decline of the Roman Empire and the establishment of the Turkish Empire, as we have already seen. Each wave of Kurgan peoples set other peoples in motion and no doubt they often led other peoples on their raids and migrations, just as the Avars or the Bulgars led the Slavs. In the chronological system which I am using here, the movements of Kurgan peoples into central Europe and parts of the Balkans may be classed under the 'Middle Kurgan' expansion (Kurgan II and III), covering the third millennium down to c. 2200, and the 'Late Kurgan' expansion (Kurgan IV), covering the last part of the third millennium and the opening part of the second millennium.

We are concerned here with the Middle Kurgan period. During it Kurgan peoples entered the Balkans on a large scale and generally imposed their own authority on the existing populations.[26] There are three particular indications which show that some Kurgan peoples were in the lakeland and adjacent areas and in parts of Greece during the period of time we have covered in this section. The first is the subterranean and semi-subterranean dwellings which were found at the very start of the settlement at Cakran. They are unique at any time in our area, as far as I am aware, and they are typically Kurgan. The second indication is provided by some burials, which are remarkable in that they are almost the only ones known during this long period in our area, and that they were made *inside* the settlement, which was certainly contrary to the established custom of the settled population. In fact they reveal the presence of newcomers, and ruling newcomers at that, who were able to dictate the place of burial (see Map 21).

The first example is at Servia, where two men were buried well within the bounds of the settlement. Each inhumation was accompanied by some possessions. The earlier man held the leg of a black four-legged cult vessel with white-filled incisions in the crook of his arm; other objects buried with him included an obsidian blade, three vases (of which one contained a red substance "perhaps ochre"), five waisted pebble-axes, a small celt, and a piece of rectangular whetstone. With the later burial were a clay phallus, an obsidian blade, two small celts, two waisted pebble-axes, part of a marble bracelet, a marble lid and two bone pins. Associated with each inhumation were ashes, bones of a sacrifice (some bones being burnt), and sherds or vessels ("some apparently broken before they were placed in the ashes"). That these were Kurgan burials is clear if we quote M. Gimbutas' brief description of Kurgan II inhumations in pits. "The dead were equipped with flint points, arrow-heads, knives, celts, axes, necklaces, beads, awls, bracelets, pendants." She mentions also "the deposition of red ochre" and the presence of animal bones and sherds as signs of a funeral feast.[27]

The manner and the relative positions of the burials were unusual. The earlier burial was in a circular pit or shaft, 1.20 m in diameter, which had been sunk first through the burnt debris of the destruction level and then 0.60 m deep into the clayey soil. The skeleton lay at the bottom of the pit in soft dark earth which had been piled over a hard earth floor. The sides of the pit had evidently been lined with cobbles (some being found cracked by fire), and a slanting layer of grey wood-ash within the entire circumference of the pit probably represented the collapse of a 'roof' of timbers, which had originally covered the 'mortuary house' and then been burnt. This manner of burial was that known as the Kurgan 'Pit-Grave'. To quote M. Gimbutas on a Kurgan III burial elsewhere: "This was a typical Kurgan grave in a larger deep shaft covered with timber planks. A piece of red ochre and sherds of a number of thin-walled, undecorated pots were found in the pit. The potsherds apparently fell into the pit after a funerary feast above the grave when the mortuary house [i.e. at the foot of the shaft] was burned."

At Servia there was a small circular hearth which lay close to the edge of the pit; this may have been used for the sacrifice or feast with fire. The cracked cobbles and the grey ash may have been the result of a ritual burning of the mortuary house. The second skeleton, described simply as "bones and a skull," may not have been complete. It was placed partly above and partly to one side of the filled-in pit; it may be conjectured that the first burial had been covered by a mound of soil, in order to protect it from animals, and that the second burial was inserted into this mound and in its turn covered by a mound of soil. As the top layer of the site was subsequently skimmed by ploughing, nothing was left of such a mound. The form of burial for the Middle Kurgan period is described as follows by M. Gimbutas: "Graves . . . were in stone cists or in pits under low earthen or stone barrows which covered single burials."

The two burials, according to Heurtley, were to be dated as follows: the first probably to Servia IIa, because "the circular cut in the burned debris on the south made it clear that the shaft followed the destruction,"[28] and the second to Servia IIb, with a question mark. If the shaft followed close on the destruction, the first burial was a very early Kurgan II burial. But in the layer of grey ash associated with it there was a varnished altar-table vase, which was of a class known in Servia IIb only, and this vase was marked by smoke;[29] if, as seems to be the case, it was marked by the fire which burnt the mortuary house, then the first burial has to be of Servia IIb. The second burial was most probably of Servia IIb because a vase beside it was dated by Heurtley to the later phase,[30] and the odds are high that the vase was associated with the burial. The second burial, anyhow, was of the Kurgan III period. Presumably the two men who were given this special honour were in some sense founders or heroes at different times in the history of the settlement.[31]

At the beginning of this century G. Soteriades remarked on the resemblance of two burials of individual men at Chaeronea to the Kurgan practice as he had seen it in a burial at Helmsdorf in Germany. The situation at Chaeronea, as at Lerna, was that the tumulus was intact within the settlement mound (not skimmed by ploughing as at Servia) and was revealed only be excavation. Soteriades found the tumulus to be some twenty metres in circumference, its periphery marked originally by a palisade of wattle and daub (we may compare the palisade at the start of Malik IIa1), and some 3.50 m in height. The tumulus had been raised over a layer of ash, on which lay the skeleton of a very young man. Soteriades did not dig lower because he reached the water table. The skeleton was covered with black earth (as at Servia), whereas the general soil was clayey. At a slightly higher level in the tumulus a part only of the skeleton of an older man lay in the clayey soil, and this part of the skeleton was lightly burnt. There were two hearths within the tumulus, and small layers of ash and animal bones were indicative of funeral feasts or sacrifices. The finds from the mound of the settlement (120 m x 120 m in extent) included objects like those at Servia: obsidian blades, a black four-legged cult vase with white-filled incisions, four-legged altar-table vases, and grey-on-grey pottery (as in the layer of ash at Servia).[32] The settlement was of the Late Neolithic period. These burials may well have been roughly contemporary with the burials at Servia; anyhow not later than the early part of Servia IIb and still within the Middle Kurgan period. As Soteriades noted, the settlers had had many sheep, and their huts were evidently of perishable material. It is probable that Kurgan leaders moved with transhumant shepherd communities down the eastern side of Greece and made this settlement in an area suitable for winter pastures and within reach of summer pastures on Parnassus and South Pindus.

Two burials within a settlement of the Late Neolithic period were found at Lerna in the Peloponnese. The skeleton of a young woman was accompanied by three vases, some encrusted with thick white paint, and "perhaps associated" with the burial were sherds of black burnished ware with incised patterns which were filled with white paint (as at Servia in the earlier burial). The second was a burial of a child, also accompanied by pottery. In both burials the pottery was strange to the locality and not paralleled by other finds. Once again the burials seem to have been made by newcomers.[33]

The burials at Chaeronea and Lerna were in the very last phase of the Greek Late Neolithic period. As the period ended earlier in Greece than in Macedonia, they were not later than the beginning of Servia IIb. Thus the wave of Kurgan-led invaders seems to have reached into the Peloponnese at that time.

The third phenomenon is the fortification of Dimini and Sesklo with massive stone walls and the building of a large house in each of the citadels at Dimini, Sesklo and Magoula Visviki near Velestino, which make such a striking contrast to the huts of the open villages. These are not only novel features in our area; they are typically Kurgan. If we are correct in seeing Kurgan burials at Servia in the north and at Chaeronea and Lerna in the south, it is most likely that they were Kurgan leaders who built these citadels. It has been recognised, for instance, by D. Theochares that "Dimini has no connection with the East or with the South (the Cyclades). The influences which contributed to its formation are probably northeastern. Precisely the same is true of the Rakhmani Culture." Or again "the use of spiraliform designs on both its impressed and painted pottery was influenced by northern ideas."[34] Theochares was thinking of Thrace, but the discoveries at Cakran and Dunavec which antedate the Dimini period and already have the continuous spiral indicate that the intermediate stages were in central Albania and southwest Macedonia.

Early Helladic I–II and Corresponding Phases in the Southwest Balkans

The terminology of chronological periods within our area is confusing because it has grown up mainly in the wake of individual discoveries in separate places. Thus we now have an 'Eneolithic period' (also called a 'Chalcolithic period') in the southwest Balkans; a Late Neolithic phase, which is sometimes called an Eneolithic Age in Thessaly; and a Late Neolithic Age in Macedonia which carried on beyond the

Early Bronze Age in southern Greece. Thus the overlap of northern Neolithic and Greek Bronze Age has to be defined. In a volume called *Relative Chronologies in Old World Archaeology*,[35] the end of the Macedonian Late Neolithic Age and the end of the Rakhmani phase of the 'Dimini' period in Thessaly were equated with the last stage of Early Helladic II, being the second phase of the Early Bronze Age in southern Greece. In a recent article on the tumuli of Leucas, I gave reasons for placing the Eneolithic period of the southwest Balkans (as exemplified at Malik) more or less within the limits of Early Helladic I and II.[36] This is shown on the chart on page 80. According to M. Gimbutas, the Kurgan IV wave of migrations began at the start of Early Helladic II.[37]

On the eastern side of Greece to the south of Mt Othrys, newcomers with copper weapons and tools, red burnished pottery and new vessel shapes, which are often regarded as imitative of metal vessels, established themselves in control and introduced new ideas and practices at the beginning of Early Helladic I. One of these, for instance, was the making of funnel-shaped cavities in the floors of their houses, which may indicate a belief in underworld deities. The origin of the newcomers, it is generally agreed, is to be sought somewhere in Asia Minor and perhaps particularly in northwestern Asia Minor.[38] They were certainly conversant with the sea, because people of the same culture began to occupy some small islands of the Aegean at about the same time. Whether they came to the mainland of Greece by sea or by land is uncertain. If by land, as is more probable, they passed through and did not occupy Thessaly either of their own will in pursuit of warmer lands or because the people of Dimini culture regained control by force. As their grip on Greece south of Mt Othrys strengthened, perhaps after some reinforcements, their culture reached a high level in the course of Early Helladic II. Houses became larger, copper was more plentiful, and settlements were founded farther afield, for instance in the west on Ithaca and Meganisi. This prosperous phase was brought to an abrupt end by invasions to which we shall return later; for these invasions began to occur at the transition from Early Helladic II to Early Helladic III.

These newcomers who entered eastern Greece and many of the Aegean islands in E. H. I and E. H. II had the initial advantage of possessing metal tools and weapons, but in most respects they had a lower standard of life than their predecessors of the Late Neolithic period. At Eutresis and Orchomenus in Boeotia, which were among their earliest settlements, they built round huts; and at Eutresis they made a more substantial round building with a funnel-shaped cavity (this building may have had a religious significance). There was a decline in the number of settlements in southern Greece and an increase in fortifications, which suggests that there was considerable fear of war. At Lerna in the Peloponnese, for instance, when the site was reoccupied after an interval, the newcomers built a double wall with towers and made it into a powerful citadel. Links between the eastern part of the mainland and the Aegean islands were particularly strong. Walled citadels were made at sites in Attica, Aegina and Syros, where Chalandriani was fortified in the same manner as Lerna. The same burial customs were practised at Ayios Kosmas in Attica and at Syros and other islands, the dead being laid in stone-lined cist (i.e. box-shaped) graves which often had a symbolical doorway and contained offerings of pottery and figurines. A distinctive vessel of the period was the so-called sauceboat, the spout in particular being imitative of a metal product, and it was widely used in E. H. II. There was some expansion towards the west before the end of E. H. II: settlements were made in Ithaca and Cephallenia, and pottery of the southern Greek type was imported to Leucas, Aphiona in Corcyra and Velcë inland of the Gulf of Valona. Settlements on the west coast of the Peloponnese suggest that ships were now sailing round the Peloponnese.

The changes which introduced the Early Bronze Age in Macedonia began probably in the course of E. H. II and ran on into E. H. III. They had the effect of cutting off the coastal areas of the Strymon and Vardar basins from all contact with Thessaly and southern Greece and of placing them within the cultural orbit of northwest Asia Minor and in particular of Troy. The newcomers came evidently from eastern Thrace and perhaps from northwest Asia Minor. They were able to work metals, slag of gold and of copper being found, for instance, at Saratse in eastern Macedonia, but the great bulk of their weapons and tools were still of stone. They had learnt the art of drilling holes in stone battle-axes, and a much improved method of mounting them on a shaft made them more effective. They prevailed over their predecessors, who had been in many ways more enterprising, by virtue of these weapons and superior numbers. As they advanced, some sites such as Akropotamos and Olynthus were abandoned, and the newcomers founded settlements for the first time at strategic points, such as Kilindir on the route from the north into the coastal plain east of the Vardar, and Vardarophtsa on the east bank by the best ford through the river in summertime. Later they advanced into the western part of the plain, where the two settlements at Nea Nikomedeia were abandoned, and sometime later still into Eordaea and Elimea where Servia was destroyed, probably by fire, and abandoned. Their influence extended northwards from there into Lyncus (e.g. to Armenokhori), Pelagonia, and the upper Vardar valley; but it was not uncontested.[39]

The people who entered and spread through Macedonia in this way differed from the peoples who had recently settled in southern Greece, in that they had no interest in seafaring or concern for trade but concentrated their efforts on agriculture. They lived at first in the simplest huts of wattle and daub and later made use of mud-bricks to form platforms for their small houses, which were reinforced by wooden poles. They had few figurines and ornaments, but one form of amulet which was distinctive to them was an anchor-shaped hook (Pl. 6a). The distribution of these and the layers in which they occur at different sites help us to reconstruct their movements.[40] For example, at Eutresis in Boeotia some 'anchors' were found in E. H. II layers but not in those of E. H. III, from which we may deduce that some anchor-people were in Macedonia in E. H. II and that some of them came into Boeotia in E. H. II.

Yet another people entered Macedonia, this time from the northeast and probably via the Preševo Pass. Their culture was called Bubanj-Hum Ia after a place of this name near Niš, and their pottery was characterised by the use of rippling and grooving, crusted paint and (on coarse ware) impressed ornament and plastic moulding. Their first conquests were on the east side of the Vardar, where they displaced the culture of Vršnik, and they and their neighbours to the east gained control of the upper Strymon valley. The Bubanj-Hum people were stockbreeders and hunters rather than agriculturalists, and it was significant of this that sites in the plain of the Bregalnitsa valley such as Anza were abandoned after their arrival. Their preference was for rocky heights, such as that on which the citadel of Skopje stands.[41] When their power was well rooted, they overthrew the culture of Kossovo and broke into Pelagonia, where the Crnobuki culture was already in decline. The Bubanj-Hum sites in Pelagonia were near Tsepicovo and at Suvodol, which lie between Prilep and Monastir, and their attempts to acquire further lands to the south were thwarted by the anchor-people, who held Armenokhori in Lyncus and were themselves on the move northwards when the Early Bronze Age was drawing to an end.

As the anchor-people and the Bubanj-Hum people made their gradual advances into the western cantons of Upper Macedonia, they not only drove refugees from deserted sites towards the west but also destroyed the trade which had made Malik and other sites in the lakeland area prosperous. It is possible, too, that the troubled conditions caused the transhumant pastoralists to take their flocks to pastures in the west rather than to those of Macedonia and Thessaly. Inevitably Malik declined in prosperity. The settlement of this period, Malik IIb, was poorer in many ways but there was no abrupt change in culture from IIa.[42] Towards the end of Malik IIb a settlement with the same culture was made at the cave of Tren beside the main route which led from the plain of Malik into the basin of the Prespa lakes and so to Macedonia. This last phase of Malik IIb seems to have extended somewhat beyond the end of E. H. II and to have ended soon after the destruction of Servia. The next phase, Malik IIIa, began within the course of E. H. III; for some pottery of Malik IIIa gives us a firm cross-dating with Cnossus.[43]

The southward movement of the Bubanj-Hum people was one of several such movements which were due to pressure from the pastoral peoples of the Russian steppes who were entering the Danube basin and expanding into the Balkans and central Europe.[44] These pastoral peoples, conveniently known as Kurgan IV peoples, were notable for bringing with them the domesticated horse, mace-heads, bored battle-axes and the distinctive form of burial by which they are named 'Kurgan'. There are traces of their presence in Pelagonia and at Malik. Among the figurines found at Porodin were unmistakable representations of horses, which being unknown in our area since the end of the Palaeolithic period, were presumably domesticated horses. As the Porodin culture lasted so long, the horse may have been brought to Porodin either in the Middle Kurgan period or at the start of the Kurgan IV period. Even more exciting is a mace-head of stone, representing a horse's head with grooves indicating the harness, which was found at Tsiplevets (Šuplevec) in Pelagonia; it is unmistakably Kurgan.[45] The site at Tsiplevets, which has been excavated but not published, has been described by M. Gimbutas as a typical Kurgan IV hill-fort. "During the excavation of 1959 this impressive hill-fort was surrounded by massive stone walls. Seventeen or eighteen houses were uncovered standing in three rows in an oval area of the hill-fort."[46] It is probable that the residents of this fort were of Kurgan origin and that the culture of the site was a mixture of Kurgan, Bubanj-Hum and local elements.[47]

At Malik IIb and especially in the transition to Malik IIIa new shapes of pottery appeared: large squat jars with dwarf handles high on the shoulders and an almost vertical collar, and bowls and jugs with vertical and almost vertical collars, decorated often with fluting. The shapes of the bowls and jugs and the fluting seem to be in imitation of metal objects. The closest analogies are to be found in the squat jars and the silver vessels of Kurgan rulers.[48] It is thus likely that Kurgan-led peoples were moving into and probably through the lakeland area in the latter part of E. H. II and in E. H. III. It was at the transition from Malik IIb to Malik IIIa that bored battle-axes appeared, displacing the earlier celts. They were found also at Kamnik in Kolonjë on the westward route towards the Adriatic Sea.[49]

It is in the western part of central Greece that we see indisputable evidence of Kurgan IV rulers in E. H. II. A large cemetery of tumuli was excavated by W. Dörpfeld at Nidhri in Leucas, where they face the harbour of the route through the Channel (see Map 21). When he published his results in 1927, little was known of the Kurgan peoples, and it is only since the war that discoveries in Russia and the northern Balkans made it clear to Balkan scholars (though not to many Aegean scholars) that the Leucas tumuli were constructed for Kurgan chieftains.[50] The earliest of the graves in the so-called "R" group of thirty-three tumuli contained sauceboats of E. H. II date and copper celts, copper fish-hooks and little plaques of copper, serving probably as amulets. The copper in the graves lacked the arsenic which has been found in objects of copper made in the Cyclades and Crete; and also the nickel which was present in copper used in Crete. Leucas then obtained its copper from a different source, i.e. from one outside the Eastern Mediterranean. As Malik IIa and IIb had copper celts and copper fish-hooks of the same types as those at Nidhri, it is likely that the people of Nidhri in Leucas obtained copper via Kamnik and Malik from the Metohija, where copper was mined at this time, and perhaps also from some source on the Adriatic sea route.[51]

Two of the earliest burials at Leucas, R 1b and R16, were inhumations, one in a pithos (a large jar) laid in a trench which had been dug below the original ground level. In another of the earliest burials, R 26c, a large mortuary chamber had been constructed below ground level; it measured 2 m x 2.10 m, was floored with pebbles and was lined with round stones (as at Servia). The skeletons of a man and a woman were found in the mortuary chamber. There had evidently been a funerary feast (as at Servia), since there was some ash in the soil of the grave, and beside the skeleton of the man there were pieces of a sheep and (probably) of a lamb. The offering of a sheep and a lamb, or a cow and a calf, or a goat and a kid was a Kurgan practice.[52]

At this point we may turn to the earliest burials yet known in tumuli in central Albania. These are at Pazhok, situated at a strategic point on the easiest route from the valley of the Shkumbi to that of the Semeni (see Map 21). Of the twenty-five or more tumuli only three were excavated. Unfortunately the only report which has appeared so far is very brief.[53] I was able to supplement this when I visited Tirana in 1972, saw some of the finds in the Exhibition and talked with some of my Albanian colleagues, including one of the excavators, Selim Islami. The central burial in each of the three tumuli had been dug below the ground level (as at Servia and Leucas); the shaft was circular or rectangular, one being about 2 m x 2 m; the sides were walled with stones and the floor was covered with gravel. Some burials were reported to be inhumations, often with two bodies in the pit. The illustrations which accompanied the report showed that the central pit of the biggest tumulus was circular (some 5 m in diameter) and had the skeletons of two or more persons (one a child), and that the bones and skull of an ox in the pit were evidence of a funeral sacrifice (Pl. 6b). The pit had been covered first with a mass of earth and then with a heap of stones.

It is evident that this burial had much in common with burial R 26c at Leucas.

When I was in Tirana, I was told that a pot on view there was from this central pit and was associated with the earliest burial, and I recognised the pot as that which had been shown on a photographic plate in the short report. Whereas I had thought it to be painted, it was in fact incised, and the incisions had been made by impressing cord or a tool giving a cord-like impression on the clay. The shape was no doubt inspired by a metal prototype. The pot has now been magnificently published.[54] The incisions are closer in kind to the earlier style of incised decoration at Servia[55] than to the later style;[56] indeed, the piece of the four-legged cult vessel which was in the crook of the skeleton's arm in the circular pit at Servia had a similar type of incised decoration.[57] When we look farther north, we find that this form of decoration was characteristic of the pottery of Kostolac near the confluence of the Morava and the Danube; it has been dated by M. Garašanin to about the end of E. H. II in Aegean chronology and by A. Benac to the Chalcolithic or Eneolithic Age of Balkan chronology.[58] The shape of the pot at Pazhok finds no echo in the pages of *Prehistoric Macedonia*. The closest parallels which I have found, but of a cruder finish, are from Bela Crkva in western Serbia; they were found there in the central burials by inhumation of Tumulus I, which has similar features to the burials of Leucas and Pazhok (one central burial having two adults and a child). These jugs and burials were also of the Balkan Eneolithic Age.[59]

It is probable, then, that the earliest burials at Pazhok were made in E. H. II and that they belonged to the same orbit as the earliest burials of Leucas and to the same cultural background as Malik IIa and IIb, which showed some Kurgan influence. Subsequent burials in the R tumuli of Leucas were mainly by cremation, some in E. H. II and others in E. H. III. Parallels for these occurred in the cemetery of tumuli of this period at Belotić in western Serbia, where the earliest burials have been dated by M. Garašanin to c. 2000 B.C., i.e. in E. H. III.[60] On the sea route up the Adriatic a tumulus with gold and silver offerings has been excavated near Tivat on the south side of the Gulf of Kotor; it has been dated to the time of or earlier than the R graves which we have been considering.[61]

Another characteristic of the Kurgan IV expansion was the spread of 'Corded Ware', in which a piece of cord or a tool was used to make a cord-like impression on the wet clay of a vessel before it was fired. This ware has been found in a cave on the coast north of Dubrovnik, where its association with Vučedol pottery dates it to late in E. H. III.[62] Corded Ware was found at Aphiona on the northwest coast of Corcyra, at the Nisos site, which belonged probably in the Late Neolithic Age or Early Bronze Age.[63] The southern limit of corded ware on the sea lanes is at Ayios Sotiros in Leucas, an occupation site in the Nidhri plain which is distinct from the cemetery of tumuli.[64] Turning inland we find a neater and shallower form of cord-impressions on pottery of Gajtan I near Scodra in northern Albania, at Kastritsa in central Epirus, and at Ayios Mamas and Kritsana in Chalcidice; these examples belong probably to E. H. III or to the Middle Bronze Age.[65]

When we consider the various movements of peoples which took place in this period (E.H. I to E.H. III in Aegean chronology and the Eneolithic period in Balkan chronology), we can see that the Kurgan IV movement was the most far-reaching, because it flowed not only into the Balkans but also into Asia Minor and into central Europe. The leaders of the migrants were evidently able and enterprising. For, although the E. H. settlers of Greece south of Mt Othrys were experienced and skilful sailors, it was a Kurgan-led group which seized the strategic point by the Leucas Channel and amassed the wealth and the weapons of which we see the signs in the burials of the chieftains. Another group succeeded in the same way near Kotor. There is evidence that Kurgan peoples later controlled the harbour at Aphiona in Corcyra (from which one could sail direct to the heel of Italy or to Sicily), as well as some of the ports on the coast of Montenegro and Dalmatia. In the same way the Albanians learnt in a comparatively short time to rival and even to surpass the sailors of the Greek mainland and islands in the eighteenth and nineteenth centuries. It is possible that the first Kurgan people to gain control of a sea route were the groups at Kotor and Leucas; they may have come down from the hills and dispossessed those who controlled the harbours on this much-used route of the Eneolithic period.

On the mainland the pastoral peoples under

Kurgan leaders who developed the resources of the lakeland and the pastures of central Albania were reinforced by other Kurgan-led peoples. On present evidence they constituted the great bulk of the population in the lakeland, and they were the first to occupy the coastal plain of central Albania. The development of Malik as an intercultural centre of trade was partly due to them, and they were able to stand firm against the Bubanj-Hum people and the anchor people, who took possession of western Macedonia. Thus a reservoir of Kurgan-led peoples was safeguarded and maintained in the area from Scodra to Velcë-Kamnik and from the Aegean watershed-range of Peristeri to the Adriatic coast. Servia too was another important point on a trade route which Kurgan chieftains seized at an earlier stage and developed. But they were dispossessed in their turn by the anchor people.

We have already mentioned the advance of some peoples from the north, which enabled Thessaly to remain independent both of the anchor-people of southern Macedonia and of the culture common to areas south of Mt Othrys. In the final phase in eastern Thessaly, named 'Rakhmani' after a village in the northeast corner, there was much use of crusted paint, which was a northern speciality. It was common at Malik IIa and less common at Malik IIb, and it was employed at Servia from which it spread into Lower Macedonia and Thessaly. Rakhmani itself had much in common with Malik and Servia in addition to the crusted ware: figurines with detachable heads, flat celts of stone, bone spoons, waisted pebble-axes and sling bullets. Copper celts and copper pins at Sesklo were like those of Malik, Kamnik and Leucas.[66] It is clear that the northern element in the population of northeast Thessaly was being progressively strengthened in the latter part of E. H. II.

One example of the use of crusted paint was at Souphli Magoula near Larissa in a group of urns and accompanying vessels, which were found outside but close to the settlement and were attributed to the 'Larissa' phase of the Dimini culture.[67] The dead had been cremated elsewhere and the remains were then placed in the urns "of middle size"; these together with smaller vessels which had contained perishable offerings were buried at a shallow depth and formed a "closed complex." Some of the pottery was encrusted with white paint, and the excavator found the closest analogies to the un-Thessalian wares in the pottery of Macedonia[68] and of the younger Vinča culture in Serbia. The closest individual pots came from Armenokhori late in the Late Neolithic period and from Malik IIb.[69]

The cemetery of urns was unique when it was reported. In 1966–67, when F. Prendi, M. Korkuti and Zh. Andrea were excavating the cave of Tren, an area in front of the cave and another area on the back of the hill, they found in the last area a closed complex of some thirty urns surrounded by stones (the whole space so occupied being 45 square metres) at a shallow depth beside the inhabited area ("à côté des habitations"). Here, however, the rites were different. Cremations had taken place on the spot, because the stones were fused into lime, and ashes and bits of charcoal lay by the urns, and these cremations and the depositions of the urns had taken place one by one over some space of time. There were apparently no human remains in the urns. These urns lay in the Early Bronze Age layer. The excavators suggested that they were connected not with burial but with some religious cult or festival. In view of the practice at Souphli Magoula, which they did not mention, it is possible that the deposition of urns at Tren was connected with burial, but that the remains of cremated corpses were placed somewhere else. The similarities anyhow suggest that the people at Souphli Magoula came from the area of the lakeland or from nearby.[70]

A remarkable discovery at Souphli Magoula was a stone stele, some two metres high, which had been reused as the lid of a Middle Helladic cist-grave and was therefore older than that grave. It is a typical Kurgan IV piece, with the spread fingers of two hands across the body and a long snake rising from below to shoulder height, and it had originally stood, one imagines, in the Kurgan manner on a tumulus over a burial.[71] It is unique in this primitive form in peninsular Greece. When I was in Bulgaria, I saw a similar stone stele, almost complete, and a piece of a second one in the yard of the small museum at Razlog (between the Strymon and the Nestus).[72] I persuaded the custodian to take me to the place of their discovery; it was a cemetery of medium-sized tumuli in a lavender field on a hillside. The almost complete one was some two metres high; it had the sun with rays, either a snake or a boat, and running spirals in triangular groups of three (such spirals figure on the stelai from Grave Circles A and B at Mycenae).[73] There was a snake, I thought, on the upper right edge by the man's shoulder, and the man himself seemed to be ithyphallic. The broken one had running spirals also and a larger sun. It seems likely that they should be dated to the Bubanj-Hum occupation of this area and regarded as a sign of Kurgan leadership; but they are probably of a later date than the stele at Souphli Magoula.[74]

The most remarkable sign of Kurgan intrusion is at Lerna near the coast of the Argolic Gulf (see Map 21). When the central house of the third settlement—the "House of Tiles," as the excavator, J. L. Caskey, called it—was destroyed by fire, part of the debris was removed but a low tumulus, circular and some 19 m in diameter, its periphery being marked by a ring of rounded stones, was made of the residue and the whole of its surface was covered over with stones. This happened at the transition of E.H. II to E.H. III. Nor was it an isolated phenomenon. At three other sites in the Argolid there was destruction by fire, and Corinth seems to have been abandoned. In Caskey's words "quite clearly, a foreign invader had conquered the land." The newcomers were different in many respects from their predecessors. Their houses of reeds and clay or some such poor material, held together by a light wooden framework, usually had an apsidal end; the shapes of their pottery were new to the Greek peninsula and islands, but pottery similar in shapes and in ornamental patterns appeared in the succeeding perod at Lianokladhi in the Spercheus valley; and anchors of clay, as in Macedonia and other places, were found now for the first time at Lerna.[75]

As Caskey remarked, the houses "point to a pastoral and semi-nomadic ancestry"; that ancestry may have been immediate if the invaders came as a pastoral and semi-nomadic people. In Macedonia and central Albania there were many signs that transhumant pastoralism was on the increase at this time with the decline of settled conditions. The link between Lerna and Lianokladhi is understandable if both peoples had been connected with transhumant pastoralist communities of Pindus. And the anchors point to a derivation of at least some of the invaders from the north. It was the leaders of the invaders who created the tumulus at the centre of the settlement, and their successors maintained it into the Middle Helladic period. In general such a tumulus at this period was the mark of a Kurgan presence. In particular this tumulus resembled the inner tumulus at Pazhok in that its surface was covered with stones, and it resembled the outer tumulus at Pazhok in size and shape and in being ringed with rounded stones. It was unusual in being a cenotaph (though cenotaphs are not uncommon in later tumuli in Albania, e.g. at Çinamak), but towards the end of the Middle Helladic period one burial was made in it and one alongside it. These burials were in mortuary chambers, lined with stones, and the floors were covered with pebbles. Again these were as at Pazhok. It was a not uncommon practice of Kurgan peoples to reuse an earlier Kurgan tumulus, as we shall see later in Albania, and this seems to have been what happened at Lerna.

Thus the last part of the Early Helladic period was a troubled time. While settled life was disrupted in western Macedonia and impoverished in the lakeland, northerners under Kurgan leadership penetrated into Thessaly (for instance at Souphli Magoula).[76] Other northerners under Kurgan leadership came probably through the Isthmus to overrun the Argolic plain and take control of Lerna and other sites.

Early Helladic III and Middle Helladic

An important feature of this period was the spread of tumulus-burial into many parts of the mainland. In order to understand the procedure involved in one kind at least of tumulus-burial, we rely less upon the archaeologist who excavates the end-result than upon a description, no doubt traditional, which Homer included in the *Iliad*. This particular procedure of burial became obsolete in Mycenaean Greece c. 1400 B.C., some six hundred years before the composition of the *Iliad*, but it was still practised in northern Epirus at the end of the Bronze Age, some three hundred years before the same event. It is therefore significant that the description was attached to Achilles, whose religious associations were with Dodona in Epirus.

When Patroclus was killed in battle, his corpse was laid upon the centre of a great pyre (*Iliad* 23. 164f). Sheep and cattle were slaughtered and skinned in front of the pyre, fat from them and their skinned carcasses were piled round the corpse. Two-handled jars of honey and oil were laid against his resting-place (literally, "his bed"). Then four horses, two dogs and twelve Trojan prisoners were killed upon the great pyre. When the pyre was lit, wine was poured upon the ground, and when it died down, it was put out with wine. But the fire did not reduce all to ashes (a very great heat being required for that). "The white bones" of Patroclus were taken up from the middle of the pyre and placed in a golden jar, which was covered with a thin veil and set in his resting-place (literally, "his hut"). Then as Achilles had ordered, as chief mourner and conductor of the ceremonies, the Achaeans made the first tumulus as follows: "They marked the circumference of the tumulus with a *tornos* [i.e. a line attached to a fixed point, which became the centre of the circle], and they laid foundation-stones (in a circle) round the pyre. And at once they heaped the piled earth over the place, and having made the tumulus they departed" (ibid. 255f). But Achilles had a further ceremony in mind for the day when he himself would be killed. Then he would be buried in the same tumulus, and thereafter the Achaeans would build a tumulus much wider and higher. Thus in the end a double tumulus was to be created over the original central burial where Patroclus—or rather his scorched bones in the jar—lay in his resting-place.[77]

Tumulus-burials in Leucas, Albania and southern Greece provide illustrations of almost every point in this epic description. The place of cremation was within the circumference of the tumulus and was often marked by a cairn of stones (e.g. in R 5, 6 and 12 in Leucas, and at Vajzë in Albania), and a sheep or an ox was sometimes laid with the dead (e.g. in R 26 in Leucas and at Pazhok). Animal bones and ash in the fill of a tumulus often showed that a funeral feast with fire had been provided; a carcass of a horse was buried alongside the resting-place of the man in the earliest of the tumuli at Marathon;[78] and Tsountas thought—perhaps rightly—that the presence of human and animal bones in the fill above the Shaft-Graves of Circle A at Mycenae was evidence of human as well as animal sacrifice. The 'bed' or 'hut' was evidently the mortuary chamber in which the remains of the dead person and the offerings of honey and oil were placed, each in the appropriate container; this bed or hut was a miniature house in the form of a round or rectangular pit, lined with cobbles and roofed over, e.g. in Leucas, at Pazhok, at Lerna or at Mycenae. When the bed or hut was ready and the containers were placed within it, the periphery of the circle round it was marked with a ring of stones, as at Pazhok and elsewhere, or with a low ring-wall (called a "Grabkreis" by Dörpfeld in Leucas), as in the S graves of Leucas. The insertion of one or more later burials was a commonplace, and there were fine examples of the double tumulus at Pazhok and Vodhinë in Albania, the smaller tumulus being marked off from the larger (upper) tumulus by shingle and stones (Pl. *6b* and *7a*).

The survival of a tumulus down to modern times has depended often upon local conditions. In Albania, where agricultural methods have been primitive until very recently, hundreds of tumuli still rise above the level of the surrounding ground, and this is true also of the three hundred tumuli at Vergina in southern Macedonia. In other areas the tumulus has disappeared as a result of ploughing or erosion. Where a tumulus lay within an ancient settlement, it was often removed in the course of reconstruction. In such cases the archaeologist cannot hope to find more than the burial chambers which lay below the ground level of the tumulus. The excavation of tumuli and the interpretation of the burials have improved with experience. At first there was a natural assumption that a tumulus was used for a relatively short period of time and that the burials should be dated by the latest objects found in them. But it became apparent that sometimes a tumulus was in use for centuries on end (for instance at Pazhok, on the interpretation of the excavators, from 1800 to late in Late Helladic, i.e. c. 1200), and that each burial had therefore to be dated separately. The making of later burials in a tumulus (some of the Early Iron Age tumuli having over a hundred burials) and/or the insertion of a second corpse into a burial led sometimes to the displacement of objects so that an object placed in one tomb might end up in or near another. As burials were made at different levels in a tumulus of stones and soil standing to a height of three to five metres, and as a shaft might be dug down from the surface at an angle other than the vertical and a mortuary chamber be made at one side of the bottom of the shaft, there was no 'stratification' of burials and a later burial could be inserted, in part at least, under an earlier burial.[79] No doubt markers, such as stelai, were placed on the surface of a tumulus to indicate approximately where burials had been made, but only a few have survived to help the modern excavator.[80]

With the increasing number of excavated tumuli

in our area a general sequence in the types of burial has emerged, and it is the same in general as that noted by M. Gimbutas in southeastern Europe. The earliest was inhumation in a pit-grave, the pit being either a simple trench (as in R 16 in Leucas and at Vodhinë in Albania) or a largish pit (as at Servia and Pazhok). Next either inhumation or cremated remains in a pithos placed in a mortuary chamber. Next inhumation or cremated remains in a cist-grave, whether the cist (literally a 'box-shaped' grave) was made of wooden planks or of stone slabs; this was the simplest form of mortuary chamber, and the choice of materials depended on what was available locally (e.g. wood at Pazhok and stone in Leucas). Equally late in the sequence and very much less common were stone-built structures, as in the F graves in Leucas and in one of the later tumuli at Marathon. Such a sequence was, however, far from rigid and it gives us only general guidelines. There were variations too in the construction of tumuli. Some had no periphery of stones (no 'Grabkreis' in Dörpfeld's terminology); others had a periphery of single roundish stones, preferably whitish; others a single row of orthostats, i.e. slabs set upright; and yet others a low ring-wall of stones, which helped to retain the soil of the tumulus.[81] A cairn of stones was set sometimes over the central burial, sometimes over all the burials; in other tumuli it was lacking altogether. 'Hearths' or 'pyres' were found in many tumuli, whether for cremation or for sacrifices with fire or for the burning of offerings, and in some cases the central cairn of stones was used for this purpose.

Tumulus-burial was the heroic form of burial in the Bronze Age, expensive, honorific and reserved for the greatest chieftains of the ruling families, apparently without sexual discrimination. At Pazhok, for instance, and in the R graves in Leucas we may infer that not every generation produced even one hero worthy of this honour. The original, central burial in a tumulus was never disturbed. Subsequent burials were placed close to it in some tumuli, and it is clear that all burials in a tumulus were made as some form of tribute to the 'founder', if we may call him so, of a line of heroes. When a second tumulus was added on top of an original tumulus, as at Pazhok, Vodhinë, R 16 in Leucas and Arnissa, further tribute was being paid to the 'founder' and his descendants in the original tumulus; for the second tumulus at Pazhok and Vodhinë seems not to have had a central burial of its own.[82] The fact that only a little sustenance, mainly in the form of honey, oil and wine,[83] was provided in the tomb suggests that the dead had need of it for only a short time. There is no evidence of subsequent offerings, and if a second burial was made within the same tomb the bones and the original offerings were casually swept aside or thrown into the fill, as if the period of quasi-survival with physical needs was already over. In the earliest burials within our area the emblems of fertility may indicate a belief in a form of rebirth or renewed existence in the underworld. Indeed the reverence shown to the 'founder' over so many generations implies something more than respect for kinship only; there may have been a belief, such as we find many centuries later in the odes of Pindar, that the founding genius had some superhuman dignity and even power in the mind of subsequent generations.

As far as excavated sites are a guide, there was sometimes a lacuna in the practice, which meant presumably a change in the ruling family. Thus in the R groups in Leucas the 'founder' seems to have been in R 26, which had the largest R tumulus, and two ruling families followed, probably contemporaneously with one another, in R 1 and R 16, which had the next largest tumuli. One of these, R 16, was covered with flat stones and then received an upper tumulus, presumably from members of the same ruling family. Later generations buried their heroes in smaller tumuli, perhaps thinking it inappropriate to vie with their ancestors in this respect, and they grouped these smaller tumuli round the two larger ones. This cemetery, comprising the thirty-three excavated R graves, was in use from c. 2500 to c. 1800. After a considerable gap a much larger tumulus, containing a stone-built structure, was made in a separate place; the burials in it, labelled F by Dörpfeld, may be dated approximately c. 1700–1650. Next came the S graves in a tumulus with a ring-wall about 12 m in diameter, made again in a separate place, and these may be dated c. 1650–1600.[84] Similarly at Pazhok there may have been a gap between those burials in the inner tumuli which were dated by the excavators to 1880–1700 and the burials in the upper tumuli which were of Late Helladic date, i.e. after 1600 B.C. On the other hand there seems to have been no lacuna at Marathon, where four tumuli have been excavated and dated from c. 1625 to "the fourteenth century" (Pl. 7b).[85]

The discovery of a number of tumuli in Attica and the Peloponnese has led me and others to a reappraisal of the two so-called Grave Circles at Mycenae, a term adopted from Dörpfeld's 'Grabkreis' in Leucas.[86] These Grave Circles, each originally having a low ring-wall about 27 m in diameter, and the graves within them have the characteristics of some tumuli and of many tumulus-burials in Leucas and to the north of Leucas. Thus Tumulus S at Leucas had a ring-wall 12.10 m in diameter. One outer tumulus at Pazhok had a diameter of some 21 m, and four tumuli at Vajzë had diameters of between 17 and 22 m. The two Grave Circles at Mycenae were for a time in contemporary use. So were pairs of tumuli at Leucas, Pazhok and probably Vajzë. The earliest graves at Mycenae, those numbered Sigma, Lambda 2, Tau and Phi in Circle B, were mortuary chambers, constructed as a miniature representation of a house, exactly as at Pazhok and elsewhere in Albania.[87] These and other similarities make it most likely that each of the Grave Circles was originally covered by a tumulus—as Tsountas, an early excavator, in the case of Circle A—and that the upper parts of the tumuli were removed in the course of reconstructions during the Late Bronze Age. In the reconstruction which took place c. 1300 above Circle A, a circular 'parapet' or ring of orthostats (i.e. slabs set upright) was made to commemorate Circle A. Such a ring was set round the inner tumulus of the double tumulus at Pazhok in Albania (Pl. *6b*), and likewise at Arnissa in western Macedonia.

At Marathon, the tumuli were succeeded by an underground tholos-tomb, itself crowned by a tumulus, which was all that was visible to a visitor. At Mycenae the Grave Circles were succeeded by underground tholos-tombs, each crowned by a tumulus, which sometimes had a circular ring-wall. The developments at Marathon and Mycenae were evidently parallel, and the continuity in each case lay in the tumulus; for in my opinion a tumulus crowned each of the Grave Circles at Mycenae. An interesting parallel occurred a thousand years later in Macedonia. Then the tumuli of the burials at Vergina in Macedonia were succeeded by the Macedonian underground built-tomb, itself always crowned by a tumulus. The design of the tholos-tomb itself, like the design of the Macedonian built-tomb, was inspired by models which were foreign to the locality.

The distribution of the E. H. III and M. H. tumuli within our area is shown on Map 21. No doubt many additions will be made in the future, but the pattern is abundantly clear. As Marinatos remarked, "such tumuli are especially abundant along the western coast of the Peloponnese; in eastern Greece they are rather rare."[88] When we compare this pattern with those shown in the other maps of this section, the inference is obvious that the origin of the tumulus-using people is to be sought in the northwest; that they were attracted, like the Albanians later, to the areas more suited to pastoral life; and that they had seafaring connections with the Sicilian and Adriatic Seas. The priority in date of the earliest tumuli of Leucas, Servia, Chaeronea and Pazhok, and the priority within the M. H. period of the tumuli of Leucas and Pazhok show that the streams of influence and of immigrants led by chieftains accustomed to tumulus-burial were flowing—no doubt intermittently—from the northwestern region into Greece from E. H. I/II onwards until the end of the M. H.[89] The relatively few tumuli in eastern Greece included one group in the Argolid and another in eastern Attica and offshore Ceos; the sites in the latter group were presumably founded by seafaring immigrants.

That the chieftains who were buried in these tumuli were speakers of an early form of the Greek language is not now to be doubted. The close correspondence between the Homeric description with which we started this section and the Bronze Age practice of tumulus-burials, about which we have learnt so much in recent decades, is a clear indication that it was a Greek ritual, characteristic of this period and revived subsequently on certain occasions to pay special honour to those who had benefited the Greeks—for instance, the Athenians, the Plataeans and the slaves who fell at the battle of Marathon.[90] The link between the chieftains who ruled Marathon, Mycenae, Argos, Asine, Lerna, the Pylos area and Malthi, for instance, in the last phase of the Middle Helladic period and those whom we know as the 'Mycenaean' rulers of these important places in the Late Helladic period is indissoluble; for they were both buried beneath tumuli, whether they lay in shaft-graves or tholos-tombs. So too there was continuity of language; and the decipherment of the Linear B script, reinforcing the whole tradition of Greek mythology, defines that language as Greek. It follows that that these Greek-speaking rulers were of Kurgan origin and had entered the Greek peninsula

Map 21

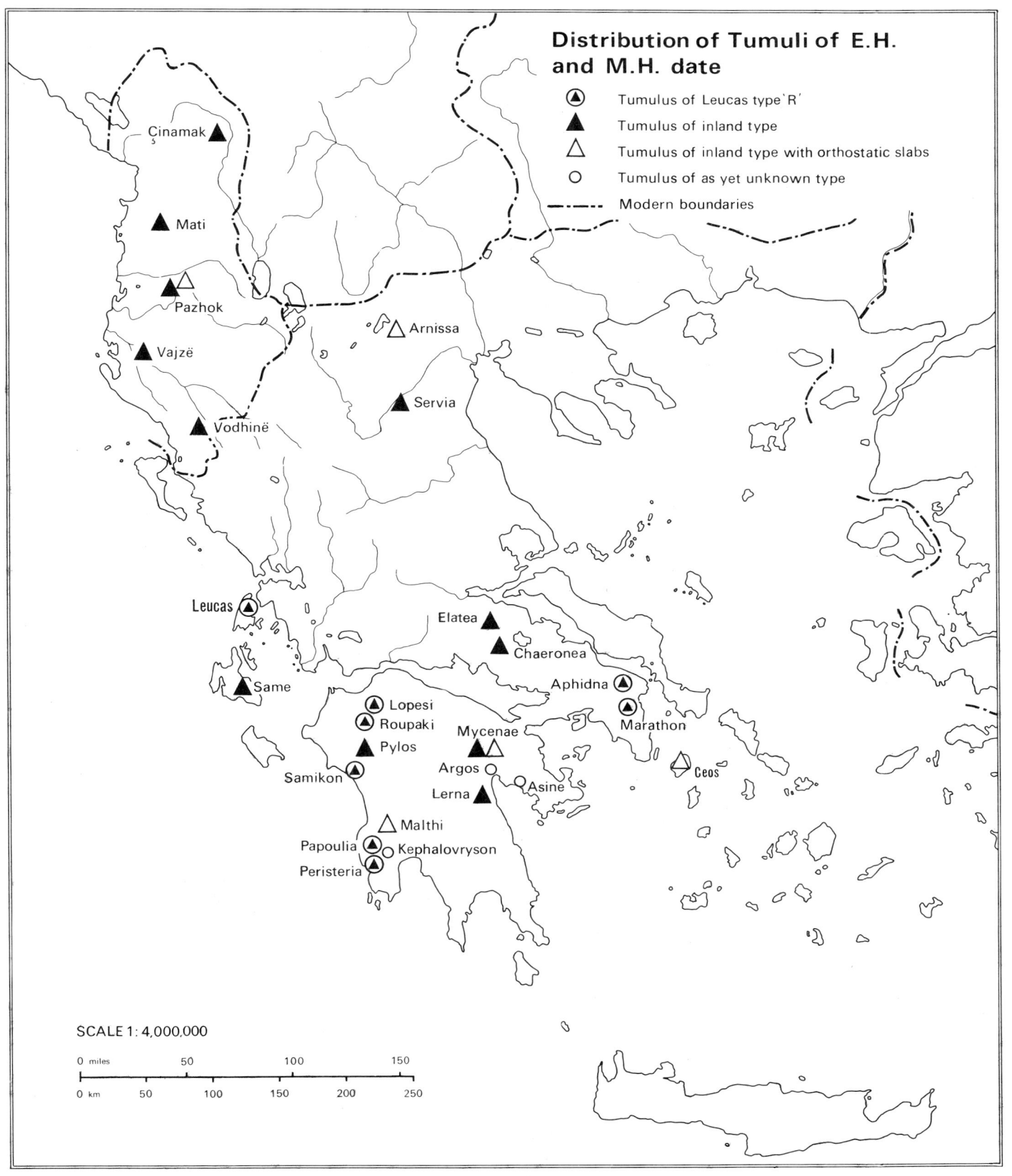

from the north and in particular from that part of the northwestern area which we know as Albania and western Macedonia.

That the dissemination of the Indo-European languages into Europe, Anatolia and Iran was to be associated with the diaspora of the Kurgan peoples was already a widely held hypothesis, before the number of tumulus-burials in our area was realised. Thus R.A. Crossland wrote as follows in 1971.

> From the linguistic standpoint there is much to be said for equating the Indo-European 'homeland' with the Pontic area or with part of the zone of steppe lands which lies to the northwest, north and northeast of it. Such an area is a likely point of departure for the migrations which brought Indo-European languages to Greece, Anatolia and Iran, and a natural centre for the radial dispersion which, in the author's opinion, best explains the similarities and differences between the historical Indo-European language groups. The identification has also been advocated on archaeological grounds. There was undoubtedly widespread disturbance of older cultures in the Danubian area and central Europe at the beginning of the second millennium, and some evidence points to warlike movements within the Pontic region and from it into the Danubian region c. 2400–1800 B.C. It is suggested that the course of these migrations is marked by the following complex of cultural features . . . . These features, all or in part, are traced back to the so-called 'Pit-Grave', 'Ochre Grave' and 'Kurgan' cultures of the Pontic region and its eastward extension.[91]

In recent years this hypothesis has crystallised into a reality in the opinion of V. Dumitrescu, writing of Rumania in this period,[92] and M. Garašanin in his *Prehistory of Serbia*. There we have already mentioned the tumulus-burials at Belotić of c. 2000 B.C., and M. Garašanin has excavated other important tumuli at Bela Crkva and Dobrača which are dated within the period known in Greece as the Middle Helladic period. Of these and other phenomena he wrote as follows: "L'interprétation historique de tous les différents éléments étudiés ci-dessus se base en premier lieu sur le rôle des mouvements successifs des peuplades venus des steppes. Ceux-ci contribuèrent dans la plus grande mesure à l'indoeuropéanisation du monde balkanique et du Sud-Est européen."[93]

We may thus see parallel developments in Yugoslavia and in the areas south of central Yugoslavia. Groups of Illyrian-speaking pastoralists, led by Kurgan chieftains, entered and came to control western Serbia from c. 2000 onwards, and they and other similar peoples gradually extended their territories southwards until, as we shall see, they reached the coast of central Albania and the coast of the Thermaic Gulf almost a millennium and a half later. Throughout this time, and indeed to some extent afterwards, they buried their heroic chieftains in tumuli. Some centuries earlier the first groups of Greek-speaking pastoralists, led by Kurgan chieftains, entered the lakeland, central Albania and western Macedonia, and they and other similar peoples gradually extended their territories southwards until the last of them, the so-called Dorians and West Greeks, reached Laconia and sailed across the Aegean.

That they were pastoralists and as transhumant pastoralists partly nomadic is clear not only from the areas in which they chose primarily to make their habitat, but also from the fact that, although the tumuli were conspicuous and some burials were rich, no corresponding settlements have been found in western Serbia,[94] central Albania, western Macedonia, Leucas and elsewhere in Greece in the Early and Middle Helladic periods. Like the Vlachs and the Albanians of the medieval period, they had little of cultural value to give to the settled peoples of peninsular Greece. "Their contribution lay in introducing or stimulating more effective political organisation."[95] In this respect the first Greek-speaking immigrants were as successful as the Dorians proved to be later; for it was they who organised the kingdoms of the Mycenaean era.

As I have argued elsewhere, it is likely that speakers of the Ionian dialect in its earliest form learnt seafaring, occupied Leucas in the R graves period, and established footholds on the western coast of the Peloponnese and on the eastern coast of Attica (see Map 21).[96] On the other hand, the speakers of Aeolian dialect in its earliest form extended their sway from central Albania and western Macedonia to include much of Thessaly in E. H. II; at that time the area of Perrhaebia on the west flank of Mt Olympus provided the main line of communication between the Haliacmon valley and the lakeland area. Extensions of the early Aeolian-speaking group reached Elatea and Chaeronea in the eastern part of central Greece (see Map 21). But the strongest wave of immigrants seems to have come in the last part of the Middle Helladic period, when speakers of Aeolian and Arcadian dialects occupied places which were to be leading Mycenaean centres such as Mycenae, Lerna, Pylos and Malthi.

Some of the traditions which the Greeks themselves preserved about their earliest days fit into this picture. The names of Kronos and Rhea, the parents of the chief god of the Mycenaean period, Zeus, were located in central Albania; for in the poetic tradition 'Kronios Kolpos' and 'Rheas Kolpos' were names of the lower part of what we call the Adriatic Sea. In classical times the Greeks used as a special name for this part of the sea 'Ionios Kolpos' or 'Ionian Gulf'. The chief location of Zeus himself was Mt Olympus and Pieria, although this area lay outside the orbit of Mycenaean culture. The oracular shrine of Zeus, the entry to the underworld, and a cult of necromancy were located at Dodona and on the Acheron river in Epirus, another region beyond the fringe of the Mycenaean world. The first Greeks to inhabit what became known as Hellas, i.e. the peninsula south of a line from the Ambracian Gulf to Mt Olympus, were located in the northeastern part of Thessaly, where three sons where born to Hellen, the eponymous ancestors of the three dialectal groups: Ionians, Aeolians and Dorians; and their cousins, Macedon and Magnes, occupied the area to the north "round Pieria and Olympus." The first hero to sail the sea, Jason, went from the Gulf of Pagasae to win the golden fleece in the Pontic region and to return by the Adriatic Sea and the Ionian Gulf. These are the traditions of peoples who lived for centuries on the northern fringes of Hellas and had entered it from the north.

We must turn now to the archaeological evidence in order to trace any large movements of *peoples* in this period, probably but not necessarily associated with the movements of Kurgan *chieftains* (see Map 22). Although J. L. Caskey did not include any tumuli north of Leucas in his consideration and made no mention of Kurgan leaders, he had no doubts about the immigration of new peoples into Greece. "A new people arrived in central Greece, probably in the twentieth century B.C. .... In some parts of Greece they settled peacefully in the communities of those who had come before, e.g. at Lerna [i.e. in E. H. II/III], while elsewhere they captured towns and killed or absorbed the older inhabitants. Before long they were spread through all the Peloponnese."[97] We have described an irruption of Kurgan-led peoples of a primitive and probably pastoralist background into the Argolic plain and the flimsy nature of their dwellings. At that time the first dwellings of Lerna IV in E. H. III had apsidal ends in many cases, and one of the first houses at nearby Tiryns in the M. H. period had an oval end. Changes at Eutresis in Boeotia at the beginning of M. H. were accompanied by the appearance of apsidal-ended houses, and recent excavations at Lianokladhi in the Spercheus valley have exposed an apsidal-ended house of M. H. date.[98] On the western side of the peninsula, houses with curving or apsidal walls appeared at Malthi early in M. H. and at Olympia probably in M. H. Oval and apsidal structures have been found at Thermum in Aetolia and on Mt Amali in Leucas. These flimsy houses and also larger structures with apsidal or oval ends were typical of a pastoral, semi-nomadic people; indeed it is noticeable that only the first generation or two of settlers made them, and that later generations built themselves rectangular houses of a permanent kind. An apsidal-ended built tomb in Tumulus II at Marathon maintained the pastoral tradition with religious conservatism.[99]

The spread of these pastoral peoples throughout the Greek peninsula lowered the standard of life and culture in E. H. III and in the early part of M. H. The decline was due to the change in local conditions and not to a change in Aegean conditions; for at this time Minoan Crete was developing apace in prosperity and trade. Throughout Greece there was a shrinkage of trade, and settlements became smaller. But there were more of them. Many of the new settlements were made in the western Peloponnese, especially in Elis and western Messenia; and these areas were no doubt chosen as being the best for transhumant pastoralism. All the indications are that pastoralist peoples were moving south from the great areas of transhumant pastoralism in Epirus, central Albania, the lakeland and southwest Macedonia and that for a time they continued to practise this way of life in central Greece and the Peloponnese.

During the M. H. period and in increasing numbers in the latter part of the period many small groups of pastoralist peoples were taking possession of Epirus, many parts of which had been almost unoccupied since the Palaeolithic Period. Their standard of life was very low and their pottery was crude. A typical encampment of the period has been found at

Thesprotikon in southern Epirus: its round huts, some 6 m in external circumference, were made of poles and thatch, and on the sloping ground each had a half-circle of flat stones as a foundation. The huts of the Sarakatsani today are much the same. These groups came from the lakeland area and western Macedonia, as far as one can judge on the present evidence, and other groups of similar people occupied Corcyra, Leucas and Aetolia. Thus the whole of the northwest region became an area of transhumant pastoralism.[100]

During the latter part of M. H. conditions improved and trade developed, especially on the eastern side of the peninsula, which traded most readily with the Cyclades and Crete. The earlier population may have played some part in the recovery. The western cemetery of the settlement at Eleusis in Attica, which was an important settlement throughout the M. H. period, reflected this growing prosperity in that the typical cist-graves of the period became larger and offerings were made in the graves in the latter phase of the period. The larger cist-graves had side openings, developed probably in the tradition of the Cycladic cist-graves with their symbolical doorway.[101]

Another group of cist-graves, at Sesklo in northeastern Thessaly, is suggestive of different contacts. In contrast to the Eleusis cist-graves these graves contained as offerings a number of objects which have been found in tumulus-burials in Albania, Leucas and Mycenae.[102] The connections here were with the northwestern area. It seems that the rulers of Sesklo in the M. H. period, and particularly at the time of the F graves late in the period, had the same cultural background as the rulers of Mycenae, Leucas and central Albania. On the inland route to the west from Sesklo the M. H. settlement at Tsangli had numerous links with the Haliacmon valley, Porodin in Pelagonia and Malik in the lakeland area, especially with the last.[103] It is evident that western Thessaly looked towards the pastoral areas of northern Pindus and made contacts there with the pastoral peoples farther north.

On the other hand, the coastal plain of Macedonia and its hinterland had hardly any contact with the south, and the M. H. period there was marked by stagnation and decline. Very few building remains or imported objects have been found. Some people may have moved south into Thessaly and central Greece, as 'anchors' have been found at Sesklo and at Cirrha near Delphi in contexts of this period. Conditions were better at Molyvopyrgo in Chalcidice, which traded with the south and imported a popular M. H. pottery, named 'Minyan' after King Minyas of Orchomenus in Boeotia, where it was first found. This pottery had a metallic sheen, which resulted probably from the invention of a hotter kiln. Its origin is disputed, but it seems to have been produced independently in several areas.[104] One of these was Pelagonia, where the influences of the Bubanj-Hum II culture were strong; it resulted in a West-Macedonian form of Minyan-type pottery.[105] Pelagonia seems to have been more fully populated and more progressive than the rest of Macedonia throughout the M. H. period. Pastoral groups from there were among those which occupied Epirus and adjacent areas; for the unpainted potteries of the two areas were almost identical, especially in the excessive use of plastic decoration.[106]

In the lakeland area the final phase of the settlement Malik IIb and the start of Malik IIIa fell within E. H. III, and the tradition was marked by the arrival of perforated hammers and hammer-axes. As we have seen above, these are among the evidences of Kurgan-led peoples coming from the north into the lakeland area. The latter part of Malik IIIa, the whole of IIIb and part of IIIc fell within the Middle Helladic period. In the excavation of Malik III no building remains were found except occasionally a hearth or a layer of mud from decayed mud-bricks, and we may infer from this that there was a further increase in pastoralism beyond that noted in Malik IIb and therefore, given the altitude of Malik, transhumant pastoralism was being practised on a large scale. The tools and weapons of the inhabitants were made of stone, horn and bone until the final phase, from which came two knives, a curved knife and a ring-pin, all of bronze. It was partly but only partly on the evidence of these weapons that the earlier part of Malik IIIc was dated by Prendi within the last part of M. H. Although metal was so rare, Malik IIIa-c was a more lively and progressive community than any in central Macedonia, and more traffic was passing through the lakeland area than through the Vardar valley at that time. The pottery of Malik III, which was very varied and advanced to a high standard by the end of IIIc (c. 1500 B.C., dated by Prendi), reflected the influences of central Macedonia (especially the wishbone handle, and more examples of the clay 'anchor' than in Malik IIb),

Pelagonia (plastic decoration and small altar-tables) and Leucas (pricked dots with incised triangles, some forms of plastic decoration and perforated ledge-lugs), and there were signs of Kurgan influence in collared jugs and fluted decoration, inspired probably by metal-work originally. Incised markings on the bases of pots resemble markings at Vučedol in northern Yugoslavia, and the bronze ring-pin in IIIc is typical of the Aunjetitz culture of Hungary at that time. The contacts of Malik reached a climax in the period of IIIc (1700–1500 B.C.) when there were many new shapes and among them high-handled cantharoi of Minyan style, as in the F graves of Leucas.[107]

It is thus clear that Malik was at the centre of a considerable amount of traffic throughout the M. H. period and in the following century. Articles of trade and perhaps immigrants came from the north, probably via Kossovo and Polog, into the lakeland. There are indications that large numbers of pastoral groups moved over from the pastures of Pelagonia and central Macedonia to those of the lakeland and lowland Albania and Epirus, and it was these groups which helped to create a great area of transhumant pastoralism extending southwestwards to Leucas and Aetolia. Malik itself served the same function as Muskopole in the acme of Vlach prosperity: it formed a centre for the meeting of transhumant shepherds who came from many quarters to the summer pastures of the region, and its people conducted the trade in the products of pastoralism, which extended northwards into central Europe. The domesticated horse was now in use for hunting, war, and transportation as a pack animal.[108]

The leaders and organisers of pastoral groups and of combinations of them became powerful and wealthy in this type of pastoral and stock-raising society, as the tribal chiefs (*phylarchi*) and the *tshelnikadzi* did in Vlach society. It was no doubt some of these leaders who were buried in the great tumuli which were constructed in most parts of Albania in the Middle Helladic period. The two largest tumuli at Pazhok, a natural centre of lowland communications, were reused, and many of the burials (made in the inner tumuli) contained daggers, long spearheads and tweezers of bronze, which the excavators, Selim Islami and Hasan Ceka, dated to the middle part of M. H. "c. 1800–1700 B.C."[109] In the very short report of the excavations there were no illustrations of these objects, but on a visit to Tirana in 1972 I saw two daggers and a broken tweezer, which, we were told, had been found together at Pazhok. One, a rapier-like poignard with three rivets set in a triangle, a very narrow blade and a strong mid-rib, bore a close resemblance to two poignards from the latest of the R graves in Leucas which belonged to the opening part of M. H.[110] The other, with three very large rivets set in a triangle, a very slight ridge and a broad blade narrowing gradually, was of a type found in Crete and of Middle Minoan II type.[111]

Tumuli which were made for the first time in the Middle Helladic period, on present evidence, range from north to south Albania (Map 21). At Çinamak on the left bank of the Black Drin, just south of its confluence with the White Drin at Kukës, a place which is a centre of communications leading to Scodra, the Metohija and the lakeland at Ochrid, there is a cemetery of sixty-seven tumuli alongside the river.[112] Of these, four have been excavated, and in them the dead man was inhumed in a pit, often lined with stones, and the pit was then covered with a layer of stones. The tumuli varied between 16 and 24 m in diameter, and the surface of them was covered with a layer of stones. The central burial of Tumulus I was in a quadrangular pit, i.e. a mortuary chamber, lined with stones and some 60 cm deep; it contained a dagger with three large rivets set in a triangle and without a mid-rib, in fine condition, which is of the same type as the second dagger at Pazhok. In the middle valley of the Mati river, through which routes from the coastal plain lead to the mountains of the interior, there are several hundred tumuli of which thirty-five were excavated before 1964. Of these two, numbered 1 and 3 by the excavators, yielded bronze knives of M. H. type, but the excavation report was of the sketchiest.[113]

At Vajzë, which lies on the route from the Gulf of Valona to the Aous valley and the interior, four tumuli, 18 to 24 m in diameter, were excavated by Frano Prendi. In Tumulus A a cairn of stones was called a 'krematorium' by Prendi and on the cairn a long rapier and a knife, both of bronze, and a high-handled cup were found, and the central burial of the tumulus had a slotted spearhead and a shoed spearhead, both of bronze. In this tumulus alone the burials were in pit-graves and the rite was cremation; in the other tumuli inhumations and cist-graves, sometimes slab-lined, were the rule. These weapons and some others in the fill of Tumulus A were of Middle Minoan, Middle Cycladic and Middle Helladic types, and they resembled specimens found in Leucas and at Sesklo.[114] At Vodhinë, on a tributary of the upper Drin, where the best route from the Drin valley leads to the upper Kalamas and the plain of Ioannina, there is a group of tumuli and one of them was excavated by Frano Prendi. The tumulus, 17 m in diameter, covered a low ring-wall of two stones set side by side, 13 m in diameter, and in the centre a cairn of stones stood over the earliest burial, which was an inhumation with no offerings. Two cremations came next, being in cist-graves lined with slabs, one situated on the cairn and the other close to the cairn. One of the cist-graves had a bronze dagger of Middle Minoan type, and each cist-grave had a set of cremation pots which have analogies at Tsangli and in Leucas of the M. H. period. These were succeeded by an inhumation in a cist-grave, also set on the cairn. This was the inner tumulus of a double tumulus, which had lost most of its upper part through ploughing.[115]

The presence of Aegean weapons in the burials of the chieftains in Albania is not surprising, when we remember the stagnation of the Vardar valley and central Macedonia and on the other hand the relative richness of the burials in the tumuli of Leucas which lay on the sea route to the Adriatic.[116] It is evident that Albania and the lakeland played the same role as they had in the Neolithic and Eneolithic periods, being intermediary stages in the passage of goods by sea and by land from the Mediterranean to central Europe. Metal weapons of Aegean types were found not only in Albania but also farther north in western Serbia, for instance in tumuli at Belotić and at Humska Čuka,[117] a site of Bubanj-Hum culture near Niš. It is evident that this traffic was organised by or passed through the hands of Kurgan chieftains, both Greek-speaking and Illyrian-speaking, and that their kindred in Leucas had a grip on the trade by sea towards the west and the north.[118] They were well armed with a variety of weapons—swords, spears, halberds, daggers and knives of metal, and bows with arrows of flint or obsidian—and they had some defensive armour to judge from the bronze discs which were probably shield-bosses.[119] They were no doubt mounted or drove in a horse-drawn car. Their followers had perforated hammers and hammer-axes of stone, slings with clay bullets, and wood-tipped spears. As shepherds the Kurgan chieftains and their followers could protect their herds from the wild beasts which were abundant in the heavily-forested western areas of Albania and Epirus and in Macedonia, and in war and raiding they were formidable enemies to the settled peoples of the peninsula. It is easy to understand their ability to migrate into southern lands and impose their rule on less warlike peoples in a period when very few persons had possession of metal weapons and horses.[120]

The tumuli have something to tell us about the organisation of the Greek-speaking inhabitants of Albania in the Middle Helladic period. The preponderance of men and of men's weapons in the burials show that it was a male-dominated society, and the continuous use of the same tumulus for centuries shows that the family tradition was very strong. It has been observed, wherever there are many tumuli, that they were made in clustered groups, indicating the association of leading families within a larger, tribal group. Although the tribal groups were related in that they buried their heroes in tumuli, they differed from one another, region by region, in the details of their ritual and customs. So too in Leucas, where the tumulus-groups R, F and S differed in practices as well as in time. The situation within Albania in the Middle Helladic period was very much the same as it was before the last war, when families, tribes and regional groups were firmly embedded in the fabric of society. In the Middle Helladic period, as in pre-war Albania, we may be confident that strong dialects were spoken in the different cantons of this mountainous country. Raiders and migrants carried their dialects with them, whether Ionic, Aeolic or Arcadian, just as the Albanians of the medieval period brought Geg, Tosk, Ljap or Tsam into the Greek peninsula.

NOTES

1. See the general accounts of S. S. Weinberg in *CAH*³ I, i, pp. 601 f. and D. Theochares in *ITEE* 1, pp. 67 f. The former has perhaps overreacted to the fame enjoyed by Dimini when it was the only such site, and Theochares has emphasised the importance of these citadels by noting that the megaron near Velestino was larger than the megara of Mycenae, Tiryns and Pylos in their days of splendour. Theochares gives a pictorial reconstruction of Dimini on p. 70.

2. See S. I. Dakaris, *Thesprotia*, pp. 48 f.

3. D. Mustilli in *Rendiconti Accad. d'Italia, Classe di Scienze Morali e Storiche* 2 (1941) 678 f., and a summary in *Epirus*, pp. 290 f. with further references.

4. As I pointed out in *Epirus*, pp. 290 f. and 293 f.; F. Prendi has come to the same conclusion in *SA* 1972, 1, 10.

5. See *PM*, p. 146, no. 62, fig. 13 (1) and *SA* 1972, 1, 30, pl. VI and pl. VIII, 13.

6. Tsountas mentioned that Thessaly imported flint from Epirus and Albania within his memory (cited in *BSA* 42, 172). I described the asphalt mines in *Epirus*, pp. 231 f.

7. Preliminary reports on Kamnik are by S. Aliu and B. Jubani in *StH*, 1969, 1, 159 f.; *Buletin Arkeologjik* 1969, 1-12 with two plates; *SA* 1971, 1, 132 f; and *Bulletin d'archéologie sud-est européenne* 2 (1971) 13-14 with fig. 2, and there is a fuller report by S. Aliu and F. Prendi in *Iliria* 1 (1971) 13-30 with sixteen plates, and a summary by F. Prendi in *SA* 1972, 1, 3-13. The primitive houses of branches and clay-daub may have been for summer use only (described in *StH* 1969, 1, 163).

8. As I wrote in *Epirus*, p. 25, before there was any report on Kamnik, "for instance, 500 Vlach families have summer pastures in the Kolonjë and rent pastures from the citizens of Konispol each winter" (Konispol owns a side valley of the Pavla).

9. So F. Prendi in *SA* 1972, 1, 12 "les rapports Maliq-Kamnik-Dimini et surtout la présence de la poterie de Dimini 'classique' à Kamnik montrent que la civilisation étudiée est synchronique à celle de la phase finale de Dimini." I give the divisions and dates put forward by V. Milojčić, *Chronologie d. jungeren Steinzeit Mittel- und Südösteuropas* (1949), as I did in *Macedonia*, p. 214.

10. The preliminary report by the excavator of the site, Frano Prendi, was in *SA* 1964, 1, 91 f., the full report in *SA* 1966, 1, 255 f. A subsidiary report on further excavations is in *SA* 1967, 1, 140 f., and an assessment of its place in the Neolithic period in *SA* 1972, 1, 3 f. I am most grateful to Frano Prendi for his kindness in sending me offprints and showing me some of the finds at Triana in 1972.

11. S. S. Weinberg in *CAH*³ I, i, p. 608 calls the crusted wares "of European derivation" (meaning central Europe), and D. Theochares in *ITEE*, p. 68 regards them as usual in northern cultures, i.e. north of Thessaly. For its presence at Malik I see *SA* 1966, 1, 256 and 268.

12. *SA* 1972, 1, 8.

13. *PM*, p. 117 with references.

14. *SA* 1966, 1, 269 for Malik. The deposit at Kamnik was twice as thick as that at Malik; Prendi did not put an absolute date for its end in *SA* 1966, but has suggested 2600 in *Iliria* 1 (1971), 30.

15. For spirals see *SA* 1972, 1, 30, pl. 6, bottom row left (Cakran); *SA* 1971, 1, 133 "le principal motif employé pour la decoration est la spirale" and *Iliria* 1, 30, pls. 10 and 11 (Kamnik); *PM*, p. 146, fig. 13,i (Servia); *Epirus*, p. 291 (Velcë). The same spirals occurred later at Tren (*Iliria* 1, 47, pl. 4). For the hearths see *Bulletin d'archéologie sud-est européenne* 1 (1969) 14.

16. Strabo 7 C 327; *Macedonia*, p. 230 with references. The settlement on Lake Ochrid at Crkveni Livadhi was by the outflow also. This was the best place for catching fish. For the importance of fish to the much later pile-settlement on Lake Prasias in the Strymon basin, see Herodotus 5.16.

17. *PM*, pp. 55, 77, 163; the only colour mentioned by Heurtley was grey.

18. See *Macedonia*, p. 231, n. 2 and the report of B. Jovanović, "Early copper metallurgy of the Central Balkans," *Actes du VIIIe congrès International des Sciences Pré- et Protohistoriques* 1(1972) 131 f. It has been suggested that copper was mined at this time at Plakalnica in northwest Bulgaria (*Archaeology* [Sofia] 1974, 1, 50); and evidence of copper-mining in the Eneolithic period has been found at Aibunar near Stara Zagora in central Bulgaria (ibid. 1971, 1, 67). Copper celts and copper hooks of the period have been found at Salmanovo in northeast Bulgaria and a pile-settlement has been excavated near Varna on the Black Sea coast. The immediate ties of Malik are likely to have been with Metohija and the north.

19. For references see *Macedonia*, pp. 222 f. Saddle-shaped weights of the Salcuta type were found at Kamnik, as at Malik II a 2 (*Iliria* 1, 30, pl. 16, 1-2, and *SA* 1966, 1, 272, pl. 3, f on the right). For Bulgaria see *Macedonia*, p. 442.

20. See *Macedonia*, pp. 220 and 229 for references.

21. Grbić, *Porodin* (Bitolj, 1960); I saw some of the material in the museum at Monastir in 1968. I give a summary in *Macedonia*, pp. 223 f.

22. Cvijić noted in 1908 that the shepherds of Pelagonia pastured 6,000 sheep on Mt Babuna (above Prilep) and took them to the plain of Thessaly for the winter.

23. M. Gimbutas in *Journal of Field Archaeology* 1 (1974) 35 and 66.

24. I had the good fortune to be shown the finds from Karanovo in 1968; see *Macedonia*, p. 442.

25. I am using the chronology which M. Gimbutas advanced in her book, *The Prehistory of Eastern Europe* (Cambridge, Mass., 1956) and in R. W. Ehrich, ed., *Chronologies in Old World Archaeology*, p. 494; and I am drawing my ac-

count from her article on the Kurgan culture in *Indo-Europeans*, pp. 155 f. I am most grateful for the help she has given me in conversations at conferences.

26. *Indo-Europeans*, pp. 178 and 180.

27. For the burials see *Macedonia*, pp. 243 f. with references. The leg of the cult vessel is illustrated in *PM*, p. 140, fig. 9, i (the cult vessel being called a "zoomorphic" vase). The quotation is from *Indo-Europeans*, p. 179.

28. *PM*, p. 54.

29. *PM*, p. 150, no. 91, p. 73, and p. 79, n. 4.

30. *PM*, p. 147, no. 76.

31. See also my discussion of the dating in *Macedonia*, pp. 243 f. It should be made clear that I am not accusing Heurtley of an error, as A. M. Snodgrass stated in *JHS* 94 (1974) 230, because there was no tumulus for him or anyone else to see in this century; for the ground above the second burial was "much broken up by ploughing" (*PM*, p. 55). Heurtley's description is, as always, meticulous. The suggestion that there was originally a tumulus is based on the method of burial inside the settlement and the need to cover up the second burial with a considerable amount of soil. Heurtley did not go beyond describing what he found.

32. See *AM* 30 (1905) 1 and *AE* 1908, 76, and my discussion in *Macedonia*, p. 262, n. 14. Snodgrass, loc. cit., has misread the last passage. He thought I accused A. J. B. Wace "of mistaking a tumulus for a small settlement-mound." In fact I said that Wace was "clearly correct." The point to grasp is that the tumulus was *inside* the settlement mound, just as at Lerna, and invisible until it was excavated. Such is the way of excavation, after all. Doubts arose about Soteriades' interpretation because only one tumulus of a prehistoric date in Greece was known at that time (at Aphidna). The situation is very different today. To translate Soteriades (*AE* 77) "after the burial the grave and the pyre were covered with a thick layer of clayey earth in the form of a tumulus (tymboeidos). Later burials were made above this cone."

33. *Hesp.* 27 (1957) 136 f. and 28 (1958) 205. One of the pots with the child was a small jug or dipper. Its high handle had a projection or broken-off horn on top; this remarkable type of handle was found at Armenokhori (to the north of Servia) and at Vardina on the left bank of the lower Vardar in the Late Neolithic period (*PM*, p. 72 and p. 151, no. 105 and p. 153, fig. 19 a-c).

34. D. Theochares in *ITEE* 1, p. 73. In *CAH*³ I, i, p. 604, S. S. Weinberg "preferred to assume that the spiral came to Thessaly from the Cyclades" (this was before the publication of the Cakran spirals) and he may be right. It is difficult however to see the Cyclades generating the concept and type of power which is indicated by the fortifications and the megara, especially if most of them were only recently settled.

35. R. W. Ehrich, ed. *Relative Chronologies in Old World Archaeology* (Chicago, 1954), p. 126.

36. *BSA* 69 (1974) 127 f. See also M. S. F. Hood in *Bronze Age Migrations in the Aegean*, ed. R. A. Crossland and Ann Birchall (London, 1973), pp. 59 f.

37. M. Gimbutas in *Indo-Europeans*, p. 186 and in *The Journal of Indo-European Studies* 1 (1973) 208.

38. J. L. Caskey in *CAH*³ I, ii, p. 805.

39. See *Macedonia*, pp. 234 f. with references. The term 'Trojan Culture' which is used in *ITEE*, 1, p. 92 seems to beg the question of origin and leadership and I have avoided it.

40. J. L. Caskey, *CAH*³ I, ii, p. 774: "These [bored hammer-axes and 'anchors'] are distinctive objects, and a proper understanding of their wide dissemination may ultimately give a useful clue to interrelationships." Pace Snodgrass in *JHS* 94, 230, these anchors are not to be confused with Kurgan cultures. For representations of those in Macedonia see *PM*, p. 203, fig. 67, f-j.

41. *AI* 4 (1963) 7f. and pl. 2, and pp. 14 f. M. Garašanin in 39 *BRGK*, pp. 53 f. and *The Prehistory of Serbia* 2, pp. 606-612 (in French).

42. For Malik II b see *SA* 1966, 1, 261 and *Macedonia*, p. 241; for Tren see *SA* 1967, 1, 142 f. and *Deuxième Conférence des études albanologiques* 2 (Tirana, 1970), p. 335 with 14 plates and 7 figures. The move to Tren cave, 856 m above sea level, was probably due to worsening conditions as the anchor-people advanced into Upper Macedonia. These people may have penetrated to the Adriatic coast via Malik, as an anchor was found at Malik II b and one was represented on a pot of Gajtan near Scodra (*Macedonia*, fig. 4 a and o). For the importance of the route by Tren see my article in *JHS* 94 (1974) 71 f.

43. *SA* 1966, 1, 263-64. There is a cross-dating with Kostolac also, see *Macedonia*, p. 242, n. 6.

44. As M. Garašanin writes in *The Prehistory of Serbia*, 2, p. 612: "Il est nécessaire une fois encore de songer à des vagues successives d'éléments nouveaux, dont le déclanchement se rattache aux mouvements des pasteurs indo-européens des steppes."

45. M. Grbić, *Porodin*, p. 54 and pl. 32, 6; the mace-head is in the Museum of Monastir, where I saw it in 1968. The figurine and the mace-head are shown in *Macedonia*, fig. 2 f. and fig. 13 j. For the mace-head see *Indo-Europeans*, p. 158 and fig. 2, 3; Gimbutas places it in the Middle Kurgan period. For others see V. Dumitrescu, *Arta Preistorica in Romania* (1974), pp. 258 f. and 504. Had there been wild horses in the area in neolithic times, some of their bones would have been found among the animal bones which have been recorded from many sites. Horse bones have been known in central Macedonia in both the Early Bronze Age and the Middle Bronze Age of Macedonia (*PM*, pp. 88 and 93), although called in question by J. L. Caskey in *CAH*³ I, ii, p. 775.

46. *Indo-Europeans*, p. 166.

47. See M. Garašanin (op. cit., note 44), 2, p. 612.

48. *Macedonia*, pp. 241; Gimbutas, *Prehistory of Eastern Europe* 1, pl. 10 and pl. 12, 5.

49. *Buletin Arkeologjik* 1969, 13, pl. 1.

50. W. Dörpfeld, *Alt-Ithaka* (Munich, 1927). For Kurgans at Leucas see M. Gimbutas in *Bronze Age Migrations in the Aegean*, p. 133. I have discussed these tumuli in two articles, "Tumulus-burial in Albania, the Grave Circles of Mycenae, and the Indo-Europeans," *BSA* 62 (1967) 77 f., and "The tumulus-burials of Leucas and their connections in the Balkans and northern Greece," *BSA* 69 (1974) 127 f.

51. Both Italy and the northern and central Balkans had copper at this time, their Chalcolithic periods. Professor A. Fol tells me that evidence of important copper-mining of this period has been found recently in the Stranca range of east Bulgaria.

52. *Indo-Europeans*, p. 170. The idea of birth and fertility and rebirth may have been involved in such a sacrifice, as in the deposition of a cult vessel and a phallus at Servia. It has been suggested that a woman and a child were buried alongside a chieftain on the same principle as a sheep and a lamb, or that a man's wife and eldest child were buried with him, e.g. at Bela Crkva (*Adriatica G. Novak dicata* [Zagreb, 1970] p. 137).

53. Selim Islami and Hasan Ceka, "Nouvelles données sur l'antiquité illyrienne en Albanie," *SA* 1964, 1, 95 f., which I have discussed in *BSA* 62, 77 f. See also *Les Illyriens et la genèse des Albanais* (Tirana, 1971), p. 91 with pl. 1.

54. *Shqiperia Arkeologjike*, plate 23.

55. *PM*, p. 66 and 140, figs. 8 and 9.

56. *PM*, pp. 74 and 204, fig. 68.

57. *PM*, p. 140, fig. 9 i; the reproduction is half the real size. The decoration of single short strokes round the collar of the Pazhok pot is the same as that below the rim in *PM*, p. 140, fig. 8 c.

58. For the Kostolac pottery see A. Benac, *Studije o kamenom i bakarnom dobu u sjeverozapadnom Balkanu* (Sarajevo, 1964), pl. 30, 3 and 6 and pl. 31, 4; see his remarks and dating on p. 176 of the summary in French.

59. M. Garašanin, *Sbornik Radova Narodnog Myzeja* 1 (1956–71), p. 48 with figs. 7 a-d, and *The Prehistory of Serbia* 2, p. 618 and pls. 44 and 45.

60. The report is in M. Garašanin, op. cit., pp. 47 and 618. I am most grateful to him for giving me copies of both works.

61. M. Gimbutas in *The Journal of Indo-European Studies* 1 (1973) 205, quoting the original publication which I have not seen by B. Jovanović, *Mokrin* II (Belgrade, 1972).

62. See M. Gimbutas, *Indo-Europeans*, p. 184 and in *Bronze Age Migrations in the Aegean*, p. 134.

63. I gave my arguments for this conclusion in *Epirus*, pp. 363 f.; for Aphiona see *AM* 59 (1934) 173 f.

64. In Bulle's words "fast identisch" with the corded ware at Aphiona; Dörpfeld described it in *Alt-Ithaka*, pp. 170 f. and Beilage 57.

65. See *Macedonia*, p. 249 and fig. 4 n for the confused site at Gajtan and the corded ware there; *Epirus* pp. 292, 309 and fig. 7, 1; and *PM*, pp. 83 and 172, fig. 46 a.

66. See *Macedonia*, p. 233 n. 1 for references; Tsountas, *Dimini and Sesklo*, pp. 351 f. figs. 292 f., and *BSA* 69 (1974) 132.

67. The preliminary report was in *Arch. Anz.* 1959, 56-74.

68. H. Biesantz gave page references in *PM* which apply to Servia II a and not to Servia II b, which would be closer in time to his date for the Souphli urns.

69. For instance, *PM*, p. 159 and pls. 7 and 8, nos. 107 and 109, and *SA* 1966, 1, 272, pls. 11, 14 and 19.

70. The account by M. Korkuti is published in *Deuxième Conférence des études albanologiques* (Tirana) 2, 337 f. with figs. 3 and 4. The urns are not described but one is seen in fig. 4 to have a high collar like those at Souphli. The practice continued into the next period at Souphli. Korkuti mentions that a similar rite to that at Tren was practised in the Iron Age at Gajtan near Scodra, but the document to which he refers is on deposit in the archaeological archives and inaccessible to me; B. Jubani says that they contained bones of children and suggests that it was so at Tren also (*Les Illyriens et la genèse des Albanais*, p. 94).

71. *Arch. Anz.* 1959, 56 f.; also an illustration in *Arch. Anz.* 1957, 54. For such stelai see Gimbutas, *Indo-Europeans*, p. 170 with fig. 13, e.g. "Kurgan house graves built of timber or of stone slabs were covered with an earthen or stone mound and then topped with a stone stela." Such a stone stele is also called a 'menhir'.

72. Dr. G. Toncheva, who was accompanying me, was a great help. At that time I was told they had not been published; they may have been published since 1970 when I was there. They are close in shape to those illustrated by M. Gimbutas.

73. Illustrated in *A Companion to Homer*, ed. A. J. B. Wace and F. H. Stubbings (1972), figs. 9 b and 33.

74. The Slavs also made such stelai, but the resemblances fit the prehistoric date. E. Vermeule, *Greece in the Bronze Age* (Chicago, 1964), p. 21 is unduly sceptical in saying it may be medieval; for it could not have been used on an M.H. grave.

75. *Hesp.* 25 (1956) 165; I discussed this mound in *BSA* 62 (1967) 90. Caskey's words are quoted from *CAH*³ I, ii, p. 785, and he mentioned on p. 777 the similarity with Lianokladhi. He illustrated five pieces of anchors in *Hesp.* 25, pl. 47 and an imitation of corded ware in pl. 44 c. There were changes also at Lefkandi in Euboea at the transition from E.H. II to E.H. III; see the preliminary reports by M. Popham and H. Sackett, p. 6.

76. At Argissa for instance, there was destruction by fire and anchors in the latest E.H. strata. As at Lerna, the Kurgans may have led others from Macedonia on the invasion and included them in the settlement.

77. The ritual is detailed and precise; only the scale is magnified. Homer's account is confused in one respect: the jars

of honey and wine and "the bed" are mentioned in connection with the pyre, but "the bed" against which the jars rested was evidently the resting-place in the mortuary chamber, "the hut" (lines 170-71 and 252-54). The confusion shows that he was not himself familiar with the procedure. The remains of Hector were placed in an urn which was covered with cloth, and the hollow trench was covered with a cairn of stones (*Iliad* 24.796 f.), as at Vodhinë in southern Albania, before the tumulus was raised up.

78. See Sp. Marinatos in *Bronze Age Migrations in the Aegean* p. 111 with pls. 13 and 14.

79. The complexity of the dating problems was not realised by the early excavators of tumuli and is still not appreciated by many whose experience has been with other forms of burial or settlements. For example, a figurine of L.H. III B type was found in a burial in Circle A at Mycenae which was otherwise of L.H. I date; in other contexts the burial might be dated rightly by the latest object in it, but in this context G. E. Mylonas, *Mycenae and the Mycenaean Age* (Princeton, N.J., 1966), pp. 95-96 was able to explain that the figurine had fallen into the burial during the filling-in of a small cave somewhat higher up. There were similar displacements in Circle B between one burial and another, e.g. *PAE* 1952, 456. It is a mistake to make no allowance for this complexity as A. M. Snodgrass wished to do in regard to two burials at Vodhinë (*JHS* 94 [1974] 230); see my note on this matter in *BSA* 69 (1974) 132, written before his review.

80. On these stelai at Mycenae see Mylonas, op. cit., pp. 93 and 107, and my comments on them in *BSA* 62 (1967) 87. The only antecedent in Greece is the 'menhir' of Kurgan type at Souphli Magoula.

81. The roundish stones and the upright slabs of the two circles at Pazhok are clearly visible in *Bronze Age Migrations in The Aegean*, pls. 28-29. For a ring-wall at Marathon see our Plate 8b.

82. For these 'double tumuli' see *StGH* 2 (Pazhok), 12 (Vodhinë), 13 (Arnissa), and 16 (Leucas).

83. G. E. Mylonas (op. cit., note 79), p. 100.

84. For my dates see *BSA* 69 (1974) 127 f.

85. So Sp. Marinatos in *Bronze Age Migrations in the Aegean*, p. 112.

86. I wrote an article on the subject in *BSA* 62 (1967) 77 f.

87. For references see my article, loc. cit.

88. Loc. cit. Twenty-five to thirty tumuli are mentioned in Messenia by K. Y. Syriopoulos in his *Prehistory of the Peloponnese* (Athens, 1964), pp. 413-414.

89. My studies here and in *BSA* 62, 66, and 69 lead me to suggest the following sequence as probable:

    E.H. I (and perhaps earlier also) Servia and Chaeronea.
    E.H. II Leucas R 1, 16, 26 c and probably others; Pazhok earliest burial.
    E.H. II/III transition Lerna tumulus (a cenotaph).
    E.H. III Leucas bulk of the R graves.
    M.H. early (c. 1900–1800) Leucas latest R graves.
    M.H. middle (c. 1800–1700) Pazhok most burials of inner tumuli; Vodhinë inner tumulus; Vajzë Tumulus A; Çinamak Tumulus I; Elatea tumulus; Peristeria near Pylos; Aphidna in Attica.
    M.H. late (c. 1700–1600) Mati T. 1 and T. 3; Pazhok latest burials of inner tumuli; Vajzë later burials of T.A; Leucas F and S graves; Mycenae earliest burials (mainly in Circle B); Papoulia and Kephalovryson near Pylos; Marathon earliest tumulus (c. 1625 onwards); Mycenae Circle A begins (c. 1620).

For the recently reported tumuli at Asine and Argos see *AR* 1972–73, 15 (*AR* 1971–72 p. 9 may also refer) and *AR* 1973–74, 10.

90. For these tumuli see *StGH*, pp. 172 f. and *AAA* 3 (1970) 357 f. Professor Marinatos kindly showed me the mound of the Plataeans and the Bronze Age tumuli in 1971; I believe the mound was raised in honour of the Plataeans and the slaves killed in the battle, and the skeletons may be those mainly of the slaves, while the corpses of the Plataeans were taken home.

91. *CAH*[3] I, ii, pp. 406 f.

92. *Arta Preistorica in Romania* (1974), p. 504. I am most grateful to him for giving me a copy of this important book.

93. *The Prehistory of Serbia*, 2, p. 621. I am most grateful to Professor Garašanin for sending me an offprint of the report on Belotić in *AI* 2 (1956) 11 f. and a copy of his important book. The tumuli of west Serbia have many features in common with the tumuli of Albania (see *Macedonia*, p. 270).

94. M. Garašanin, op. cit., 2, p. 617: "les formes d'habitats du groupe sont encore absolument inconnues."

95. R. A. Crossland in *CAH*[3] I, ii, p. 875.

96. The Aphidna tumulus is earlier than those at Marathon; for points in common with Leucas see *Macedonia*, p. 260 n. 14, and p. 261.

97. J. L. Caskey, *CAH*[3] II, i (1973), p. 139.

98. *AR* 1973–74, 21 with fig. 34.

99. For Leucas see Dörpfeld, *Alt-Ithaka* 1, pp. 201 f. with fig. 12; also Sp. Marinatos in *Bronze Age Migrations in the Aegean*, p. 112 with pl. 16.

100. For Epirus see *Epirus*, p. 308 and *PM*, p. 111 (Heurtley dated the movement to the Macedonian E.B.A., being unaware of discoveries made later in Epirus); for Corcyra, *Kerkyraika Khronika* 14 (1968) 80-81 with reference to several sites; for Leucas, Dörpfeld *Alt-Ithaka*; and for Aetolia, *DgL* 2, 2, p. 601. For the round huts see S. I. Dakaris, *Cassopaia and the Elean Colonies*, p. 29 and fig. 48 with references.

101. See Mylonas (op. cit. note 79), pp. 89 f. for a short description and for references to the excavation reports.

102. See *Macedonia*, pp. 265 f. and *BSA* 69 (1974) 136 f.; such objects in common include ear-rings, hair-rings, shoed spearheads, halberd blades, tweezers, knives, and the use of copper occasionally for weapons and pins.

103. See *Macedonia*, p. 267.

104. See J. L. Caskey in *CAH*³ II, i, pp. 118 f., p. 132 (Minyan ware of Troy VI) and p. 139; and J. Mellaart in *CAH*³ I, ii, pp. 682 and 700 f.

105. See *Macedonia*, p. 252 with references, to which should now be added M. Garašanin, *The Prehistory of Serbia*, 2, pp. 609-611.

106. See *Macedonia*, p. 253 with figs. 6-8.

107. The preliminary report on Malik was in *SA* 1964, 1, 91 f., and the main report, an excellent one by Frano Prendi was in *SA* 1966, 1, 255-80. I gave a very brief summary of it in *Macedonia*. Subsequent excavations at Malik have been reported by Muzafer Korkuti and Skender Anamali in *Bulletin d'archéologie sud-est européenne* (Bucarest) 1969, 1, 12 f. Both Prendi and Korkuti-Anamali mention Malik III c having "minoenne" pottery, by which they evidently meant Minyan and not Minoan pottery. It is possible that the end of Malik III c may have been earlier than 1500 B.C. for reasons which have been given by me in *Macedonia*, pp. 281 f., but the point is not of significance in the present context. 'Anchors' spread to Italy at this time, perhaps from Albania (see M. S. F. Hood in *Bronze Age Migrations in the Aegean*, p. 62).

108. See p. 110, above for the mace-head of a harnessed horse from Tsiplevets, the horse figurine from Porodin and the report of horse bones in Macedonia in both Early and Middle Bronze Age. In peninsular Greece horse bones were found in Lerna V, which is of M.H. date; a horse was buried in Tumulus I at Marathon near the end of M.H.; and horse and horse-drawn cars figured on stelai and gold rings at Mycenae. See *Macedonia*, pp. 267-68.

109. In *SA* 1964, 1, 96.

110. See *BSA* 69 (1974), pp. 129, 136, and 139.

111. See K. Branigan, *Aegean Metalwork of the Early and Middle Bronze Age* (Oxford, 1974), p. 88 for the large-sized rivets and no. 141 (from the Heraklion Museum) on pl. 3 for the arrangement of the rivets and the shape of the blade.

112. Reports are in *Buletin Arkeologjik* 1969, 37-48 with pl. 1 showing the dagger from Tumulus 1, in *SA* 1971, 1, 150 and in *Bulletin d'archéologie sud-est européenne* 2 (Bucarest, 1971) 27.

113. There are short reports in *BUSS* 1955, 1 and *SA* 1964, 1, 101 f. One of the knives is shown in the latter on pl. 12 as no. 3; it resembles a knife of M.H.–L.H. date from Sesklo with four rivets similarly set, but the Mati one had apparently six rivets. At Tirana in 1972 I was shown another such knife with five rivets similarly set, which came from Bazjë in the middle valley of the Mati. I mentioned the Mati knives and daggers in *Epirus*, pp. 329 f. with fig. 21, G. They are illustrated and discussed by M. Korkuti in *StH* 1970, 4, 159 f. with pl. 2.

114. Prendi's report on the Vajzë tumuli is in *BUSS* 1957, 2, 76 f.; I gave a summary in *Epirus*, pp. 228 f., 348 f. and passim, with figs. 20, 21, and 23 and I have discussed the weapons etc. in *BSA* 62, 83 f.; 66, 229 f.; and 69, 127 f.

115. Prendi's report is in *BUSS* 1956, 1, 180 f.; for my summary and discussion see *Epirus*, pp. 201 f., 350 f. and passim with figs. 20 f., and the articles in *BSA* cited in the preceding note.

116. Indeed, the Leucas graves are unique as far as peninsular Greece is concerned in the wealth of gold, silver, copper, flint and obsidian, so much so that K. Branigan has recently suggested in his valuable book (op. cit., note 111), pp. 110 ff. that there was "a small but distinctive metal industry" in or near Leucas and that its products were also found in Ithaca, Corcyra, Epirus and Albania. He also suggested that the two famous gold sauceboats in the Louvre and at Jerusalem came originally from Leucas and this suggestion may be supported by the finds of gold and silver vessels in a tumulus at Tivat on the south side of the Gulf of Kotor, which are either earlier or of about the same period. As regards weapons, he attributes the shoed spearhead, the straight-backed square-ended knife with three or more rivets, and the collared double-axe to the metal industries of the north and west (p. 123); the first two of these have been found in the tumuli of Albania.

117. For instance, see *AI* 2 (1956) 12, fig. 3; M. Garašanin, *Prehistory of Serbia*, p. 2, pl. 48; *AI* 1 (1954) 19 f., fig. 4 a and c.

118. The view of the Albanian archaeologists has been different from mine all along. Although weapons of M.H. type (including Middle Minoan and Middle Cycladic) were recognised to be of M.H. date in adjacent areas, such as Leucas, southern Greece and western Serbia, the Albanian view was that exactly similar weapons found in Albania in tumuli were all of Early Iron Age date. An exception to this isolationist view had to be made later when the weapons found in an inner tumulus at Pazhok had to antedate L.H. I–II weapons and pottery found in the outer (later) tumulus. The idea was that Illyrian metalworkers of the Early Iron Age made concurrently both *iron* weapons of up-to-date types and *bronze* weapons of antique M.H. types, and so in Albania one finds both varieties in Early Iron Age tumuli. In my opinion to make a shoed or slotted spearhead when a socketed spearhead had been in use for centuries would be analogous to making a breechloader when a sten-gun had been in use; nor would anyone prefer a badly-hafted small bronze knife to an iron cutlass. Nor is their view compatible with the facts that only a very few of the very numerous Early Iron Age tumuli had bronze weapons and that in those tumuli the bronze weapons of M.H. type were usually in the central burial only; for on their theory bronze and iron weapons should have turned up together in most burials and sporadically in all or most Early Iron Age tumuli. My views have been stated in *Epirus*, pp. 202 f., and fully in *BSA* 66 (1971) 229 f., while Muzafer Korkuti has put the opposite view, for instance, in *StH* 1970, 4, 159 f. (also expressed at the Second International Congress of South-east European Studies of 1970). His conclusion in the French version was as follows:

Au commencement de la première période du fer, à un temps où la civilisation mycénienne était complètement détruite, la civilisation illyrienne marquait des pas importants à tout égard. Un grand épanouissement connaissait l'extraction et le traitement des métaux, où le pays fut favorisé par ses ressources de fer, cuivre et autres métaux rares. Ce développement général de l'artisanat et l'accroissement sensible des demandes pour les armes de plus en plus nombreuses, comme conséquence de l'approfondissement de la différenciation de classe et la plus grande fréquence des guerres, ont entrainé l'accroissment quantitatif et qualitatif des objets métalliques illyriens et aussi l'imitation et la réplique des produits connus des armes mycéniennes. Les artisans illyriens sont parvenus à fabriquer ainsi des épées, des couteaux, des fers de lances de bronze et de fer mycénien, qui se font distinguer pour l'excellente qualité de fabrication et leurs formes parfaites.

119. Three round bronze phalara, 4.5 cm in diameter, were found in Leucas in Tumulus S Grave 8, which is to be dated late in M.H.; being "by the head and somewhat deeper" they evidently had been on a shield of perishable material, laid over the head and chest of the dead man. A bronze shield-boss was found in Tumulus 1 and Grave 1 at Bela Crkva near Belotić in West Serbia, being 4.4 cm in diameter; see M. and D. Garašanin in *Sbornik Radova Narodnog Muzeja* I (1956–57) 38 and 50 with fig. 15 b. These early examples should be added to the list given by V. R. d'A. Desborough, *The Last Mycenaeans and Their Successors* (Oxford, 1964), pp. 65 f. and A. M. Snodgrass, *Early Greek Armour* (Edinburgh, 1964), pp. 38 f., because they virtually answer the question of origin.

120. In the *Acta of the Second International Colloquium on Aegean Prehistory* (Athens, 1972) p. 184 Sp. Marinatos depicted the "first Greeks" as they entered Greek soil. "They were not numerous groups of professional warriors, perhaps a few hundreds every time. But they brought with them the revolutionary new war machine, the chariot. They possessed horses; they were armed with long bodyshields, long spears and long swords. They were, moreover, renowned bowmen . . . . They inspired holy terror among the labourers and herdsmen."

VI

Destruction and Migration in the So-Called Dark Age of the Southwest Balkans

The Decline of the Mycenaean World

In the last two chapters we have made no use of the fashionable term 'substrate' and very little use of any concept of race and racial origin, for which the modern word is 'ethnogenesis'. The substrate, as I understand it, is that element of the population of a region which has not arrived recently by invasion, immigration, invitation or the like but is resident itself and is descended from residents who were there before the last invasion etc. In the early stages of a country's history or in colonial territories the substrate is a recognisable entity, at least in theory; for example, mesolithic hunters and persons descended from them may have been as distinct from the first neolithic settlers of Thessaly as the Red Indians were from the followers of Columbus or the aborigines of Australia from the first generation of English convicts. But as time goes on, the waters of the substrate become muddied. Or, to change the metaphor, the layers of the substrate become both numerous and confused. By the Middle Helladic period, let us say, the layers, e.g. in Thessaly, were (on the assumption of optimum survival) mesolithic hunter stock, preceramic neolithic stock, early neolithic stock, 'barbotino' stock, middle neolithic seafaring stock, pastoralist stock, Dimini stock, metal-using Early Helladicites, northern Rakhmanites, Kurgan stock, and cistgravers at Sesklo. But, nature being what it is, intermarriage within the substrate must have fused the lot into an indistinguishable mixture, except for the latest wave or perhaps two waves of immigrants. Nor is the situation any different today in countries of Europe, such as Britain, Germany and Greece. Any area of transit, such as lowland Macedonia, was as mixed in 1500 B.C. as it is in 1975.

One preserver of race is endogamy. As we have seen in the cases of the Sarakatsani, the Vlachs while nomadic or semi-nomadic, and some regional groups of Albanians, there was until very recently a strict observance of endogamy, and practically no one went outside his or her group to marry. In the first two cases the way of life—transhumant pastoralism—favoured the exclusion of rival pastoral groups and of settled peoples from the marriage stakes, as they were all potential enemies. It is probable, then, that the Kurgan steppe-peoples and the neolithic transhumants of Dunavec-Cakran likewise practised endogamy, as long as they were living the pastoral life and were living it in rival groups. Regional groups of settled peoples, as in south Albania, were something different. Free range vendetta, until very recently, was a symptom and a product of intense family, clan and tribal feeling. It prevailed among the inhabitants of that region and of Tsamouria on the Greek side of the frontier, whether they spoke Albanian or Greek. They were very probably descended from groups of transhumant pastoralists who had practised endogamy, and the adoption of a settled agricultural life did not change the tradition in the course of a few generations. Endogamy and vendetta were certainly hard-set before the coming of the Stalinist-Maoist regime.

In a trading community, more especially if it is engaged in seafaring, and in the urban conditions which usually follow in the wake of extensive trade, racial distinctions are not treasured so highly. Money may count for more than blood when it comes to arranging a marriage, and in general "wealth puts birth to confusion," as the Greek writer Theognis remarked. One can see that in historical times in Greece 'race' in the restricted sense of family, clan and tribe counted for less and less with the growth of trade and urbanisation and democracy. Then within the Greek peninsula the contrast became very marked between the tribal groupings of the western areas, such as the Molossians (in Epirus) and the Eurytanes (in Aetolia), and the mixed populations of commercial centres such as Athens and Corinth, which were grouped mainly on the eastern side of the peninsula.[1] So too there was a contrast between the hill-tribes on the fringes of Thessaly and the plain-dwellers of Thessaly who had become urbanised and often money-minded. The situation in Macedonia was somewhat similar. Most of the upland country, in which pastoral life predominated, until the conquests of Philip and Alexander the Great brought revolutionary changes, was occupied by small tribal groups which coalesced into tribal states. On the other hand, the lowlands of the coastal plain were remarkable for a large number of cities, each with its own territory, within which tribal distinctions seem to have disappeared in very early times.[2] Similar contrasts between hill-tribes and city-dwelling plainsmen were to be observed also in the basin of the Strymon valley.

Nationalism is of course a different concept. It grew often at the expense of racial distinctions in the narrower sense. In the fifth century B.C., when Athens was at its most nationalistic stage, racial tribes were virtually defunct in the community. And the Macedonian kingdom reached its zenith when it was an amalgam of races united only by loyalty to the king.

It is necessary to make these definitions because we are moving into a period when they are relevant. In the period prior to Middle Helladic we have been able to name peoples only by the local or regional culture which differentiated them from their neighbours. Thus we have written of the peoples of Dunavec-Cakran as distinct from those of Malik or Dimini or Rakhmani. Then in the Middle Helladic period we have gone on to speak of language, whether Illyrian or Greek, and also of the dialects of Greek. Speech and race, however, are not conterminous. The Greek language, for instance, has been spoken by a plethora of races between the third millennium B.C. and today. It is indeed language itself which often subsumes the substrate and welds it into the national amalgam. Fragments of the substrate which retained their traditional language tended in ancient times to hive off and betake themselves to remote places. This is how Thucydides described the inhabitants of the small places on the rocky coast of Mt Athos: "These places are inhabited by a mixture of races, bilingual but non-Greek; they include a small Chalcidic element, and the main element is Pelasgic, Bisaltic, Crestonic and Edonian" (4.109.4).

By the time of the war of the Greeks against Troy, which I date c. 1200 B.C.,[3] it is probable that the substrate was linguistically subsumed and that we may speak correctly of the inhabitants of the peninsula south of Mt Olympus in the east and south of Leucas in the west as 'Greeks', in the sense that they spoke the Greek language and that they shared a common form of Greek civilisation, which we have labelled 'Mycenaean'. The label should be treated in the same way as the later labels 'Classical' and 'Hellenistic'. There were no 'Mycenaeans' in a general sense,[4] just as there were no 'Classicals' or 'Hellenistics'. Mycenaeans in a particular sense were the citizens of Mycenae only.

We gain a remarkable insight into the peoples and the places of this Mycenaean civilisation from the so-called Catalogue of Ships in the second book of the *Iliad*. The leaders and the sizes of the contingents which mustered against Troy were enumerated in this Catalogue with many details which do not agree at all with the pattern of peoples and places of Classical civilisation. It is generally believed that the author of the Catalogue as we have it drew upon a traditional lay, composed near the time of the Trojan War[5] Some peoples were named as tribes, and others took their names from a place. Thus 'Cephallenes' and 'Epeioi' occupied Dulichium, Ithaca, Samos and Zacynthos (the later Leucas, Ithaca, Cephallenia and Zacynthos), and also the coasts of the mainland opposite. 'Aitoloi, Lokroi, Phokeeis, Boiotoi' (the last being very recent immigrants) and 'Abantes' (in Euboea) held the bulk of central Greece. Other tribes inhabited the fringes and the hinterland of the Thessalian plain: 'Enienes' reaching westwards as far as Dodona in Epirus, 'Peraiboi' by the river Titaresius, 'Magnetes' by the river Peneus and Mt Pelion, and 'Myrmidones, Akhaioi and Hellenes' to the south of the plain. The last group had Peleus as their king and were led by Achilles. On the other hand, the contingents from the plains (except in the case of the Boeotian plain) were named after their city: for instance, Athenaioi after Athens, Argeioi after Argos, and Pylioi after Pylos. And the cities were most numerous in the plains which had been occupied for the longest time (as shown in our Maps 20 and 22): twenty-three in the plain of Thessaly, thirty-one in that of Boeotia, twenty in the plains of northeastern Peloponnese, and eighteen in those of the southern Peloponnese. The contingents from the Aegean islands were named also by locality, e.g. Rhodioi and Kretes. Crete, the oldest centre of civilised life, had a hundred cities.

The contingents of the tribal peoples in the Catalogue were almost as powerful as those of the cities. In this respect there was a resemblance between the last phase of the Bronze Age and the last phase of the Classical Age, when tribal states such as Molossoi, Aitoloi and Athamanes began to play an important role. There was a difference too between the northwestern area and the northeastern area. What we know as Corcyra, Epirus and Acarnania was almost entirely excluded from the Catalogue, and all the peoples in or adjacent to the northwestern area were tribal. The northeastern area south of Mt Olympus was completely included, and many of the peoples took their names from the cities only. This difference is an indication that the peoples at the tribal stage of development were the latest incomers into the Mycenaean area, and that they had come from the northwestern area. The Cephallenes, for instance, were frozen in mid-stride, one foot on the northwestern mainland and the other on the islands; and the Boiotoi had come into the land of Cadmus recently, after the sack of Thebes by the Epigoni. Of the tribes round Thessaly the Peraiboi had a tribal name related to the river Aias (later Aous),[6] the Magnetes had come recently from the area round Mt Olympus,[7] and the Hellenes were connected with the region round Dodona in Epirus.[8] Indeed their leader, Achilles, in a moment of stress, made the following prayer to Zeus of Dodona (*Iliad* 16.233 f.):

> High Zeus, lord of Dodona, Pelasgian, living afar off, brooding over wintry Dodona, your prophets about you living, the Selloi who sleep on the ground with feet unwashed. Hear me.

These tribes and those behind them in the northwestern area, were engaged both in transhumant pastoralism and in stock-raising rather than in agriculture, and their standard of life, like that of the Selloi, was low in comparison to that of the people who lived in cities and enjoyed the full flowering of Mycenaean culture. Yet they were powerful; for the Boiotoi were able to take possession of the very rich plain, when a coalition of Greeks from southern Mycenaean centres prepared the way for them by sacking Thebes.

The Catalogue of Ships is a striking example of the purposes for which epic poetry in hexameter verse was employed towards the end of the Bronze Age. The singers of the poems were recording facts, not fantasies, and geographical features, genealogical details and military strengths were no less relevant than the deeds and quarrels of men in the field of history, the *klea andron* of *Odyssey* 8.73. Thus a framework of fact was transmitted by the singers, however much they might develop the characters of the warriors or add religious colouring. The most rational of ancient historians, Thucydides, had no hesitation in accepting that framework, for instance at 1.3 and 10-11 and he, no less than Hesiod, believed in the weakening of what we call 'the Mycenaean world' by internal wars such as that of the Epigoni at Thebes and external forays such as the war against Troy. "A part were destroyed by evil war and dread battle, some beneath the walls of seven-gated Thebes in the land of Cadmus as they fought for the flocks of Oedipus, others at Troy whither they were borne on ships over the great gulf of the sea."[9]

The epic poems were focused mainly on a relatively short period c. 1250–1150, although there were extensions into earlier memories and later an awareness of the final collapse which was effected by 1100 B.C. One reason for this is, on the analogy of other epic poems, that the making of epic songs "originated in the introduction of less cultured but more virile warriors into a developed but declining civilisation,"[10] and ended (apart from the reworking of old material) with the passing of that civilisation. As an analogy for the first stage, we have already had occasion to mention passages in the *Chanson de Roland* which were composed when the Crusaders entered the Byzantine Empire and the bards recorded the names and events of the time. On this interpretation it is not surprising that the world of the epic saga dif-

Map 22

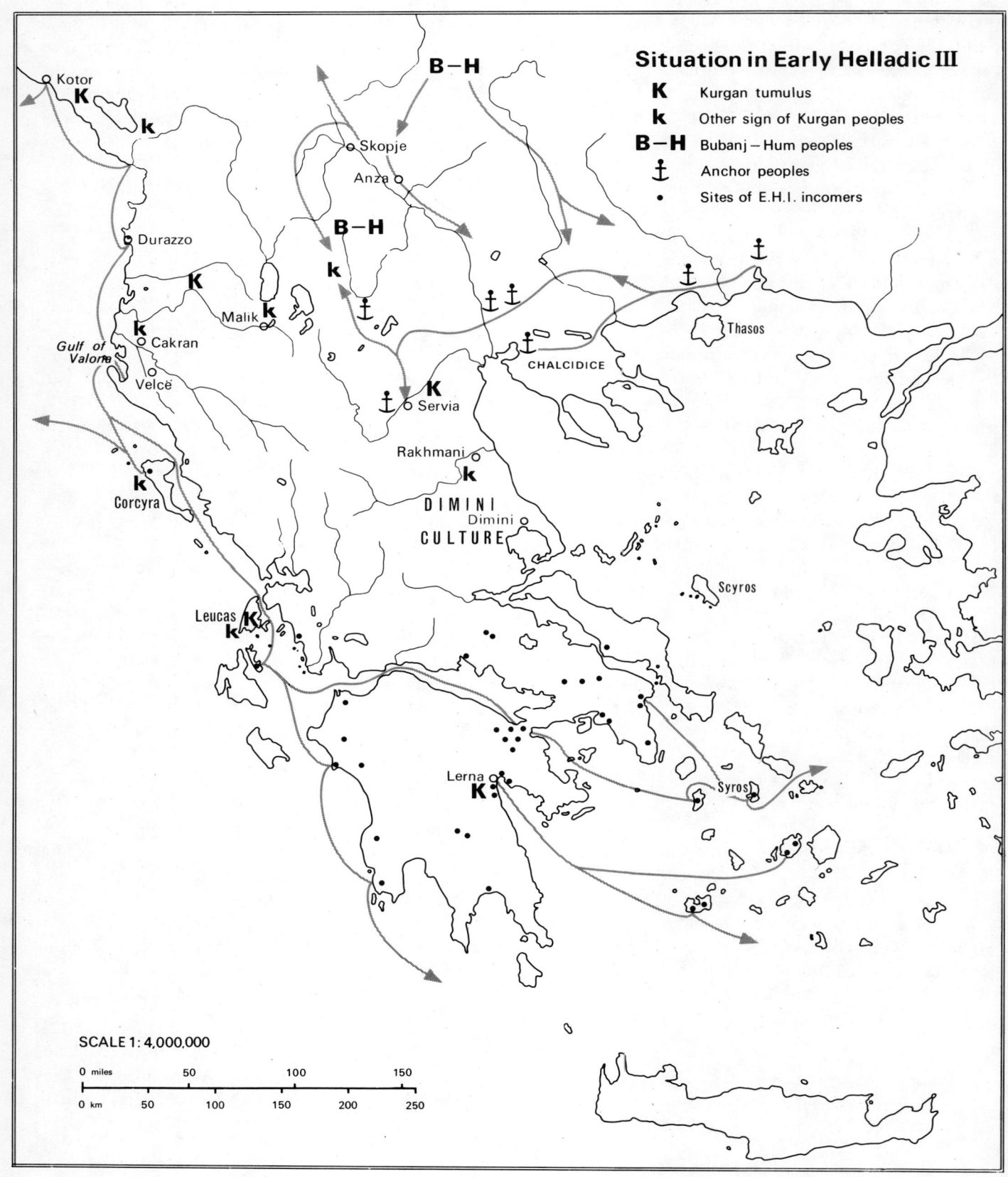

fered in some respects from the bureaucratic system of the city-palaces, which we know from the decipherment of the Linear B tablets; epic poetry came with the intruders and was not itself invented by the settled people of the cities.[11]

As far then as our knowledge of the epic saga goes, the thirteenth century was a troubled period. The thrones of Argos, Mycenae, Sparta and Pylos were usurped by adventurers who relied on armed force; Thebes was destroyed and the Boiotoi took control of the rich plain; and new dynasties established themselves in Ithaca, the Spercheus valley, Salamis and Crete.[12] The Trojan War sowed the seeds of further disorder at home. The *Nostoi* or 'Homecomings' of the heroes provided the singers with new and exciting themes in which adventures, assassinations, intrigues and inter-state wars were prominent. The *Odyssey* is a greatly elaborated form of such a *Nostos*. The phase of original composition ended with the lives of the sons of the heroes, such as Orestes, Telemachus and Telegonus (who died c. 1125–1100 B.C. at the latest). Events thereafter seem not to have been recorded in the epic songs. Rather the original lays, composed in an early form of the Aeolic dialect, were carried overseas and were transformed there into the Ionic dialect in the course of transmission and elaboration over a period of three or four centuries. The final form as we see it in the *Iliad* and the *Odyssey* was due to the artistic genius of Athens and the related Ionians, which transformed the epic lays into a sophisticated form, even as it adopted and transformed 'tragedy' if, as Aristotle reported, tragedy was originally a Dorian invention.

To return to our main theme, the account of invasions and migrations which Thucydides gave (for the period c. 1200–1100 B.C.) was derived from his sober interpretation of epic songs, originally composed during the twelfth century but later reworked during oral transmission. It was as follows (1.12):

> After the Trojan War Greece was still subject to migrations and settlements, so that it could not enjoy the tranquillity needed for growth. Thus the Greek return from Troy was long drawn-out and caused many revolutions, and the civil wars which ensued in almost all of the states led to the foundation of [new] states by those who were driven out. Thus too the Thessaloi made the Boiotoi as we know them today remove from Arne sixty years after the sack of Troy [c. 1140 B.C.], and these Boiotoi settled in what we now call Boeotia but was previously known as Cadmeïs (there had been an offshoot of them there before, and some of them had campaigned against Troy), and the Dorians together with the Heracleidae took the Peloponnese eighty years after the sack of Troy [c. 1120 B.C.].

In this passage the foundation of new states is of some importance. Evidently there were accounts of these enterprises, transmitted no doubt by the epic singers in some cases and preserved in the oral tradition of religious shrines or families in other cases. For example, Mopsus was said to have founded Aspendus in Pamphylia and Mallus in Cilicia. Recently his name has appeared as 'Mukshush' on a Hittite tablet of his period, while the house of 'Mukshush' in Hittite and of 'Mupsh' in Phoenician was mentioned in a much later inscription found at Karatepe in Cilicia.[13] In the northwestern area Amphilochus was said by Hecataeus and Thucydides (2.68.3) to have founded Amphilochian Argos on the eastern shore of the Gulf of Arta; Neoptolemus, son of Achilles, was said by Pindar to have ruled in Molossia in central Epirus; and Odysseus was involved in helping the Thesprotoi against the Brygi according to Eugammon's *Telegony*, written c. 565 B.C. This group shows an extension of Mycenaean influence into Epirus after the Trojan War.

Oral tradition, as opposed to the orally transmitted epic songs, was also cited by Thucydides, e.g. at 1.9.2, when he wrote "those who have received the clearest account in the Peloponnese by hearsay from those who lived before them say as follows." The citation was with reference to events some eight hundred years before his time; yet he believed in the tradition so far that he based his arguments upon it. One detail in this piece of oral tradition was the presence of the Heracleidae in Attica and the fear with which the Heracleidae were regarded at Mycenae in the generation before that of the Trojan War. Another example of oral tradition in the Peloponnese referred to the Heracleidae shortly before the Trojan War, when they tried to enter the Peloponnese and their leader Hyllus was killed in single combat. Both the Tegeans and the Athenians appealed to this tradition at the battle of Plataea in 479 B.C.[14] Such traditions should not be dismissed on the grounds that they were orally transmitted. We have analogies in the illiterate society (until recently) of Albania. There the epic songs concerning the deeds of Skanderbeg and the unwritten laws of his contemporary Lek Dukagjini have been orally transmitted for some five hundred years, and no one can deny the historicity of the two men and much of what they did. The Vlachs too cited from oral tradition the names of the families which combined to form the *synoikismos* of Samarina some four centuries ago, and there are no grounds for supposing the names to be fictitious.

When we turn to the archaeological evidence for the Greek mainland, we find clear signs of a general decline which started around the middle of L.H. III B, i.e. c. 1250 B.C., and continued down to the end of L.H. III C, i.e. c. 1100 B.C. On the chronology which I am using the Trojan War fell c. 1200 B.C. and the start of L.H. III C was c. 1180 B.C. Let us deal first with L.H. III B. Massive fortifications were made or extended in the course of L.H. III B, and special precautions were taken to ensure a water-supply which was accessible from within the walls; there was evidently fear of siege-warfare. The most fortified of all areas was the Argolid—at Mycenae, Tiryns, Midea and Argos; Athens and Gla in Boeotia were also heavily fortified. On the other hand Iolcus in Thessaly was unfortified. If we think of the Classical period, the deduction is clear that these places were fortified one against another. The Greeks of the Mycenaean age were specialists in the sieging and sacking of cities, and not unnaturally in self-protection they became highly skilled in the art of fortification. But the peoples to the north of the Mycenaean sphere were innocent of this art. They had no fortifications and were inexperienced in siegecraft; it was for that reason that Iolcus did not feel the need to build massive walls. The same thing happened between 450 and 350 B.C.: immense fortifications on the Greek mainland, and none at all among the northern tribes which inhabited Epirus and Macedonia.

Again the archaeological record is one of destruction and partial destruction at a number of Mycenaean centres: Thebes, Mycenae, Tiryns, Ano-Englianos in Messenia, Teichos Dymaion in Achaea, Gla in Boeotia, and Crisa in Phocis. In some cases it is not certain whether it occurred before or after the Trojan War.[15] At some of the sites occupation was resumed after the catastrophe. Nowhere is there archaeological trace of an intruder from outside the Mycenaean world. The literary tradition is entirely clear. Before the Trojan War coalitions were formed to destroy cities and the Epigoni succeeded in destroying Thebes, and after the Trojan War it was an age of inter-state war and internal faction. Where the archaeological record and the literary tradition are both so clear, it seems gratuitous to postulate a traceless invader as an alternative wreaker of destruction.

It may be thought desirable to make one exception. A wall of fortification has been discovered by excavation across the neck of the Isthmus, and it has been dated on archaeological grounds to the thirteenth century B.C. Against what enemy was it made? In terms of pure speculation either against a foreign enemy, as later in 480 B.C. against the Persians, or against a coalition of Greek states, as in the 390s. The literary tradition recorded an unsuccessful attempt by the Dorians, led by Hyllus, to force their way into the Peloponnese a hundred years before the successful invasion of c. 1120 B.C. (Herodotus 9.26-27; Pausanias 8.5.1 and 6), but it attributed the failure not to any wall but to a single combat between two champions. All we can say with confidence is that the peoples of the Peloponnese—Arcadians, Achaeans and Ionians according to the literary tradition—were afraid of enemies farther north, who were geographically Greeks of Mycenaean culture in the first place and Greeks of non-Mycenaean culture in the second place.

That there were considerable movements of peoples within L.H. III B is clear both from the literary evidence and from archaeological discovery. We have already referred to changes of dynasty at many Mycenaean centres (e.g. Tydeus from Aetolia becoming a prince at Argos), the movement of pastoralist and stock-raising tribes from the north and particularly from the northwest into the orbit of Mycenaean civilisation before the Trojan War, and the emigration of adventurers and their followers in the decade or two after the sack of Troy. We should add the earlier emigrations which were reported specifically in the Catalogue of Ships: Tlepolemus, a Heraclid, and "much people" (probably from southwest Epirus) to Rhodes, and two sons of Thessalus, another Heraclid (probably from the same region) to Cos and other islands of the Dodecanese.[16] It seems that some 'Dorieis' went to Crete (*Odyssey* 19.177). These movements of tribal peoples by land and by sea in the course of L.H. III B bear a strong resemblance to the later movements of the Albanians by land and by sea. Excavation has lent support to the tradition of emigrations at the end of L.H. III B, e.g. to Cyprus and to Tarsus in Cilicia,[17] and to the extension of Mycenaean culture into Epirus, e.g. at Kiperi near Parga in L.H. III B and at the Oracle of the Dead by the Acheron probably also in L.H. III B.[18]

The Decisive Invasions

The literary tradition concerning what we call L.H. III C was that the period of civil wars in the Mycenaean states continued; that new states were founded by émigrés, who doubtless took "much people" with them, as Tlepolemus had done earlier; and that the movements of tribes from the northwestern area into Mycenaean areas increased in scale and swamped such areas as southwest Thessaly, Boeotia and later the Peloponnese (Map 23). The tradition of these last movements seems to have come from Mycenaean sources and to have been transmitted orally. It contained a geographical account, of which we know only fragments from classical authors. The Thessaloi, coming from Thesprotia in south Epirus, occupied southwest Thessaly, while the Phokeeis built a wall across the pass at Thermopylae to head them off. During this incursion the Boiotoi were driven out of Arne in southwestern Thessaly, and they occupied the plain which came to be called Boeotia (joining their predecessors of the same name). Then c. 1120, as we have seen, the Dorieis issuing from the high plateau of Doris "took the Peloponnese." The routes used by these peoples are likely to have been respectively those from Arta to Gomphi and to Karpenisi near the head of the Spercheus valley; from Arne via the pass of Gravia to Delphi and thence to Chaeronea and Coronea; and from Doris again to Delphi and thence to Naupactus and Rhium.

At Naupactus the Dorieis joined forces with other peoples who had come from Aetolia to Rhium. In the Peloponnese they divided, the Dorieis heading for the Argolid and the Aetolian peoples taking possession of Elis. The Dorieis marched through Arcadia and then via Lerna and Nauplia into the Argive plain, where they defeated "Tisamenus and the Achaeans" and founded the Temenium in honour of their Heraclid leader, Temenus. Heraclid twin brothers, Eurysthenes and Procles, led the forces which invaded Laconia; and another Heraclid, Cresphontes, and his followers overran Messenia. An uncle of the twins led an expedition which captured Thera and probably seized Melos en route. Thus within a matter of ten or twenty years (c. 1120–1100 B.C.) most of the main Mycenaean areas were conquered—not necessarily the citadels—and Dorian bands set off overseas into the Aegean. For the moment most of Achaea, the Isthmus countries, Attica, some parts of Phocis, and northeastern Thessaly were by-passed.[19]

Excavation has shown that Tiryns and Mycenae suffered their third catastrophes at about the same time in the middle of L.H. III C, c. 1150 B.C. Thereafter Tiryns was unimportant. Mycenae revived but was finally destroyed c. 1120 B.C. or later;[20] it then ceased to be of importance. Teichos Dymaion, a strongly-fortified citadel on the coast route from Rhium into Elis, was destroyed towards the end probably of the twelfth century, and it has been noted by Desborough that two vases in the destruction layer were of a type which was popular in Cephallenia, Ithaca and Epirus.[21] In northeast Thessaly Iolcus was destroyed, but not until the first quarter of the eleventh century in the opinion of the excavator. The most remarkable feature of L.H. III C, which has emerged from a careful and extensive survey by Hope Simpson,[22] is the sharp decline in the number of settlements in the Mycenaean area as compared with those of III B. It is very marked in some districts: in the Peloponnese a fall from 150 in III B to 56 in III C and in Boeotia from 28 to 5. On the other hand in Attica and Euboea the decline was from 24 to 13 and 11 to 6 respectively, and in Thessaly much the same, from 25 to 17. In Cephallenia, Ithaca and Zacynthos the settlements remained the same in number, and in Achaea they even increased from 10 to 11.

When we put the literary tradition and the archaeological evidence together, that is for the area south of Mt Olympus and of central Epirus, we can see that they are in remarkably close agreement. The warring principalities of the Mycenaean mainland damaged one another and on occasions, but rarely, wiped out a great centre. During these wars some relatively backward tribes which practised stock-raising and pastoralism in the northwestern area (Epirus, Pindus, Acarnania, Aetolia and Doris) moved forward into some of the less populous or devastated areas and took control.

The war against Troy did not create any lasting unity of purpose. The next stage was one of intense party-faction and civil war (*stasis*). Some cities were partly destroyed; others were deserted.[23] The situation may have been aggravated by further inter-state wars (as in fourth century Sicily). Further infiltrations and invasions by pastoral tribes, which were some within and others outside the limits of the orbit of full Mycenaean civilisation, lowered the standard of life by reducing great tracts of territory to a form of semi-nomadic pastoralism, in which there were no regular settlements. As conditions worsened for the settled population, many of them went overseas in search of new lands. Others took refuge in relatively safe areas such as Achaea and later Attica. The final invasion which broke the back of Mycenaean power in the Peloponnese was made by the Dorians and the west Greeks c. 1120 B.C. They defeated their opponents in the field. It was enough to destroy Teichos Dymaion and Mycenae; other citadels could be left to surrender or wither away.

This long period of decline and infiltration over 150 years or so was very like a period which we have already described, namely that of the Albanians and the Vlachs who were so terrifying to the settled peoples of the Byzantine world. Then too the warring principalities weakened one another and unintentionally prepared the way for the invaders, sometimes even importing them to further their own cause in an internecine war. The number of inhabited centres declined and there was widespread impoverishment, as more and more of the countryside was taken over by semi-nomadic pastoralist tribes. Even the stages of the Albanian-Vlach invasion were very similar. First the advance into the northwestern area; then the occupation of the country as far as Naupactus, but by-passing the fortified centres at Ioannina and Arta; then infiltration of the Peloponnese, and an attempt to take control which almost succeeded. Other groups entered Thessaly and Boeotia and spread outwards from there. They owed much to the able leadership of the Vlachs.

We turn next to the northern parts of our area. In Lower Macedonia almost all the Late Bronze Age sites were east of the Vardar valley, and they were in close contact with the sites in Chalcidice. These Macedonian sites were reached by Mycenaean traders c. 1350 B.C., and local versions of Mycenaean pottery were made at Vardarophtsa and Vardina on the Vardar and exported inland from c. 1300 B.C. to c. 1125 B.C. These versions were true to type throughout this period of time, which implies a regular trade.[24] But the trade was not in weapons of Mycenaean types (only one has been found, at Vardina). In general this part of Macedonia was conservative and unenterprising. At some time "before the Trojan War" the Teucri of Troy and the Mysi entered Europe, conquered all Thrace and advanced to the Ionian Sea in the west and the river Peneus in the south.[25] In this advance they must have crossed the Balkan range via Malik, Ochrid or Dibër. We may compare their advance with that of the Bulgars and that of the Turks. The southward advance may have driven the Magnetes from the plain east of Mt Olympus into the area between the Peneus and Mt Pelion and introduced Thracians in their place.[26] By the time of the Trojan War, as we learn from the Trojan Catalogue, the suzerainty of Troy extended to the Axius (Vardar); her allies there were the Paeonians, and she planted Paeonian settlers in the Strymon basin. The weapons of the Paeonians in the *Iliad* were the long spear and the bow, and they were the only people who were called 'fighters from chariots' (*hippokorystai*). They may have used the battle-axe also, but apparently not the sword.[27]

In the opening phase of the Late Bronze Age the important site of Malik in the lakeland area developed a style of matt-painted pottery, which was marked by the use of linear geometric designs such as the pendent triangle, criss-crossed lines and parallel lines, and by the setting of these designs in such a way as to enhance the shapes of the vessels. It was a fine, if austere style, and it had an excellent appreciation of shapes. At first it was painted after firing. This was so with most of the pieces at Malik, but with relatively few of those at Tren. Thereafter, wherever it was adopted, the painting was done before the pottery was fired. It has been found, usually as the only form of painted pottery, over a very large area and over a very long period (not necessarily concurrently in time): from Gajtan (near Scodra) and Ochrid in the north to the plain of Ioannina in the south, and from Pateli (in Eordaea) to the Adriatic coast of Albania.[28] It has been called "northwestern geometric pottery," a name appropriate to its area of use (Pl. 9). The common feature which explains the widespread adoption of this pottery is the system of transhumant pastoralism, which had been established in this area since the Middle Bronze Age; for the shepherds came into contact with one another in the summer months when they brought their flocks to the summer pastures of the Candavian mountains, Grammus and Pindus.

It is most probable that the people of this large area used the wool of their sheep and goats for the weaving of rugs and for making articles of clothing, as their successors did until very recently in Albania, Epirus and Western Macedonia. The designs on the 'northwestern geometric pottery' seem to me to have been inspired in the main by designs which were employed in rugs and in articles of clothing. Some of them are illustrated in Plate 10. They are in fact very similar to the designs used in contemporary weaving in this area. In her special study of the Sarakatsani Mrs Hadzimichalis described their sense of design as "simple, static and geometric," and she saw a close similarity between it and that of the Geometric style in Greece c. 900 to 700 B.C. She was not aware at that time of the 'northwestern geometric style', which has a closer similarity still. It seems highly probable that the origins of both of these styles are to be found in the practice of nomadic pastoralism and in the transference of woven designs to become painted designs on pottery.

'Northwestern geometric pottery' was in use throughout the lakeland area in the Late Bronze Age, as we know from finds at Malik IIId, Tren and Barç. It originated probably at Malik itself, which served as the chief commercial centre for trade in pastoral products, just as Muskopole (near Malik) did in the flourishing period of Vlach trade. It travelled with transhumant pastoralists into central Albania, where it has been found in tumulus-burials of this period at Pazhok and farther south. The spread of it into the Haliacmon valley, for instance to Boubousti, and into the plain of Ioannina may have occurred at this time or later; for the earliest associated finds so far are of the Early Iron Age. Wherever it came into use, it lasted down to the fourth century B.C., so that it had a very long and static life. It disappeared at the time when pastoralism was giving way to agriculture and urbanisation increased, as we see for instance in the speech of Alexander in Arrian, *Anabasis* 7.9.2.

There was a marked increase of pastoralism in the Late Bronze Age. Heurtley noted that the town-settlements of the Pelagonian plain were abandoned c. 1500 B.C., and he suggested that the people moved to hill-sites and engaged mainly in pastoral life,[29] which at that altitude involved the practice of transhumance. The same thing happened at Malik, when the large settlement known as IIId was abandoned and the people moved, in the opinion of the excavators, to a new hill-site at Symizë nearby and to an easily defended site at Tren, which had been unoccupied since the Early Bronze Age. The move from Malik occurred before the end of the Late Bronze Age, because the pottery at Tren was of a later stage than that found at Malik IIId and because "a pot of L.H. date, imported from the Aegean world" was unearthed in the Tren deposit.[30] The desertion of the open site of Malik in the plain and the choice of two higher, defensible sites which lay at the strategic entries from the east into the plain of Poloskë and from the west into the plain of Malik were certainly prompted by the danger of invasion, and it is possible that we should associate the end of Malik IIId with the incursion of the Teucri and Mysi, in c. 1250, who went through to the Adriatic coast. Large settlements in open situations were thereafter a thing of the past in the lakeland area. A movement of people from Lower Macedonia into central Epirus has been inferred from the finding of typically Macedonian Late Bronze Age painted pottery at Kastritsa near Ioannina.[31] Once again the pastoral way of life seems to have been reinforced.

To the west of the lakeland area the most surprising phenomenon was the reuse of old tumuli and the making of new tumuli for burials from the beginning of L.H. III C approximately and on into the Early Iron Age. At Krume near Kukës in northeast Albania two tumuli were made in the last phase of the Bronze Age according to the excavator, Bep Jubani, who has not yet published a full report.[32] The central burials, over which the tumuli were raised originally, were cremations made directly on the ground, covering an area some 4 m in diameter; one such area was covered with a pavement of slabs, and the other was not. The other burials in the tumuli were inhumations in graves made of 'travertins' (probably cist-graves with slabs of this porous stone). Only pottery was found with the burials. The outer tumulus of the great double tumulus at Pazhok in central Albania received at least one burial, an inhumation in a cist of wood or trellis, which was dated by a spearhead to L.H. III B or C. At Vajzë, inland of the Gulf of Valona, Tumulus A was reused in a similar manner at some time in L.H. III C, and a new tumulus (Tumulus B) was made of which one burial had a spearhead of L.H. III C type. Other objects from the soil of Tumulus B were of L.H. III C types, one of them being a piece of gold leaf with a design of concentric circles impressed in relief and in dots, as on the piece of a helmet from Tiryns. Two other tumuli had burials which were probably of the Early Iron Age. These four tumuli seem to have run in sequence, like the four tumuli at Marathon. At Vodhinë in the Kseria valley in south Albania the earlier tumulus was reused and a burial, an inhumation in a simple trench, was inserted close to the cairn (Grave 17); it contained a fiddle-shaped javelin-head with a facetted shaft, which may be of LH. III C type. Other burials of this period, inhumations in slab-lined cists, were added, and then a layer of stones was laid over it. Subsequently, in the Early Iron Age, an outer tumulus was added, and burials were made in slab-lined cist-graves in it, one of which contained a bronze spectacle-fibula. In the same valley one tumulus was excavated at Kakavi and two more at Bodrishtë; one burial in the former may be of L.H. III C date, and the burials at Bodrishtë were of the Early Iron Age.[33]

A remarkable tumulus, 41 m in diameter and containing 112 burials, has been excavated recently at Barç by Korçë in the plain near Malik, and the range in time according to the excavator, Zhaneta Andrea, was from c. 1200 to perhaps c. 850 B.C.[34] One burial (Grave 18) contained a Mycenaean stirrup-jar of L. H. III C type and a short bronze sword of a kind which had been found in other tumulus-burials which we have already mentioned. When I was in Tirana in 1972, I saw some of the finds in the Exhibition. They included two gold hair-coils of some twelve spirals each, with loop-ends at the top and bottom and with the two coils at the top twisted, and a jug with cutaway neck and pointed foot, decorated in 'northwestern geometric style'. The design running round the surface just below the lip of the jug represented a veil, formally arranged, and I remembered that when the white bones of Patroclus were put in a golden jar in his resting-place, above which the tumulus was to be made, the jar was covered with a thin veil (*Iliad* 23.254; see p. 114 above).

As in the Middle Bronze Age, so at this time no settlements were found in the vicinity of the tumuli. The way of life was predominantly pastoral. The warriors buried in the tumuli were no doubt leaders of pastoral groups, and the continuity of use arose from the hereditary principle in the leading families of the groups, who were no doubt organised in tribes. The equipment of these warriors was connected mainly with the north and had very little to do with the Mycenaean world. The five bronze swords had features which have been found and classified in Mycenaean swords, but they were much shorter, more crude in workmanship and evidently made somewhere in the vicinity, probably in the Metohija-Kossovo area, where copper was abundant. As they imitated dateable features of Mycenaean swords, although they were in many respects 'uncanonical' by Mediterranean standards, I argued that they should be dated approximately to the same period as their Mycenaean models, and the discovery at Barç of a Mycenaean stirrup-jar of L.H. III C type together with a short sword of L.H. III C features in one burial adds strength to my argument.[35]

These short swords are all members of the Naue Type II class which was used for slashing and thrusting. The warrior at Kakavi had not only one of these swords but also an iron knife with curved back and a bronze rivet, pieces of bronze sheet, bone-plaques and hammer-pins, all characteristically northern in type. He evidently had worn a baldric with ornamental plaques[36] and perhaps some form of leather armour tied by the pins. Javelin-heads and spearheads of bronze were also in use, and those with the facetted type of socket came probably from the same local workshop as the uncanonical swords. Long bronze pins—up to 33 cm long—often decorated with engraved zig-zags and usually of an early type—were found in tumulus-burials at Vajzë (in nine burials spread over three tumuli), Vodhinë and Barç, and also in graves (unpublished) at Leskoviq; they were appropriate for fastening thick clothing of goat-hair and wool, such as is traditional among the Vlachs living in the open, and the slight swellings were enough to prevent the pins from pulling out of the thick stuff. Similar long pins have been found at Diakata in Cephallenia in a burial trench which may be dated around 1125 B.C. As Cephallenia had strong links with the north in other respects, it is likely that the pins of Diakata, Vajzë, Vodhinë and Barç came from a common source in the north.[37]

In Epirus south of the watershed between the Drin valley and the upper Kalamas no tumuli have been found. There are cist-graves, as in the Albanian tumuli, which have been dated by the excavators, S. I. Dakaris and I. P. Vokotopoulou, to late in L.H. III B and early in L.H. III C, i.e. on either side of 1180 B.C.

on my chronology. One group is at Kalbaki, Mazaraki and Elaphotopos, situated high up the Kalamas valley and the last near the pass leading to Konitsa; and another, containing a Mycenaean stirrup-jar, is at Kastritsa near Ioannina. Another two were nearer to the coast, one being close to the Oracle of the Dead at the confluence of the Cocytus and Acheron rivers, and the other near Paramythia at the head of the Cocytus valley. Moreover, in this area a small tholos-tomb with Mycenaean pottery of III B style and a Mycenaean acropolis have been reported at Kiperi near Parga, and another Mycenaean acropolis lay above the Oracle of the Dead on the hill called Xylokastro.[38] Thus the plain of the Acheron with its entry to the underworld and the adjacent coast, from which the Thesprotoi sailed their ships, was very much a part of the last phase of the Mycenaean world, familiar to people in the *Odyssey*, for whom Dodona was "quite close" (19.301). It was from this area that the Heraclid Tlepolemus set out with "much people" to make a settlement in Rhodes before the Trojan War, and it was here that Odysseus was active after his long-delayed return from Troy.

In southern Epirus the so-called Mycenaean class of short swords with square shoulders, known as F ii, was much in use. The distribution of these swords was strong in Elis, Cephallenia and southern Epirus, and they passed northwards into Europe; one was found as far away as Pelynt in Cornwall.[39] The admixture of northern elements in Epirus was very strong. The tholos-tomb at Kiperi contained a leaf-shaped spearhead of northern (Hallstatt) type, and more examples of the leaf-shaped and flame-shaped spearheads have been found in Epirus south of the Albanian border than in the rest of L.H. III C Greece. The warrior with the F ii sword at Kalbaki had a curving-backed knife of a Hungarian type, and there was another such knife in a cist-grave at Elaphotopos. Beads of amber were found in the cist-graves at Kalbaki, Elaphotopos and Mazaraki—a material which came from the north and was abundant later in tumulus-burials of the Mati valley in central Albania. No less important were five types of bronze battle-axe which have been found in Albania and southern Epirus, not in tumulus-burials but as stray objects or dedications (at Dodona). They were of Hungarian types or had marked Hungarian features and most probably had been brought to this area by invaders from the north, either bearers of a Lausitz culture or associated with them, in the period c. 1250–1150 B.C.[40]

Particular interest attaches to the cist-graves in the upper Kalamas valley because they have distinctive features which have not been found either in the tumuli of the nearby Drin valley nor in the plain of the Acheron. Thus armlets of bronze wire with spiralling ends were in the graves at Kalbaki and Elaphotopos; finger-rings of bronze band with spiralling ends at Mazaraki and Elaphotopos; and finger-rings of bronze band with incised or grooved decoration at Mazaraki and Elaphotopos. Whence did this group of warriors come to the upper Kalamas valley in the early decades of the twelfth century? The geographical pointer is towards Konitsa and western Macedonia, because most of Albania was held by equally well-armed but differently equipped warriors. In Pelagonia cist-graves with similar objects have been dated to the same period. Grave xi at Saraj on the bank of the Cerna Reka contained an armlet of bronze band with four grooves, and a grave near Prilep a finger-ring of bronze band and a piece of spiralling end which had belonged to the ring, and two amber beads. At least one finger-ring of bronze band with spiralling ends has been found recently in the tumulus at Barç. A child-burial in a cist-grave at Demir Kapu in the middle Vardar valley contained two bronze armlets with overlapping ends, resembling one at Elaphotopos.[41] The graves at Elaphotopos, Mazaraki and Saraj had handmade cups, round-bottomed, with one handle, usually high-rising, and the cups at Elaphotopos had two or three nipple-shaped knobs on the body.

The ultimate origin of the bronze ornaments and the knobbed pottery was in Hungary, from which peoples of the 'Lausitz culture'—a portmanteau term covering many separable groups—spread out into the Balkans from the late thirteenth to the late twelfth century. The ornaments, like the battle-axes, were features of the Vattina group in Yugoslavia; for instance, a hoard of this group at Lovas in Croatia contained finger-rings with spiralling ends, armlets with spiralling ends, small shield-bosses and buttons, all of bronze, and spiralling hair-coils of gold.[42] All of these have been found in tumulus-burials in Epirus-in-Albania and Barç or in cist-graves in Epirus-in-Greece.

Pottery with knobs, known as Buckelkeramik or Knobbed Ware, was a fairly general characteristic, it seems, of the migrating peoples with Lausitz culture, whereas the bronze ornaments we have mentioned were of a more restricted distribution. We may turn then to the pottery with knobs, both the smaller nipple-shaped knobs and the horn-like projections, and with the fluted and grooved forms of decoration which are also Lausitz features. All these forms have been found at Gajtan near Scodra in layer III, which extended from the last period of the Bronze Age into the Early Iron Age.[43] Fluted pottery was very prominent in the tumulus-burials of the Mati valley, and the shapes of the vessels led the excavators to date some to the end of the Bronze Age, but most are likely to be of the Early Iron Age; in many cases the fluting of the handles was so marked that they resembled "a goat's horn" in the words of the excavators, Selim Islami and Hasan Ceka.[44] Other such handles were found in tumulus-burials at Çinamak and Këneta near Kukës. The recent excavations at Barç near Korçë produced knobbed ware with both large and small knobs. Such Lausitz elements were often found on pots which were decorated with the northwestern geometric designs, and it is evident that the Lausitz influence was absorbed into the local style to a considerable extent. On the other hand there has been no mention of knobbed ware in the tumulus-burials of southern Albania.

In the coastal plain of Macedonia pottery with Lausitz characteristics was found at Vardarophtsa on the east bank of the Vardar in a layer containing two settlements, a layer which began and ended apparently with conflagrations. Heurtley dated the beginning of this layer to c. 1150 B.C., partly on the presence in it of Mycenaean pottery of the Granary class, and such a date is now seen to be compatible with the derivation of its Lausitz pottery, especially the 'turban-dish' (a bowl with fluted rim), from the Mediana group of southern Yugoslavia. I have suggested elsewhere that the period of the Lausitz occupation of Vardarophtsa and nearby Vardina, where the same pottery appeared, was c. 1140 to c. 1080 B.C. Lausitz pottery spread later to Vergina, which is on the south bank of the Haliacmon river in the coastal plain.[45]

Knobbed ware has been found at Strumsko on the lower Strymon and at many sites in central Bulgaria, where it occurred first in the twelfth century. And also at Troy in the settlement known as VIIb 2, which had some pottery of the Mycenaean Granary style and may be dated c. 1150–1070 B.C.[46] There were other similarities between the pottery found at Vardarophtsa-Vardina and the pottery of Troy VIIb 2, to which I have drawn attention.[47]

The literary evidence helps us to give a name to the peoples of Lausitz culture in our area. From a summary of Eugammon's *Telegony*, an epic based on traditional material and written c. 565 B.C., we learn that Odysseus led the Thesprotians against the 'Brygi' after his return from Troy, i.e. c. 1180 B.C.; and in the foundation-legend of Epidamnus (later Dyrrachium), which was seized by Greeks c. 627 B.C., some 'Briges' took the place and its territory at some time after Heracles had been there, and these Briges were displaced by the Taulantii, 'an Illyrian tribe', and they by the Liburni, after whom came the Greeks. In classical times there were 'Brygi' inland of Epidamnus, 'Briges' in the northernmost part of Pelagonia, 'Briges' adjoining the Macedones (then in Pieria) and having their capital below Mt Bermium (probably at Edessa, a Phrygian word), and 'Brygi Thrakes' somewhere north of Chalcidice. Herodotus remarked that the 'Phryges' were called 'Briges' while they were in Europe, and Strabo, drawing upon Hecataeus probably, mentioned that Mt Bermium was held earlier by 'Briges, a Thracian tribe', of whom some crossed to Asia and were there called 'Phryges'. There were earlier 'Phryges' who crossed from Europe into Asia "after the Trojan War," according to Xanthus, writing c. 460 B.C.[48] These fragments of an early tradition from the period of the *Nostoi* "after the Trojan War" touch upon the extreme points at which we have found peoples with the intrusive Lausitz culture, namely south Epirus and the Troad, and the pattern of the surviving peoples with the name Briges or Brygi in Europe coincides well with the finds of Lausitz pottery and ornaments of the twelfth century B.C. It was in fact an invasion on a very large scale, analogous to that of the Slavs (see pp. 66 f.). Thus the situation to the north of the Greek peninsula fits into the general picture of the great land raids and sea raids of the twelfth century, which destroyed the structure of Late Bronze Age civilisation in the countries bordering the Eastern Mediterranean. The name 'Brygi' may be used as a generic term for the migrating peoples who pressed southwards through the Balkans and set other peoples in motion.

We are now in a position to summarise the antecedents and the course of the so-called Dorian invasion (Map 23). At the time approximately of the Trojan War, c. 1200 B.C., the first groups of the Brygi advanced from the Danube basin, probably by the Kačanik pass, into the upper Vardar valley and then into the high plateau of Pelagonia. Like the Goths in A.D. 479, they turned west and entered the lakeland. One group went on to seize the territory which belonged later to Epidamnus (Dyrrachium), and another group penetrated southwestwards via Korcë, Leskoviq and Konitsa (see Map 4). The area between these two thrusts was occupied by pastoral peoples who spoke a dialect of Greek and buried their chieftains in tumuli. The area to the south was occupied by Greek-speaking peoples who differed from their kindred farther north in that they were in touch with the Mycenaean world, did not practise tumulus-burial and engaged in seafaring as well as in transhumant pastoralism, their chief means of livelihood. They had a common name 'Thesprotoi', and their land, Thesprotia, covered then what is now Epirus-in-Greece and the hill-country beyond (ancient Parauaea, modern Danglli).[49]

In the previous generation the Heracleidae, a clan of Achaean stock, originally native to the Argolid but then in exile, had been the ruling power in Epirus, and members of the clan had led settlers overseas to Rhodes and the Dodecanese. The head of the clan, Hyllus, had led a large force against the Peloponnese but had been killed in single combat c. 1220 B.C. When the Brygi invaded Thesprotia, resistance was led by the queen of the Thesprotoi, Callidice, and her ally, Odysseus, now back from Troy. But the Brygi prevailed to the extent that they established themselves in the basin of the upper Kalamas from c. 1180 B.C. onwards. A third group of Brygi went southeastwards (as the Goths did later) and broke into the coastal plain by Edessa, which became the centre of their kingdom "below Mt Bermium." Some of them pressed on eastwards, forced the passage of the Vardar and burnt the Paeonian settlements at Vardarophtsa and Vardina c. 1140 B.C.

The invasions of the Brygi set up a chain-reaction. What Thucydides rightly said of the earliest period in Greece, was eminently true of the northwestern area from central Albania to the Gulf of Corinth in the twelfth century B.C.: "the country had no settled population; on the contrary, migrations were of frequent occurrence, the several tribes readily abandoning their homes under the pressure of superior numbers"

(1.2.1) But could they force their way into the Mycenaean world? One tribe at least, the Boiotoi, had already done so successfully. By 1150 B.C. the tribal leaders in the northwestern area were heavily armed with javelins, thrusting-spears, short swords and knives and they wore some form of protective armour; their followers were hardy shepherds using slings, bows and wooden spears. In battle the leaders counted most; for personal combat was decisive in epic warfare.[50] The outstanding leaders c. 1140-20 B.C. were the Heraclids. They supplied the "kings" of the Thessaloi and the Dorieis; and it seems that they were able to form a temporary coalition with other tribes in the northwestern area.[51] The Heraclids and some of the other chieftains had experience of Mycenaean warfare, whether in battle against Mycenaean peoples or as their allies or mercenaries, but they lacked the means of carrying out a siege.

The Thessaloi were the first to move out of Thesprotia (Map 23). They took their families and flocks through the passes of southern Pindus which led to Karpenisi and the Spercheus valley and to Mouzaki (anc. Gomphi) on the edge of the southwestern plain of Thessaly. With this broad front they could have moved either north or south. As the Phocians held the pass at Thermopylae, the Thessaloi entered southwestern Thessaly c. 1140 B.C. Their invasion set the Boiotoi in motion. The Boiotoi left Arne (Cierium) in this part of the plain (henceforward called Thessaliotis) and migrated probably via the Gravia pass and Delphi into Boeotia, where they settled first at Chaeronea and Coronea, joining forces with their kinsmen of the same name. The way was now clear in central Greece for the mounting of an invasion of the Peloponnese. The strongest group of tribes was called "The Dorieis." It consisted of three tribes—Hylleis, Dymanes and Pamphyloi—and its three kings, presumably reflecting a tradition of three tribal kings, were all Heraclids (Temenus, Cresphontes and Aristomachus, who died at the time of the invasion and was succeeded by twin sons). The Dorians, then, moved from Doris to Delphi and Naupactus, and there joined forces with Oxylus, king of the Aitoloi, a tribe within the Mycenaean world (for they had figured in the Catalogue of Ships against Troy). As Doris is a small canton, high and inhospitable in winter, only a few Dorians can have lived there. The others simply used it as their last staging point before invading the Mycenaean area. It is most likely that

Map 23

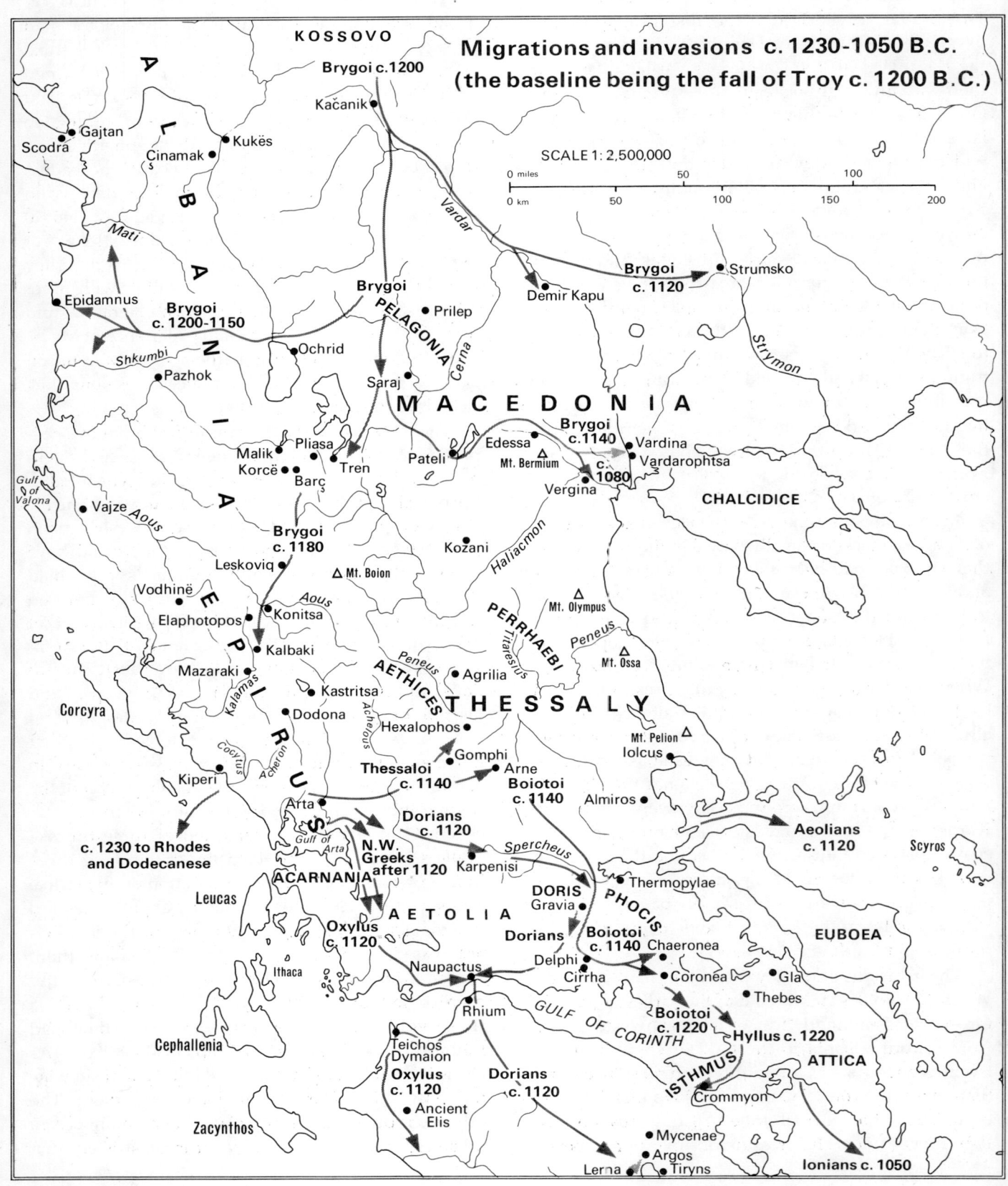

they came to Doris from southern Epirus,[52] following the route of the successful Thessaloi into the Spercheus valley and then swinging south into Doris.

On crossing over to the Peloponnese the invaders split into their original two forces. Oxylus and his followers occupied Elis. The Dorians marched through Arcadia and invaded the Argolid from Lerna, fortified a base near Nauplia and defeated the Achaeans who were commanded by Tisamenus, son of Orestes. While Temenus kept the Argolid as his kingdom, Cresphontes conquered and acquired part of Messenia, and the twins, as nominal commanders, defeated the Achaeans in Laconia. From there some of the Dorians went overseas to occupy Thera and *en route* Melos, where the Mycenaean site at Phylakopi was deserted just before the end of L.H. III C. At 5.112.2 Thucydides dated this last event c. 1116 B.C. Thus the first sweep was rapid; for the invaders won the open countryside and then went at once to another area. But the actual conquest, as opposed to the claims of the kings and their followers, was very far from complete. Two generations passed before the last of the citadels in the Argolid fell, according to the Greek tradition; and many more generations passed before Amyclae in Laconia was captured. We may compare the ability of Arta and Ioannina to hold their own against the migrating Albanians.

The period which followed has been called by modern scholars 'The Dark Age'. The lights of Mycenaean civilisation, dimmed already by internecine wars and internal revolutions, were finally extinguished in most parts of the Greek mainland. Even the art of writing seems to have disappeared, presumably because it had been practised mainly in the service of Mycenaean kings. Presumably those kings and kingdoms also ceased to exist. The Dorians and the Aetolians were not the only invaders; for when they had opened the way, other migrations followed. The later waves of migrants spoke a dialect known as Northwest-Greek, which was closer to the Doric dialect than to any other dialect of Greek. No doubt they too came from Epirus, and certainly in part from Epirus-in-Albania. The common feature of all these invaders—Thessaloi, Boiotoi, Dorieis, Aitoloi and Northwest-Greek speakers—was that they were pastoralists predominantly and lived a semi-nomadic, open-air life, exactly as the Albanians did when they invaded the Peloponnese on the decline of the Byzantine world.

When they obtained their new lands in the Peloponnese they continued their old way of life, living in small groups and building nothing more than temporary encampments. Many of them, like the Vlachs, scorned agriculture; so they made the defeated peoples into serfs, who tilled the land and gave most of the produce to their masters—alike in Thessaliotis and in Laconia. Equally they scorned urban life and such aspects of urban life as retail trading; thus one of the immediate and lasting effects of their invasions was a complete disruption of normal commerce. Moreover, the invasions were set within the framework of the raids by sea and migrations by land which had impoverished the whole of the Eastern Mediterranean area. Recuperation even for countries which had not been invaded, such as Attica, was to be a very slow process.

Some other pieces of evidence which have a bearing on the Dorian invasion must be mentioned. In the picture of pre-invasion Greece which the *Iliad* and the *Odyssey* provide, the 'Perhaebi' lived by the river Titaresius (*Iliad* 2.749 f.) and they were there after the invasion; as they controlled the main route from Macedonia to Thessaly via the Volustana pass and the valley of the Titaresius, and as they were not displaced, we may infer that the great mass of invaders did not come through the territory of the Perrhaebi. The same holds, but with less certainty, for the Aethices. They were on the Thessalian side of Pindus in pre-invasion times (*Iliad* 2.744) and in historic times in the same area, towards the sources of the Peneus (Strabo 327); as they held that side of the Zygos pass and as they were not displaced, we may infer again that the great mass of invaders did not use that pass. With the 'Enienes' (in the later dialect the 'Aenianes') it was different. They lived round Dodona (*Iliad* 2.749 f.); in later times some of them were in the Spercheus valley and others near Cirrha by Delphi. It is evident that the great wave of invasion carried them from central Epirus and deposited them like driftwood on the side of its course. The Dolopes lived "at the extremity of Phthia," i.e. at the head of the Spercheus valley (*Iliad* 9.484), and were found later in two parts, one in the headwaters of the Achelous and the other on the island of Scyros (Thucydides 2.102.2 and 1.98.2). The Locrians too were a single people opposite Euboea, but in historic times they were split into two parts, east and west of the route from Doris to Delphi. It seems then that the great mass of invaders came through the passes into the upper Spercheus valley and from there into the eastern part of central Greece. Similarly on the western side the Cephallenes were on the mainland and on three islands—Ithaca, 'Samos' and Zacynthos (*Iliad* 2.631 f.), but later only on Cephallenia, the classical name of the Homeric 'Samos'. Here too the invasion seems to have displaced most of the Cephallenes, and we may infer that there were movements both by sea and by land which made the Cephallenes withdraw into the one island.

We may recall a practice of the Vlachs of Almiros in Thessaly. Each year they sent a party to their earlier summer home, Pliasa near Korcë. So too the Aenianes sent a party of maidens driving an ox to Cassopaea in southern Epirus, where they made sacrifice to Apollo and gave the ox to Zeus (Plutarch, *Moralia* 297 B = *GQ* 26); the reason was, according to Plutarch, that they had had their home in Cassopaea in the interval between their removal from Molossia (in central Epirus) and their coming to Cirrha. The analogy of the Vlachs suggests that the reason was a true one. The same reason may have underlain the sending each year of a tripod to Dodona by the Boiotoi; for they seem to have come from Epirus also, and their name may be connected with Mt Boion (the part of Pindus overlooking the upper Haliacmon valley) and the Boioi (on the south shore of Lake Ochrid).[53]

The names of Greek tribes fall into groups in accordance with the form of the endings. One such is the group of names ending in *-enes* or *-anes*. In Classical times this group was found almost entirely in the northwestern area: Athamanes, Atintanes, Arctanes and Talaeanes in Epirus; Acarnanes, Eitanes and Eurytanes in Aetolo-Acarnania; and Cephallenes in Cephallenia. The Aenianes and Cylicrenes were on the eastern side in the Spercheus valley. The only tribal names with this ending in the *Iliad* were the Enienes by Dodona, the Cephallenes then still in part on the northwestern mainland, and the Hellenes of Achilles in the Spercheus valley;[54] and their proximity to the source of such names suggests that they had emigrated from the homeland of *-anes* tribes. So too one of the three tribes which made up the Dorians was the Dymanes, and the inference is that the Dymanes had come from the same homeland, namely the northwestern area.

The Greeks of the fifth century were interested in the fact that they spoke a variety of strongly marked dialects, and that their literature was expressed dialectically and had been even in the earliest epic lays and choral songs.[55] That the speakers of the dialects were all of one *race* was not in doubt; this belief was expressed in the form of a genealogical tree of eponymous ancestors for each group of tribes, all descended from Zeus. But Greek writers assumed that there had always been a strong link between *tribes* and dialects. No doubt they could see that this was so in backward parts of the peninsula in their own day. So too we can see that tribe and dialect were closely linked among the Vlachs and the Albanians and that groups of tribes coincided with the divisions of dialect-groups in Albania. Greek writers realised also that, when one tribe held another in subjection over a long period, its dialect might become dominant and that to this extent tribal distinctions might become blurred.[56] But that was exceptional.

Herodotus and Thucydides drew a tribal-dialectal map of *pre-invasion* Greece with complete confidence, using the oral traditions and the earliest literature, and no doubt making inferences from the contemporary situation. Dialects of the Aeolic group were spoken then in Thessaly, Boeotia, Euboea, South Aetolia, Corinthia, Argolis (the Homeric "Achaioi" of Argolis being "an Aeolic tribe" in Strabo 333), and Elis.[57] Dialects of the Ionic group were spoken in Attica and in the Isthmus area as far south as Crommyon, and also in some parts of the Peloponnese, such as Cynuria and Achaea.[58] Arcadian was spoken in some parts of the Peloponnese (see Map 24a). One source which Herodotus and Thucydides could not use was the language of Linear B script, but their views have received support from our decipherment of Linear B, which has shown that the literary language of palace circles at Thebes, Mycenae and Ano-Englianos in Messenia was close to Aeolic and had affinities with Arcadian. Another literary language, that of the Homeric epic, has fossil forms of these two dialects, Aeolic and Arcadian, which indicates—if we are correct in supposing that epic lays existed before the Dorian invasion—that the poetical language then was of the same general character as the official language of these three palace centres.

The existence of Arcadian as a developed dialect in the Peloponnese during the Late Bronze Age is demonstrated by the speaking of a form of Arcadian in Cyprus, which was introduced there by emigrants from the Peloponnese; according to Greek tradition

Map 24a

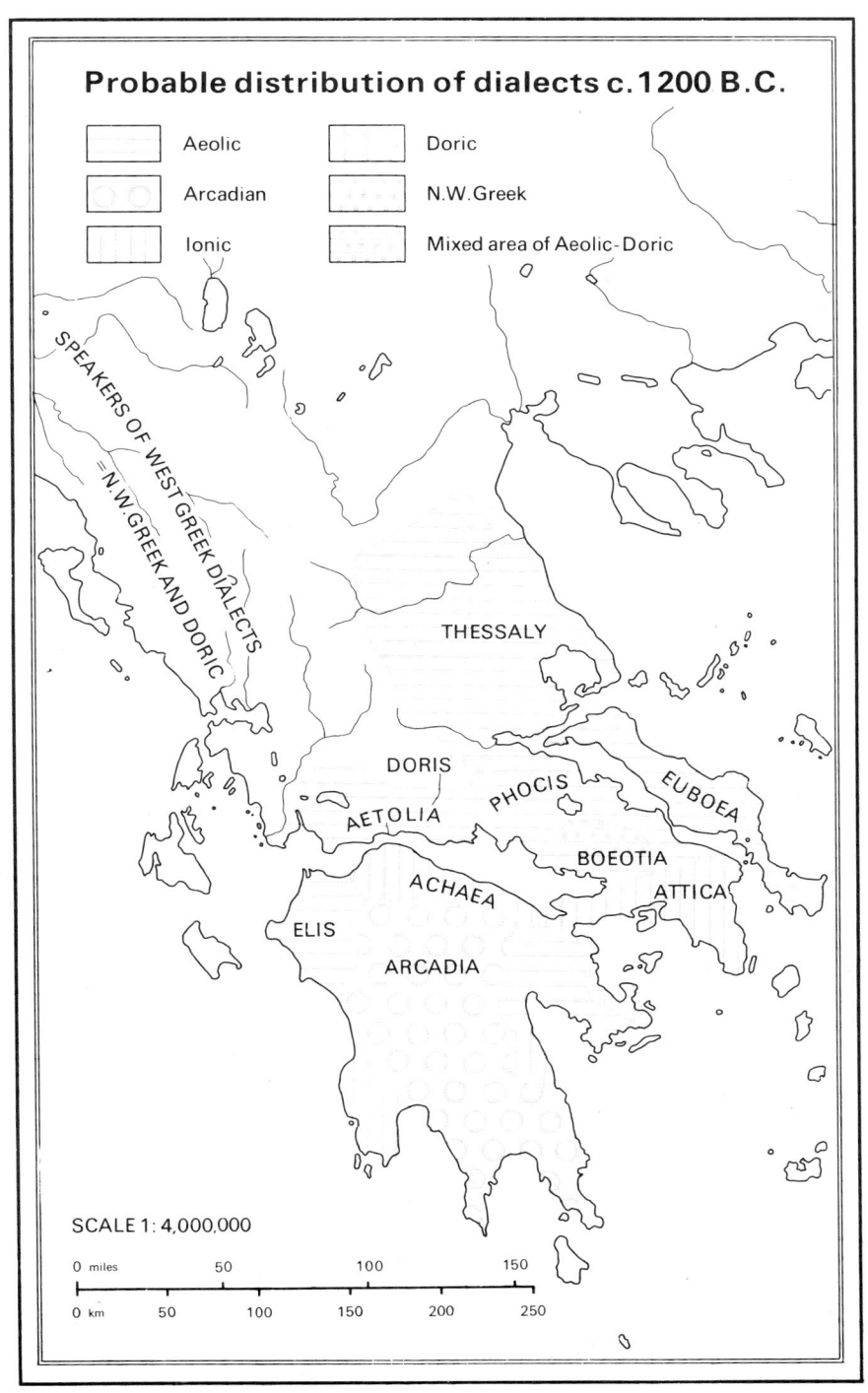

and archaeological evidence this happened before the collapse of the Mycenaean world. A dialect which was a mixture of Arcadian and Aeolic was spoken in classical times in Pamphylia, a country in Asia Minor, which may have received Greek settlers from the Peloponnese at the same time, more or less, as Cyprus. If the Greek writers were correct about the Aeolic and Arcadian parts of their tribal-dialectal map, as we are maintaining, then the odds are high that they were correct also about the place of Ionic as the earliest of all dialects to be spoken in Greece[59] and about the absence of Doric and Northwest-Greek dialects from the areas which they mentioned in the pre-invasion period.

The tribal-dialectal map of *post-invasion* Greece also was drawn by ancient writers. They preserved traditions of tribal movements in what we call the Dark Age, such as the advance of the Dorians to Corinthia and to the Isthmus territory, where the Doric dialect ousted the Ionic dialect, and they noted some occasions when one dialect dominated another, Doric for instance gaining over Aeolic in parts of the Peloponnese and subduing Ionic in Cynuria.[60] Their map has been supported by the study of inscriptions, where they are available for the period before the decline or overlaying of dialects (see Map 24b).

A comparison of the pre-invasion map and the post-invasion map shows very clearly what happened during the initial invasons and the Dark Age. As C. D. Buck wrote[61] "even if there were no tradition of a Dorian invasion, such a movement would have to be assumed." Indeed the comparison shows us one point which was not preserved in the Greek tradition, namely the follow-up of the Dorian-Aetolian success by speakers of Northwest-Greek who flooded a great part of central Greece, northern and western Peloponnese, and three of the Ionian islands. Behind them too were other Greek-speaking tribes whom we find in possession of Epirus at the start of the historic period.

When we ask what the invaders did once they were in possession of the land, the answer of archaeology is expressed mainly in negative terms. In general they had no effect on developments in pottery. The development from the Mycenaean style to what is called Sub-Mycenaean was direct and uninterrupted both in invaded areas, such as Boeotia, Corinthia, Argolis and Elis, and in Attica which escaped invason; and the completely new style, Protogeometric, evolved in northeast Thessaly and in Attica c. 1050 B.C. and spread out from there. This lack of influence by the invaders was no doubt due to their not making fine pottery themselves in the land from which they came, and this in itself means that they were semi-nomadic pastoralists, who, like their modern counterparts, the Vlachs and Sarakatsani, had wooden vessels, skins and gourds as bowls and containers and made only coarse cooking pots of pottery. Most of those who came from southwest Epirus and Aetolo-Acanania were familiar already with Mycenaean pottery, even if they rarely owned it, and they readily adopted such pottery from the people they conquered in the Greek peninsula.[62] Next, the invaders did not build any citadels or fortifications and seem to have let the Mycenaean fortresses fall into decay. This must mean that they had come from an area which did not have such things, and that they depended for their supremacy upon their weapons, like the Dorian Hybrias in Crete, who sang as follows:[63] "My riches are spear, sword and stout protective shield; with them I plough, with them I reap, with them I tread the sweet wine from the grape, with them I am entitled master of the serfs."

Nor did they build settlements. Indeed the number of settlements in the whole of the Greek peninsula declined considerably in the Sub-Mycenaean period from the already small number present in L.H. III C.[64] The invaders evidently lived in the open, making temporary encampments, such as leave little or no trace, and depended mainly on the products of transhumant pastoralism and stock-raising. There had been a similar decline for very much the same reasons in E. H. III and the first phase of M. H.

A change in burial customs came with the break-up of the Mycenaean communities. For example, at Mycenae no new chamber-tombs were made in L.H. III C and the old chamber-tombs which had served as family vaults for generations received no new burials after the end of L.H. III C I (c. 1140 B.C.); subsequent burials were each in a single grave, whether earth-pit, pithos, larnax or cist-grave, the last being usual for a child.[65] At one extremity of the Mycenaean world, however, the old custom continued in northeastern Thessaly, which seems not to have been overrun, even after the destruction of Iolcus c. 1075 B.C. Thus the tholos-tombs at Marmariani on the western side of Mt Ossa and elsewhere in Magnesia and the tholos-tombs in Perrhaebia were in use for a long

Map 24b

time. But throughout the mainland, including Attica, the cist-grave became the norm. The change in custom could have been due in theory to invaders from the north; for cist-graves had been common in Leucas (E. H. III and M. H.), Epirus including southern and central Albania (L. H.), the Haliacmon valley e.g. at Kozani (L. H.) and northern Thessaly e.g. at Sesklo, Iolcus and Agrilia (M. H. and L. H.) But the cist-grave had a long life also in the Cyclades, and even on the mainland it had not gone out of use in the Mycenaean period. With the decline in family life and the general improverishment which followed the invasion it is very likely that the cist-grave became popular as the simplest and cheapest form of burial.[66]

When we turn to particular instances, only a few point to the origin of some of the invaders. At Hexalophos in southwestern Thessaly a tumulus of soil, 27 m in diameter, has been partly excavated and two cist-graves have been opened. The offerings with the dead were a sword of F ii type, a leaf-shaped javelin-head, a long knife, a ring with spiralling ends and bits of a shield-boss—all of bronze—and high-footed kylikes of pottery, poorly made. There was some evidence of a pyre in connection with one of the burials. The excavator, D. Theochares, has dated the burials within the period 1150–1100 B.C. As the tumulus and its contents are unparalleled in Thessaly, and as every detail has been found in Epirus-in-Albania and in the cist-graves of the upper Kalamas valley, it is clear that the tumulus at Hexalophos was constructed by newcomers from Epirus. As both the area and the time fit the invasion of the Thessaloi, led by Heraclids, according to the literary tradition, we may regard the dead as Heraclids or other champions to whom this honorific form of burial was granted. As one of them wore a Lausitz ring, he may have been a Lausitz warrior.[67]

At Mycenae some burials were made at some time after the last destruction (of c. 1120 B.C. or later) within the confines of the citadel. It is most probable that those who lived there and buried their dead within the walls were the conquerors rather than the conquered. The details of the burials in the Citadel House are therefore important for our purpose. One was the cist-grave of a child, eight or nine years old, possibly female, made within a wall which was partly demolished to provide a cavity. The offerings were a finger-ring of bronze strip with spiralling ends, two long pins with slight swellings below the small heads and incised grooves above and below the swellings, three arched fibulae of a simple type, and seven vases which Desborough has dated late in the Sub-Mycenaean period, i.e. c. 1075 B.C.[68] Such finger-rings were found in cist-graves in the upper Kalamas valley in Epirus and in a cist-grave at Prilep in Pelagonia, similar but more primitive long pins in tumulus-burials at Vajzë in south Albania, and arched fibulae of a different type in the same cist-grave at Prilep. Thus the contents of this grave at Mycenae suggest a northern origin with some Lausitz association for the occupants of the citadel. The placing of the burial of a child against or within a wall has been noted at Gajtan near Scodra and at Tren in the lakeland (Early Iron Age and Early Bronze Age respectively), and it has been suggested there that it was a sacrifice "de caractère de culte . . . pour la solidité des murs de ceinture."[69] Perhaps it was the same with this burial at Mycenae, except that the wall was an internal wall.

Another cist-grave inside the Citadel House at Mycenae was covered by long boulders of which "the undersides showed signs of fierce burning," and the walls of the cist showed similar signs of burning. The bones of the corpse, a young woman, had been affected by the fire. Fragments of an iron pin were found, which led Desborough to date the burial "just possibly at the very end of Sub-Mycenaean but more probably during the Protogeometric period."[70] The burning of the mortuary chamber and the affecting of the bones by fire were noted in Kurgan IV burials of a much earlier date, and something similar continued into the Early Iron Age in the tumulus-burials of the Mati valley in central Albania, where "ont éte déposés les restes non entièrement incinérés des ossements et de l'inventaire qui a subi le même sort." Iron pins occurred early in tumulus-burials at Vajzë in south Albania.[71] At Ancient Elis burials of up to three persons in earth pits with covers or upright markers of unworked stone have been attributed to "the time of the Dorian coming" by N. Yialouris and to the early eleventh century by Desborough. One had two bronze pins of early types; one pin with a very slight swelling resembled a pin from Vajzë. Another burial had two pins with a bulb, and there were arched fibulae of the plainest type, as at Mycenae in the child burial, and bronze rings in other burials.[72] At Tsaleika, in Elis inland, a preliminary report was made of a possible tumulus-burial, made in a pithos with a cairn of stones set over it, dated "perhaps to L.H. III

C"; if it was a tumulus-burial of that period, we may see it as an indication of invaders coming from north of the Kalamas valley in Epirus.[73]

In Cephallenia three cemeteries have been excavated which were in use in L.H. III C and probably until the end of the twelfth century. In any case they provide evidence for the period before and for a short time after the invasion of the Peloponnese. The dead were laid in parallel rectangular trenches cut in soft rock. No one, I think, has suggested a parallel but there may be at least two: one at Palia Goritsa near Konitsa in Epirus where two such trenches cut in limestone had been opened and small mounds nearby appeared to cover some others, and the other at Treskavtsa in western Yugoslavia.[74]

It is then probable that those who used these cemeteries, like the users of the R Graves in Leucas earlier, had come to Cephallenia from the coast of the Adriatic Sea. In one trench with several dead at Lakkithra, numbered A, there were remains of a pyre with offerings of gold objects and animal bones, but the dead were inhumed, not cremated; this rite is reminiscent of Kurgan burials of much earlier date. The objects in the burials showed a mixture of Mycenaean and non-Mycenaean elements, the latter including amber beads, leaf-shaped bronze spearheads, long bronze pins, and a piece of ridged bronze band which was a part probably of a Lausitz-type finger-ring. Amber was particularly common in the Mati valley burials; the spearheads were like some found in Epirus; and the long bronze pins included pins with a slight swelling and one roll-top pin, of which the former were found in tumulus-burials at Vajzë and the latter were reported in tumulus-burials at Barç near Korcë as "Rollenkopfnadeln."[75] If these burials spanned both sides of the Dorian invasion, they show that Cephallenia was in contact with the north and in particular with Albania throughout that time, and that the Cephallenes were not ejected from the island. Rather, as we have seen from the literary evidence, the effect of the invasion was to concentrate them within the island which now took their name. The other point of interest is that these burials may help to show the northern origin of some of the objects which occurred in other burials also of the post-invasion part of L.H. III C or the Sub-Mycenaean period.

To sum up, the invasions which ended the Mycenaean era are singularly well attested. The epic and the oral traditions concerning the wars and troubles of the Mycenaean states from the time of the Seven against Thebes to the deaths of the Trojan War heroes and their sons, and in particular the detailed lists of the Catalogue of Ships mustered against Troy, give us a remarkable insight into the state of affairs before the invasions. The archaeological picture, now reasonably firm, of the latter half of L.H. III B and of L.H. III C reveals a distribution and relative strength of sites in confirmation of the Catalogue and supports other traditions such as the sack of Thebes. The literary traditions about the invasions themselves indicate clearly the area from which the invaders came, the routes they followed, and the areas which they conquered and occupied. Again such archaeological evidence as there is—not enough *by itself* to give much of an insight—is consistent with the traditions. Then we have good clues to the distribution of dialects both before and after the invasions, as to a lesser degree in the case of the Albanian invasions; a comparison of these dialect distributions reveals clearly the origin, direction and extent of the invasions in a manner consistent with the other, entirely independent evidences. Contemporary movements of peoples in the Balkans help to explain why the invasions occurred; these movements have been revealed by excavations which Aegean scholars have to take into account, and the literary tradition helps to explain their impact on the lands north of the Mycenaean sphere. Some of the post-invasion burials in conquered areas give clues to the origins of some invaders and suggest that some Balkan warriors accompanied the Greek-speaking invaders.

The Subsequent Migrations

(See Map 25)

The invasion of the Peloponnese was followed by two generations of turmoil. The Arcadians fought for their independence successfully but were penned up in the centre of the Peloponnese. The Achaeans of the Argolid, led by Tisamenus, son of Orestes, were driven first out of their own land and then out of Laconia, which they tried to defend. Next they found a refuge in Achaea from which they expelled the Ionian population. Even there they were not safe; for further waves of Northwest-Greek speakers over-

Map 25

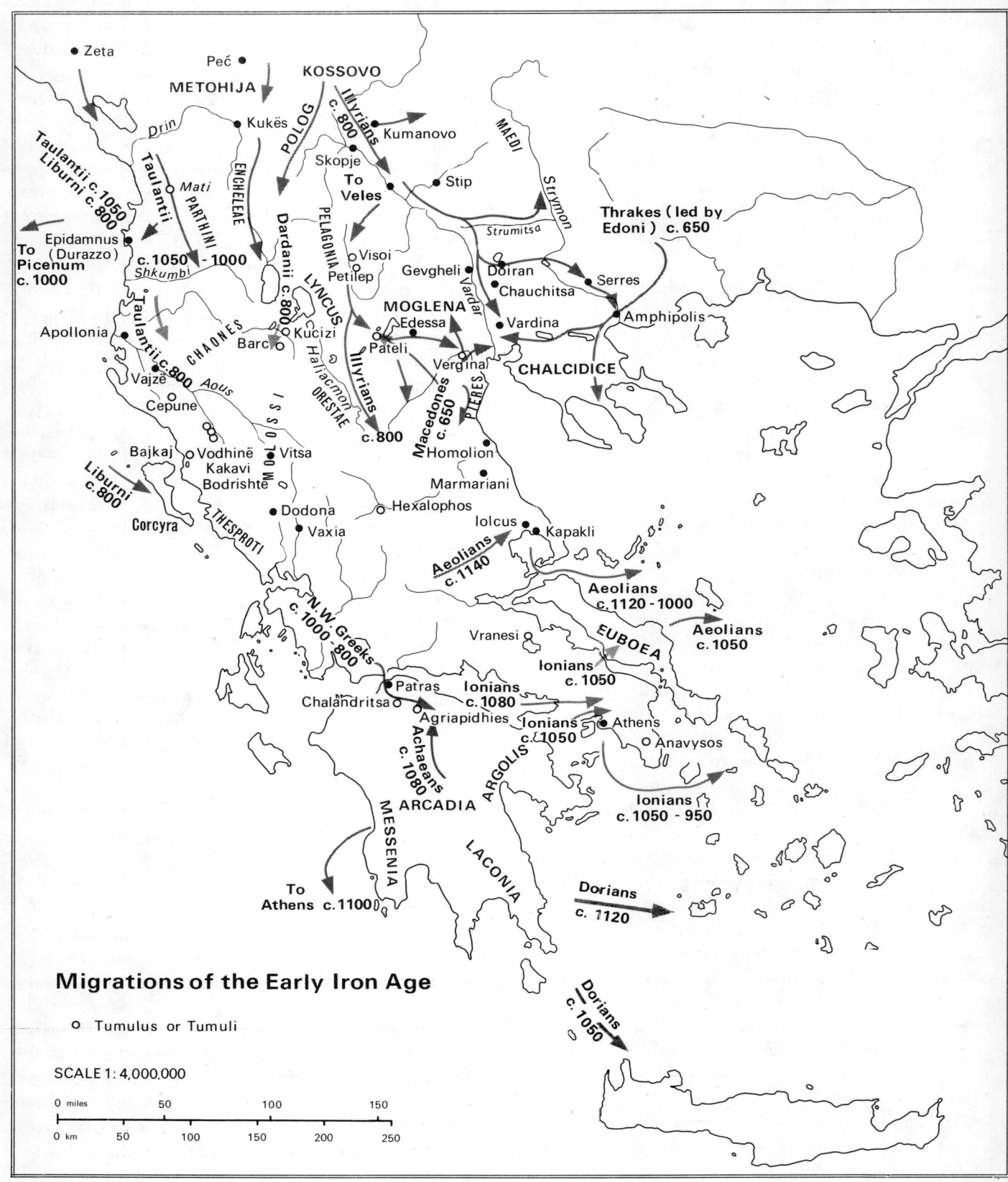

Migrations of the Early Iron Age

○ Tumulus or Tumuli

SCALE 1: 4,000,000

powered them. Some of the leading Messenian families escaped from Messenia and were accepted at Athens. The Ionians who had been expelled from Achaea took refuge at Athens in approximately 1080 B.C.; and other Ionians followed from the Isthmus territory, which was seized by the Dorians of the northeastern Peloponnese c. 1050 B.C.. Athens had the courage and the intelligence to accept and enfranchise the refugees, a step which, in Thucydides' words, "made the state still greater through its increased population, so that Attica became insufficient and emigrants were subsequently sent off to Ionia" (1.2.6). This emigration started soon after 1050 B.C. But it was not the first emigration from the Greek mainland in this troubled period.[76]

In central Greece Athens held firm against attack by the Boiotoi. Indeed the Boiotoi and other speakers of Northwest-Greek had to recognise the independence of many of the Aeolic-speaking communities in Boeotia, Phocis and Locris. The haven for Aeolian refugees, both from central Greece and from southwestern Thessaly, was Iolcus and the northeastern part of the Thessalian plain. The first shocks of the invasion caused this area to become overpopulated, and the first emigrants, led by another son of Orestes, went overseas before the end of the twelfth century. The so-called Aeolian migration went on for several generations and ended in the occupation by Aeolian Greeks of the rich island of Lesbos and points on the adjacent Asiatic coast by the end of the eleventh century. Meanwhile the Ionian migration from Athens was well under way. It too lasted for a century or more. The insecurity and the violence which attended these two migrations were features of most parts of the eastern Mediterranean. The spirit of the period was epitomised by the words of an Ionian poet: "with overmastering might we settled at beloved Colophon, pioneers of boisterous violence, and from there . . . by the grace of the gods we captured Aeolian Smyrna." The Ionians also drove the Aeolians out of Euboea and occupied it themselves. In the southern part of the Aegean archipelago the descendants of the Dorian invaders continued their successful invasion, becoming masters of the small southern islands, of Crete and Rhodes and of the mainland adjacent to Rhodes.[77]

Thus the Dorian invasion led to migrations eastwards which were of the greatest historical significance. For the Greeks won then the islands which they hold to this day, and a Greek population was planted in Asia Minor which was destined to play an important part in the history of the Eastern Mediterranean until it was expelled in 1923.

Within the Peloponnese the number of known settlements declined from fifty-six in L.H. III C to twenty-three in the post-invasion period and did not rise steadily until after 800 B.C. The decline was due not only to the expulsion and emigration of previously settled peoples but also to the reversion of great areas of coastland and mountain valley to pastoralism of a semi-nomadic nature. Further peoples with this way of life entered Achaea late in the period and drove out the Achaeans (originally of the Argolid), who had themselves expelled an Ionian population. These newcomers spoke Northwest-Greek which became the dialect of Achaea in the Classical period. Coming from Epirus and Aetolo-Acarnania, they were typical of this large and warlike group in that they contributed nothing to the Greek achievement in literature and culture but formed the toughest communities of the Hellenistic period. It is probable that we may see traces of the newcomers in two cemeteries. At Agriapidhies, some twenty kilometres south of Patras, a number of slab-lined cist-graves were found within a circular area, marked by a *peribolos* of slab-like stones; as the excavator saw, it probably had had a tumulus originally. The graves contained little of interest except four crude hand-made jugs and containers, which were probably of a type usual in the north. At Chalandritsa in the same region several tumuli were reported, and the two which were excavated had cist-graves lined with stones and one of these had an apsidal end. Tentative dates for the two cemeteries were the tenth century and the eighth century respectively; as they were unique at these dates in the Peloponnese, they probably were connected with the coming of Northwest-Greek speakers from a tumulus-using area such as Epirus.[78]

Let us now turn to the north. The peoples of northeastern Thessaly became relatively prosperous by creating an orbit of trade to the northeast, as their predecessors had done in the Dimini period; for in the course of the Aeolian migration they established contact with the ports of the Thermaic Gulf, Chalcidice, the Thracian coast and the Troad. They developed their own style of Protogeometric pottery very early,[79] and they exported it to the east side of the inner Thermaic Gulf, from which it reached the interior. Whereas these contacts were made and maintained by sea, there was certainly a movement of people between the middle Haliacmon valley and northern Thessaly, which was based primarily on the transhumance of sheep. The chief sign was the offering of hand-made pottery painted in the 'northwestern geometric' style in five tholos-tombs which were in use regularly for a long period—from somewhere in the eleventh century down to 800 B.C.—and occasionally thereafter into the sixth century. The hand-made pottery belonged to the early burials, and a continuing influence from farther north was apparent in certain bronze ornaments. The site of the tholos-tombs is at Marmariani on the foothills of Mt Ossa, looking towards the plain of Larissa. The peculiar qualities of the site and its long use are best explained on the supposition that the leaders of pastoral groups, like the Vlach *tshelnikadzi*, kept their flocks there during the winter season for generation after generation, and that some who died in the winter were buried in the tholos-tombs. At another site, Kapakli near Volos on the Gulf of Pagasae, similar contact with the Haliacmon valley was indicated by pottery in a tholos-tomb, but the main influences came by sea from the coastal plain of Macedonia.[80]

In Macedonia it seems that the Brygi were driven back from Vardarophtsa and Vardina c. 1080 B.C. and their frontier with the Paeonians was drawn at the river Vardar. The important unit of power in Macedonia west of the river was the kingdom of the Brygi, of which the capital was below Mt Bermium, where the gardens of Midas, son of Gordias, were famous for their sixty-petalled roses. It is probable that the gardens are those of Vodena, the ancient Edessa, which stands on the main route (that of the Via Egnatia) from the western part of the coastal plain to the Monastir gap from which routes lead into the lakeland and to the head of the Vardar valley.[81] As we have seen, the Brygi established themselves also in Pelagonia, in the lakeland area at Barç, and in the vicinity of Epidamnus on the Adriatic coast of central Albania. We can thus discern the outlines of a large system of Phrygian power, which gave some sort of stability to this area for a period of some 350 years. The end came with the mass emigration of the Phrygians from Europe to northwestern Asia, where they founded a new empire and made their capital at Gordium. The date was approximately c. 800 B.C.

During the long period of Phrygian power in Europe the Brygi were the neighbours of the Macedones, a Greek-speaking tribe or group of small tribes which occupied the hill country of Pieria as their homeland and engaged mainly in pastoral life.[82] Its coastal plain was the land of Thracian peoples, known as 'Pieres'; they were famed for their music, and Orpheus was said to be buried near Dium. A number of cist-graves with unusual features and each with a small mound above it, at Koundouriotissa in this area, was a memorial to their presence; for Herodotus recorded such individual burial with a mound as customary for Thracian leaders (5.8). The most remarkable cemetery in Macedonia west of the Vardar is a group of some 300 large tumuli, situated below a terrace-site called Palatitsa which overlooks the plain, and close to the right bank of the Haliacmon.[83] As the cemetery was open and undefended and lay beside the main road which led from Pieria to Edessa and so to the Vardar, it must have been made by a people which was undisputed master of the western plain. As the richest period of the cemetery of 'Vergina', as it is called, was that of the Phrygian kingdom in Europe, we may be confident that it was the cemetery of the kings and nobles of the Brygi. When they crossed to Asia they made a royal cemetery of eventually some eighty large tumuli at Gordium.

Tumulus-burial was a feature also of the inland principalities of the Phrygian system of power. A large cemetery at Pateli (Ayios Pandeleëmon) near the southern end of Lake Ostrovo was excavated in the 1890s by Russian scholars who opened 376 graves but left a confused and meagre record. Of these the 'royal' burials, in the opinion of the excavators, were fourteen cist-graves within a circular area which was bounded by a thick circular wall, and the offerings were of gold, bronze and pottery. We may infer that there was originally a tumulus over this circular wall. Farther north at Visoï in Pelagonia there is a cemetery of tumuli, and a model of one which has been excavated is on show in the Museum at Monastir. It too had a circular wall, of which the thickness was made up of two or three large, dark stones, and there were nearly forty cist-graves within the enclosed space of the tumulus. At the centre two burials had their own small circular *peribolos* of single whitish stones.[84] Moving to the west, we have already mentioned the large tumulus at Barç which contained some 112 burials, ranging from the twelfth century to c. 800 B.C. It too had a complete ring-wall. The offerings included diadems of fine bronze plaque, as at Vergina and Pateli, hair-coils of gold wire, as at Vergina, and twin-vases and triplet-vases, as at Pateli. In the Mati valley, where thirty-six tumuli ranging from 12 to 30 m in diameter have so far been excavated, more than twenty-five belonged to the Early Iron Age but it is not stated how many were of the period before 800 B.C. Some tumuli were constructed above circles of stones, and the offerings included diadems and a pair of hair-coils of gold, which were found together with "two swords of a Mycenaean type."[85]

There were differences in the offerings which were made in these cemeteries of tumuli. The differences indicate that the principalities enjoyed considerable independence and that the ruling class was merged with the native population to some extent in each case. For example, Vergina had an elaborate headdress with a broad diadem for a priestess and examples of a miniature double-axe, which both seem to be related to the claim of the local people, the Bottiaeans, to have been of Cretan origin.[86] Pateli was remarkable for a unique system of arranging the skulls of the dead. Visoï was closer in offerings to Vergina than to Pateli, despite the fact that Pateli lay geographically between them. Barç had more long pins of bronze than Visoï and Pateli and fewer weapons in the burials. Mati had most weapons, including battle-axes of iron which were not found in the other cemeteries. There were differences also in the pottery as between principality and principality. Thus Mati stood aside from the others, in that striation rather than paint was used for decoration and small vases predominated.[87]

During this period there are indications that Illyrian tribes were migrating from farther north into northern and central Albania. Peculiarities of the tumulus-burials at Mati were shared by numerous tumulus-burials near Kukës (at Çinamak, Këneta and Krume). In both areas pottery-containers were broken as part of a ritual performed during the construction of the upper part of a tumulus, and the burials themselves were usually covered with stones of moderate size; these practices were not found in tumuli farther south. A genealogy of the sons and daughters of Illyrius, the eponymous ancestor of the race in the Greek manner, has come down to us, transmitted probably from the foundation-story of Epidamnus, in which the Brygi were followed by "the Taulantii, an Illyrian tribe" (Appian, Bella Civilia 2.39 and Illyrica 2). Among the sons and daughters were Taulas, ancestor of the Taulantii, who lived in classical times inland of Epidamnus; Partho, the eponym of the Parthini, who lived then in the middle Shkumbi valley, and Encheleus, ancestor of the Encheleae, who lived then near Lake Ochrid. Illyrius himself was the eponymous ancestor of a tribe, called by Roman writers 'the Illyrians proper' (Illyrii proprie dicti), and this tribe lived in Classical times to the north of the Taulantii.[88] It seems probable that these Illyrii were the southernmost of the Illyrian-speaking tribes at the time when their name became known to Greek-speaking peoples and was applied to other tribes of similar speech and manners.

The advance of the Taulantii, Parthini and Encheleae, which left the Illyrii proper behind, occurred probably c. 1050–1000 B.C., for 'Illyrian' burial customs made their appearance in Peucetia on the Italian side of the Adriatic c. 1000 B.C. and somewhat later in Picenum; these included burial areas ringed with slabs or large stones, and the slab-lined cists or simple trenches within the circle were covered with a low tumulus of stones, on top of which there may originally have been a higher tumulus of soil. Bari in Peucetia is the counterpart of Epidamnus at the safest crossing of the southern Adriatic, and the Museum of Bari has a number of pots typical of the 'northwestern geometric style' which was in use, for instance, at Pazhok and farther south. This pottery in Peucetia has been dated early in the first millennium B.C.[89] Thus it seems that the overseas expansion of some Illyrian peoples into Italy took place in the same period as the advance of Illyrian peoples into northern Albania. While we may assume that one stream of Illyrians came south by the Zeta valley and Lake Scodra, others seem to have come from Peć in Metohija and entered the Drin valley in the vicinity of Kukës and ascended it to near Lake Ochrid. Hill-fortresses near Kukës and the cemeteries of tumuli have been associated with this advance.

The connections of the tumulus-burials at Barç in the southern part of the lakeland were not with the Kukës or Mati tumuli but with those of Vajzë and southern Albania; for example, in the long bronze pins, roll-top pins, twin-vessels, handles divided by a cross-bar, and small spectacle-fibulae of an early type (1 g). Moreover, the pottery of the 'northwestern geometric style' which was typical of Barç was current not in north but in central and south Albania and also in the plain of Ioannina at this time. It is probable that the peoples to the south of the Shkumbi valley and Lake Ochrid spoke Northwest-Greek, being the residue left behind when the migrations carried many of their kindred into the Greek peninsula. The interrelationships within this large group of Greek tribes led Hecataeus, writing c. 500 B.C., to describe them as "Molossian tribes" or "Chaonian tribes." Thus the Orestae of the upper Haliacmon valley were "Molossian," and the Dexaroi "a tribe of the Chaones, adjacent to the Encheleae." The latter, under the variant form Dassaretai, occupied the southern part of the lakeland in Classical times. The most northerly of this group of speakers of Northwest-Greek were the Pelagones.[90]

The departure of the Brygi c. 800 B.C. may have been hastened by renewed pressure from Illyrian tribes which had already advanced into central Albania and the lakeland. The period of Illyrian control in the plain of Macedonia lasted from c. 800 to c. 650 B.C. The evidence has survived almost entirely in warrior-graves and women's graves which were much less numerous. There were cremations sometimes in urns, as well as inhumations; large pithoi were used as coffins, e.g. at Vergina; and burials were grouped together, sometimes under a tumulus and sometimes not. New articles were bronze pendants of various kinds, bronze belt-plates, large bronze spectacle-fibulae, armlets of thin bronze wire and armlets of heavy bronze metal with incised decoration, and many bronze beads of various shapes (Pl. 11). At Vergina, where the same cemetery was used for Illyrian chieftains, two new forms of bowl were evidently copied from wooden prototypes, such as are made by the Vlachs in modern times. New tumuli constructed for Illyrian chieftains contained many spearheads and spear-butts, sickle-shaped knives and heavy bracelets. The homeland of these new elements was in central Yugoslavia, and the typical site there was Glasinac, where the tumuli were numbered in thousands.

Thus the expansion of the Illyrian-speaking tribes went on over a long period, as that of the Albanians was to do. They moved first down the western flank, occupying the country as far south as the Shkumbi valley and Lake Ochrid c. 1050–1000 B.C. and crossing over into Italy c. 1000 B.C. The area between the Shkumbi and the outflow of the Aous may have been in dispute for centuries, but it was acquired by the Illyrians who were there before 600 B.C. when Apollonia was founded probably as a mixed settlement of Greeks and Illyrians. It is likely that the Illyrian tribes who expanded in this way were based on the Zeta valley area and the Metohija, and used these areas as their launching grounds for expansion by land and sea, as the Ardiaeans were to do some centuries later.[91] When we compare the Illyrian advance with that of the Albanians, there is the remarkable difference that the Illyrians failed to drive southwards through Epirus.

The state of affairs in Epirus is known also from tumulus-burials. This form of burial was originally common to both the Illyrian-speaking and the Greek-speaking branches of the Indo-European peoples, when they entered the southwest Balkans, and it was maintained by the descendants of both on this flank of the peninsula. Tumuli of Middle Bronze Age date at Vajzë just south of the lower Aous and at Vodhinë in the Kseria valley farther south were re-used from the last stage of the Bronze Age onwards into the Early Iron Age perhaps by leading families which returned to power in these regions. New tumuli were constructed in the Early Iron Age: probably C and D at Vajzë, and two at Bodrishtë near Vodhinë.[92] Altogether new centres developed around the end of the twelfth century and went on into the Early Iron Age. At Çepune near Kardhiq in the Kurvelesh a tumulus 22 m in diameter has been excavated recently. Of its 63 burials the earliest were three inhumations and one cremation inside slab-lined cist-graves, the actual cremation having been done outside the cist, and from these came spearheads, javelin-heads and long pins of bronze. One fiddle-shaped javelin-head with a facetted socket is like one from Vodhinë, and the long pins resemble those at Vajzë. This tumulus remained in use into the third century B.C.[93] At Bajkaj near Delvino a tumulus 20 m in diameter had 43 burials which extended from the late twelfth to the ninth century B.C. according to the excavator, Dhimosten Budina. The earliest burial was a cremation. The pottery included a pot of knobbed ware and a jug influenced by Protogeometric style; and a bronze pin, a javelin-head and a spearhead were similar to those in other tumulus-burials of northern Epirus.[94] With the exception of Çepune, which is in an exceptionally remote part, it seems on present evidence that tumulus-burial was declining from 900 B.C. onwards and may have ended in the course of the ninth century.

The tribal groups, of which the warrior-chieftains were buried in tumuli at these four places, were evidently strong enough to keep the Illyrians at bay. In fact they had begun the important task which they were to discharge for some centuries. The groups were combined under the name 'Chaones', when they first figured in literary records, and they ruled over the whole of Epirus at the beginning of the historical period.[95] Their territory extended northeastwards into the lakeland area, where the 'Dexaroi' lived, and it was there that the next Illyrian breakthrough occurred.

The tumulus at Barç went out of use perhaps by 850 B.C. Another tumulus, 29 m in diameter, was made some eight km away at Kuçi Zi; the burials there have been dated by Zhaneta Andrea to the eighth and seventh centuries B.C. Five of them were cremations in urns; the rest were inhumations in a trench either bare or stone-lined. The offerings were indisputably Illyrian: spearheads, arrow-heads, swords, knives and cutlasses, and a variety of bronze pendants and bronze beads (Pls. *11* and *12*). The excavator compared them with those of Illyrian tumulus-burials at Suva Reka and with objects from Priština, both in Kossovo. It is probable, then, that Illyrian tribes from Kossovo came via Polog, Kitsevo and Ochrid to the plain of Korçë. Some pendants were found also at Tren. One of the six sons of Illyrius was Dardanus, the eponym of the Dardanians, and it is possible that the Dardanii and the Encheleae combined at this time, because a tradition has survived of one Bato (later a dynastic name in the Dardanian royal house) having founded a city among the Encheleae. The offerings were richer than they had been at Barç.[96]

The advance into the plain of Korçë c. 850/800 B.C. put the Illyrians in a strong position to intervene, when the Brygi left Macedonia c. 800 B.C. One route of Illyrian invasion was certainly down the Vardar valley, proceeding via Valandovo to avoid the Demir Kapu. Several groups of warrior-graves have been found on both sides of the lower Vardar between Gevgheli and Axioupolis (Bohemica), which is a district of the greatest strategic importance. At Chauchitsa thirty-six burials were made probably in wooden coffins or wood-lined trenches, each burial being covered by a cairn of rough stones and the central one being placed within a larger cairn. The corpses lay on their backs in an extended position, and three bronze bosses—all that remained of a perishable shield—were found on the chest of the man in the central burial. The burials were grouped together on a low rock-outcrop and had probably been covered originally by a tumulus of soil. There were other burials in the vicinity made in slab-lined cist-graves. Across the river at Axioupolis more than twenty burials in pithoi or in slab-lined cist-graves contained many beads of amber. A woman's grave contained a bronze boss, similar to that used on a shield. It had been attached to her belt or apron. Another group of graves was opened near Gevgheli. The men in these groups of graves had been equipped with swords, knives and shields (Chauchitsa) and spears (Axioupolis); and they and their women had an astonishing number of bronze ornaments, hung as pendants from shoulder or belt.[97]

In the cemetery at Vergina the period of greatest prosperity, c. 900–800 B.C., was followed by radical changes and a growing impoverishment. In some tumuli the partly cremated remains were placed in urns, and sickle-shaped knives with whetstones and spears over two metres in length with iron head and iron butt accompanied some of the warriors. In Upper Macedonia the presence of Illyrian rulers was shown by burials with similar weapons and ornaments at Visoï and Petilep in Pelagonia; at Pateli in Eordaea; and at Vučedol near Skopje and by Titov Veles. Objects typical of them have been found in small numbers at Kozani and at sites in the middle Haliacmon valley. To the east of the Vardar they seem to have driven the Paeonians back towards the Strymon valley, and there are concentrations of Illyrian objects at Kumanovo and at Radanja near Štip. Large numbers of tumuli are reported in this area; some at least were made probably for Illyrian warriors. Other groups of Illyrians established themselves in the middle Strymon valley, where their name in Classical times was the Maedi; in the Kumli valley between Doiran and Serres; and in the vicinity of Amphipolis. There were penetrations also into northwest Bulgaria and even beyond the Danube in Rumania.[98]

The expansion of the Illyrian tribes had some effects also on northern and central Greece. At Vitsa in Zagori burials were made in shallow trenches, or in cist-graves roofed with branches on which stones were placed, or under a cairn of stones. The burials were close-packed, set in three layers, and very close to the settlement, and the cemetery was in use from just before 900 B.C. into the fifth century B.C. To judge from the objects buried with the dead this community had contacts with Barç, Vergina, Vodhinë, the Illyrians, and also southern Greece. The explanation is to be found in the situation of Vitsa, 1000 m above sea level, close to the summer pastures used in modern times by the Sarakatsani; for it was evidently through the practice of transhumant pastoralism that the people of Vitsa ranged from the lakeland to the Gulf of Arta. The site was certainly not inhabitable in the winter. At Dodona and at Vaxia southeast of Dodona Illyrian objects of the eighth and seventh centuries have been found, and they are indicative of peaceful and perhaps sometimes warring penetration by Illyrians. At sea too the Illyrians controlled the outlet of the Adriatic Sea; the Liburni, for instance, gained control of Epidamnus and Corcyra, at some time before 730 B.C., and it is probable that they carried their raids into the Mediterranean. At Halus on the coastal route of southeastern Thessaly a tumulus, some 20 m in diameter, contained sixteen cairns of stones over cremated remains and offerings. The men had swords, spears and knives, and the women had small knives, as later in the medieval Illyrian-Albanian culture. This tumulus was constructed probably in the eighth century, and the warriors came from the north. It is uncertain whether they were Illyrians or Thracians; for some gold hair-rings (Pl. 12), found also at Marmariani and Homolion at this period, were of a Thracian type.[99]

At Vranesi in Boeotia, close to Lake Copaïs, one of at least two tumuli was excavated early in this century, and the report is very thin. There was a cairn of stones in the centre; the burials were cremations and inhumations in trenches lined with stones and covered with slabs; and offerings included bronze swords, gold ear-rings and diadems, and pieces of bronze bowls. The tumulus was in use probably from the tenth century to the eighth century B.C. At Anavysos in Attica many tumuli were reported. One was excavated which contained both crudely incised hand-made pottery and Attic Geometric pottery of the eighth century. Burials were apparently of partly cremated remains in urns, laid in wooden coffins, and they were at different depths in the fill of the tumulus. In the Kerameikos at Athens, where citizens of foreign descent or resident aliens of distinction were probably buried, there were many signs of contacts with Illyrians and Thracians during this period, as one would expect.[100]

The tumulus at Halus was the memorial of an invasion. In other cases we may see examples of peaceful penetration through the practice particularly of transhumant pastoralism. Sites such as Vitsa in Zagori, Marmariani in Thessaly, Vranesi in Boeotia and even Anavysos in Attica were probably used by semi-nomadic peoples of Northwest-Greek origin, who returned to the same summer and winter stations over the centuries in pursuit of their own way of life. Some of their customs, including tumulus-burial, were common to the southern Illyrian tribes. Indeed in this period of Illyrian expansion it is probable that the way of life in southern Illyria was based on pastoralism and stock-raising. In one respect there are striking analogies between the warrior-groups of the Illyrians and the leaders of the Vlachs. Both peoples carried their wealth on the persons of themselves and their womenfolk in the form of jewelry, pendants and especially belt-ornaments; for they had no houses and no fortresses.

The power of the Illyrians was destroyed during a series of raids and migrations by the Cimmerians, themselves impelled by Scythian migrants from southern Russia, during the decades down to c. 650 B.C. The Cimmerians and the allies they acquired in Thrace have left traces of their raids in Macedonia, for instance at Titov Veles, and in Epirus at Dodona; but they did not come to stay. The vacuum of power which they caused was soon filled by the Thracians, the Paeonians and the Macedones.

A group of Thracian tribes, led by the Edoni, occupied most of the territory between Mt Belasitsa and the sea as far west as the Vardar, including much of the peninsula of Chalcidice, and also the Strumitsa valley north of Mt Belasitsa. Some of the Paeonian tribes recovered possession of their old lands east of the middle Vardar and made their capital near Astibus (Štip). In the lakeland area the Illyrians disappeared from Kuçi Zi, and another large tumulus was made there which received 18 burials. The offerings were different: no weapons except one spearhead, some double-pins and beads of different shapes and material and wheel-made pottery showing contact with southern Greece. Two gold mouthpieces with strings for attachment over the mouth of the corpse were typically Thracian and may represent a time of Thracian rule.[101] But it is to be inferred from the fragments of Hecataeus that the southern part of the lakeland was recovered by the Chaonian group of tribes and that they linked up with the Greek-speaking tribes in Pelagonia in the sixth century B.C.

The movement which was destined to have the greatest consequences was that of the Macedones from the hill-country of Pieria to the western edge of the coastal plain by Vergina, which became their capital under the name Aegeae. They drove the Thracian Pieres out of coastal Pieria and the Bottiaei out of the coastal plain as far as the Vardar; and the refugees settled east of the Vardar, the Bottiaei in the centre of Chalcidice and the Pieres near Mt Pangaeum. Next they attacked the Eordi and destroyed most of them; a few survivors settled east of the Vardar near the lakes north of Chalcidice. They expelled also the Almopes from the district of Moglena. By these ruthless methods the Macedones carved out for themselves a large and continuous kingdom up to the Vardar by 550 B.C., and they became adjacent to the speakers of Northwest-Greek who were in possession of the middle and upper Haliacmon valley and of Lyncus-Pelagonia.[102] In this way a shield of backward, even primitive Greek-speaking peoples in northern Epirus and western Macedonia was formed to resist the constant pressures of Illyrians, Dardanians, Paeonians and Thracians which enabled the civilisation of the city-states in the Greek peninsula to grow to maturity in comparative safety.

NOTES

1. Residence instead of race became the basis of political organisation in these countries. See *HG²*, pp. 104 and 187.

2. I have given grounds for this view in *Macedonia* II, which is in the press.

3. See *HG²*, pp. 653 f. and *CAH³* I, i, pp. 246 f.; an approximate date is deduced from the statement in Thucydides 5.112.2 that Melos in 416 B.C. had been inhabited for 700 years by Dorians, and the tradition is that the Dorians went on from Laconia to occupy that island. The alternative date is c. 1250 B.C., which is favoured by V. R. d'A. Desborough, *The Greek Dark Ages* (London, 1972), p. 23; this extends the last part of L.H. III B to an unusual length, as he puts the transition to L.H. III C at about 1200 B.C. (p. 32), and creates a large gap between the end of the Trojan War and the main sea raids of the 1190s.

4. The word can be used as an abbreviation for Greeks of Mycenaean culture, but I see no grounds for regarding some of the inhabitants of Thessaly as "of Mycenaean stock" and others as of "native" stock, as for instance Desborough does, op. cit., pp. 103, 106 and passim.

5. As E. A. Freeman wrote in 1873, "we have never doubted for a moment that the Catalogue in the *Iliad* is a real picture of the Greek geography of the time" (*Historical Essays*, pp. 60 f.); and excavation has fully substantiated his view, whether in 1921 when T. W. Allen wrote *The Homeric Catalogue of Ships*, pp. 171 f., or in 1970 when R. Hope Simpson and J. F. Lazenby wrote *The Catalogue of Ships in Homer's Iliad*, pp. 153 f.

6. The name evidently means 'those beyond the Aias', and we may compare in the historical period the Parauaioi 'those beside the Aias' or 'Auas', as the river Aous was also called (see *Epirus*, pp. 394 and 680).

7. In his genealogy of eponyms of Greek-speaking tribes Hesiod fr. 7 put Magnes and Macedon respectively by Mt Olympus and Pieria; the Catalogue shows a later position for the Magnetes (see *Macedonia*, p. 298).

8. See *Epirus*, pp. 370 and 382.

9. Hesiod, *Works and Days* 161 f.

10. As I wrote in *HG²*, p. 61, where I owed most to H. M. and N. K. Chadwick, *The Growth of Literature* I (Cambridge, 1932).

11. Or indeed in the Dark Age, as G. S. Kirk, *The Songs of Homer* (Cambridge, 1962), pp. 150 f. has suggested; for in the Homeric poems the bards were represented as singing of the most recent events, shortly after their happening, and it is most likely that epic poetry came into being on the heels of a great event and not a century or more after the Trojan War.

12. For the genealogies of the kings in Homer see *HG²*, p. 60.

13. See my account in *CAH³* II, ii, pp. 679 f.

14. Herodotus 9.26-27; Pausanias 1.44.10, 8.5.1, 8.53.10.

15. See Desborough (op. cit., note 3), pp. 19 f. The destructions are, as he says there, "not many"; there were some seven in L.H. III B, spread over perhaps 100 years on his chronology and 70 years on my chronology. See also *ITEE* 1, pp. 285 f.

16. *Iliad* 2.653 f. and 676 f. See *CAH*³ II, ii, pp. 686 f. and 844 for a different view, where the migrations are transferred by a century and more to the end of the Bronze Age.

17. See *CAH*³ II, ii, pp. 216 and 659.

18. See S. I. Dakaris, *Thesprotia* (1972), p. 63 f.

19. See my account, citing references, in *CAH*³ II, ii, pp. 678 f.

20. Desborough (op. cit., note 3), p. 79 n.10: "recent excavations by Mylonas at Mycenae have led him to conclude that the date of the final destruction there was later than supposed, c. 1120 or after," (see *PAE* 1968, 11).

21. Ibid, p. 94.

22. R. Hope Simpson, *A Gazetteer and Atlas of Mycenaean Sites* (London, 1965).

23. Desborough (op. cit., note 3), pp. 21 f. has attributed the decline to a great invasion late in III B—an invasion remarkable for the complete withdrawal of the invaders, which has to be postulated because the continuity between III B and III C was unbroken; and R. Carpenter, *Discontinuity in Greek Civilization* (1968), attributed it to a climatic change. These are both hypotheses which it is impossible to prove or disprove within their own posits; but if we attach any value to the literary evidence, the first is unacceptable and the second is unnecessary. For criticism of these two hypotheses see S. Jakovidhis in *ITEE* 1, pp. 258 f. and J. Bouzek, *Homerisches Griechenland* (Prague, 1969), pp. 85 f.

24. *PM*, p. 93.

25. Herodotus 7.20.2; see *Macedonia*, p. 297.

26. See *Macedonia*, pp. 416 f.; some traditions recorded infiltration of Thracians into Phocis and Boeotia, and they may refer to this period.

27. *Iliad* 2.848 f.; for the Trojan Catalogue see *HG*², p. 63. On the Paeones see *Macedonia*, pp. 296 f. When the Persians invaded Europe they found the Paeones in the same strategic areas, and the early Paeonian coins showed a god or hero in an ox-drawn car.

28. Reports are in *SA* 1967, 1, 142 f. with figs. 3 and 4; *Bulletin d'archéologie sud-est européenne* 1 (1969) 15 f. and 2 (1971) 15 f.; and *Iliria* 1 (1971) 31 f. with pls. 6 and 7.

29. See *PM*, p. 93 and references in *Macedonia*, pp. 281 f.

30. The date is founded upon the large site at Malik and its successor at Tren (see *SA* 1966, 1, 274 f. and note 28 above). Heurtley put the beginning of this pottery at Boubousti in the last phase of the L.B.A. and I did so in *Macedonia*, pp. 280 f. S. Dakaris did likewise for Kastritsa near Ioannina (*PAE* 1952, 378), but the dates have been called into question. For the relationship between Malik IIId and Tren see M. Korkuti in *Deuxième Conférence des études albanologiques* (Tirana, 1968) 2, 340 f.; cf. *SA* 1972, 2, 198 f. For discussion of this pottery see *Macedonia*, pp. 280 f., M. Korkuti in *Les Illyriens et la genèse des Albanais*, pp. 55., and K. Rhomaiopoulou in *BSA* 66 (1971) 353 f.

31. *PAE* 1952, 378 f. and *Epirus*, p. 297 (category 4b).

32. My account is from his article in *Les Illyriens et la genèse des Albanais*, pp. 90 f.

33. *BSA* 62 (1967) 82 for Pazhok; *Epirus*, pp. 346 f. for Vajzë, pp. 349 f. for Vodhinë, Kakavi and Bodrishtë (also pp. 201 f.). See n. 29 in *BSA* 69 (1974) 132 for the dating of the facetted javelin-head.

34. There is a preliminary report in *Buletin Arkeologjik* 1971, 31 f. and remarks by the excavator in *SA* 1972, 2, 187 f. Albanian archaeologists attribute the twelfth century B.C. to the Albanian Iron Age, because they hold that iron was used first in Albania; but the dating by centuries is as in Aegean chronology, where the Iron Age commences with the eleventh century.

35. See *Epirus*, pp. 318 f. with references to the Albanian periodicals; for the dating of the swords see H. W. Catling in *BSA* 63 (1968) 98 f. and my article in *BSA* 66 (1971) 234 f. For the northern connections see *Epirus*, p. 352.

36. The baldric was a piece of equipment mentioned in the Homeric poems and not found in the Mycenaean area c. 1200 B.C.; like tumulus-burial, it was at home in the northwestern area.

37. By now it is probable that more of these pins have been found in the northwestern area than in the Greek peninsula. When used in the warmer climate of Attica with less thick clothing, a round bulb took the place of the slight swelling. See Desborough (op. cit., note 3), pp. 295 f. on the subject of pins but without mention of those in the tumuli of northern Epirus.

38. *AE* 1956, 114 f.; *PPS* 33 (1967) 35f.; *AE* 1969, 179 f.; *AD* 19 (1964) 312 (Kastritsa); *Ergon* 1963, 62 (Nekyomanteion); *AD* 20, 2, 349 f. (Paramythia); *Ergon* 1960, 110 (Kiperi) and *PAE* 1960, 123 f.

39. See S. I. Dakaris in *AE* 1956, 139 f. and H. W. Catling in *BSA* 63, 96. The Cornish specimen is in the Truro museum.

40. See *Epirus*, pp. 331 f. and fig. 22, where I discussed their affinities. To these should be added the hoard found in Lakkasouli (*Ergon* 1972, 112 f.), an important hoard at Petralona in Crousis (unpublished but see *Macedonia*, pp. 299 f.) and a mould and axes from Kravari in Pelagonia (ibid). In Albania in 1972 I saw a collared double-axe from Mokra near Kukës, and another from Kukës, and I was told of one of the same kind and a single-bladed axe in the museum at Argyrokastro. Such axes were not in use in the Mycenaean world.

41. *Starinar* 11 (1960) 199 f. for Saraj Grave xi, dated c. 1200 B.C. by V. Trbuhović; ibid. pp. 209 f. with figs. 13 and 15

(Prilep); 12 (1961) 229 f. and 243. fig. 24 (Demir Kapu); *Buletin Arkeologjik* 1974, 26 and fig. 1, 2 (Barç). The Prilep and Demir Kapu graves were dated by arching fibulae of an early type to Hallstatt A, c. 1200–1000 B.C. See *Macedonia*, p. 321.

42. See J. Schránil, *Die Vorgeschichte Böhmens und Mährens* (Berlin, 1928), pp. 143 f., pl. xxviii 16, 32, 37; pl. xxx 35, 37, 44; pl. xxv 6 and 8; and pl. xxviii 45. For the date see M. Gimbutas, *Bronze Age Cultures in Central and Eastern Europe* (The Hague, 1965), p. 131. For Lovas see M. Garašanin, *Prehistory of Serbia* 2, p. 626 with pl. 56.

43. *SA* 1964, 1, 100 and *StH* 1966, 1, 41-70; see also *Macedonia*, pp. 307 f.

44. *SA* 1964, 1, 103 and pl. 16, 8-10 (typical small knobs on pl. 16, 11); two are admirably illustrated in *Shqiperia Arkeologjike* (Tirana, 1971), pl. 51.

45. For Çinamak, see *Buletin Arkeologjik* 1971, p. 53; for Këneta, *Shqiperia Arkeologjike*, pl. 50 (also in *Les Illyriens et la genèse des Albanais*, p. 107, pl. iv, 5); for Barç, see *Buletin Arkeologjik* 1971, 39 f. pl. ii, 3 (a triplet-vessel) and iii, 1. When at Tirana in 1972, I was told that the horn-like knobs occurred at Barç. For Macedonia, see *PM*, pp. 35, 39, 96 n. 5, and 124-29; *Macedonia*, pp. 305 f. and *StGH*, p. 40; J. Bouzek, *Homerisches Griechenland*, p. 66 with fig. 25 and *Op. Ath.* 9 (1969) 41 and 48, n. 33 (on Vergina beginning in L.H. III C); and M. Garašanin, *Prehistory of Serbia* 1, p. 315 (map); 2, p. 624 with pls. 53-54, and his comments on the Mediana group e.g. "les analogies étroites avec la céramique de Vardaroftsa démontrent le rôle important joué par le groupe de Mediana au cours de la migration égéene"; and in *Bronze Age Migrations in the Aegean*, pp. 120 f.; M. Andronikos, *Vergina* 1, pp. 185 f.

46. *Archaeology* (Sofia) 12 (1970) 81 for Strumsko; 6 (1964) 2, 72 for Kozloduj; *Troy* 4, 1, 144; *Macedonia*, pp. 318 f. Other elements were also involved in Troy VIIb2, as M. Garašanin has pointed out (loc. cit.).

47. *Macedonia*, pp. 318 f.

48. Oxford Classical Text of Homer, V, p. 109 (*Telegony*); Appian, *Bella Civilia* 2.39 (Epidamnus); Ps-Scymnus 434; Steph. Byz. s.v. *Brygias* and *Bryx*; Herodotus 7.73 and 8.138.2-3; Herodotus 6.45 and Strabo 7 fr. 25; *FGrH* 765 (Xanthus) F 14; Strabo 473 (see *Macedonia*, p. 318).

49. See *Epirus*, pp. 701 f. for the geographical significance of the term 'Thesprotos' in Rhianus, *Thessalika*, and its reference to archaic times.

50. This is obvious from the Homeric epics. In the traditions of the migrations single combats were mentioned between Hyllus and Echedemus at the Isthmus; Pyraechmes, an Aetolian, and Degmenus, an Epeian "in accordance with an old custom of the Greeks" (Strabo 357); and Melanthus, king of Athens, and Xanthus, king of the Boiotoi.

51. The account given by Herodotus 1.56 of the wanderings of the people eventually called 'Dorieis' implies a stay in Epirus before their vanguard reached Doris. I discussed the passage in *BSA* 32 (1932) 151 f.

52. Burials at Mouliana tomb A in Crete (*EA* 1904, 21 f.) and at Kaloriziki tomb 40 in Cyprus (*AJA* 58 [1954] 140 f.) contained weapons, plaques and edging strip as in tumulus-burials in southern Albania, and my deduction is that the burials were those of successful mercenaries or more probably adventurers who became kings and that they had come from the northwestern area, so equipped. See my discussion in *Epirus*, pp. 356 f.

53. See *BSA* 32 (1932) 160 f.

54. The Hellenes and Achilles had close links with Dodona and its vicinity; see *Epirus*, pp. 382 f.

55. The language of Homeric epic was an amalgam of Aeolic, Arcadian and Ionic (the last very much predominating), and although Hesiod was not Ionian and wrote in a non-Ionian land, this language was adopted by him with only a minimum of imported Aeolisms and Dorisms of a local type. Choral lyric was Dorian in dialect, and Athenian tragedians composed lyric passages for the Chorus at Athens in the Dorian dialect.

56. For instance, Herodotus 8.73.3 and Strabo 333.

57. Herodotus 7.176.4; Thucydides 7.57.5; Pausanias 10.8.4; Strabo 447; Thucydides 3.102.5; 4.42.2; Strabo 333.

58. Strabo 392; Herodotus 8.73.3; 1.145.

59. The theory of Risch, *Mus. Helv.* 12 (1955) 61 f. and others that Ionic was the latest of the dialects and grew out of Arcadian after the Dorian invasion seems to me incorrect. As Page pointed out in *History and the Homeric Iliad* (California, 1959), p. 220, it does not explain the presence of dialectal fossils in the epic language. It flies in the face of all ancient tradition, and it requires a new dialect to develop common forms in widely separated places within a relatively short period of time, between say 1000 and 800 B.C. It is simpler to accept the ancient tradition and allow the two hundred years for the full adaptation of the epic lays from Aeolic-Arcadian to the Ionian form.

60. Strabo 333; Herodotus 8.73.3.

61. C. D. Buck, *CP* 21 (1926) 18.

62. It is interesting that there was no sign of the 'northwestern geometric painted pottery' in the area of conquest. It was, on present evidence, in use at this time only in areas north of the Kalamas valley, from which probably a small proportion of the invaders came. From the account in the literary sources the campaign was such that one would not have taken one's pots with one. J. Bouzek, *Op. Ath.* 9 (1969) 45 makes this point also.

63. Athenaeus 695 f.

64. See the table in J. Bouzek, *Homerisches Griechenland*, p. 51.

65. R. Hägg, *Die Gräber der Argolis* (Uppsala, 1974), pp. 64 f.

66. See V. R. d'A. Desborough, *The Last Mycenaeans and Their Successors*, pp. 38 f. and 289, and *The Greek Dark Ages*, pp. 269 ff. for a discussion of the cist-grave and its connection with the north. I have not discussed the appear-

ance of cremation which is too late in the conquered areas for my purpose.

67. *AAA* 1, 289 f.; *AD* 23, 2, 263 f. See *Macedonia*, p. 407 and Desborough, *The Greek Dark Ages*, pp. 98 and 104.

68. Full publication by Desborough in *BSA* 68 (1973) 91 f. with commentary; see *Macedonia*, p. 406 for references. Absolute dates at this time are uncertain by a factor of some fifty years, as Desborough remarks in *The Greek Dark Ages* p. 134, for the end of Protogeometric.

69. Bep Jubani, "Traits communs dans les rites d'inhumation," in *Les Illyriens et la genèse des Albanais*, p. 94. He dated the urns at Tren much earlier than the fortification wall, for which see below.

70. *BSA* 68, 92.

71. *SA* 1964, 1, 102; for Vajzë see *Epirus*, pp. 228 f. and 346 f.

72. *AD* 17, 2, 125 f. with pl. 146 e (a) for the early pins; Desborough, *The Greek Dark Ages*, p. 376. Also *Ergon* 1963, 117 f.

73. *AD* 23 (1968) 2, 1, 179.

74. The Palia Goritsa mounds were seen by S. S. Clark and reported by me in *Epirus*, p. 273. Three rock-cut graves at Treskavtsa were illustrated in *Spomenik* 98 (1941–48) 193 f.

75. *AD* 5 (1919) 92 f.; *AE* 1932, 17 f. and 1933, 73 f.; Desborough, *The Last Mycenaeans and Their Successors*, pp. 103 f.; *Epirus*, p. 347 for the pin from Vajzë Tumulus A, Grave 10, shown in fig. 25 e; *SA* 1972, 2, 188 for Barç. The piece of ridged bronze band is shown in the centre of pl. 14, 3 of *AE* 1932.

76. For the literary evidence and the calculation of approximate dates see my remarks in *CAH*³ II, ii (1975), pp. 702 f.

77. See *CAH*³ II, ii, pp. 703 f. and 773 f. (J. M. Cook).

78. *PAE* 1930, 85 f.; *Op. Ath.* 5, 101 and for Chalandritsa, *BCH* 85, 682. For the dates see Desborough, *The Greek Dark Ages*, p. 92 and Snodgrass, *The Dark Age of Greece*, p. 171; for statistics of settlements (including cemeteries) J. Bouzek, *Homerisches Griechenland*, p. 51 and *Op. Ath.* 9, 57.

79. Perhaps earlier than Athens, as Verdelis had suggested; see *Macedonia*, p. 400 for references.

80. *BSA* 31 (1930–31) 1 f.; *AE* 1914, 141; *Macedonia*, pp. 401 f. for further references.

81. A rose in modern Greek is a 'thirty-petaller'; Herodotus 8.138.2-3.

82. Herodotus 7.73. My reasons for considering the Macedones to have been Greek-speaking are set out in *Macedonia* II which is awaiting publication.

83. For this cemetery see M. Andronikos, *Vergina* I (Athens, 1969), and articles on other tumuli by Ph. Petsas; I study the work of both in *Macedonia*, pp. 328 f.

84. Described in *Macedonia*, pp. 316 f. and 337 f.; see I. Mikulčić, *Pelagonija* (Skopje, 1966) who dates the central burials later than I do.

85. *SA* 1964, 1, 101 f.

86. See Andronikos, *Vergina* 1, p. 51 and *Macedonia*, pp. 393 f. and 335 f.

87. *SA* 1964, 1, 103.

88. On this subject see my article in *BSA* 61 (1966) 239 f.

89. When I saw this pottery in Bari, the relationship was obvious; Zhaneta Andrea drew attention to it in her report on Barç in *SA* 1972, 2, 200 f. See *Macedonia*, pp. 381 f. and M. Garašanin in *Starinar* 19 (1968) 294 for the dating.

90. *FGrH* 1 (Hecataeus) F 103 and 107; see *Epirus*, pp. 460 f.

91. For Ardiaean warrior-graves in the Zeta valley see *Glasnik zem Muzeja Sarajevu Arh.* 24 (1969) 5 f.

92. See *Epirus*, pp. 201 f., 228 f. and 346 f.

93. Short reports in *Buletin Arkeologjik* 1969, 49 f., *SA* 1971, 1, 152 and *Bulletin d'archéologie sud-est européenne* 2 (1971) 29 f. For Kardhiq see *Epirus*, p. 215.

94. *Buletin Arkeologjik* 1971, 57; *Iliria* 1 (1971) 350. I saw some of the finds at Tirana in 1972.

95. Strabo 323 fin.; cf. *Epirus*, pp. 463 f.

96. Reports in *SA* 1972, 2, 190 f.; *Bulletin d'archéologie sud-est européenne* 2 (1971) 28; and the best illustrations in *StH* 1972, 4, 81 f. *Iliria* 1 (1971) 42 and pl. 15 for Tren.

97. *Macedonia*, pp. 348 f. with references to the original publications.

98. *Macedonia*, pp. 420 f. I saw the material from Gevgheli and the Bulgarian sites in the Museum at Sofia, and the material from Amphipolis in the Museum at Vienna.

99. *Macedonia*, pp. 372 f.; the final report of Vitsa by Mrs Vokotopoulou will soon be published, and I am grateful to her for discussions and for showing me the site and some of her finds. *Epirus*, pp. 179 f. and 427 f. for Dodona and Vaxia. *BSA* 18 (1911–12) 1 f. and *Macedonia*, pp. 403 f. for Halus; *Macedonia*, fig. 20, u-v and p. 443 for the hair-rings.

100. *PAE* 1904, 39 f. and 1907, 109; *AM* 30, 132 for Vranesi. *PAE* 1911, 110 f. for Anavysos near Thoricus (different from the cemetery there of *AD* 21, 2, 97 f.). Thracian mercenaries may have brought to the Kerameikos the bell-shaped clay idols incised with dot-centred circles; for these were common in Bulgaria but have not been found in Macedonia west of the Vardar. One may compare the hiring of Albanian mercenaries c. 1400 A.D. (p. 59, above).

101. *Macedonia*, pp. 427 f.; *SA* 1972, 2, 193 f. (Kuçi Zi); I saw the mouthpieces in the exhibition at Tirana in 1972. Best illustrations are in *StH* 1972, 4, 86 f. figs. 12 and 13.

102. For the placing of Aegeae at Vergina-Palatitsa see my arguments in *Macedonia*, p. 156; and for the expansion of the Macedones, *Macedonia* pp. 430 f., citing especially the account in Thucydides 2.99.

RETROSPECT

It is not possible to generalise about the relationship between a migrating people which conquers a territory and any substratum of conquered people which may remain. Let us take some extreme cases from the borderline between prehistory and history, where we have literary evidence as well as archaeological evidence. The population of Achaea in the northern Peloponnese seems to have changed entirely twice within a matter of two or three centuries at the most: from the Ionian occupants of Mycenaean times to the 'Achaeans' under Tisamenus, and from them to a Northwest-Greek-speaking population which was there in Classical times. It is unlikely that any substratum of Ionians and Achaeans survived into the period of the Northwest-Greek speakers. At that time migrations led to migrations: Thessaloi displacing Boiotoi who migrated southwards, Dorians displacing 'Achaeans' who migrated northwards, and migration and expansion on the mainland leading to the Aeolian and Ionian migrations eastwards. Some of these cases fall within the picture which Thucydides drew with such perspicacity:

> It is obvious that the land now called Hellas was not securely settled in ancient times, and that migrations occurred in the earlier phases and individual peoples left their land easily through the pressure of more numerous peoples. In the absence of commerce, peaceful interchange by land and sea, capital resources and arboriculture . . . men obtained only a bare subsistence from the land and so had no difficulty in moving away in the belief that they could get the bare necessities of their daily existence anywhere (1.2.2).

What Thucydides had to say on this subject may have been inspired by his knowledge of conditions in the country to the north of Greece, where his family owned property. For it fitted the movements of the Macedones, Pieres, Eordi and Bottiaei in the period c. 650–550 B.C. In their cases there seems to have been no substratum left *in loco*, and the reason was that the conquered peoples were not rooted to the spot by capital possessions but were ready to move on to new lands. For this to be so their way of life must have been primarily that of the pastoralist, who takes his herds along with himself and his family in time of war, as he had been accustomed to do during seasonal migrations in time of peace.

Wherever, therefore, pastoralists impinged on pastoralists and one migration led to another, we can be fairly confident that no substratum was left *in loco*. For example, in the Early Bronze Age of Macedonia the impact of the migrating peoples with the anchor-amulet culture and with the Bubanj-Hum culture caused other peoples to migrate from parts of western Macedonia into central Albania and Epirus in pursuit of new pasturelands. And in medieval times Albanians moving with their herds pushed groups of Vlachs into the search for other areas, just as the Vlachs themselves had pushed the ancestors of the Sarakatsani off the pastures of northern Pindus.

The position is less simple when the conquerors are primarily pastoralists but the lands they invade are occupied by settled peoples. This was so in many parts of the Peloponnese at the time of the Dorian invasion; for the decipherment of the Mycenaean tablets has shown the presence of the very activities which Thucydides mentioned as absent in his picture of migratory movements: commerce based on agricultural surpluses, trade in luxury goods as well as basic needs, accumulation of capital in whatever form, and arboriculture which required skilful husbandry and long-term planning. Even where the conquering race preferred to continue in its own pastoral way of life, it could see the advantage of subjugating the settled peasants and keeping them at work for their new masters. The Dorians reduced some of the peasants to a position of serfdom in most of the areas which they conquered, and they did so not as individuals acquiring slaves but as a community obtaining a communal service. Thus the Spartan state owned the Helots, each Dorian city-state in Crete owned its 'Klarotai' and 'Mnoitai,' and Argos had its class of 'Gymnetes'; and the state assigned to its citizens a stated amount of the serfs' produce. In the first instance, the peasant families had stayed on their land, because their livelihood depended on being where they were; their means of life was not transferable. Under the Dorian system they remained as peasant families and peasant communities, enjoying only a few aspects of freedom, much like the *fellahin* of the Egyptian delta.

The serf populations in the conquered areas may have left more trace in the archaeological record of the Dark Age than the Dorian masters. For the serfs carried on the Mycenaean traditions in the making of tools, terracotta figurines and pottery. But it would be a mistake to suppose that they had any significant influence on the course of historical development in the Dorian states; for the Dorians were racially exclusive and their ideas were radically different from those of the Mycenaean world. Even when the original type of Dorian society was modified by revolutionary developments and the serfs were absorbed sometimes into the franchised community, it was clear that Dorian elements, for instance at Sicyon, were for long the dominant ones.

We know much less about the migrations of the Greek-speaking peoples into the peninsula in Early Helladic III and the Middle Helladic period. Although they came from a background of pastoralism and their Kurgan leaders seem to have resembled Vlachic *tshelnikadzi*, the conquerors of this period behaved very differently from their successors, the Dorians. The fact that they built citadels, whereas they had not done so in Albania and the lakeland, shows that they were a relatively small minority and that the bulk of the earlier population had not migrated but stayed in their peacetime occupations, which were primarily those of agriculture and arboriculture. We may assert with some confidence that there was a large substratum of pre-Greek-speaking peoples of various origins in Greece at the end of the Middle Helladic period. For instance, the plain of Marathon had been cultivated by local people since the beginning of the Early Helladic period, their settlement being situated then close to the coast, and the arrival of Kurgan rulers with a limited number of followers who were primarily pastoralists may not have caused a major displacement of the local people. It seems rather that the founders of the Mycenaean citadels and the rulers whose presence is known from their tumuli formed, together with their followers, an overlay of authority and control, rather as the Normans did in England. Yet by the middle of the Late Helladic period it was the overlay and not the substratum which provided the universal language and the power-structure for what we call 'Mycenaean civilisation'. Once again the material culture of the period was much affected by the substratum which carried on the earlier traditions of art and architecture, but it was the Greek-speaking element which determined the future course of history.

The migrations of the medieval period were less far-reaching in terms both of geography and ideas. During the long course of the Albanian migrations some oases of Greek civilisation survived either by retaining their independence, as Ioannina did, or on sufferance in mountainous areas, such as Zagori. In the end the migrations of such peoples as the Slavs, Avars, Bulgars, Koumani and Albanians did not end in domination but in co-existence. And with co-existence a phenomenon which was first noted by Isocrates c. 380 B.C. began to affect the overall situation:

> Our city (Athens) has outstripped the rest of the world in intellectual insight and power of expression to such an extent that her pupils have become the teachers of all others. She has brought it about that the term 'Greek' has a connotation of outlook and not of race any longer, and that those who share our culture are called 'Greeks' rather than those who share a common blood (*Panegyricus* 50).

Athens and the land she represents have not always been politically independent but they have never lost their cultural independence since the time of Isocrates. When the migrants settled down to a peaceful existence, the waters of Greek culture flowed back into the ravaged areas and in the course of time they overlaid the original distinctions of race. The qualities which had the miraculous power of yeast in relation to dough were correctly summarised by Isocrates as "intellectual"—above all the capacity for inquiry (*historia*)—and "power of expression" in a language which has shown unparalleled ability to adapt itself to changing conditions through four millennia.

Illyrian has survived for as long as Greek within our area. Geography has played a large part in that survival; for the mountains of Montenegro and northern Albania have supplied the almost impenetrable home base of the Illyrian-speaking peoples. They were probably the first occupants, apart from nomadic hunters, of the Accursed Mountains and their fellow-peaks, and they maintained their independence when migrants such as the Slavs occupied the more fertile lowlands and the highland basins. Their language may lack the cultural qualities of Greek, but it has equalled it in its power to survive and it too is adapting itself under the name of Albanian to the conditions of the modern world.

PLATES

Plate 1a: Korakou bridge on the Achelous, designed for pack-horses. Note effects of erosion. See p. 31.

Plate 1b: The Acheron cutting its way through limestone ranges in a series of impassable gorges. View taken from above Gourana (Trikastron), looking west.

Plate 2a: Alpine pastures on limestone ranges near the sources of the Achelous. Looking east towards Khaliki from the pass above Sirrakou. See p. 43.

Plate 2b: Alpine pastures on greenstone (mainly serpentine) formation. Looking south from the pass between Metsovo and Milea. See p. 43.

Plate 3a: Shepherd, wearing homespun cloak (kāpă), and sheep in the plain of Ioannina, the ridge of Kastritsa showing behind him and the lake to the left. The sheep were on the spring migration. See pp. 40 and 83.

Plate 3b: Vlach shepherds showing off their rams near the summer pastures of Khaliki on the uppermost Achelous. See p. 41.

Plate 4a: Threshing in Albania in 1932, with wooden saddles in the foreground. The horses tread the corn and the men throw up the chaff with wooden forks. See p. 53.

Plate 4b: Albanian-speaking family in Tsamouria, southwest of Paramythia. See p. 63.

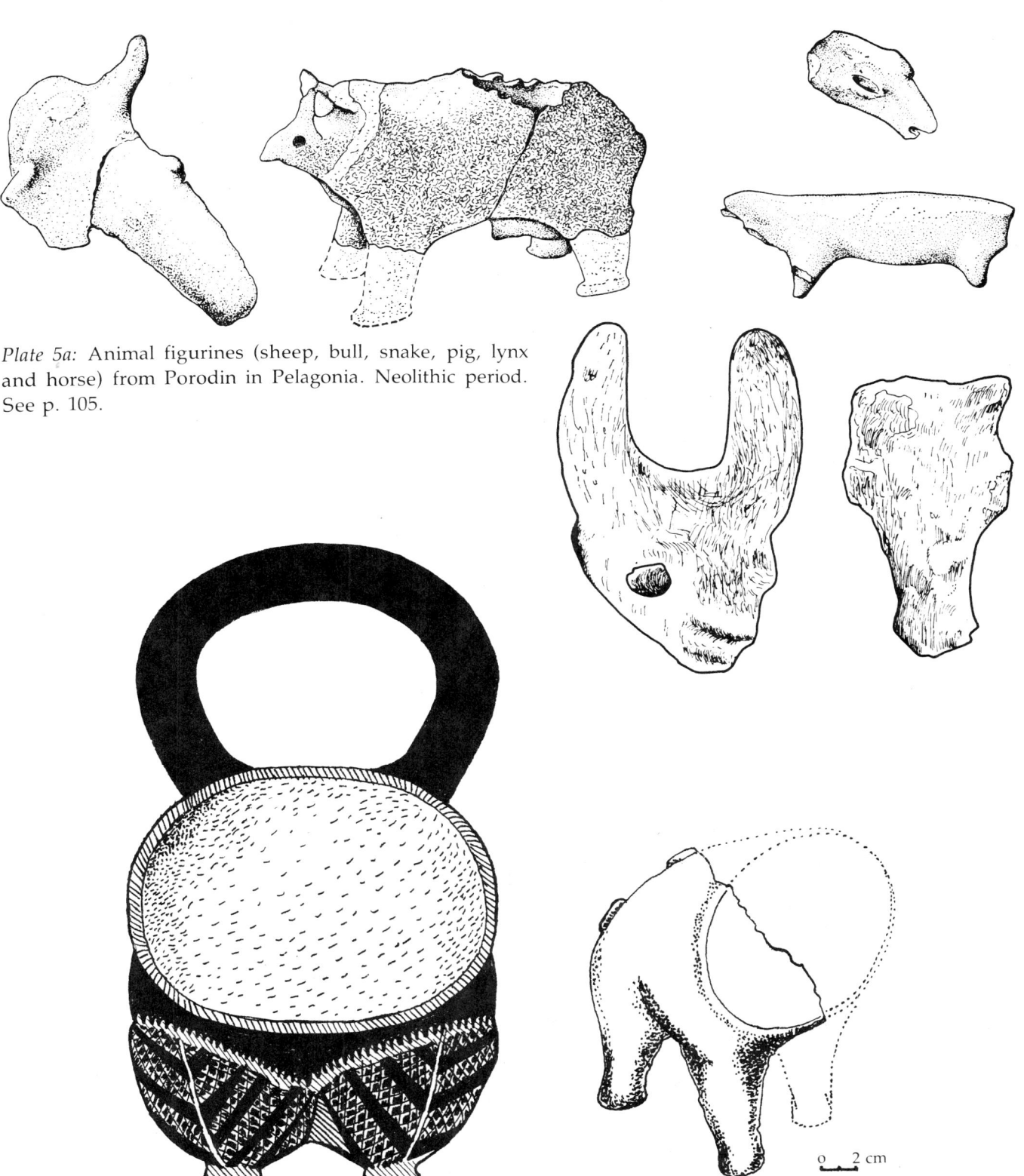

Plate 5a: Animal figurines (sheep, bull, snake, pig, lynx and horse) from Porodin in Pelagonia. Neolithic period. See p. 105.

Plate 5b: Four-legged fertility vases, used probably in a ritual for the increase of the flocks. Middle and Late Neolithic periods. See p. 93.

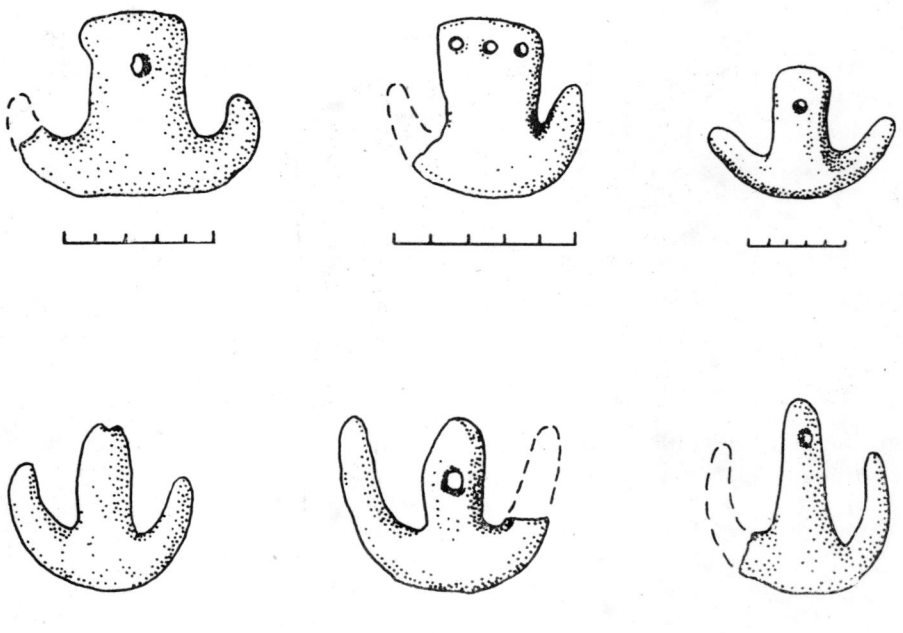

Plate 6a: Anchor-amulets of clay, typical of intruders from the east into Macedonia and Greece. Early Bronze Age. Scale in centimetres. From Eutresis, Lerna, Servia and sites in Thessaly. See p. 109.

Plate 6b: Double tumulus at Pazhok in central Albania, the earliest burial in the central pit being probably of the Balkan Eneolithic period and the burials in the outer tumulus extending over the Late Bronze Age. See pp. 110 and 114.

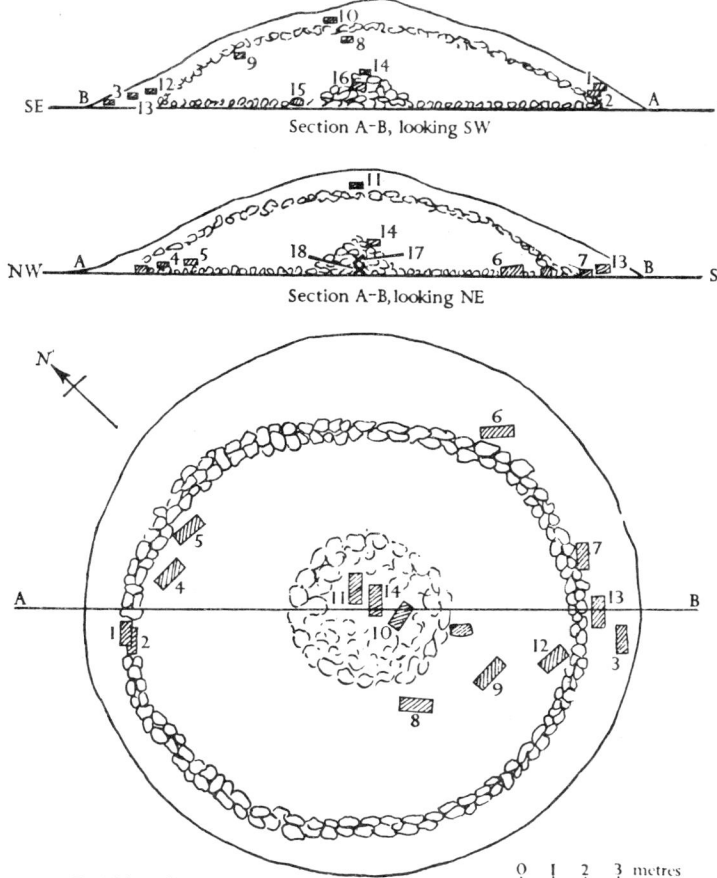

Plate 7a: Double tumulus at Vodhinë in south Albania, the earliest burial being of the Middle Bronze Age and the latest in the Early Iron Age. See p. 114.

Plate 7b: A tumulus with two circles at Marathon in Attica. Late in the Middle Helladic period. See p. 115.

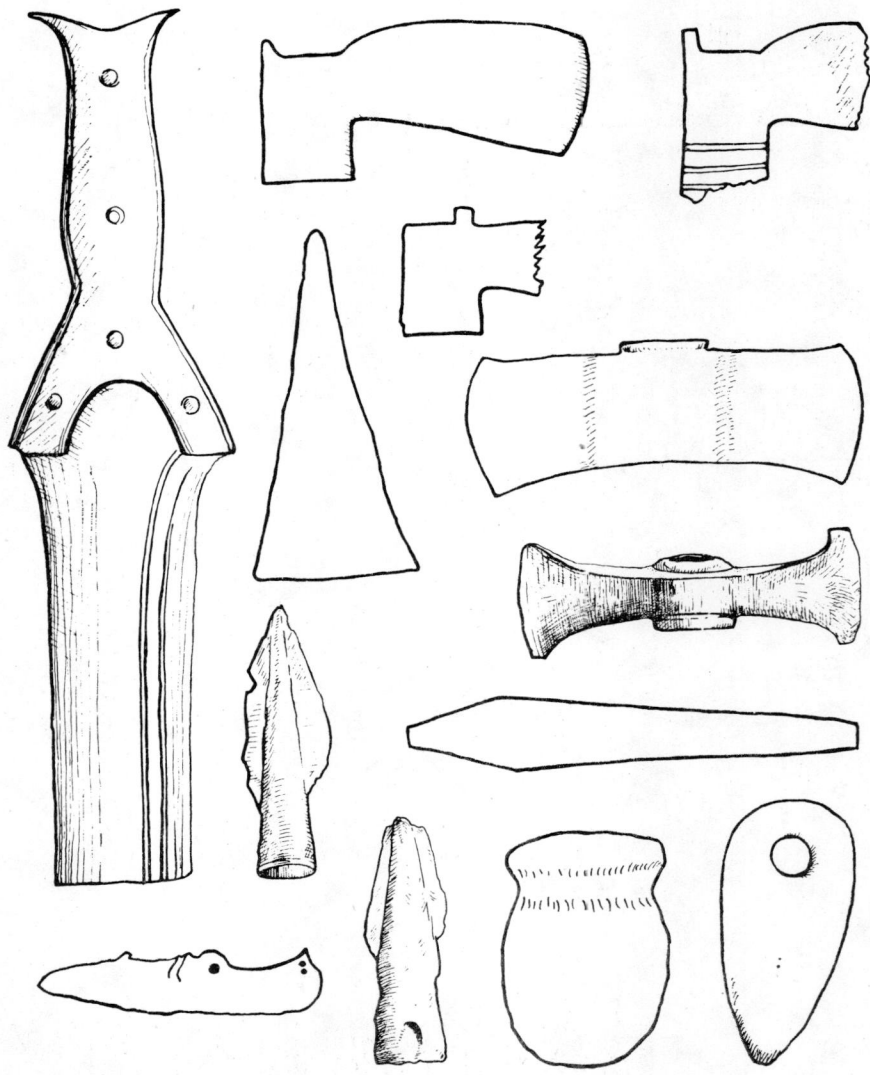

Plate 8: Bronze and stone objects from Macedonia. Sword (Vergina CΔ). Axes and chisel (Petralona). Collared axes (Kravari, Kilindir). Javelin-heads (Prilep, Vardina). Stone sceptre-head, representing a horse (Tsiplevets). Cold chisel (Petralona). Stone hammer, waisted for binding, and stone hammer-axe, bored for hafting (Kravari).

Plate 9: Pottery of "northwest geometric style" and fluted ware. The former from Kilindir, Boubousti, Pateli, Tren, Kastritsa, Vodhinë and Lianokladhi, and the latter from Gajtan. The large bowl at the bottom, from a tumulus-burial at Aphidna in Attica, is much earlier in date but has the same idiom of matt-painted decoration. See pp. 136 f.

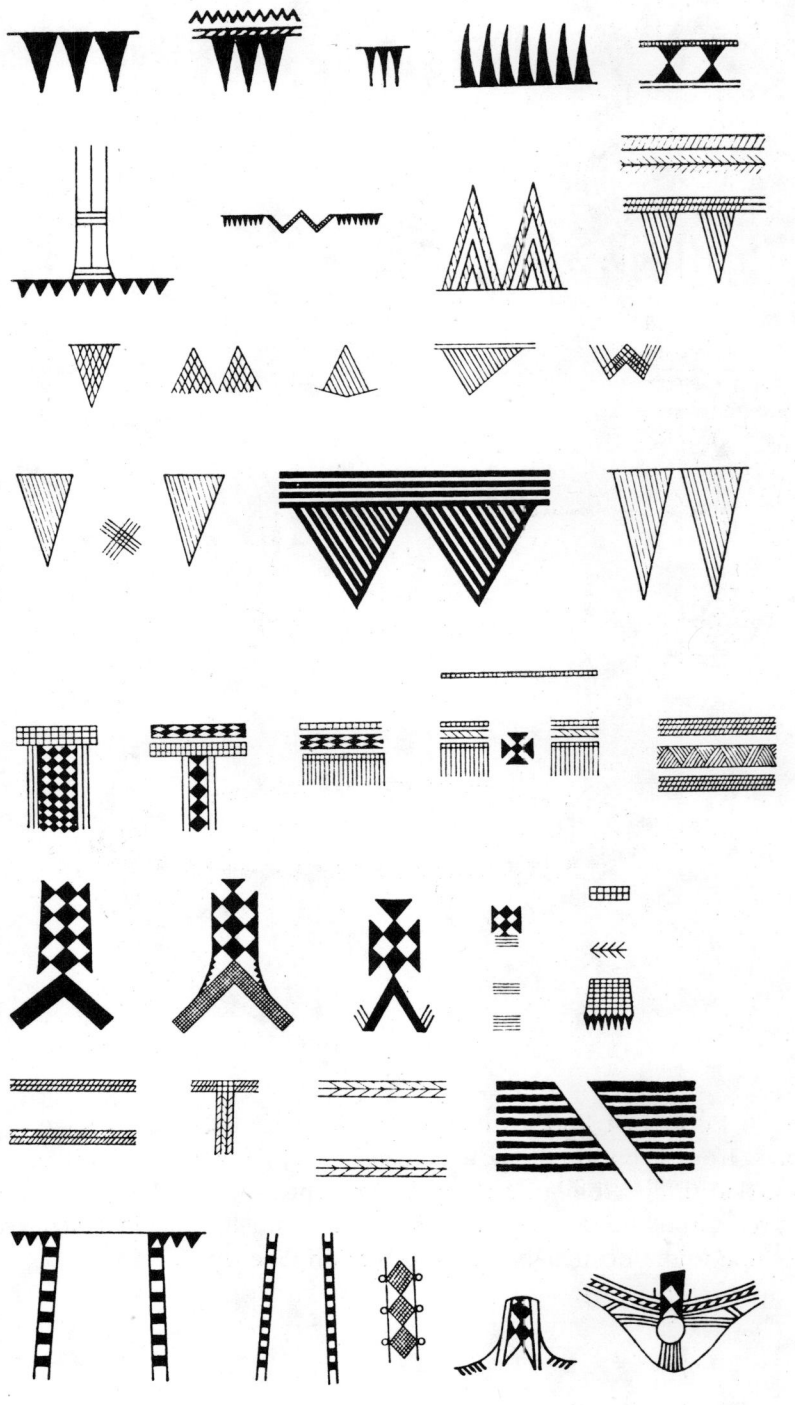

Plate 10: Designs on "northwest geometric style" pottery from Malik and Tren. See p. 137.

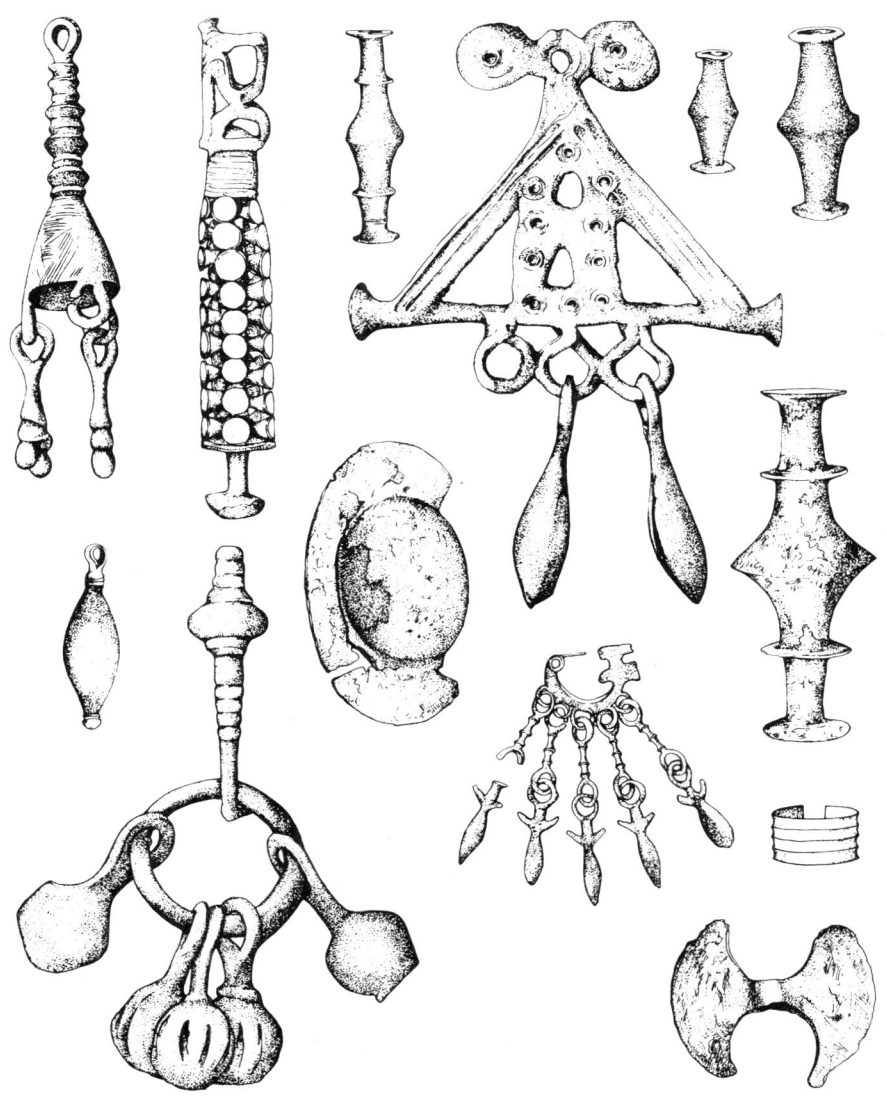

Plate 11: Illyrian pendants of bronze and other objects. Early Iron Age. Pendants (Axioupolis, Kozani and Mati valley). Typical biconical beads. Phalaron (Axioupolis). Armband (Saraj). Miniature double-axe with pierced waist (Olynthus). See p. 155.

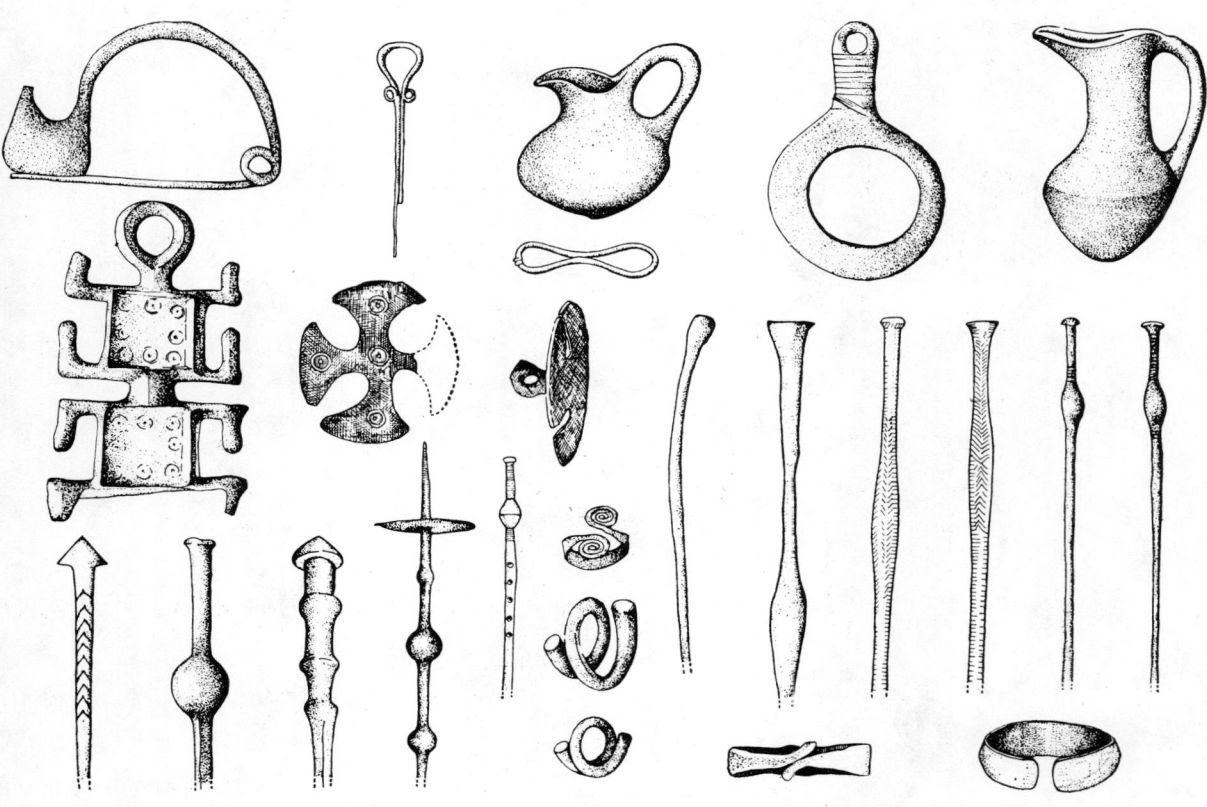

Plate 12: Early Iron Age bronzes, and hair-grips of gold and iron. Fibula, pin, miniature jugs, horse-trapping, iron hair-grip, pendant, button, dress-pins, finger-rings with spiralling ends (one with ends broken off), hair-rings of gold, and open-ended armlet. See pp. 154 f.

Index

Reference is usually made to only one map number, although a name may appear on several maps.

Abantes: 130
Acarnania: Map 9; 25, 27, 35, 42f, 45f, 51, 59, 61, 66, 68, 73, 81, 96, 100, 102, 131, 135, 144, 151
Accursed Alps: 19, 163
Achaea: Map 24a; 66, 134f, 141-4, 151, 161
Achaea, Prince of: 29
Achelous R.: Map 5; 22, 24f, 27, 31, 42f, 48, 50, 143
Acheron R.: Map 5; 23, 83, 119, 139
Acherusian L.: 96
Achilleiou I.: 27
Achilles: 113f, 131, 144, 159
Achris, see Ochrid
Acichorius: 70f
Acontisma Pass: 20f, 30
Acroceraunia Mts: Map 4; 22f, 26, 35, 52f
Actium: 25, 71
Adrianople: 63, 68
Adriatic Sea: Map 1; 29, 34, 67, 69, 73, 81, 84, 88, 96, 104, 110f, 116, 119, 122, 136f, 152f, 156
Aegeae: 157
Aegina: Map 8; 108
Aeginium, see Nea Kutsufliani
Aenianes: 50, 130, 143f
Aeolian dialect: 118f, 122, 133, 144-6, 151, 159
Aeolian migration: Maps 23 and 25; 161f
Aethices: Map 23; 143
Aetolia: Map 6; 25, 32, 35, 43, 59, 61, 66, 68, 70, 73, 77, 102, 119f, 121, 130f, 134f, 141-6, 151, 159
Agraei, Agraïs: 27, 33
Agrapha: Map 10; 41
Agraphiotikos R.: 31
Agrianes: 20, 32
Agriapidhies: Map 25; 151
Agrilia: Map 23; 148
Aias, see Aous
Aibunar: 123
Akhaioi: 130, 144
Akropotamos: 109
Alans: 63
Albania and Albanians: 19f, 34, 39, 42f, 49f, 52-63; early mention of: 50f, 67, 68f, 70; culture c. 600–800 A.D.: 74f, 81, 83, 88f, 92, 95f, 102, 112, 114, 118, 120f, 122, 127, 129, 133f, 136f, 139, 148, 152, 159, 161, 163
Albanians, migrations of: Maps 11, 12, 13; 49, 57-63, 71, 73, 111, 122, 143f, 161
Albanopolis: 56f, 76
Albeigne: Map 12; 56, 74
Alexander I, of Macedon: 73
Alexander III, of Macedon: 23, 68, 130, 137
Alexander, of Molossia: 78
Alexius: 26, 32, 38, 56
Ali Pasha: 41, 43, 48, 62
Almiros (Pherae): Map 9; 62f, 45, 144
Almopes: 157
Alpheus R.: 84
Amali Mt: 119
Ambelokhori: 24
Amber: 139, 149, 155
Ambracia, see Arta
Ammotopos: Map 5; 33
Amphilochus: 133
Amphipolis: Map 25; 30, 32, 155, 160
Amphissa: Map 6; 25, 28

Amyclae: 143
Amyntaion (Cellis): 29
Amyntas I, of Macedon: 73
Anatolia: 85, 96f, 99, 118
Anavysos: Map 25; 156
Ancient Elis: Map 23; 148
Andrea, Zh.: 93, 112, 128, 155
Andronikos III: 39, 57
Andros: 62
Angeli: 57
Animali, Skendër: 74
Anna Comnena: 56
Ano Englianos: 134, 144
Ano Selcë: 29
Antigonea, Pass of: Map 4; 32
Antirrhium: Map 6; 25, 71
Anza: Map 22; 88, 92, 105, 109
Aoi Stena: Map 4; 27, 78
Aous R. (Vijosë and Vojousa) Map 4; 21, 26f, 29, 32, 43, 59, 63, 71, 78, 83, 93f, 96, 102, 121, 131, 154, 157
Aphidna: Map 21; 124, 126
Aphiona: Map 20; 108, 111, 125
Apollo: 144
Apollonia Illyrica (Poyan): Map 4; 23, 26, 29, 78, 81, 84, 93, 98, 154
Apsus R. (Semeni): Map 4; 21; see Semeni
Apulia: 35, 84
Arachova: 32, 73
Arachthus R.: Map 5; 23, 25, 33, 71
Arbana, Arbanon: Map 11; 56f, 63, 74
Arbonë: Map 11; 76
Arcades: 49, 83f
Arcadia: Map 24a; 66, 84, 119, 134f, 143-6, 149
Arcadian dialect: 119, 122, 143f, 159
Arctanes: 144
Ardiaei: 32, 34, 69, 154, 160
Argissa: 85, 125
Argolis and Argos: Map 8; 49, 63, 66, 89, 93, 100, 113, 116, 119, 126, 131f, 134f, 141-4, 151, 162
Argos, Amphilochian: 133
Argyrokastro: Map 4; 26, 61, 158
Aristomachus: 141
Armenokhori: 109, 112, 124
Arne (Cierium): Map 23; 133, 135, 141
Arnissa: Map 21; 34, 36, 115f
Arta (Ambracia): Map 5; 23, 25, 27f, 31, 33, 36, 48, 59, 61, 66, 71, 73, 77, 135f, 143
Arta, Gulf of: 22, 54, 61, 95, 119, 133, 156
Arumani: 45, 76
Arvanitovlachi: 39
Aryithea: Map 5; 31f
Arzen R.: Map 11; 56, 61
Asan, John, II: 68
Asan, the Vlach: 39, 42, 68
Asia: 59, 68, 91f, 105, 108, 111, 140, 146, 151f
Asine: Map 21; 116, 126
Asopus R.: Map 7; 29
Asparagium: 26
Aspendus: 133
Asphaka: Map 18; 86
Asphalt or bitumen: 102, 123
Asprokhaliko: 83f
Aspropotamos R., see Achelous: Map 9
Astakos: Map 19; 95, 98, 100, 102
Astibus, see Štip
Astraeus R., see Vodhas
Athamanes, Athamania: 26, 28, 50, 144

177

Athens: Map 7; 46, 73, 81, 116, 130f, 151, 159, 162f
Athens, Duke of: 29
Athos, Mt: Map 9; 38, 130
Atintanes: 144
Attica: Map 13; 26, 29, 43; Sarakatsani in: 49f, 59, 61, 63; Slavs in: 66, 73, 77; 86, 89, 91f, 95f, 108, 116, 118, 120, 126, 133, 135f, 143-8, 156, 158
Aulon: Map 4; 22, 29, 54
Aunjetitz: 121
Australia: 129
Austria: 104
Avars: 38, 65, 67, 73f, 78, 105, 162
Avdhella: 38, 42f
Avgo, Mt: Map 5; 33
Axios R., see Vardar
Axioupolis (Bohemica): 24, 155
Ayios Kosmas: 108
Ayios Mamas: 111
Ayios Pandeleëmon, see Pateli
Ayios Petros: 86
Ayios Sotiros: 111
Azov, Sea of: 65, 67
Babië: Map 1; 29, 32, 34
Babuna, Mt and Pass: Map 2; 24, 34, 123
Baietan: 42
Bajkaj: Map 25; 154
Balagrita (Berat): 57
Barbotine ware: 88f, 93, 98
Barç: Map 33; 137-140, 149, 152f, 155f, 159
Bari: 35, 153
Barnous, Mt: 24, 29
Basil I: 67f
Basil II: 67
Bato: 155
Bayezid: 73
Bazje: 127
Begorritis, L., see Ostrovo
Bela Crkva: 111, 118, 125, 128
Belasitsa, Mt (Orbelus): 24, 30, 71, 156
Belgrade: Map 12; 67, 88
Belotić: 111, 118, 122, 126, 128
Benac, A.: 111
Benjamin, of Tudela: 39, 42
Berat: Map 4; 21, 30, 36, 42, 50, 57, 68, 73
Bermium Mt (Bermion): Map 23; 30, 33, 86, 140f, 152
Beroea, see Verria
Beuaei: 39, 42
Bevus R., see Molca
Beycesultan: Map 19; 91f
Bilisht: Map 2; 27, 30, 32, 103
Bisaltae: 130
Bistritsa R.: Map 4; 23, 35
Bitola (Butella), see Monastir, Map 11
Blagoevgrad: 20
Blato R.: Map 1; 24
Bodrishtë: Map 25; 138, 154
Boebe, L.: Map 17; 84f, 95
Boeotia: 25, 28f, 32, 43, 50, 59, 61, 63, 66, 71, 73, 84, 88, 91f, 95, 108, 119, 131, 134f, 141, 144-6, 151, 156, 158
Bogë: 20
Boion, Mt, see Voion, Map 23
Boiotoi: Map 23; 130, 133, 144, 159, 161
Bolgius: 70, 78
Boncoes: 61
Bosnia: Map 15; 67f, 92f, 103f
Botoko R.: Map 6; 25
Bottiaei: 153, 157, 161
Boubousti: 137, 158
Bouii: Map 11; 39, 50
Boursina: 59
Bozhigrad: 22

Bradashesh: Map 1; 21, 26
Branigan, K.: 127
Brasidas: 36
Bregalnitsa R.: Map 3; 30, 70f, 88, 92, 94f, 97f, 109
Brennus: 70f, 73, 78
Brezhdan: 27
Briaza: 96
Briges: 140
Brizza: 35
Brygoi: Map 23; 133, 141, 153-5
Bubanj-Hum: 109f, 112f, 120, 122, 161
Buck, C. D.: 146
Buckelkeramik, see Knobbed ware
Budina, D.: 154
Bulgaria, Vlachs in: 45; Sarakatsani in: 49f, 84, 112, 125, 140, 155
Bulgarian Empire, First: 67, 70, 74
Bulgarian Empire, Second: 68, 70
Bulgars: 21, 35, 38, 49, 54, 59, 61, 63, 65f; invasions by: 67-8, 69f, 73, 105, 136, 162
Butkova, L.: Map 3; see Prasias
Butmir: 104
Butrinto: 31, 43, 81f, 96
Bylazora, see Titov Veles: Map 2
Byron: 62
Byzantium (Constantinople) and Byzantines: 21, 30, 39f, 42, 56f, 61f, 63, 65, 68, 74f, 131, 136, 143
Cadmeïs: 133
Cadmus: 131
Caesar, see Julius Caesar
Cakran: Map 19; 93f, 98f, 102f, 106f, 124, 129f
Calabria: 69
Callidice: 141
Callidromus Mt: Map 6; 25, 28
Caloecini: 22
Cambunian Mts: 28
Campbell, J. K.: 47f, 49, 51
Candavian Mts: 29, 32, 137
Can Hasan: 91
Cantacuzenus, John: 39, 42, 57, 59, 61
Cantacuzenus, Manuel: 61f
Cardium ware: 88f, 93
Carnelian: 83, 85
Carpenter, R.: 158
Caskey, J. L.: 113, 119
Casos: 62
Cassopaea: 50, 144
Catalans: 59, 62
Çatal Hüyük: 86, 88f
Catalogue of Ships, in the Iliad: 130f, 141, 149
Cecaumenus: 37f
Çeka, H.: 121, 140
Celetrum, see Kastoria
Ceos: Map 21; 62, 116
Cephallenes, Cephallenia: Map 13; 35, 108, 130f, 135, 138f, 144, 149
Cephissus R.: Map 6; 25, 28, 71, 73, 91f, 95f
Çepune: Map 25; 154
Ceramiae: 65
Cercine, Mt: 22
Cercinitis, L.: 30
Çermenikë: Map 16; 53, 56
Cerna R. (Erigon): Map 1; 24, 95, 139
Chaeronea: Map 6; 25, 28, 71, 91, 93f, 107, 116, 118, 126, 135, 141
Chaeronea ware: 91
Chalandriani: 108
Chalandritsa: Map 25; 151
Chalcidice: Map 20; 81, 84, 93, 104f, 120, 136, 151, 156f
Chalcis: Map 7
Chalcocondylas, L.: 61
Chanson de Roland: 56, 74, 131
Chaones: Map 25; 32, 154f, 157

Charzanes R.: Map 11; 56
Chauchitsa: Map 25; 155
Childe, G.: 91
Choirospilia: 86, 100
Cierium, see Arne
Cilicia: 86, 91, 100, 133, 135
Cimmerians: 38, 156
Çinamak: Map 21; 113, 121, 126, 140, 153
Cirrha: Map 23; 120, 143f
Cist-graves: 108, 115, 120-2, 137-9, 146-8, 151-5, 159
Cithaeron Mt: Map 7; 25, 28, 35, 71, 95
Citium: 36
Citius, Mt: 33
Cnossus: 109
Cocytus R.: Map 4; 83, 102, 139
Codrion: 32
Colonia, see Kolonjë
Colophon: 151
Columbus: 129
Constantine IV: 65, 67
Constantinople, see Byzantium, Map 15
Copaïs, L.: 63, 84, 88, 93, 95f, 156
Copper: Map 16; 104f, 108, 110, 112, 123, 125f, 127, 138
Corcyra: Map 4; 22, 35, 69, 78, 81, 83f, 88, 97, 100, 108, 111, 120, 127, 131, 156
Corded ware: 111, 125
Corfu, see Corcyra
Corinth: Map 6; 35, 49, 54, 59, 61, 63, 67, 89, 92f, 95, 100, 102, 113, 130, 144-6
Cornwall: 139
Coronea: Map 23; 135, 141
Cos: 134
Cresphontes: 135, 141
Crestonia: 130
Crete: 49, 62, 66, 97, 110, 119f, 131, 133f, 146, 151, 153, 159, 162
Crisa: 134
Crkveni Livadhi: 123
Crna Gora: 19
Crnobuki: 105, 109
Črnomen: 68
Croae: Map 11
Croats: 67, 139
Crommyon: 144
Crossland, R. A.: 118
Crousis: 158
Crusades: 26f, 56f, 69, 71, 131
Crusted ware: 94, 103, 105, 107, 109, 112, 123
Crvena Stijena: Map 18; 84f, 88, 92, 97
Cyclades: 49, 62, 66, 107, 110, 120, 124, 148
Cylicrenes: 144
Cynuria: 144, 146
Cyprus: 62, 135, 144, 159
Cyrrus: 34
Cythnos: 62
Dacia: 37f
Dajti, Mt: Map 11; 56
Dakaris, S. I.: 98, 138
Dalmace: Map 16; 74, 78
Dalmatia: 34, 42, 45, 67, 88, 92, 104, 111
Danglli: Map 5; 27, 141
Danilo: Map 19; 91f, 103
Danube R.: Map 12; 19f, 37, 56, 63, 65, 68, 88, 92, 95, 99, 103f, 109, 111, 118, 141
Daphnus R.: see Mornos
Dardanians: Map 25; 20, 34, 70, 78, 155, 157
Dardanus: 155
Darius: 71
Dassaretae: 154
Degmenus: 159
Delphi: Map 6; 25, 32, 70, 73, 120, 135, 141

Delvino: Map 4; 102, 154
Demetrios: 57
Demosthenes: 28
Desborough, V. R. D'A.: 135, 148, 157f
Deshnicë R.: 21
Devoll R. (Eordaicus): Maps 2, 4, and 5; 21, 24, 30, 103f
Dexaroi: 154f
Dhafnis R.: 31
Dhamasi: 24
Dhëmbel, Mt: 23
Dhespotikon: Map 13; 59
Dhipotamos R.: 31
Dhriskos: Map 5; 31
Diabolis R., see Devoll: Map 11
Diakata: 138
Diavat Pass: Map 1; 29
Dibër (Dibra): Map 1; 30, 32, 50, 53, 56, 61f, 63, 68, 136
Dikili Tash: 104
Dimini: Map 20; 100, 102f, 107f, 123, 129f, 151
Diocletian: 54
Dionysus: 20
Dium: 25, 34, 152
Djakova: 35
Dniester R.: 63
Doberus, region: 34
Doberus R., see Strumitsa
Dobrača: 118
Doclea, Presbyter of: 45
Dodecanese: 134, 141
Dodona: Map 5; 23, 71, 96, 113, 119, 130f, 139, 143f, 156, 159
Doiran, L.: Map 3
Dolopes: 143
Domitius: 28
Domousova: 29
Dorians: Maps 23 and 25; 89, 118f, 133, 151
Doris: Map 6; 25, 28, 73
Dörpfeld, W.: 110, 114, 116
dosis probatōn: 50
Drama: Map 15; 30, 68, 92, 104
Drenova: 30
Drin (Drilon), Black R.: Map 1; 19f, 29f, 56, 121, 153
Drin (Drilon), White R.: Map 1; 20, 121
Drin, Gulf of the: 34f, 81
Drin, tributary of Aous R.: Map 4; 23, 26f, 31f, 62, 71, 122, 138f
Druinopolis, see Hadrianopolis
Dubrovnik (Ragusa): Map 12; 19, 42, 57, 74, 111
Ducas, John: 39, 62
Dukagjin: 74
Dukagjini: 53, 56, 74, 76, 134
Duka Planina: 19
Dukat: Maps 4 and 11; 52
Dulichium: 130
Dumitrescu, V.: 118
Dunavec: Map 20; 92f, 94, 98, 103, 107, 129f
Durazzo (Durrës), see Dyrrachium, Map 9
Dymanes: 141, 144
Dyrrachium (Durazzo): Map 1; 21, 29, 34, 54, 56f, 59, 61, 66f, 69f, 74, 76f, 78, 84, 140f, 152f, 156
Dzhumaia: Map 9; 45
Echedemus: 159
Echedorus R., see Gallikos
Echinus: Map 6; 25, 141
Edessa: Map 2; 30, 34, 36, 66, 70, 73, 104, 140, 152
Edonians: Map 25; 130, 156
Egnatia, Via, see Via Egnatia
Eidomene, see Gevgheli
Eitanes: 144
Elaphotopos: Map 23; 139
Elassona: Map 9; 24, 28, 97
Elatea: Map 19; 88, 92f, 118, 126
Elbasan: Map 1; 21, 29, 76, 78

Eleusis: Map 7; 26, 120
Elimea: 33, 109
Elis: Map 13; 61, 66, 81, 84, 95, 119, 135, 139, 143-8
Ellopie: 77
Encheleae: Map 25; 153-5
Encheleus: 153
Englianos, Ano, see Ano-Englianos
Enienes, see Aenianes
ennomion: 50
Enver Hoxha: 53
Eordaea: 24, 29, 34, 109, 136, 155, 157, 161
Epeioi: 130, 159
Epic lays, in Albania: 76, 78, 131, 134
Epidamnus, see Durazzo, Map 23
Epidaurus: 63
Epigoni: 131, 134
Epirus: 22, 26, 28, 31f, 35, 39, 43, 46, 49, 53, 57, 59, 61f, 63; Slavs in: 66, 67f, 70, 73, 77; 81, 83f, 95f, 97, 102, 113, 119f, 122, 126f, 130f, 133f, 135, 137, 140f, 143f, 146-151, 153f, 156-9, 161
Epirus Nova: Map 11; 54f, 57, 63, 74, 76
Epirus Vetus: Map 11; 56, 63
Erigon R., see Cerna Reka, Map 2
Ersekë: Map 4; 23, 26, 93, 102
Euboea: Map 13; 49, 61f, 63, 66, 89, 91f, 95, 100, 130, 135, 143f, 151
Euenius: 93
Euenus R. (Phidaris): 25
Europus: 34
Eurymenae: 31
Eurysthenes: 135
Eurytanes: 130, 144
Eutresis: 108f, 119
Evans, Arthur: 42
Ezeritae: 66
Fan R.: Map 1
Filiates: Map 4; 31, 102
Flambourari: 48
Flamininus: 71
Flint: 83, 86, 91, 96, 102, 105, 122f, 127
Florina: 28, 43
Fol, A.: 125
Fourka: Map 9; 40f, 43
Franchthi Cave: 84, 97
Frashër: Map 4; 42
Frasherots: 42f
Fratar: Map 9; 27, 42
Gajtan: Map 23; 111, 124f, 136, 140, 146
Gallikos R. (Echedorus): 25
Gallipoli: 67
Gamila, Mt: Map 10; 23, 48
Garašanin, M.: 111, 118, 125f
Gardhiki: Map 9; 31f, 42f
Gauls: 69-71, 73, 78
Gegs: 53f, 63, 122
Gemellomuntes: 38
Genoese: 35
Genthius: 32
Genusus R. (Shkumbi): Map 4; see Shkumbi
Geometric style of pottery: 156
Gerania, Mt: Map 6; 26, 29, 71, 95
German forces in 1941: 27f
Getae: 78
Gevgheli (Eidomene): Map 2; 30, 73, 155, 160
Ghin: 56f
Gimbutas, M.: 105f, 108, 110, 114, 123
Gjalicë, Mt: 20
Gla: Map 23; 134
Glasinac: 154
Glossa, Cape: Map 11; 54, 56
Golaj: 74, 78
Golemiskr R.: 73
Gomphi (Mouzaki): Map 5; 28, 31f, 135, 141

Gopeš: Map 9; 42f
Gordias: 152
Gordium: 152
Goricë: 54
Gostivar: Map 1; 20f, 30
Goths: Map 12; 33f, 35f, 63, 65f, 68, 70, 73, 78, 141
Gourana (Trikastron): 96
Grabak Cave: 104
Gradec: Map 2; 22
Gradeska, Mt: 24
Gradevo: 20
Gradisht: Map 17; 83
Gradsko (Stcbi): Map 2; 24, 30
Grammus, Mt: Map 10; 22f, 36, 42, 45, 47, 81, 95, 102f, 137
Gramosteani: 43, 45
Gramosti: Map 9
Gramsh: Map 2; 27, 30, 32, 103
Granary style of pottery: 140
Gravia Pass: Map 6; 25, 28, 73, 135, 141
Grdelica gorge: 20
Greece and Greeks: 54, 68f, 144, 162f; passim
Grevena: Map 5; 24, 28, 31, 36, 43f, 51
Greveniti: Map 5; 31, 48
Gumani: 83
Gymnetes: 162
Hadrian: 26
Hadrianopolis: 26, 61
Hadzimichalis, A.: 49, 137
Haemus, Mt: 66f, 68, 71
Haliacmon R. (Vistritsa): Maps 2, 5 and 9; 24f, 30, 33, 36, 42f, 86, 89, 91f, 93, 102f, 118, 120, 137, 140, 144, 148, 152, 154f, 157
Halonnesos: Map 7; 84
Halus: Map 6; 25, 70, 156
Hasluck, M.: 19, 74, 81
Hassunah: 91
Hebrus R., see Maritsa R.
Hecataeus: 133, 140, 154, 157
Hector: 126
Hellen: 119
Hellenes: 130f, 144, 159
Helmsdorf: 107
Helots: 162
Heraclea, see Monastir
Heracleidae: 133f, 135, 139f, 141, 148
Heracles: 140
Hermione: 84
Herodotus: 144
Hesiod: 131, 157
Heurtley, W. A.: 33, 94, 99, 106, 124, 126, 137, 140
Heuzey: 83
Hexalophos: Map 23; 148
Higgs, E. S.: 83
Himarrë: Map 4; 27, 53, 69, 102
Hoeg, C.: 46
Homeric epic: 76, 91, 125, 144, 149, 158f
Homolion: Map 25; 156
Hope Simpson, R.: 135
Hostilius: 32
Hourmouziadis, G.: 89
Humska Ćuka: 122
Hunavia: Map 11; 56
Hungary: 38, 67, 74, 103, 121, 139
Huns: 35, 63
Hvar: 104
Hybrias: 146
Hydra: 62, 69
Hylleis: 141
Hyllus: Map 23: 49, 133f, 159
Hypate: 39
Ibar R.: Maps 1 and 12; 29, 93

Igoumenitsa: 83
Iliad: 113, 143f
Illyrians: 20, 35, 54, 69, 118, 122, 130, 153-6, 163
Illyricum: 54f, 57
Illyrii, tribe: 153
Illyrius, 153
Inachus R., tributary of Achelous, see Sindekiniotikos
Indo-European languages: 118, 154
Ioannina: Map 9; 24, 26f, 31f, 40, 43, 48, 59, 61, 71, 73, 77, 81, 83, 86, 89, 122, 136f, 139, 143, 162
Ioannina, L.: 96
Iolcus: Map 23; 92, 99, 134f, 146-8, 151
Ionian dialect: 118f, 122, 133, 144, 159
Ionian gulf: 67, 104, 119, 136
Ionian islands: 100, 146
Ionian migration: Maps 23 and 25; 151, 161
Ionians: 135, 146, 151, 161
Ios: 62
Iran: 118
Isaou, of Ioannina: 61
Islami, Selim: 110, 121, 140
Isocrates: 69, 162f
Isthmus, wall at: Map 13; 26, 29, 59, 61, 63, 70, 73, 92, 95, 102, 134f, 144, 146, 151, 159
Istria: 34, 42f, 45
Italy: 35, 54, 61, 69, 100, 111, 153f
Itea: Map 6; 25, 32
Ithaca: Map 23; 35, 108, 127, 130, 135, 144
Jericho: 56, 91
Jerusalem: 127
Jezerce, Mt: 19
Jubani, B.: 125, 137
Julius Caesar: 23, 26, 28, 32
Kačanik Pass: Map 1; 20f, 35, 37, 66, 70, 73, 78, 88, 92, 144
Kakanj: 92f, 103f
Kakarditsa, Mt: 22
Kakavi: Map 25; 138
Kakiskala: 26, 29
Kalabaka: Map 5; 24, 28, 31, 83
Kalaja Rrmait: 32
Kalamas, R.: Map 4; 23, 31f, 59, 61, 71, 83, 102, 122, 138f, 141, 148f, 159
Kalamata: Map 8
Kalarritai: 40, 45
Kalasë, R.: Map 4; 23
Kalbaki: Map 23; 139
Kalenji: 33
Kaloriziki: 159
Kamnik: Map 20; 93, 102f, 104, 110, 112, 123
Kanalit: Map 20; 102
Kanina: Map 11; 56f
Kapakli: Map 25; 152
Kapesovo; 48
Kapoutzedhes: 105
Karaburnu, Mt: 29
Karanovo: 92, 104f
Karatepe: 133
Karava, Mt: 22
Karavassara (Limnaea): Map 6; 25, 27, 33, 71
Karidhi, Mt: Map 7; 25, 29, 71
Kardhiq: 154
Kardhitsa: Map 5; 66, 88
Karpenisi: Map 6; 31f, 135, 141
Kastania: 24
Kastoria (Celetrum): Map 5; 24, 26f, 31f, 43, 69, 104
Kastritsa (Eurymenae): Map 5; 31, 83, 89, 96, 111, 137, 139, 158
Katavothra: 31
Katerini: Map 9; 28, 45
Kavadarci (Tikvetch): Map 2; 22
Kavalla (Neapolis): 30

kefalovrysia: 83
Kelcyrë Map 4; 21, 23, 27
Kemal Attaturk: 69
Keneta: 140
Kent: 56
Kephalovryson: 126
Kerameikos: 156
Keramopoullos: 104
Khaliki: Map 9
Khalkopouloi: 31, 33
Khasia: Map 5; 24, 28, 89, 96
Khazars: 65, 67
Kiafa R.: 33
Kilindir: 28
Kilkis: 28
Kineta: 153
Kiperi: Map 23; 135, 139
Kipourio: Map 9; 45
Kirli Dirven Pass: Map 2; 24, 28, 34, 70
Kissavos Mt (Ossa): 25, 86, 97f, 148, 152
Kitsevo (Uscana) Map 1; 21, 29f, 32, 36, 68, 92
Kjustendil (Pataulia): Map 3; 22, 30, 32, 68, 70, 73, 94, 103f, 155
Klidhi: Map 2; 24, 28, 35
Klidhi Pass: Map 3; 32, 67
Klimatia, see Veltsista
Klinovos: Map 5; 24
Klisoura, in Macedonia: Map 9; 43
Klisura Pass, in Aetolia: Map 6; 25, 27, 71
Klisura Pass, on the Isthmus: Map 8; 29
Klisura Pass, on the Strymon R.: 22, 30
Klos: Map 16; 23
Knobbed ware: 139f, 154, 159
Kolatë Mt: 19
Kolonjë: Map 10; 42f, 45, 102f, 110, 123
Koman: 78
Komiskortas: 56
Komotini: Map 19; 92
Konisbalte: Map 9
Konispol: 123
Konitsa: Map 4; 21, 24, 26f, 31, 61, 77, 83f, 96, 139, 141, 149
Konya plain: 86, 91
Korab, Mt: 20, 30
Korakou: Map 5; 31
Korcë (Koritsa): Map 4; 21, 23f, 26f, 29f, 36, 42f, 61, 98, 138f, 141, 144, 155
Koritsa, see Korcë
Korkuti, M.: 93, 112, 125, 127
Kosovë: Map 16; 74
Kossovo: Map 25; 20, 22, 34, 54, 63; battle of: 68, 73, 92f, 103, 109, 121, 138, 155
Kossovo Polje: 68
Kostolac: 111, 124
Kotor: Map 12; 19, 34, 111, 127
Koumani: 38f, 49, 68, 162
Koundouriotissa: 152
Kouphovouno: 92, 99
Kozani: Map 5; 28, 33, 148, 155
Krabista: 38
Krania: Map 5; 24, 43
Kratovo (Tranupara): 30
Kravari: 158
Krekapak: 20
Kresna defile (Klisura Pass): Map 3; 22, 35
Kretzounista: 59
Kritsana: 105, 111
Kriva R.: 30
Krivodol: 104
Kroai, see Krujë
Kronos: 119

Krujë (Croae): Map 11; 56, 62, 68, 73f, 76, 78
Krume: 137, 153
Kseria R.: 23, 138, 154
Ktismata: 23
Kuç, near Himarrë: Map 11; 53
Kuç, on the Semeni: Map 4; 26, 32
Kuci Zi: Map 25; 155f
Kudhes: 53
Kukës: Map 1; 20f, 121, 137, 140, 153, 158
Kumanovo: Map 2; 73, 155
Kumli R.: Map 3; 30, 32, 73, 155
Kupatshari: Map 10; 45, 50f
kupatshu: 45
Kurgans: 89, 105f, 109, 111f, 118f, 120f, 122, 124f, 126f, 129, 148, 162
Kurvelesh: 23, 27, 52, 54, 62, 154
Kutrigurs: 67
Laconia: 66, 89, 95, 118, 135, 143, 157
Laeaei: 22
lahute: 76
Laibach, see Ljubljana
Lakkasouli: 83, 96, 158
Lamia: Map 6; 25
Langadha basin: 30, 32, 71, 73
Larissa: Map 6; 34, 39, 81, 83f, 85, 98, 112, 143, 152
Lausitz: 139f, 148
Lavra monastery: 45, 49
Leake, W. M.: 33, 76
Lebadea: Map 6; 32, 73
Lefkandi: 125
Lek Dukagjini, see Dukagjini
Lengyel: 104
Leo VI: 67
Leo, the Wise: 68
Leonidas: 28
Leosas, Peter: 59
Lepenac R.: Map 1; 20
Lepenski Vir: 88
Lerna: Map 8; 91, 107f, 113f, 116, 119, 124, 135, 143
Lesbos: 151
Lesh (Lissus): Map 1; 21, 35, 57, 69, 74, 78, 84
Leskoviq: Map 23; 23, 26, 138, 141
Leucas: Map 9; 35, 86, 97, 100, 108, 110f, 112, 114, 116, 118f, 120f, 122, 125f, 127f, 130, 148f
Lianokladhi: 113, 119, 125
Libisda: 59
Liburni: Map 25; 69, 156
Lidhoriki: 78
Lidizda: Map 13; see Libisda
Limnaea, see Karavassara
Lin: Map 1; 22
Linear B script: 116, 133, 144, 161
Lipari isles: 104
Lipljan, see Ulpiana
Lissus: Map 11, see Lesh
Ljapokhori: 77
Ljaps: 53, 63, 122
Ljubljana (Laibach): 104
Llogora Pass: Map 4; 23, 26
Locris: 130, 151
Lopova: Map 9; 45
Louros R.: Maps 5 and 10; 23, 27, 83f
Loutro R.: Map 6
Louvre: 127
Lovas: 139
Ludias R.: 25
Lumnitsa: Map 9; 45
Lunka: Map 9; 42f
Lycaonia: 86
Lychnidus, see Ochrid

Lyncus: Map 25; 24, 30, 32, 105, 109, 157
Lysimachea: 78
Macedon: 119, 157
Macedones: Map 25; 28, 152, 156f, 161f
Macedonia: 46, 62, 66, 69f, 77, 86, 89, 91, 97, 103f, 105, 109, 112f, 118, 120f, 122, 127, 130, 134, 136, 152, 155f
Maedi: Map 25; 32, 155
Magnes: 119, 157
Magnesia and Magnetes: Map 6; 71, 78, 130f, 136, 146
Magoula Visviki, 107
Magoulitsa: Map 18; 88f, 95
Magyars: 38
mahalas: 54
Makrinoros, Mt: Map 6; 25, 27, 71
Malakasa, see Malakastër, Map 11
Malakasi: Map 5; 31, 42f
Malakasii: 39, 42, 50, 57, 59, 61
Malakastër plain: Map 9; 39, 43, 50, 61, 77, 83f, 93
Maliac gulf: 25
Malik: Map 2; 21, 30, 32, 42, 92, 94f, 102f, 105, 107f, 110, 112, 120f, 123f, 127, 130, 136f, 138, 158
Malik, L.: Map 10; 21, 104
Mali me Gropë, Mt: 56
Mallus: 133
Malthi: Map 18; 116, 119
Mandra: 21
mandriatikou dekatia: 50
Maniakis, G.: 57
Manolis bridge: Map 6; 31
Mantinea: 49
Marathon: Map 7; 114, 116, 119, 126f, 138, 162
Margariti: Map 4; 27, 83
Marinatos, Sp.: 116, 126, 128
Maritsa R. (Hebous R.): Map 3; 68, 92
Mark Antony: 26
Marmara, Sea of: 29f
Marmariani: Map 25; 146, 152, 156
Marseilles: 40
Massagetae: 38
Mati R.: Map 16; 21, 30, 56, 60f, 74, 78, 121, 126f, 139f, 148f, 153
Mazaraki: Map 13; 59, 61, 139
Mediana: 140, 159
Megalopolis: Map 8; 84
Meganisi: 100, 108
Megara: Map 8; 28
Megaris: 28f, 49
Megaron: 91, 97, 100, 123f
Megdovas R.: 31
Melanthus, king of Athens: 159
Melingi: 66
Melos: 85f, 135, 143, 157
Menhir: 125f
Mersin: 86
Mesaritae: 39
Mesokhora: Map 5; 31
Mesolonghi: Map 6; 25, 27
Mesopotamo: 51
Mesoyefira: 61
Messapium, Mt (Osogovska Planina): 19
Messenia: 119, 126, 134f, 143f, 151
Mesta R., see Nestus
Metaxas: 47, 49, 77
Meteora: 31
Methone: 34
Metohija: Map 25; 20, 22, 29, 39, 54, 63, 92, 104, 110, 121, 123, 138, 153f
Metsovo: Map 5; 31, 41, 43, 45, 48, 96
Mezilo: 31

182

Midas: 152
Midea: 134
Mijele: 74
Mikanis R., see Murganis
Milea: 41
Minyan ware: 120f, 127
Mirakë: 32
Mirditë: Map 16; 74f, 78
Mirditë-Mati culture: Map 16; 74-6
Mistra: 61
Mithridates: 69
Mnoitae: 162
Mogila: 88
Moglena: Map 25; 38, 43, 45, 157
Mokra: 158
Molca R. (Bevus): 32
Molossi: 31f, 130f, 133, 144, 154
Molovistë: 43
Molyvopyrgos: 120
Monakhiti: 24, 33
Monastir: Map 2; 24, 28f, 30f, 32, 34, 43, 45, 68, 88, 98, 109, 152
Mondsee: 104
Monemvasia: Map 8; 66
Mongols: 68
Montenegro: 19f, 29, 57, 84, 111, 163
Mopsus: 133
Morava R.: Map 12; 111
Morlachs (Black Vlachs): 42, 45
Mornos R. (Daphnus): Map 6; 70
Moscow: 40
Mouliana: 159
Mousterian artefacts: 81, 84
Mouzaki, see Gomphi
Murad, Sultan: 68, 71
Murë: Map 1; 30
Murgani: Map 5; 31
Murganis R. (Mikanis): Map 6; 24, 28
Muskopole: Map 9; 40f, 42f, 45, 92, 96, 121, 137
Muzeqijë plain: 42
Mycenae: Map 8; 112, 114, 116, 119f, 123, 126, 133f, 135, 144-8, 158
Mylonas, G. E.: 158
Myrmidones: 130
Mysi: 137
Naissus, see Nis
Naupactus: Map 6; 27, 59, 61, 135f, 141
Nauplia: 135, 143
Ndermajnë Pass: 20
Nea Kutsufliani (Aeginium): Map 5; 28, 31
Nea Makri: 86, 96
Neanderthal man: 83
Nea Nikomedeia: Map 18; 24, 86f, 89, 91, 95f, 105, 109
Neapolis, see Kavalla
Nekyomanteion: 135, 139
Nemanja: 57
Nemea: Map 18
Neoptolemus: 49, 133
Nestus R. (Mesta): Map 9; 20, 30
Nevropolis: 31
Nicaea: 57
Nidhri: 110f
Nigrita: 45
Nikaj: 20
Nikšić: 19, 84
Niš (Naissus): Map 12; 20, 34, 46, 68, 109
Nisos: 111
Normans: 56, 69, 71, 162
Northwestern Geometric pottery: 50, 136, 159
Northwest-Greek dialect: 143, 146, 149, 151, 154, 157, 161
Nostoi: 133
Nounesation: 102

Novi Pazar: 93
Obsidian: 85f, 96, 104, 106f, 122, 127
Ochre: 116, 118
Ochrid (Lychnidus): Map 1; 20, 26, 28, 32, 34, 41, 54, 56, 62, 66f, 68, 73f, 121, 136, 144, 155
Ochrid, L. (Lychnitis): Map 1; 21, 27, 29, 39, 42, 56, 61, 92, 104, 123, 153f
Odessa: 40
Odrysians: 22
Odysseus: 49, 133, 139f
Odyssey: 131, 139, 143
Oedipus: 131
Oeta, Mt: Map 6; 25, 28
Olympia: 119
Olympus, Mt: Map 9; 25, 35, 45, 86, 91, 118f, 130f, 135f, 157
Olynthus: Map 19; 92f, 98, 109
Olytsika, Mt (Tomarus); Map 10; 48
Onchesmus, see Santi Quaranta
Onogurs: 67
Optičare: Map 18; 88
Opus: Map 6; 25
Oracle of the Dead, see Nekyomanteion
Orbelus, Mt, see Belasitsa
Orchomenus, in Boeotia: 108, 120
Orestae: Map 25; 154
Orestes: 133, 143, 149, 151
Oricum: Map 4; 26, 56
Orpheus: 152
Osogovska Planina (Mt Messapium): 19f
Osovo, Mt: 20
Ossa, Mt, see Kissavos: Map 7
Ostrog Pass: 19
Ostrogoths: 63
Ostrovo, L. (Begorritis): Map 2; 29, 36, 70, 152
Osum R.: Map 4; 21
Othrys, Mt: Map 6; 25, 47, 108, 111f
Otzaki: 91
Ovče Polje: 92, 95f, 97, 105
Oxylus: Map 23; 141, 143
Paeonia: 20, 22, 32, 69f, 77, 136, 152, 155f, 157f
Pagasae: Map 6; 25, 31, 35, 85f, 100, 102, 104, 119, 152
Paiko, Mt: 45
Palatitsa: 152
Pale, Cape: Map 11, 56
Palermo: 23
Palia Goritsa: 149, 160
Paliokaria: 31
Paliokhori: 31
Pamphyliai: 133
Pamphyloi: 141
Pandora: 49
Pangaeum, Mt: 19f, 30, 157
Papingo: 48, 61
Papoulia: Map 21; 126
Paradimi: 105
Paramythia: 61, 83, 102
Parapotamii: Map 6; 25, 28, 32
Parauaioi: 141, 157
parea: 48
Parga: Map 12; 62, 69, 135, 139
Parnassus, Mt: Map 6; 29, 32, 47, 61, 95, 107
Parthini: Map 25; 153
Partho: 153
Passaron: Map 5; 31
Pataulia, see Kjustendil
Pateli (Ayios Pandeleëmon): 136, 152f, 155
Patras: 66, 151
Patroclus: 113f, 138
Pavla R.: Map 4; 83, 102f

183

Pazhok: Map 4; 26, 111, 113f, 116, 121, 125f, 127, 137, 153
Peć: Map 1; 20, 29f, 32, 39, 42, 95, 104, 153
Pecinj R.: Map 2; 20, 70f
Pejë Pass: 20
Pekinj: 78
Pelagonia: Map 18; 24, 34, 37, 52, 66, 86, 88f, 91, 93, 95, 104f, 109, 111, 120f, 137, 139f, 148, 154f, 157f
Pelasgic: 130f
Peleus: 131
Pelion, Mt: Map 23; 86, 97, 130, 136
Pelium: 32
Pella: 24, 34
Pelynt: 139
Pende Pigadhia: 27, 33
Peneus R.: Maps 5, 6 and 9; 24, 28, 31, 43, 71, 83f, 85, 91, 103, 130, 143
Perachora: 63
Perama: Map 17; 83, 96
Peristeri, Mt, in Epirus: 22
Peristeri, Mt, in Macedonia: 29f, 112
Peristeria: Map 21; 126
Perivoli: 41f, 43
Permet (Premedi): Map 4; 27, 77
Pernik: 20
Perrhaebia: Map 5; 24, 28, 36, 89, 91, 95, 97, 103, 118, 130f, 143
Perseus of Macedon: 32, 36
Persians: 28, 35, 69f, 71, 73, 134, 158
Pertouli: 24
Peter Leosas: 62
Peter, the Lame: 62
Peter, the Vlach: 39, 42, 68
Petilep: Map 25, 155
Petra, in Albania: 26
Petra, in Macedonia: 28, 33
Petralona: Map 17; 83f, 97, 157
Petres: 34
Petrina, Mt: 29f
Peucetia: 153
Phalara: 128, 155
Phanote, see Raveni
Pharsalus: Map 6; 25
Phidaris R., see Euenus: Map 6
Philip II, of Macedon: 28, 130
Philip V, of Macedon: 32
Philippaei: Map 10; 45
Philippi: 30
Philippoupolis, see Plovdiv
Phocis: Map 24a; 88, 91f, 93f, 130, 134f, 141, 151, 158
Phoenice: 32
Phoenicians: 133
Photice: Map 13; 61
Phrygians: 92, 140, 152
Phthiotis: 78
Phylakopi: 143
phylarchi: 42
Picenum: Map 25; 153
Pieres: Map 25; 152, 157, 161
Pieria: 25, 28, 33; Vlachs of: 45; 73, 81, 91, 119, 140, 152, 157
Pindar: 114, 133
Pindus, Mt: Map 13; 22f, 31f, 33, 38, 41, 43, 45, 47f, 62, 66, 77f, 81, 84f, 86, 91, 95, 98, 102, 107, 113, 120, 135, 137, 141, 143f, 161
Pirin, Mt (Rhodope): 19f, 43, 71
Pisodherion Pass: Map 2; 28, 30, 32, 43
Plakalnitsa: 123
Plataea: 29, 126, 133
Plataeans, Mound of the: 116
Platamona (Heracleum): 25, 28
Platanos: 26

Pletvar Pass: Map 2; 24, 30, 34
Pliasa: Map 9; 42f, 50, 144
Plovdiv (Philippoupolis): Map 15; 22, 68, 70f
Pogoniani: Map 11; 24, 59
Pogradec: Map 2; 27, 92, 98
Poland: 63
Polog: Map 1; 20, 32, 88, 92, 103f, 120, 155
Poloskë: 24, 30, 137
Polykastro: 28
Pompey: 26, 28, 32
poriatikon: 50
Porodin: Map 20; 94, 98, 104f, 109f, 120, 127
Porphyrogennitus: 68
Porta Panayia: 31
Poyan (Apollonia): Map 4; 21f
Prasias, L.: Map 3; 123
Preceramic period: 85f
Prendi, F.: 98, 103f, 112, 120f, 122f
Preševo Pass: Map 1; 20f, 42f, 88, 92, 109
Prespa, L.: Maps 1, 2; 21, 29, 42, 62, 67, 73, 104, 109
Prespa, Little L. (Ventrok): Map 2; 21, 27, 30
Preveza: Map 9; 25, 43, 61, 66, 71, 77, 83f, 96, 102
Prilep: Map 2; 24, 28, 30, 32, 34, 56, 66, 68, 73, 93, 109, 139, 148
Priština: Map 11; 29, 88, 93, 104, 155
Prizren: Map 1; 20f, 67f, 73, 77
Procles: 135
Prodromos: 86, 88f, 95
Prometheus: 49
Protogeometric ware: 151, 154
Psara: 62
Ptolemaïs: 28
Ptolemy, geographer: 56f, 76
Pydna: 34
Pylon Pass: Map 1
Pylos: Map 21; 116, 119, 123, 126, 131f
Pyraechmes: 159
Pyrasos: 88
Pyrrhus: 78
Qeparo: 53
Qukës: Map 1, 29
Radanja: 155
Radohinë, Mt.: 19
Radomir: Map 3; 20f, 70
Ragusa, see Dubrovnik
Rakhmani: Map 22; 105, 112, 129f
Raveni (Phanote): Map 4; 31
Razlog: 20, 112
Rendina Pass: 30
Resen: Map 1; 29f, 41, 43, 45
Rhea: 119
Rhium: 135
Rhodes: 131, 134, 139, 141, 151
Rhodope, Mt; see Pirin
Rila, Mt: 19f, 22, 35, 71
Rodoni, Cape and town: Map 16; 56
Romanelli Cave: 84
Romano: 96
Rosh, Mt: 19
Rremull: Map 16; 74
Rudnik, L.: 104
Rumania: 37, 104, 118, 155
Runchini: 66
Rupel Pass: Map 3; 27, 30
Russia: 63, 105, 109f, 152, 156
Sagoudatae: 66
Saint Erasmus: 21f
Salamis: Map 8; 133

Salcuta: 104, 123
Salmanovo: 123
Salonica: Map 9; 28, 30, 34, 46, 57, 65-8, 71, 78, 105
Samarina: Map 9; 27, 41f, 43, 84, 96, 98, 134
Samarra: 91, 97
Samo: 67
Samokov: Map 3; 73
Samos: 62
Samos, in Homer: 130, 144
Samuel, the Bulgar: 32, 67
Santi Quaranta: Map 4; 23, 31
Saraj: Map 23; 139
Sarajevo: 92
Sarakatsani: Map 10; 37f, 47-51, 69, 83, 102, 120, 129, 137, 156, 161
Sarandaporos R., in Epirus: 23
Sarandaporos R., in Perrhaebia, see Titaresius
Saratse: 108
Sarda, see Shurdhah
Šar Planina (Mt Scardus): Map 1; 19, 29f, 32, 57
Save R., 67
Scampia: 34
Scardus, Mt: (Šar): Map 1
Sceptecasas: 38
Scironian Cliffs: Map 8; 26
Sclaveni: 66
Scodra (Shkodër): Map 1; 19f, 54, 57, 73, 77, 111f, 121, 124f, 136, 140, 148, 153
Scodra, L. (Skutari): Map 1; 19, 74, 78
Scombros, Mt (Vitosha): 19f
Scopelos: 62
Scupi, see Skopje
Scyros: Map 18; 143
Scythians: 34, 38, 65, 71, 156
Seidi Cave: Map 17; 84
Selenicë: 102
Selia: Map 9
Selloi: 131
Semeni R. (Apsus): Maps 4 and 9; 21, 26, 32, 61, 110
Serbs: 20, 40, 57, 59, 61, 67f, 73f, 111f, 118, 122, 126
Serdica (Sofia): 67
Serpentine: 85f, 98
Serres: Map 3; 19, 30, 39, 45f, 68, 73, 155
Servia: Map 5; 24, 28, 33, 36, 86, 89, 91, 93-8, 102f, 106f, 109f, 112, 116, 125f
Sesklo: Map 18; 85f, 88f, 91f, 97, 100, 107, 112, 120, 122, 127, 129, 148
Seven against Thebes: 149
Shalë: 19
Sheep Track Pass: 20
Shipiska: Map 9; 40, 42, 45, 92
Shkumbi R. (Genusus): Maps 1, 4 and 9; 21, 26, 35, 54, 61f, 74, 110, 153f
Shpat: 41
Shqipërë: 52
Shqiptars: 54, 76
Shtish-Tufina: Map 16; 74
Shurdhah (Sarda): Map 16; 74
Shushicë R (Polyanthes): 23, 83, 96
Siatista: Maps 5 and 10; 46, 83f
Siatista Pass: Map 5; 28
Siberia: 92
Siberia: 105
Sicilian Sea: 69, 116
Sicily: 78, 111, 136
Sicyon: 162
Sidari: Map 17; 85f, 88
Sidimund the Goth: 34
Sindekiniotikos R. (Inachus): Map 6; 33
Sirmium: 67

Sirrakou: Map 9; 40, 45
Sisanion: Map 10; 43
Sistrounion: 96
Sitalces: 22, 34, 71
Skamneli: Map 10; 48
Skanderbeg, George: 32, 53, 62, 76, 134
Skirtos R.: 30
Skopje (Scupi): Map 1; 20f, 24, 67f, 109, 155
Skoulikaria: 33
Skutari, see Scodra: Map 9
Skydhra: 28
Slavs: 35, 63; invasions by: 65, 67, 68, 70, 73, 76, 85, 105, 140, 162f
Smilčić: 98
Smixi: Map 10
Smolika, Mt: 23, 27
Smyrna: 151
Snodgrass, A. M.: 97f, 124, 126
Sofia (Serdica): Map 15; 20f, 30, 32, 46, 67f, 70, 73, 92, 160
Sordinas, A.: 96
Sosthenes: 70
Soteriades, G.: 107, 124
Souli: 62, 69
Soulopoulon: Map 4; 23
Souphli Magoula: 85, 112f, 125f
Soutista Mt: 23, 27
Spahiu, Hena: 74
Sparta: Map 8; 28, 133, 162
Spatas, John: 59, 62
Spercheus R.: Map 9; 25, 31, 39, 70f, 73, 113, 119, 133, 135, 141-4
Spetsae: 62
Spilë: 102
Spilio: 98
spondylus gaederopus: 92
Sporades, Northern: Map 18; 49, 62, 86, 95
Srejović, D.: 92
stani: 48
Stara Zagora: 123
Starčevo: Map 19; 86, 88f, 91-4, 105
stele: 72, 114
Stena Aoi Pass: Map 4; see Aoi Stena
Stena Dov Tepe Pass: Map 3; 28, 30, 73
Stena Portas Pass: Map 5; 24
Stephen I: 67
Stephen Dusan: 59, 68
Štip (Astibus): Map 2; 30, 32, 68, 73, 88, 92, 155f
Stobi, see Gradsko: Map 2; 32, 34
Stournareïka: 31
Stranca Mts: 125
Stratus: Map 6; 25, 27, 33, 42, 45
Strongili: 27
Strouga: Map 1; 21
Struma R., see Strymon
Strumitsa R. (Doberus): Map 3; 24, 28, 69, 71, 92, 156
Strumitsa town: Map 2; 28, 30
Strumsko: Map 23; 105, 140
Strymonii: 66
Strymon R.: Maps 3, 9 and 12; 19f, 22, 27, 30, 32, 39, 43, 45, 66, 68, 73, 108f, 130, 136, 140, 155
Šuplevec, see Tsiplevets
Suva Reka: 155
Suvodol: 109
Sveti Naum: 22
Symeon, the Bulgar: 45, 67
Symizë: 137
Synoikismos: 50, 134
Syria: 91, 100
Syros: Map 22; 108
Talaeanes: 144

185

Tanagra: Map 7; 29
Taron: 39
Tarsus: 135
Tartars: 63, 65, 68
Tatarna Bridge: Map 6
Taulantii: Map 25; 57, 140, 153
Taygetus, Mt.: 66
Tegea: 133
Teichos Dymaion: Map 23; 134f
Telegonus: 133
Telegony: 133, 139
Telemachus: 133
Temenium: 135
Temenus: 135, 141f
Tempe Pass: 25, 28, 70
Tepelenë: 41
Tetovo: Map 1; 20, 68
Teucri: 136f
Thasos: Map 15
Thaumaci: Map 6; 24f
Thebes: Map 7; 131, 144
Theochares, D. R.: 86, 107, 123, 148
Theodimund, the Goth: 34
Theodore: 59
Theodoric, the Goth: 33f
Theogephyra: 23
Theognis: 130
Theopetra: 83
Thera: 135, 143
Thermaic Gulf: Map 9; 81, 86, 104, 118, 151f
Therme: 28
Thermopylae Pass: Map 6; 25, 28, 43, 63, 70f, 73, 78, 135, 141
Thermum: 119
Thesprotia: Map 25; 133, 135, 139f
Thesprotikon: 120
Thessaliotis: 141
Thessaloi: Map 23; 133, 161
Thessalonica: see Salonica
Thessaly: Map 23; 26, 36, 38, 42f, 45f, 57, 59, 62, 66f, 68, 70, 73, 83f, 85f, 88f, 91, 93f, 95f, 100, 102f, 108f, 112f, 119f, 129f, 131, 134f, 136, 141-6, 151f, 156
Thiudimer, the Goth: 70
Tholos tomb: 116, 146, 152
Thomas, Despot of Ioannina: 59
Thrace and Thracians: Map 25; 20, 45, 49f, 63, 67, 69, 71, 76, 85, 92f, 98, 104f, 107, 136, 151f, 156f
Thucydides: 131f, 141-4, 151, 161f
Thyamis R., see Kalamas
Thyamus, Mt: 25
Tigris R.: 91
Tikvetch, see Kavadarci
Tirana: Map 11; 21, 26, 40, 57, 74, 84, 110f, 121, 127, 138
Tirnavos: Map 9; 97
Tiryns: Map 23; 119, 123, 134f, 138
Tisamenus: 135, 143, 149, 161
Titaresius R. (Sarandaporos): Map 9; 24, 43, 91, 97, 130, 143
Titov Veles (Bylazora): 22, 66, 68, 155f
Tivat: 111, 127
Tlepolemus: 134, 139
Toncheva, G.: 125
Toplana: 35
Toskesi: 77
Tosks: 53, 63, 122
Tranupara, see Kratovo
Trebenište: 21f
Trebeshin, Mt: 23
Tren Cave and site: Map 23; 109, 112, 124f, 136f, 148, 155, 158, 160
Tren Pass: 30

Tresca R.: Map 1
Treskavtsa: 149, 160
Tria Khania: 31
Triballians: 70, 78
Tricca, see Trikkala
Trikastron, see Gourana
Trikkala (Tricca): Map 5; 24, 40, 46, 66
Tringia, Mt.: 22
Tripolis, in Peloponnese: Map 8
Tripolis, in Perrhaebia: 36
Trnovo: 68
Troezen: 62
Troy: 108, 130f, 133f, 136, 139f, 149, 151, 157
Truro: 158
Tsaleika: 148
Tsamouria: 39, 46, 63, 129
Tsams: 53, 63, 76, 122
Tsangli: Map 19; 91, 93f, 98, 120, 122
Tsangon Pass: Maps 2, 4, and 5; 24, 30
tselingas: 48
Tsepelevo: 48
Tsepicovo: 109
Tserovo: 22
tshelniku: 42, 152, 162
Tsiplevets: 93, 98, 110, 127
Tsoumerka, Mt: Map 10; 22f, 48
Tsountas: 114, 116, 123
Tumulus-burial: 105-7, 110-22, 124-8, 137-40, 148f, 151-6
Turkey and Turks: 35, 40, 43, 45, 48, 52, 56, 59, 62f, 65; invasion by: 68f, 71, 73, 76, 86, 92, 95, 105, 136
Tydeus: 134
Tymphrestus, Mt.: Map 6; 31f
Tzernikos: Map 11
Ukraine: 63, 105
Ulpiana (Lipljan) Map 1; 29f, 34f
Urfirnis ware: 91f
Uroš: 57, 68
Uscana, see Kitsevo: Map 1
Utigurs: 67
Vajzë: Map 17; 83f, 96, 114, 116, 121, 126, 137f, 148, 153f
Valandovo: Map 2; 24, 28, 34, 71, 78, 155
Valens: 63
Valona (Vlorë): Map 4; 23, 42, 57, 62, 68f, 100
Valona, Gulf of: Map 4; 19, 21f, 26, 29, 35, 42, 52, 54, 61, 81, 96, 102, 104, 108, 121, 137
Valtetsini, see Arcades
Vardar R.; maps 1, 2, 3, 9 and 12; 19f, 25, 29f, 34, 46, 66f, 69f, 71f, 73, 88, 92, 94, 105, 108f, 122, 136, 139, 152, 155f, 157
Vardarophtsa: Map 23; 109, 136, 140f, 152, 159
Vardina: Map 23; 124, 136, 140f, 152
Varna: 39, 123
Varytimidhes: 86, 91
Vashtemi: 92
Vasilaki: Map 17; 84
Vatokhorion Pass: Maps 2 and 5; 30
Vattina: 139
Vaxia: Map 25; 156
Vazovir, L.: Map 3
Vela: Map 13; 59, 61
Velcë: 94, 102f, 104, 108, 112
Velemishti Pass: 24
Veles, see Titov Veles: Map 2
Velestino: 100, 107, 123
Veltsiotikos R.: 31
Veltsista: Map 4; 131
Venetians: 35, 57, 61f, 69
Venetikos R.: Map 5; 24, 28
Ventrok, L., see Prespa, Little L.

Vergina: Map 23; 114, 116, 140, 152f, 157, 159
Vermion, Mt. see Bermium Mt.
Verria (Beroea): Map 2; 25, 28, 34, 43, 67f, 104
Via Egnatia: 29, 32, 34, 54, 78, 152
Vidin: 68
Vienna: 40, 160
Vijosë R., see Aous: Map 4
Vinča: 88, 112
Viniani: Map 5; 31
Visigoths: 63
Visoï: Map 25; 152, 155
Vistritsa R., see Haliacmon
Vistula R.: 63
Vitosha, Mt (Scombrus): 19f
Vitsa: Map 25; 155f
Vivari, L.: 96
Vlachia, Great: 43
Vlachia, Little: 43
Vlachs: Maps 10, 11, 12, 13; 20, 31, 37-46, 59, 61f, 73f, 76f, 83f, 88f, 92, 95, 97, 103f, 118, 121, 123, 129, 134, 136f, 138, 152, 154-6, 161f
Vlakholivadhi: Map 9; 45
Vodhas R. (Astraeus): 25
Vodhena, see Edessa
Vodhinë: Map 21; 23, 114, 122, 126, 138, 154, 156
Voïdhomati R.: 23, 27, 61
Voïon, Mt (Boion): 144
Vokotopoulou, I. P.: 138, 160
Volos: Map 17; 31, 41, 152
Volustana Pass: Map 5; 24, 86, 89, 91, 143
Vonitsa: 27
Voulgareli: Map 5; 31
Voutonosi: 31
Vovousa: Map 5; 27, 40, 42f, 48, 96
Vradeto: 48

Vranesi: Map 25; 156
Vrap: 78
Vrondismeni: 59
Vrousina: 59
Vršnik: Map 18; 88, 92, 105, 109
Vučedol: 111, 121, 155
Wace, A. J. B.: 38, 43, 45, 50, 124
Wallachs, see Vlachs
Weigand, G.: 38f, 41, 52
Weinberg, S. S.: 85f, 89
Wittman, B.: 98
Xanthus, historian: 140
Xanthus, king of the Boiotoi: 159
Xerakia: 31
Xerovouni, Mt.: 23
Xerxes: 28, 33, 69, 73
Xylokastro: 139
Yialouris, N.: 148
Yiannitsa, L.: 24
Yugoslavia: 54, 74, 92, 97, 104, 119, 121, 139f, 149, 154
Yuruks: 45, 99
Zacynthos: Map 13; 35, 130, 135, 144
Zadrimë: Map 16
Zagori: Map 9; 31, 47f, 61, 77, 83, 102, 155f, 162
Zagorië: Map 4; 61, 77
Zagoritikos R.: 23, 31
Zalongo, Mt: 22
Zelenikovo: 92
Zeta valley: 19, 29, 32, 67, 74, 84f, 88, 92, 95, 153f, 160
Zeus: 119, 131, 144
Zitsa: Map 4; 23
Zog, king of Albania: 52, 54
Zoödokos Pege: 33, 36
Zygos Pass: Maps 5 and 10; 22f, 31, 41, 86, 96, 143